Oklahoma

Arkansas

Red River

VERNON

TEXARKANA

Louisiana

•DALLAS
•WILLS
POINT

FORT
WORTH

•ABILENE

•WACO

•COLLEGE
STATION

BEAUMONT

☆AUSTIN

•MOUNTAIN
HOME

KERRVILLE

HOUSTON

GALVESTON

•SAN
ANTONIO

•VICTORIA

Gulf of Mexico

CORPUS
CHRISTI

Rio Grande

•LAREDO

KINGSVILLE

•MISSION

•BROWNSVILLE

TEXAS BIG RICH

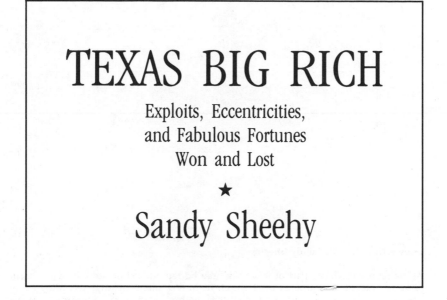

TEXAS BIG RICH

Exploits, Eccentricities,
and Fabulous Fortunes
Won and Lost

★

Sandy Sheehy

William Morrow and Company, Inc.
New York

Library of Congress Cataloging-in-Publication Data

Sheehy, Sandy.
    Texas big rich: exploits, eccentricities, and fabulous fortunes won and lost/Sandy Sheehy.
        p. cm.
    Includes bibliographical references.
    ISBN 0-688-04819-6
    1. Wealth—Texas. 2. Millionaires—Texas—Biography. I. Title.
HC107.T43W47   1990
332'.092'2764—dc20   89-13975
                                                                                              CIP

Printed in the United States of America

First Edition

1 2 3 4 5 6 7 8 9 10

BOOK DESIGN BY J. PONSIGLIONE

To my mother,
Jean D. Granville,
who taught me to read
and to love books

ACKNOWLEDGMENTS

CRAIG NELSON SUGGESTED this book and its organization. Evan Marshall found it a home and helped me get it going. Scores of busy Texans allowed me to interview them as subjects or sources. My magazine editors—particularly Frank Zachary, the late Arnold Ehrlich, and Kim Waller at *Town & Country* and Chris Andrews and Kathryn Casey at *Ultra*—gave me the encouragement, assignments, and financial freedom I needed to complete the work. Some of the material appearing here first saw print, in different form, in those or other publications.

Friends and fellow writers, especially Bill Barrett, Paul Burka, Alison Cook, Alan Field, Joe Nocera, and Mimi Swartz, shared their insights with me along the way. Morrow's editor in chief, Jim Landis, was extraordinarily patient and enthusiastic. My agent, Stuart Krichevsky, was always there for me, urging me along and guiding me through the baffling process of getting a book published. My husband, Tom Curtis, believed in me, if not always in the wisdom of this enterprise; he gave unstintingly of his good counsel and made it unthinkable for me to leave this book undone. My editor, Jeanne Bernkopf, was every author's dream. With her wry wit, keen ear, deft pencil, and gentle wisdom, she made this a far better book than it would have been otherwise.

My heartfelt thanks to them all.

CONTENTS

In order to gain and to hold the esteem of men, it is not sufficient to possess wealth or power. The wealth or power must be put in evidence.

—Thorstein Veblen, *The Theory of the Leisure Class* (1899)

Texas is a new boy, standing in relation to the rest of the United States as the United States stands to Europe. . . . To be sure, the widespread mockery of Texas, like the old European custom of patronizing America, originally stemmed from the newcomer's relative immaturity, but something much more provocative has come into play: envy.

—John Bainbridge, *The Super-Americans* (1961)

How do you become a Texas millionaire? Start off as a Texas billionaire.

—Joke making the rounds in Houston in late 1986

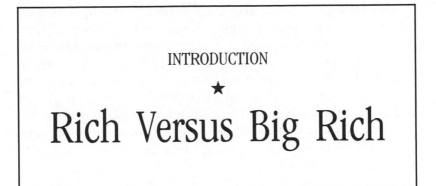

INTRODUCTION

★

Rich Versus Big Rich

For months the date had been set aside in Houston's *Black Book*, the leather-bound calendar that regulates the ebb and flow of social life among the city's *haut monde*. On the evening of Friday, January 22, 1988, the only place to be was at opening night of John and Nellie Connally's four-day bankruptcy auction.

By six-thirty BMWs, Rolls-Royces, and Chevy Suburbans packed the parking lot surrounding Hart Galleries, a thirty-thousand-square-foot erstwhile supermarket a few blocks from the mansions of River Oaks. In a line that wrapped around the building, men in custom-made alligator cowboy boots and women clutching Judith Leiber handbags to their Black-glama mink coats waited to fork over the fifteen-dollar admission fee. As hot tickets go, it was the bargain of the season.

To help repay forty-one million dollars to the former

Texas governor's unsecured creditors, high bidders would snatch up three housefuls of furniture and accessories—among them fourteen sets of china, scores of original paintings, exquisite Oriental rugs, elaborately carved and gilded French antiques, even a pair of eighty-five-inch-long tusks (which went for eighteen thousand dollars) from an elephant he'd shot in Tanzania. There were pieces of Texana, like hinges (which brought forty-five hundred dollars), a window (seventeen thousand dollars), and even a brick (seven hundred dollars) from the original State Capitol, which burned in 1881. But no collection of objects, however impressive, could have ginned up the interest this sale attracted. That was due to the man John Connally.

From the time he was elected governor in 1961 at a youthful forty-four, Big John embodied Texas to much of the world. Not the Texas of Compaq Computer and biotechnology and H. Ross Perot. He represented the Texas in which fortunes in oil and gas and cattle and real estate were won by Cowboy Capitalists who thought big, loved a high-stakes gamble, and took brash optimism as an article of faith. It wasn't just Governor Connally's possessions that were going on the block that chilly Friday night; it was a whole era of Texas social and economic history.

John Connally's tragedy was Texas's tragedy; his hubris was the state's. In 1979, when he announced his retirement from public life, his net worth fell somewhere between six million and thirteen million dollars. Rich. But for Connally, as for Texas, rich wasn't enough. He wanted to be Big Rich.

The Big Rich count their assets in the tens and even hundreds of millions. In making and spending their money, in taking chances, in wielding behind-the-scenes political power, they operate on a scale the merely rich can only dream of. President George Bush, with his five million dollars, is not Big Rich. But unsuccessful vice presidential candidate Senator Lloyd Bentsen, Jr., is; he inherited a hefty chunk of his late father's $190 million fortune.

The drive to be Big Rich fueled the Texas boom. It also precipitated the bust.

*   *   *

On March 31, 1986, one of the most entertaining, extravagant, and in many ways disturbing eras in the annals of American society came to a shuddering halt. That was the day the price of a barrel of West Texas intermediate crude, the benchmark of the American petroleum industry, fell below ten dollars for the first time in a decade. As petroleum prices plummeted, they brought with them many of the Texas Big Rich, those whose annual *incomes*, not their assets, were measured in the millions.

In the thirteen years between the first major OPEC price hike in 1973 and that collapse, the richest Texans had wielded their wealth with an abandon unparalleled, even by the state's generous standards. So many people were getting so rich so quickly—not just from escalating oil but from the real estate boom which accompanied it—that lavish, and often inventive, public displays of wealth became the accepted way for the Texas Big Rich to introduce themselves to their peers and trumpet their mounting success. "Better *nouveau* than never" was their rallying cry.

Such flashy spending was often so diverting that even Old Texas Money began emulating New Texas Money. When Camilla Blaffer-Royall (whose grandfather had helped found the Humble Oil Company [now Exxon]) married blue-blooded Boston financier Herbert Mallard, Jr., in 1984, the couple had an authentic Hindu ceremony in the lavish garden of the Sisodia Rani Palace in Jaipur, India. The bride wore a pink and gold sari-inspired gown and a diamond ring—in her nose. The groom sported a towering turban and white silk tunic with a red overskirt. As his bride waited demurely in the garden, he approached astride an elephant, leading a procession of two more pachyderms, four camels, eight horses, and sixteen warriors in elaborate battle dress.

Being rich in Texas has always been more fun than being rich anywhere else in the United States because Texans, unfettered by pressures to conform, have felt free to show off with abandon. The essential difference between the Texas Rich and their economic peers elsewhere in the country is a difference in myths. Most of the American upper class is reared on legends of the family founder—a hardworking,

intelligent, pleasure-shunning captain of industry who created a corporation producing useful goods and employing
large numbers of people. He got rich either because God in
his wisdom rewarded his extraordinary efforts or because his
innate abilities gave him a Social Darwinian edge. With the
fortune resulting from his endeavors, he established a dynasty of well-educated, prudent, public-spirited patricians
who understood the adage that from those to whom much
is given, much is expected. Never mind that the family founder
may have been a robber baron who ran roughshod over his
competitors and held the American economy for ransom to
get where he was; by the end of his life he had atoned for
his sins by willing a hefty chunk of his money to a charitable
foundation. Besides, it's the edifying message that counts.

But for Texans, rich and otherwise, the key mythic figure
has long been the cowboy, alone and independent, no man's
lackey and no man's boss, unhampered by conventions and
restrictions. Like the early oil wildcatters, he stood alone
against the vagaries of nature. He was comfortable with risks
but uncomfortable with moral ambiguity, long on native intelligence but short on formal learning—especially when it
had no obvious practical application. The cowboy disdained
those who couldn't provide for themselves, unless they had
obvious physical disabilities. If he got rich, it was partly through
luck and partly a matter of recognizing opportunity and having the courage to make the most of it. He won a ranch in
a poker game, then struck oil while digging for water. To
celebrate, he spent freely but indiscriminately. If he could
become a multimillionaire, everyone else had a chance to; so
the system was just, and there was no need to feel guilty
about his wealth. He enjoyed it while he had it and didn't
worry much about the future.

The cowboy myth was compounded by an eccentricity
of history: Texas is the only state in the Union that was first
a fully functioning, representative republic. Combine that
heritage with Texas's size—east to west, a third of the girth
of the United States—and the result is something approaching national consciousness. With seventeen million people
and 266,807 square miles of area, the state is bigger than

most European nations, and the variations in climate, topography, and ethnic influences within its borders are more dramatic.

On the same January day that a blizzard blasts across the Panhandle, the temperature can reach 80°F in the grapefruit groves of the Lower Rio Grande Valley. The eastern fifth of the state is a dense woods, long-needled pines laced with dogwoods, live oaks, and magnolias. Texas's vast midsection is an extension of the Midwest and the Great Plains. With its desert canyons and high, arid mountains, Texas's western third is as much a part of the Southwest as New Mexico.

Yet despite its internal diversity, Texas is a region unto itself and clings to its separateness. For example, although they could afford the tuition at the most expensive East or West Coast schools, most rich Texans educate their children within the state. The Texas Rich want their young to stay Texan.

These scions of privilege emerge from UT and SMU flashing their wealth with an unparalleled exuberance and sense of theater.

"Nowhere else would you put on pink shorts, a lynx coat, a seventeen-carat diamond, and get into a white Rolls-Royce to go to the Safeway," said Dallas boutique owner Loretta Blum as she maneuvered through the racks of $4,000 dresses and displays of $390 shoes. A former buyer for Bergdorf Goodman in New York and then for Neiman Marcus in Dallas, Ms. Blum opened her own store in 1973—the year of the OPEC oil embargo—and rode the gusher of wealth to its peak in 1981, when oil cost $35 a barrel and its Texas producers talked of its reaching $85 by 1990.

"I chased the oil rich throughout my career," she said. "If the money was from oil royalty checks, it was play money. With earned money—I don't care *how* much you make—it isn't the same. They threw it up in the air and bought anything their little hearts desired—clothing, furs, jewels, stadium boxes. Just because you had a Mercedes convertible, that didn't mean you didn't want a Rolls-Royce to show up at a ball."

The price of oil had risen so rapidly that the merely well heeled became as rich as Saudi sheikhs virtually overnight.

The skyrocketing price of energy pushed up prices throughout the economy, including the cost of drilling oil wells and
the interest on the money to finance exploration and production. But the incurably optimistic Cowboy Capitalists bet
on continued escalation. Who cared whether it cost $108 a
foot to sink a well in 1982 (up from $12 a foot twenty years
earlier) and whether that expense carried with it a 20 percent
interest rate? At $35 a barrel, it was worth it. And once oil
got to $50, there'd be that much more gravy to go around.
Texans slapped bumper stickers on their pickups that read
"Secede and join OPEC" and "Drive 80—Freeze a Yankee."
Recession could hit the rest of the nation, this message im-
plied, but the Lone Star Republic was immune.

When the oil-fueled orgy ended, it took awhile before
most people noticed. Gradually at first, and then with the
ominous momentum of an avalanche, the price of petroleum
dropped. From an average of $31.77 a barrel in 1981, it skit-
tered down a dollar or two a year until 1985, when it averaged
$24.09. As the price slid, there were occasional bankruptcies,
especially among small operators who were still paying off
expensive oil-field equipment purchased with high-interest
loans. An operation that made money with oil at $28 a barrel
could lose it at $25, but the bank still had to be paid. Most
of those failures were quickly rationalized; unscrupulous
bankers had pushed that money on those poor oilmen, practically forcing them to become overextended. The problems
were individual rather than global. In Texas optimism is such
an article of faith that the slump was called a minor correction;
any more gloomy appellation was heresy. Businesses reorganized under Chapter 11 of the Federal Bankruptcy Code,
and a few small and medium-size banks cratered; but personal life-styles didn't change.

Then, triggered by the collapse of discipline within OPEC
and the flood of Middle Eastern petroleum on the world
market, oil took a swan dive. On that fateful day in March
1986 the psychological impact was devastating.

The people hurt worst weren't the Texas Big Rich at all,
but those who worked in the oil industry. During the boom
the Oil Patch—from giant multinationals like Exxon to medium size companies that made drilling pipe—based its hir-

ing guidelines on the assumption that the price of a barrel of crude would rise to at least ninety dollars by the year 2000. From petroleum engineers to training specialists, success-dressed young professionals from across the country swarmed into Texas to work for the major oil corporations and the banks and law firms that supported them. In many cases the companies didn't need their services immediately but were afraid that if they didn't hire skilled people fresh out of grad-uate school, they wouldn't have the talent they would require to unlock the hard-to-get reserves that fifty-dollar-a-barrel oil would make feasible. At the same time laid-off Rust Belt auto- and steelworkers rushed to Texas to drill wells and man refineries. Still more came to build the shimmering glass-skinned office towers that sprang up as fast as mushrooms in an East Texas cow pasture. All those people needed places to live, clothes to wear, cars to drive.

Fortunes made in apartments and shopping centers dur-ing the late seventies and early eighties rivaled those made in oil. So did the bankruptcies in those fields when that era ended.

Yet to assume that the Texas Big Rich are now broke would be an error. In fact, the 1989 *Forbes* 400, that catalog of the nation's richest individuals, listed thirty-one Texans with net worths exceeding $275 million. Twelve of those were oilmen. Eight were billionaires: computer services magnate H. Ross Perot; investor Harold Simmons; oil heirs Ray Hunt and Margaret Hunt Hill (unscathed by their brothers' finan-cial woes); and corporate traders Bob, Sid, and Lee Bass and their futurist brother, Ed. And three *Forbes* 400 Texans were new entries. Only New York and California boasted more names on that enviable roll.

For one thing, oil is coming back. By the end of 1989 prices had stabilized around eighteen dollars a barrel, and the cost of drilling was down to two thirds of what it had been in 1982. For another, Texas has always had plenty of Big Rich people whose money had nothing to do with oil. Nevertheless, the state has seen a sharp reduction in blatant, exuberant, competitive displays of wealth. The once-foreign concepts of restraint and good form are creeping in. With

even a few of one's friends on the verge of personal bankruptcy, showing off loses some of its zest. What seems to be
emerging is a more staid and circumspect Texas elite, as if
the whole Big Rich subculture were passing from adolescence
into adulthood.

By the turn of the millennium it may be hard to tell a
Texas tycoon in New York, Tokyo, or London from any other
rich American businessman. He will wear the same elegant
Italian or Savile Row suit, the same handcrafted wing tips
and probably even speak with the same network television
accent. Texas may become homogenized with the rest of the
country, and America will lose the last vestige of its brash
innocence.

Yet, even stripped of such surface trappings as ermine
Stetsons, diamond-bezeled Rolexes, and alligator cowboy
boots, the traditional Texas traits of enthusiasm, optimism,
humor, and willingness to take risks may remain and may
even leaven the rest of the American economy and culture.
These, after all, are the characteristics that are most adaptive
in the long run—and most worth saving.

★

CHAPTER ONE

Clayton Williams

The King of the Cowboy Capitalists Moves On

Galloping down a red-rock draw, the man in the well-worn leather chaps and dust-streaked white Resistol cowboy hat reined in his bay gelding. He swung down from the saddle, looked the camera square in the eye, and promised in a broad West Texas drawl, "We're gonna take care of it for you. And at the right price."

Multimillionaire Clayton W. Williams, Jr.—oil- and gas-man, real estate developer, rancher, banker, alfalfa farmer, safari outfitter, and epic party giver—had taken on AT&T. He was starring in nine television commercials for his latest venture, Texas's first statewide long-distance company. Like many of his corporate entities, ClayDesta Communications took its homespun handle from his own first name and that of his vivacious brunette wife, Modesta.

By September 1988, four years after Williams founded ClayDesta Communications, television viewers everywhere in Texas had been exposed to his country-boy charisma. "If you've got a problem with your phone system, you can't call up Mr. AT&T," he explained, sitting in his office at the ClayDesta National Bank in Midland. "You don't even know who he is. But if you have trouble with ClayDesta Communications, you can call Clayton Williams."

The commercials showed Williams rounding up oceans of coal black Brangus cattle, hunkered down by a campfire, circling in his Bell JetRanger helicopter over ClayDesta Plaza—his 183-acre Midland commercial complex. It took thirty-six takes to get the scene where he jumped off his horse, but Williams gamely kept repeating it until both he and the director were satisfied. "The damned old horse wore out," he recalled. "His shoulder went lame."

Williams even rewrote the scripts, putting them in the ranch vernacular. "I Claytieized them," he explained, evoking the moniker bestowed by his grandmother.

Claytie Williams seemed to be having more fun in his commercials than Chrysler chairman Lee Iacocca seemed to be having in *his*. "I'm better than him," Williams asserted. "I've made a lot more money than he has, if you want to know the truth."

How much money had he made? About $150 million more than he'd lost, spent, or owed banks, he said. "From early memory I just wanted to accomplish something," he explained. "I had no idea I'd ever be able to owe so much money."

At one time that debt totaled almost half a billion dollars, but in May 1989 he shoveled away the last chunk when he sold ClayDesta Communications to Advanced Telecommunications Corporation for $33 million in cash, $10 million in stock, and a seat on the ATC board. With 150,000 customers and annual revenues of $168 million, the Atlanta-based long-distance company was almost three times ClayDesta's size. ClayDesta would keep its name, and Claytie Williams would continue as its spokesman.

Flashing the wraparound grin that made him look a little like Kirk Douglas, Williams claimed that *Forbes* overestimated his wealth in 1982, when it first included him in its list of the 400 richest Americans, and underestimated it when it dropped him in 1985, when the cutoff was above $150 million. In 1983 he'd told a *Houston Chronicle* reporter that he wasn't a billionaire—yet, adding, "Everybody needs a goal."

On March 17, 1989, Clayton W. Williams, Jr., unofficially announced another goal: He planned to run for governor on the Republican ticket in 1990. Sporting a green glitter St. Patrick's Day hat, he'd just addressed the Texas Railroad Commission, which regulates the state's energy industry. To demonstrate the plight of the independent oil- and gasman, Williams had in tow seven weeping cowboys, some on crutches, others with arrows through their hats. They represented, he said, the seven worst years in the recent history of the business.

The message was serious, but the packaging was pure Claytie, a harbinger of what was to come as November 1990 drew closer. He anted up six million dollars of his own money for the March primary alone and flooded the state with campaign commercials that bathed him in golden light. Never mind that Williams was bald or that his ears stuck out. By managing to look both homely and heroic and to sound both conservative and populist, he galloped off with 61 percent of the Republican primary vote.

The first time I met him, Clayton Williams seemed like the quintessential Cowboy Capitalist. Although he stood a modest five feet nine inches and his hairline was receding, his aquiline nose, unwavering blue eyes, and ready, toothy grin inspired confidence. He sported a white Stetson and black ostrich-skin boots with his suit. He laughed readily, and his idea of a good party was one where the food, drink, and entertainment were extravagant but everyone wore jeans. But he was also a for-real cowboy—or, more precisely, a rancher. He'd rounded up 482,000 acres under his half circle W brand.

Along with the Cowboy Capitalist's willingness to take risks and act decisively, Williams had two major characteristics rare among that breed: foresight and adaptability. In many of the businesses he'd started, he'd been able to sense when a downturn was coming and had sold out six to eight months beforehand.

Even when he *did* hold on too long, Williams was quick

to change directions once events proved him mistaken. "Ego
is a powerful son of a gun," he said. Settling philosophically
into a leather armchair in his office, decorated with hunting
trophies and bronzes of cowboys on horses, he continued:
"A lot of significant, wealthy men have reached the pinnacle
of success and gone on to the depth of failure because their
ego wouldn't let them say, 'I'm not such a big deal. I'd better
back up. I may be wrong.' I've not had that ego that drives
some people off a cliff rather than admit they're wrong."

Claytie Williams had changed business directions at least
five times in his life. Born in 1931, he grew up on the southwest edge of the Permian Basin in Fort Stockton. Halfway
between San Antonio and El Paso, Fort Stockton lies sixty
miles west of the Pecos River, which meanders down from
southeastern New Mexico, slicing off the part of Texas that
definitively belongs to the West. Along with a museum depicting the rigors of pioneer life in Comanche country, the
town's main claims to fame are abundant tumbleweeds and
Paisano Pete—an eleven-foot-tall polychrome fiber glass
sculpture billed as the world's largest roadrunner.

By local standards, the Williams family was unusually
cultured, something Claytie disguised well beneath his buc-
olic manner. His grandfather, Judge O. W. Williams—an
Illinois-born, Harvard-educated lawyer drawn to West Texas
in 1877 by respiratory problems—had the first library in that
part of the state. Claytie Williams's late father, Clayton Wheat
Williams, Sr., graduated from Texas A&M College (now University) with a degree in electrical engineering and later
farmed cotton and alfalfa and dabbled in oil, without much
success. "He didn't go broke in the oil business," Williams
said, "but he went bent."

To keep himself in pocket change during high school,
young Claytie farmed cotton on some of his father's irrigated
land. He took so well to agriculture that he decided to go to
A&M and major in animal husbandry. Despite that institution's countrified reputation, A&M has produced a surprising number of the state's richest and most successful self-
made men. University of Texas graduates run the state, the
saying goes; A&M graduates own it.

Texas A&M has always had its own culture, and that

culture has always been eccentric, especially for a public university. Until 1963 the school was all male, and unlike ROTC groups on other campuses, the quasi-military Corps of Cadets remains its most elite student group. Especially during his first two years Claytic Williams, who enjoyed playing his guitar and singing sentimental Mexican ballads in bars, bridled against the strict discipline in the dorms. When he left for Christmas and summer break, he'd salute the campus with an elevated middle finger and vow never to return. But he always came back and eventually finished his degree.

Thirty years later Claytie Williams was Texas's most ardent Aggie. All his aircraft, including his sporty Sabreliner jet, were painted the school's maroon and white colors and bore the thumbs-up GIG 'EM AGGIES sign on their tails. As a signal that he was at home in Midland, he flew a seven-foot-by-nine-foot A&M flag from the roof of his twelve-story office building. His cars and trucks sported maroon and white bumper stickers that read: "We believe in God, Aggies, and Brangus cattle." Even the steam shovels he used on construction projects flaunted his alma mater's maroon and white logo. The swimming pool at his Happy Cove Ranch in the Davis Mountains was shaped like the boots worn by seniors in A&M's Corps of Cadets, and the surrounding concrete apron was carpeted with a worn piece of AstroTurf that once adorned the fifty-yard line at A&M's Kyle Field football stadium.

Williams was also one of the school's biggest benefactors. He funded everything from scholarships to an experimental program to increase the population of wild sheep through the use of embryo transfers. Along with author James Michener, he bankrolled a project of Texas A&M Press to publish works examining everyday life in Texas from Spanish colonial times to the early oil boom. When Michener was researching his novel *Texas*, Williams ferried him around the Trans-Pecos in his helicopter, gave him insights into the oil and gas business, and lent him books written by his father, an amateur local historian.

Shortly after that epic tome appeared, Michener joked that one of the most interesting things about Clayton Williams was "that medical operation where they drained out all his blood and replaced it with paint the color of the A&M flag."

Williams donated $2.5 million toward building the $7 million former student center, which bears his name. Asked to speak at the groundbreaking, he became so choked with sentiment that he could barely finish crediting his alma mater with his success. The school gave him three invaluable things, he said: Despite his natural predilection for partying, it forced him to work hard on his studies; its military orientation taught him leadership; and the camaraderie and school spirit helped him forge a tight bond with the other students.

The gung ho patriotism and pro-free-enterprise attitude that have always pervaded the campus also fitted nicely with William's brand of political conservatism. In the late 1960's, when students at A&M's archrival the University of Texas at Austin, seventy miles to the west, were staging protest marches, Aggie corpsmen were singing "Green Berets." "During the Vietnam War A&M epitomized what Texans and Americans were supposed to be," Williams said. "We never changed. We were who we were. We stood tall."

After graduating from college in 1954, Williams spent a two-year hitch in the Army. One evening, while he was moonlighting from his soldierly duties by waiting tables at a café in Mineral Wells, he met a man who sold insurance. The salesman persuaded the young West Texan that peddling insurance would be the best way to earn the money he needed to buy a ranch. When Williams got out of the service, he followed the advice and made pretty good money, about ten thousand dollars a year, until he ran out of family and friends who needed policies. Then it got harder. "The insurance salesman is the best salesman of all," he opined three decades later. "He can talk some old boy into giving up his beer money and paying an insurance premium so that if he dies, his wife can go live with some other man."

As his insurance income fell off, Williams and his partner Johnny May began brokering oil and gas leases, trying to get the best prices for the ranchers around Fort Stockton and saving their commissions to begin their own explorations. Together they founded Clajon Gas. In 1965 Williams bought out his partner for twenty-five hundred dollars; he eventually built Clajon into the largest individually held natural gas company in Texas.

Williams was a wildcatter—a romantic-sounding term that simply refers to anyone who finds oil and gas by sinking wells without knowing for sure what lies beneath the surface. The average industry success ratio for wildcats is one producing well for every nine dry holes; a single well can cost one million dollars or more to drill. Williams's record was a bit better—between one in six and one in seven. Asked why he was able to stay afloat while others in the Oil Patch went under, he replied, "Blind, staggering luck. I've had periods of *horrible* luck, but I had good luck starting out, when I needed it."

His luckiest strike was Gataga No.2, one of the biggest natural gas wells in the world. It came in on December 31, 1975, blowing out with such force that the nearby town of Mentone had to be evacuated. Williams, his wife, and the local sheriff went from door to door, warning people that if they didn't leave, they could be killed by deadly hydrogen sulfide gas. The entire community spent New Year's Eve in motels in nearby Pecos and Monahans, with Clayton Williams cheerfully picking up the tab. In those days, natural gas was selling for $2.25 a thousand cubic feet, and Gataga #2 spewed 220 million cubic feet—$495,000 worth—through the drill pipe daily.

"An oil or gas discovery is euphoric," Williams said, his blue-gray eyes lighting up. "You've created wealth that wasn't there except for you and your people's own efforts. I bet it's like getting on dope. Wanting to do it again has driven many, many men to the poor farm."

By the mid-1970's Williams was operating oil and gas leases all over Texas. His Gig 'Em Aggies flag flew from wells north of Houston, across the Permian Basin, and south of San Antonio to the Mexican border. To transport that gas, he built thousands of miles of pipeline.

Williams generally negotiated a flat fee for the right to lay his pipe across ranchland, and most of the ranchers were more than happy to receive ten or twenty thousand dollars for no outlay of expense or effort. Then he ran into Clinton

Manges, a multimillionaire rancher and bankroller of some
prominent Democratic politicians. Manges, who owned a
sizable chunk of brush country just east of Laredo, was as
tough and thorny as the cactus that covered his land. He'd
started out pumping gas and ended up suing Mobil Oil for
a billion dollars, claiming that the petroleum giant had failed
to fulfill its contractual obligation on a sixty-four-thousand-
acre oil lease.

Since people in South Texas had warned Williams about
Manges, he wasn't surprised when his lawyers couldn't ne-
gotiate a deal for the right-of-way. Williams was afraid to
take the wily rancher to court in South Texas, because Texas
judges are elected and Manges was in the habit of contributing generously to judicial campaigns. So, putting his faith
in his own homespun charm, Claytie Williams went down
to Freer and called on Manges personally.

Greeting him cordially, Manges took the Midland wildcatter out back to see the Danish domestic hogs he was crossbreeding with javelinas (Texas wild boars). Then he
introduced Williams to his wife, offered him a drink, and
invited him to go deer hunting.

"I figured anybody who was crossbreeding hogs has got
to be a pretty good fella," Williams said as he sat beside a
campfire on one of his four Davis Mountain ranches recounting the story. "I thought, 'They've misjudged this man.' He
said, 'Son, I like you.' And I said, 'Mr. Manges, I like you,
too, sir.' Then he said, 'I'll tell you what I'm going to do.
You just buy me a new Cadillac, and we'll write that right-
of-way off.' My little ol' Aggie mind went buzz. Modesta
and I had a Cadillac at the time that cost twelve thousand
dollars. I knew there were fancier ones, but I figured they
were maybe twenty, twenty-two thousand."

Estimating that the right-of-way was worth at least
twenty-two thousand dollars, Williams accepted the deal,
thinking he'd gotten off cheap. They agreed that Manges
would go to Houston the next day, choose the car he wanted,
and have the dealership arrange for Clayton Williams to pick
up the tab. The following afternoon the car dealer called
Williams's office in Fort Stockton saying that a customer
was claiming Williams would pay for the fifty-five-thousand-

dollar Cadillac stretch limousine he was ordering. Gritting his teeth, Williams told the salesman he was good for it. "I was just glad there weren't any hundred-thousand-dollar Cadillacs," Williams said on reflection.

In 1981 Williams owned seventeen companies, but as the decade wore on, he began cutting back. In early 1987 he even sold Clajon Gas, his biggest corporation, to pay off his bank notes.

Williams's own bank—ClayDesta National, the largest independent bank in West Texas—remained healthy, partly because of timing. Its doors opened in 1982, too late to be tempted to make loans on the assumption that oil would be seventy-five dollars a barrel by 1990, as many banks that later failed had done. A year after ClayDesta came on the scene, the First National Bank of Midland, a financial pillar of the community for almost a century, cratered. The city's two other big banks were owned by huge Houston and Dallas holding companies (branch banking was outlawed in Texas until 1987), and many former Midland First National depositors shifted their accounts to ClayDesta out of community loyalty.

Surprisingly, one thing Clayton Williams got back into in 1986 was oil. With the cost of drilling down, his fields south of San Antonio were money-makers again, even at ten dollars a barrel. "In 1986, by drilling wells using secondhand pipe and secondhand pumpjacks, we managed to increase our reserves for virtually no money," he announced proudly.

He also cut office rents for his ClayDesta National Bank Building, so that for every tenant who left, typically because of bankruptcy, another was there to take his place. By 1983, that 600,000-square-foot structure was the nerve center of Williams's corporations and the anchor of his 183-acre commercial complex two miles north of downtown Midland. In 1981 this patch of prairie had been the site of a drive-in theater.

ClayDesta Plaza's biggest draw was the bank lobby. In true Texas tradition, it boasted the vastest atrium and the tallest houseplants in the United States. Under a skylight composed of dozens of glass pyramids, speckled brown ducks splashed in an artificial stream fed by its own waterfall and waddled beneath towering rubber plants, thirty-foot ficus trees, Brobdingnagian philodendrons, and three-story Norfolk pines. At the center was a fountain spurting fifty feet into the air. In an arid, pancake-flat city where contact with nature often meant enduring dust storms and dodging tumbleweeds, the atrium acted like a magnet. People strolled down its flagstone paths and ate their lunches on its wooden park benches. But pleasant as it was, this indoor oasis seemed otherworldly, as if it were plunked down on some distant planet to remind deracinated interstellar colonists what Earth was like.

Back in easier times, on December 10, 1984, America had gotten a taste of Claytie Williams's flamboyant showmanship when the *CBS Morning News* covered his December 7 Cowboy Christmas Classic—a black-tie cattle auction staged in the ClayDesta atrium and topped off with a style show featuring evening dresses by Dallas designer Jay Jacks. Williams wore a dinner jacket by New York high-fashion guru Oscar de la Renta; it was covered with magenta sequins—the closest Williams could find to Aggie maroon. The stars of the show—nineteen of Williams's best registered Brangus heifers—made their bows, their glossy black coats gleaming with Purple Oil, a bovine cosmetic that made them look even blacker. To the television audience, it appeared that each cow paraded in her own pearl necklace. In reality, it was just one sixty-five-hundred-dollar strand of pearls passed from cow to cow. The single bull paraded unadorned.

When the glitter cleared, Clayton Williams had grossed $362,000.

What makes a cow worth more than a Porsche? Genetics and hyperbole. The true economic worth of even the best cow or bull lies in how much more meat that animal enables a rancher to send to market. But it takes a number of years of a sophisticated breeding program for a cattleman to recoup a forty-thousand-dollar investment by producing slightly heavier, somewhat more disease-resistant animals. And no one is going to turn a forty-thousand-dollar heifer into hamburger—not until she's produced scores of hefty calves. Using state-of-the-art breeding techniques, a canny rancher can see to it that she lends her most desirable traits—vigorous health, fertility, and efficiency in transforming grass into prime beef—to as many as twenty-eight offspring a year, all carried and delivered by less valuable recipient cows.

So, many breeders make back their money and turn a profit by concentrating on using their expensive registered cattle to produce more expensive registered cattle. At that level, ranching resembles setting up an Amway distributorship.

"As long as you've got *new* people wanting to build *their* herds, it goes well," Clayton Williams explained. "But if your breed ever becomes unpopular and new people aren't buying the best, you can drift into uneconomic times."

The breed Williams concentrated on was Brangus—a cross between the heat-resistant Brahma cattle worshiped in India and the Angus meat factories native to temperate Scottish moors. Brangus thrive in Texas despite the long, searing summers, and their shiny, solid black coats and sturdy conformation make them look, well, classy standing out in the pasture, as if a fancy Dallas interior designer had suggested they'd be the perfect complement for that green grass.

Ranchers who raise all the beef breeds popular in Texas—Santa Gertrudis, Limousin, Charolais, Saler, even wily longhorns—hold fancy auctions, complete with four-color catalogs, to sell their best breeding stock. But nobody puts on a more extravagant show than Brangus breeders.

"You get a lot of Texans flying out here in their planes and you fill 'em full of whiskey, they'll pay a lot of money for a cow," Williams said, explaining the philosophy behind the event held annually during the boom and known simply as Claytie's Party. By 1984 the guest list for the August bash held at Williams's Happy Cove Ranch between Alpine and mile-high Fort Davis, ninety miles north of Big Bend National Park, had grown to eight thousand—this in a county with a population of fifteen hundred.

Although its ostensible purpose was a cattle sale, the Party also functioned as a company picnic and a way for Williams to say thank-you to everyone from his plumber in Midland to his Mexican ranch hands. Many of Williams's neighbors received invitations—but not all. Not everyone in that normally quiet, churchgoing western enclave found that drinking and carrying-on in tune with community values— not to mention the traffic jams along the Alpine–Fort Davis highway, where a person could generally fly down the road at ninety miles an hour. That may have been why, when Williams tried in 1981 to get the sale of liquor legalized in the dry precinct of Jeff Davis County where his ranch house sat, local voters defeated the measure 112 to 44. While anyone can give a private party—however large—in a dry Texas precinct, beer and liquor distributors can't deliver their beverages there. Williams got around that inconvenience by having the kegs dropped off at his foreman's house, which lay ten miles away in wet Brewster County.

Along with two thousand pounds of beef, guests at this Texas version of a potlatch consumed oceans of beer, whiskey, and tequila dispensed at way stations along the twelve miles of dirt road leading from the highway to the party site, a box canyon shaded by cottonwoods and lined with lichen-spattered red volcanic rock. To keep the dust on the road from becoming unbearable, trucks watered it down—a practice that raised further controversy in this semiarid land where water was precious. Lit by floodlights, a giant American flag waved from a peak behind the ranch house. Williams's fleet of five maroon and white corporate aircraft flew overhead in formation; after dark a full-scale fireworks display lit up the clear mountain sky.

To help get cattlemen in the mood for heavy bidding, Williams brought in such big-name country and western entertainers as Charley Pride, Merle Haggard, Tom T. Hall, and Janie Fricke, who performed on a permanent covered and lighted outdoor stage. And Claytie Williams got in on the act himself. After a few drinks "to loosen him up," as his wife, Modesta, put it, he'd tuck his trousers legs into the tops of his maroon and white cowboy boots and sing the "Aggie Fight Song," "God Bless America," and his favorite Spanish ballads—all in a clear tenor warm with emotion. One year he donned a red Stewart tartan kilt to lead a parade of bagpipers; another time he got down on all fours and pawed the straw to imitate a Brangus bull.

In 1984 such antics brought a staggering average of fifty-two thousand dollars per animal. But there was no party in 1985. That spring Claytie and Modesta Williams sold their eleven-thousand-head registered Brangus herd for five million dollars, keeping three hundred pregnant cows to restart the herd. One reason for the dispersal was to raise money to pay bank service charges (Williams shelled out forty million dollars in interest alone in 1984); another was that he suspected that the price of registered Brangus might be close to its peak. "In the boom people started throwing money," he explained a year later. "At the prices they were paying, there was no way you could make your money back out of those cattle."

Yet Williams didn't get out of the cattle business entirely. Far from it. He kept his quarter million acres of ranchland under his half circle W brand—eighty-two thousand acres in the Davis Mountains, a hundred thousand acres in Wyoming, and the rest in three ranches south of San Antonio.

"I don't know that I'm a cowboy," he said, sipping a cup of coffee from a tin cup as he rested from working cattle on his High Lonesome Ranch near Marfa. "I might be a fair cowman. A cowboy is a good roper, a good bronc rider, a good spitter. A cowman's one who's able to raise cattle at a profit."

Williams looked forward to getting out on his ranches twice a year for a week or two of grueling dawn-to-dusk physical labor. He'd roll out of his sleeping bag before sunup, eat a chuck wagon breakfast of tortillas and *huevos con chili roja*, and spend the day rounding up his herd and separating the mother cows from their calves. Dressed in a battered hat, scuffed boots and chaps, and a frayed button-down shirt, he'd work alongside his foreman, Chapo Ramirez, and three ranch hands. All five men would flap their jackets and shout at the recalcitrant cows, swearing exuberantly in Spanish and English.

By 1989 Williams was running about two thousand commercial Brangus—animals of undistinguished parentage bred for slaughter—at his cow-calf operation in the Davis Mountains. He also had three hundred registered Brangus, from the embryos he'd kept when he liquidated his herd. And when other ranchers sold their yearlings cheap to avoid feeding them during droughts, Williams bought them and shipped them to his greenest grassland, where he fattened them for sale the next year at heftier prices.

Williams kept his three-pronged cattle enterprise profitable by not letting nature take its course. He poisoned the catclaw—a treacherous shrub bristling with needle-sharp thorns—and water-greedy mesquite that invaded his pastures and starved the nutritious native grama grasses. He root-plowed and planted a strain of South African Klein grass specially developed by Texas A&M for the Trans-Pecos, where it stays green and tender longer than ordinary range varieties. He staggered dams across washes, deflecting the runoff to water the grass instead of eroding the hillside. And he cross-fenced and rotated his grassland, allowing the cattle to graze one pasture down to the roots, then moving them to another while the first recovered.

He also employed an astute businessman's sense of timing, holding his cattle until the spring instead of selling them in the fall, when most ranchers do.

When Williams hit a particularly dry year, he'd truck his herd to his ranch in Wyoming or eighty-five miles northeast to his thirty-five-hundred-acre irrigated farm near Fort Stockton, where he also grew alfalfa to fatten his stock. The land once belonged to Williams's father, who had to sell it during the serious drought that hit Texas in the early 1950's. Between 1978 and 1984 Claytie Williams bought the land back parcel by parcel.

In the Davis Mountains Williams's ranching methods were considered controversial. For one thing, he was raising coal black cattle where traditionally white-faced red highland Herefords had grazed. For another, his love for the latest in Aggie agricultural technology went against the local grain. This country was right out of a Marlboro ad, and many of the ranches operated much as they did a century ago. The spreads were big enough and the grass nutritious enough to make old-style ranching economically feasible—provided the land was paid off a generation or two ago and no one had borrowed against it since.

But some neighbors had more serious concerns about what long-range impact Williams's approach would have on the land. The Davis Mountains pastures may look as green as those in central Wyoming, but in reality they're an oasis in the vast Chihuahuan Desert—the most arid stretch of real estate in North America. The ecosystem here is extremely fragile.

Yet Clayton Williams insisted that by killing the moisture-sucking invaders like catclaw and mesquite and deflecting runoff, he was *improving* the land, not degrading it. He expressed some respect for neighboring ranchers but no patience with hard-line environmentalists urging him to leave the land in its natural state. "I despise those people, and they don't like me back," he said bluntly. "They're really fighting free enterprise, rather than looking after the land."

Knowing his opinions, many of Williams's friends and associates were surprised to learn that he'd become one of the primary backers of the Chihuahuan Desert Research Institute, an organization based in Alpine and noted, at least in its early days, for its shaggy-headed environmentalist bent. "I was able to help the Chihuahuan Desert group to steer a moderate course, but they can still research and grow hair," he conceded wryly, glancing up at his own retreating hairline. In 1984, "back when everybody was rich," Williams actually auctioned the shirt off his back to raise twenty-five thousand dollars to help the CDRI establish a nature center featuring realistic wildlife dioramas. But once he became involved with the group, its research into such topics as the effects of pesticides on the endangered peregrine falcon went by the board.

Clayton Williams seemed less a rancher than a cattle entrepreneur. In fact, he was possessed of an entrepreneurial passion so strong that almost anything provided him with a new business concept. "You can throw out an idea to Claytie, and it's just like igniting a can of gasoline," said his wife.

When Frank Velasco, foreman at Williams's Fort Stockton alfalfa farm, suggested the alfalfa crop might sell better mixed with molasses and fashioned into little cakes, Williams founded ClayDesta Feeds. When he learned that Parkview —one of Midland's two hospitals—was for sale, he cooked up a joint venture with forty-one doctors to buy the out-

moded institution and move it to new quarters in the
ClayDesta Plaza complex.

Though he put in fourteen-hour days on his ranches,
Williams denied being a workaholic. "When I work, I work
very intensely, and when I stop, I stop very intensely," he
explained at the end of a hectic weekday, treating himself to
a whiskey from the bar in his Midland office.

But some of his closest associates questioned whether
Clayton Williams ever really stopped. He had no interest in
gambling in Las Vegas, skiing in Vail or Aspen, or lounging
on a beach in the Bahamas—all popular escapes for the Texas
Big Rich. He'd never been to Western Europe. His idea of
relaxation was taking Modesta on a three-week hunting trip
to someplace like Afghanistan or Nepal, where they'd bag
the his-and-hers trophies arranged by continent on the rock
walls of the living room of their twelve-thousand-square-foot
house.

Once a year Williams and his wife would ride hundreds of miles across seventeen-thousand-foot-high steppes
or hike for days through dense jungle. Yet even these strenuous vacations provided grist for his entrepreneurial imagination. When he and Modesta had an especially enjoyable
safari staged by Hunters Africa in Botswana, he bought the
company.

"You'll find more entrepreneurs in Texas than just about
anywhere," Williams said. "Texas values are good. Being a
Texan is important. It's *something*. That carries us further than
some people. We *think* that we're special, and because we
think we are, we are."

In the interest of nurturing these attitudes in the young,
Clayton Williams served as an entrepreneur-in-residence at
Texas A&M, teaching a class in the College of Business. Eight
times a semester he flew to College Station in his Sabreliner
jet and spent a couple of days lecturing on his successes and
failures, to give seniors and graduate students practical perspective to balance textbook theory. "Those kids are about
at the age where they won't listen to their fathers, but any
stranger's an expert," he said.

Clayton Williams received something more than intellectual stimulation and ego massage from being an Aggie

entrepreneur-in-residence. Dr. Ella Van Fleet insisted that Williams read all the books on her syllabus before he started his seminar. If he hadn't been exposed to current business theory, especially to John Naisbitt's *Megatrends*, he admitted, he wouldn't have been receptive to the idea of moving from oil and gas into long-distance communication.

"When some of my young fellows came to me and said, 'You should go into the long-distance phone bidness [as he pronounced it],' I said, 'My God, you guys must've been smoking marijuana,' " Williams recalled with a grin.

ClayDesta Communications was born when AT&T told Williams that it would take three or four months to provide phone service to tenants in the ClayDesta National Bank Building, which was about to open. Joe Mitchell and Jamie Winkel, two Young Turks working for his real estate company, suggested Williams develop his own long-distance system based on the latest technology—converting sound into digital signals that could be turned back into speech at the receiving end.

Clayton Williams embraced concepts like high tech, high touch, and the expansion of the service sector with the zeal of a religious convert. As for the industry that brought him his first wealth, he was less sanguine. "I think this economy is tellin' us that we've left manufacturing—oil and gas production, steel production—as a major part of our economy," he told a roomful of anxious Midland Jaycees in November 1985, waving his arms around as if he were trying to separate a Brangus calf from its mother. "The strength is coming from services—information and that kind of thing. You can import a barrel of oil, but you can't import a service."

Then oilman Clayton W. Williams, Jr., flashed his toothy, wraparound grin and added: "The nice thing about the long-distance bidness is it doesn't deplete."

★

CHAPTER TWO

Houston

High Times in Petro Metro

On May 20, 1985, gossip columnist Maxine Mesinger stood on the balcony of Mary Elizabeth Mecom's mansion in River Oaks—Houston's most expensive neighborhood—and intoned in her husky, theatrical voice, "You don't have to be a blueblood to be in Houston society, enough of that green stuff will turn anybody's blood blue." Across the country seven million viewers of the *Today* show watched.

Maxine was saying something that everyone in Texas already knew. For well over a decade Houston had boomed. And boomtown Houston was a city of limitless potential and endless opportunity, a place where ordinary middle-class people, without exceptional talents or even good educations, could become multimillionaires in a few short years. Examples were everywhere: in Maxine's column; in the Rolls-Royces and Mercedes that crowded the freeways; in the mansions, newly built to look old, along River Oaks Boulevard and Kirby Drive, standing right out there where everyone could see the money.

And everyone had to be able to see the money; otherwise no one would know who was rich and who wasn't. New people were flocking into town in such numbers and rising from the obscure local ooze at such a rate that the only way to tell who was worth bothering with (all too often that meant who could help one up the business or social ladder) was to engage in a competitive display of the trappings of wealth: houses; cars; clothes; jewels; parties; even charitable donations. Worthy causes published lists of their supporters, with the names ranked by the size of the contributions.

The endless status game was a field day for fancy restaurants, pricey specialty shops, florists, caterers, hairdressers, publicists, and carriage-trade real estate agents earning sixty-thousand-dollar commissions on million-dollar homes. New York and European jewelers and couturiers galloped in to scoop up that freely spent green. To capitalize on the city's fascination with imported aristocrats—even if they'd bought their titles— boutiques catering to the Big Rich had viscounts and baronets for managers.

Houston had always been fascinated with Baron Ricky di Portanova. And why not? He had a title. He was an heir to one of Houston's biggest and oldest oil fortunes. He had suave Clark Gable looks. He spent his money with an ostentation that would put a Greek shipping tycoon to shame. And his pretty, voluptuous brunette wife—Sandy "Buckets" Hovas when she was a student at Houston's Lamar High, now the baroness Sandra—was a local girl catapulted to social stardom.

Baron Ricky di Portanova was a throwback to a type seldom seen, at least on this continent, since the 1920's: the globe-trotting playboy. That may be why he had to battle so hard against his own family for his full fortune.

In 1928 the baron's maternal grandfather, a fifth-grade dropout named Hugh Roy Cullen, struck a billion-dollar pool of petroleum near Houston. He quickly became one of those legendary larger-than-life wildcatters, unbelievably wealthy in the Depression-ravaged 1930's.

Cullen built an immense mansion on six acres in River

Oaks; the place required fourteen servants to maintain it. He also founded Quintana Petroleum as an umbrella for his oil interests. Then, like the Yankee robber baron industrialists of a generation or so before him, Hugh Roy Cullen developed a social conscience. In 1936 he turned from ostentatious display to philanthropy. Over the next two decades he and his wife, Lillie, gave the University of Houston more than two hundred million dollars, almost single-handedly building it into an institution where children of the city's working class could get decent educations. The Cullens also contributed substantially to Houston's hospitals and arts groups.

Hugh Roy and Lillie Cullen had four daughters. (Their son, Roy, had died in a drilling rig accident in 1936.) The three younger girls married sober types who worked in the family banking business. But the eldest daughter, named for her mother, went to Hollywood, where she met Paolo di Portanova, a swooningly handsome Italian bit actor who claimed a title dating back to 1740 but obscurely documented. They married on December 16, 1932. Their first child was born eight months later.

In those days such a circumstance was scandalous, especially when it occurred in what was probably the richest family in Baptist-dominated Houston. While the Cullens didn't legally disown Lillie di Portanova, they had little to do with her from then on. The titled Italian actor and the American oil heiress had two sons: Enrique, who inherited his father's title, and Ugo, who grew up to become a large man dedicated to rewriting the Bible to reflect a kind rather than a vindictive God. Eventually the marriage broke up, and Lillie Cullen di Portanova moved to New York, where she lived out her years in a modest hotel on Times Square, fattening herself to almost four hundred pounds on sweet cream and Coca-Cola. Although she kept more than a million dollars in the bank, she wandered the streets dressed as a bag lady. She would buy good cloth coats at Bergdorf Goodman, then replace the collars with scraps of velvet, the buttons with safety pins. She gave legendary tips to the porters who brought her Cokes.

Living in Rome, Baron Ricky had no idea he was heir to a vast fortune. Then, after Hugh Roy Cullen died in 1957, he began receiving checks for five thousand dollars every month—enough to make him curious about his grandfather's estate and to give him the leisure to try to satisfy his curiosity. In 1961 he came to Houston.

While Enrique's aunts treated him pleasantly enough, they refused to give him an accounting of the family trusts. As he attempted to dig deeper into the Cullen affairs, he and his first wife, Ljuba—a tall, dark-haired beauty who'd ducked out of Yugoslavia as a member of a women's basketball team—made a social splash in Houston. He won several relatively minor financial victories. In 1965 the Cullens gave him $841,425, and in 1966 his mother died, and he and Ugo inherited her $4.8 million estate. Meanwhile, Baron Ricky was playing the stock market with great success, multiplying his millions. And he spent freely, using his twin-engine plane to ferry friends three hundred miles each way to lunch at the Cadillac Bar in Nuevo Laredo.

In 1967 Enrique and Ljuba di Portanova went through a messy divorce. Ljuba got $1.01 million, her jewelry, her furs, and a town house; Ricky had to pay a fee of $300,000 to her lawyer, Houston courtroom giant Percy Foreman, who had accepted three star sapphires and a diamond necklace as a down payment. The baron, though, got to keep most of his substantial fortune; the trusts were then paying him $64,000 a month. And he got to marry his new *amore*, Sandy Hovas.

In 1980 Ricky hit on an inventive birthday present for his beloved: controlling interest in her favorite nightclub, New York's posh "21." The very public deal fell through, but to jet set gossip columnists, it was the romantic gesture that counted.

During the seventies and eighties Baron Ricky continued to fight for his and Ugo's share of what had grown to be a two-billion-dollar pie. He hired bulldog-mean New York superlawyer Roy Cohn to do battle for him, asking for five hundred million dollars in punitive damages. The case, still in court in 1989 (three years after Cohn's death,) represented, as much as anything, a clash in life-styles.

While the rest of the Cullen family led decorous, low-key lives (the only cousin of Ricky's whose name regularly made the papers was Mary Cullen, a marathon runner), the Di Portanovas flaunted their money with open exuberance. Their primary residence was an opulent two-story apartment in Rome with a roof garden and a seventy-five-foot-long living room. During the three months a year they spent in Houston, they stayed at the white Mediterranean mansion they bought for the baroness's mother. Because they found the muggy Houston summers oppressive, they enclosed the entire backyard in an ultramodern steel and glass extension.

Because the house sat smack out on River Oaks Boulevard for all the world to see, the air-conditioned addition sent aesthetic shock waves through that moneyed enclave. Two gigantic crystal chandeliers hung over the forty-by-forty-foot swimming pool. It looked, neighbors sniffed, like something an Arab prince might erect in Beverly Hills.

But the Hovas house was a modest bungalow compared with Arabesque, the breathtaking villa the Di Portanovas built in the fashionable Las Brisas section of Acapulco. Viewed from across the bay on the terrace of the Villa Vera Racquet Club, the house looked like a Berber palace gleaming white against the dark blue water. It had thirty-two bedrooms, twenty-six baths, four kitchens, two indoor waterfalls, and its own discotheque with pulsating lights under the dance floor. The roof was adorned with life-size marble camels and a gun turret.

During the winter months Arabesque was a virtually continuous house party, with the Di Portanovas entertaining such celebrity guests as Henry and Nancy Kissinger, Paloma Picasso, Titi von Furstenberg, and Harold and Nancy Robbins.

While this Moorish fantasy was under construction, CBS News reported that it was being built for the shah of Iran, then in exile a couple of hundred miles away in Cuernavaca. The mistake was understandable—the shah's sister had a less impressive villa next door—but it was the Di Portanovas' machine-gun-toting guards, not the remnants of the shah's SAVAK, who patroled the drive leading to the house.

Private parties were a major event in the social Olympics during the Houston boom. As tough as the competition was and as hard as many hostesses (and hosts) trained for the games, the gold medal belonged to Lorraine McMurrey, a fiftyish blond with a good, leggy figure and an equally well-developed instinct for the dramatic. Flush with Big Money from oil, gas, ranching, and racehorses, she threw a party a week when she was in town. In 1983, to fete legendary Dallas hostess Nancy Hammond on her sixty-fifth birthday, Ms. McMurrey took over the swank Rio Room, then the hottest club in Dallas, and re-created highlights from the honoree's top parties. That was no mean challenge. For years Mrs. Hammond had staged lavish birthday parties for her husband, Jake. Each of them had a creative theme. One, for example, was a circus party that required elephants to be tethered to the side of Dallas's exclusive Brookhollow Country Club.

For the thirty of the 150 guests at the Hammond party who were traveling the 260 miles from Houston, Ms. McMurrey chartered two jets, plus a bus to take the celebrants from Love Field, where they landed, to the Rio Room. To get the Houstonians in the mood, the bus driver wore a burnoose, and a belly dancer undulated her navel in the aisle. At the nightclub, clowns, acrobats, jugglers, weight lifters, and sword swallowers entertained under paper palm trees and a ceiling-hung model of the *Spirit of St. Louis* while guests feasted on whole roast lamb.

Even Lorraine McMurrey's less ambitious parties contained elements of surprise and fantasy. Since she gave *at least* a brunch or dinner every week, she kept the towering ficus and rubber trees in her two-story living room strung with little white Tivoli lights, ready to be plugged in at the drop of an invitation. The tile fountain that decorated one wall of the square living room doubled as a tub to ice champagne and white wine, and the backyard converted into a croquet court for leisurely brunches.

To add glitter to her guest list for her larger dos, Ms. McMurrey always included Big Names. "You've got to have a cross section of people," she asserted. "You've got to have your country ranchers, your socialites, your entrepreneurs, your professional people. And you've *got* to have stars. I don't believe in having *you* be the only one who's pretty or glamorous."

Lorraine McMurrey's chief rival for the Houston Hostess

crown was her decidedly glamorous friend Lynn Wyatt, a
true member of the international jet set. Mrs. Wyatt's Houston house was a Big Rich landmark—the grand château the
late Houston society architect John Staub had designed for
Hugh Roy Cullen. When she entertained there, it was normally a seated dinner for twenty, without a theme or floor
show but with an interesting mix of people—say, a princess
or two and Mick Jagger.

"Why not?" Mrs. Wyatt declared. "Royalty likes Mick
Jagger as much as Mick Jagger likes royalty."

In the more innocent days before windfall profit taxes
and OPEC, Houstonians didn't pull their punches when it
came to showing off. During the forties and fifties Houston
timber and real estate baron "Silver Dollar" Jim West kept
thousands of silver dollars in the basement of his River Oaks
mansion. He had his pockets specially constructed so he
could carry the coins and throw them, fifty and a hundred
at a time, in public places. West delighted in tossing handfuls
into swimming pools and watching children dive for them.
Houston's grandest *grande dame*, Miss Ima Hogg (her name
was real, but her fabled siblings Ura, Sheza, and Heza never
existed), had a passion for pink and a fondness for riding an
oversize tricycle up and down the halls of her luxury high
rise. She ordered the help around with a whistle, with a
different number of tweets for each servant.

About 1950 Sheppard King III called society jeweler
Steve Chazanow out of bed at 3:00 A.M. to deliver a diamond
to fit the navel of his intended, belly dancer Samia Gamal,
a former favorite of Egyptian King Farouk. They tried stone
after stone, but none was quite right—and it had to be *perfect*.
The superrich playboy was so enamored of the dark-eyed
beauty that he converted to Islam and changed his first name
to Abdullah. And he was heir to a cotton fortune—*really* Old
Money by Texas standards.

Until she sold the *Houston Post* to the group that owns
Toronto's *Sun* newspaper chain for $130 million in 1983,
Oveta Culp Hobby, whose wealth *Forbes* pegged at $650 mil-
lion in 1989, was the most powerful woman in Texas. During
World War II she headed the Women's Army Corps, and
she was President Dwight Eisenhower's secretary of health,

education, and welfare. Still, when her neighbors in the very old guard and deed-restricted subdivision of Southampton, which predated River Oaks, refused to approve her plans to replace her Tudor mansion with a contemporary design, she tore the old house down and left the unsightly rubble on the lot for years.

No orgy of ostentation before or since equaled the impact Houston wildcatter Glenn McCarthy made in 1949 when he opened his outrageously opulent $21.5 million Shamrock Hotel. Before that single event Houston, with 619,000 people, was the largest city in the South and the business heart of the oil industry. Afterward it was the undisputed world capital of the *nouveau riche*.

At the time the forty-one-year-old oilman's net worth was about $212 million. He had 150 million barrels of oil in the ground. He owned a chemical plant, a natural gas company, a radio station, seventeen weekly newspapers, the South's most opulent hotel, two downtown office buildings, and five thousand acres of Houston real estate. And his planes had placed first, second, and fourth in the 1948 Bendix races—the airborne equivalent of the Indianapolis 500.

With a genius for publicity, McCarthy (who served as the inspiration for the hard-drinking, two-fisted upstart James Dean played in the film version of Edna Ferber's Texas epic *Giant*) had the nation primed. Months before the green-roofed monument to oil was ready for occupancy, newspapers nationwide trumpeted the Shamrock's amenities. It boasted the world's largest hotel swimming pool. Fifty meters long and fifty meters wide at its broadest point, it was shaped like an Irish harp. Each guest room had its own TV, although Houston had only one television station. The hotel had three kitchens and two bakeries—one for breads, the other for sweets. In the basement was a special disposal facility that chilled the garbage and loaded it onto trucks, protecting the noses of guests and neighbors. The Shamrock lobby was paneled in twenty-two thousand feet of Honduran mahogany, all cut from the same huge tree, and the decor featured sixty-three shades of green.

The grand opening was set for St. Patrick's Day, March 17, 1949. As the date got closer, newspapers showed the debonair oilman, with his wavy hair and fashionably thin mustache, buying all three top steers in the Chicago Livestock Show to provide steaks for the party. And when a nursery refused to sell him enough grass to sod the twenty-two acres around the Shamrock, McCarthy bought the company; the press loved it.

For high-rolling excess and outlandish behavior America had never seen anything to match that $1.5 million bash. In its wake *The New York Times* archly described the blowout as "a county fair in ermine," and *Fortune* magazine haughtily observed: "The state's great oilfields have spurted forth a number of newly rich characters who have conducted themselves with all the shy reserve of so many flagpole-sitters."

McCarthy, who sat on the board of Eastern Airlines, chartered three Constellations—then the *dernier cri* in commercial aviation luxury—to transport celebrities from New York and Chicago, and he hired a Santa Fe Chief with sixteen Pullmans to fetch the Hollywood crowd. McCarthy himself arrived for the festivities in the country's only private Stratoliner. The plane had a lounge, a bar, and a bedroom; his longtime friend Howard Hughes, Jr., was at the controls. (Two months later McCarthy bought the Stratoliner from Hughes for six hundred thousand dollars)

Small wonder, then, that Houston jammed the Shamrock that March 17. The *Houston Chronicle* counted a hundred multimillionaires in the crush. By nightfall some fifty thousand people had crowded around the hotel, hoping to catch a glimpse of the celebrities as they returned from the premiere of *Green Promise*, the first and only film McCarthy ever bankrolled. Starring Walter Brennan and a ten-year-old newcomer named Natalie Wood, the movie extolled the virtues of the 4-H clubs. But the real drama was in the Shamrock Emerald Room, where actress Dorothy Lamour was due to broadcast her nationally popular weekly live radio show.

"The whole hotel was full," McCarthy said thirty-seven years later. "People couldn't get a drink and everybody was thirsty, so we sent the whiskey out in the hallway." Those who couldn't make it to the whiskey simply dipped their glasses in the "river of champagne"—fountains of bubbly arrayed on tables down the hall.

Then, as airtime for the Lamour show got closer and the guests got tipsier, the public-address system failed. Fred Nahas, who managed McCarthy's radio station, had intended to announce that those holding certain tickets (including the VIPs present) should go to the Emerald Room, while others should take their reserved seats in nearby banquet rooms. But there was no way to get word to the crowd. Finally, like a flock of berserk penguins, scores of tuxedo-clad Houstonians rushed the Emerald Room, where the show was about to go on the air coast to coast. They grabbed the stanchions strung with velvet rope that cordoned off the entrance and began hitting each other with them.

An irate woman grabbed Miss Lamour's microphone and announced coast to coast: "I don't care about your damned broadcast. I paid to get in. I want my seat." Then, mistakenly assuming he was talking into a safe line, a harried NBC engineer complained that the Houston end was "fucking up" the broadcast. The "word" vaulted into America's living rooms; seconds later the network pulled the plug.

Frustrated and angry, Glenn McCarthy sought out his friend Eastern Airlines chairman and flying ace Captain Eddie Rickenbacker. "I said, 'Isn't this one hell of a thing to run into? They're just tearing up the whole show,' " recalled McCarthy. "And he said, 'Oh, no. Don't let it bother you. If there wasn't something like this happening, it wouldn't be worth a damn.' "

"I don't think Houston even *has* what other cities would call society," opined Dody Resnick, flashing a diamond the size of a grape as she dipped into her endive salad at Tony's, the pricey French restaurant that served as a kind of malt shop for the Houston rich. Mrs. Resnick's husband, Bob, was one of Texas's new breed of multimillionaire entrepreneurs. In 1985 he sold his communications company, TSI, to Atlantic Bell for twenty-three million dollars.

"Houston society is just a lot of people spending a lot of money and having a good time," Mrs. Resnick continued. "I've met people who did volunteer work for charities and didn't know what the charity *did*."

Small wonder. During the boom years of the late seventies and early eighties there was a major benefit gala several times a month. The attendant preliminary cocktail parties, plus the exhausting rounds of birthday bashes, little lunches, and soirees to honor titled persons flogging fragrances, piled up to the point where the socially active were dropping in on as many as five parties a night, pausing at each just long enough to register their presence.

In March 1985 divorcée Franelle Rogers, whose Beaumont-based family fortune was founded on Texas State Optical, an eyeglass chain, rocketed onto the big-city social scene as chairman of the Houston Grand Opera Ball. As a tie-in with HGO's production of *Eugene Onegin*, she transformed the ballroom of the Warwick Post Oak into a scene from czarist Russia, complete with mounds of beluga caviar and salmon and oceans of chilled Stolichnaya vodka. Mounted Cossack guards paraded in front of the entrance; Russian wolfhounds on leashes patrolled the lobby. A four-story onion-dome set replicated St. Petersburg in 1879. The Warwick Club became a knock-off of New York's Russian Tea Room, down to the exotic dessert menu. After Russian-born ballet star Rudolf Nureyev had wowed the four hundred guests, the orchestra broke into Strauss waltzes. "People don't want to think they're spending all their money on decoration, but they *do* like to walk into a fantasy," Ms. Rogers said afterward.

After the collapse of oil prices the charity ball merry-go-round slowed down. By 1986 it was customary for five couples to share the cost of a twenty-five-thousand-dollar table for ten—something that was *never* done in the early eighties.

There *were* rich Houstonians whose tastes and sensibilities were as cultivated as any in the world. Take Dominique de Menil, the Paris-born heiress to the oil tool fortune founded by Conrad Schlumberger (pronounced SCHLUM-ber-zhay). She amassed one of the world's outstanding collections of surrealist and contemporary art, and in June 1987 she opened a museum to house it, a museum to rival the Frick in New York, the Phillips in Washington, and the Gardner in Boston. Fifteen years earlier she and her late husband, John de Menil, younger son of a French baron, had commissioned New York architect Philip Johnson to design an

ecumenical chapel to house some of the last, profoundly
somber paintings by the Abstract Expressionist Mark Rothko.

Both for the source of her two-hundred-million-dollar
fortune and for her strong will, Mrs. de Menil was known
as the "steel butterfly." She wasn't just an art collector; she
was an art scholar. In 1979 she published *The Image of the
Black in Western Art*, her own two-volume treatise with lavish
photographs; a third volume appeared in 1986. A slender
gray-haired woman who dressed simply, Dominique de
Menil looked as regal balancing a bowl of gumbo on her
knees as she did standing next to former President Jimmy
Carter handing out the Carter-De Menil Human Rights
Award to mothers of Argentina's Disappeared.

Unlike most of the Texas Big Rich, whose politics ranged
from middle-of-the-road Democratic to the farthest right
reaches of Republicanism, Mrs. de Menil had been a lifelong
supporter of liberal and even radical causes. "Broken Obe-
lisk," the Barnett Newman sculpture she and her late husband commissioned for the reflecting pool in front of the
Rothko Chapel, was dedicated to the fallen civil rights leader
the Reverend Martin Luther King, Jr. Even Black Panthers
paid their respects at John de Menil's funeral in 1973. And
like George Bernard Shaw's Professor Henry Higgins, the
couple took a dashiki-clad young black activist named Mickey
Leland, sent him to France to give him a sophisticated world
view, and polished him up to the point where he became a
U.S. representative from Houston. (Congressman Leland
died in July 1989 on a fact-finding mission to Ethiopia, when
the light plane ferrying his party to remote, famine-ravaged
refugee camps crashed.)

The De Menils weren't the only fabulously wealthy
Houstonians with politically liberal leanings. Libby Rice
Winston—whose mother was the first wife of Houston's
most mysterious millionaire, the late Howard Hughes—used
her inherited fortune to found the Peaceable Kingdom, a
utopian arts, crafts, and agricultural commune an hour north
of the city.

What Dominique de Menil did for Houston's visual arts,
commercial developer Gerald Hines, Medici of the New Architecture, did for its skyline. He started out modestly, a

Purdue engineer fond of horn-rimmed glasses, penny loafers, and motorcycles. When he first came to Houston in the
early sixties, he lived in the YMCA. But perhaps by marrying
Dot Schwarz of the FAO Schwarz clan, Hines acquired a
certain upper-class sensibility and top-drawer taste. He also
acquired, through his own efforts, assets worth an estimated
$225 million

In the early seventies Hines decided that the city's top
law and accounting firms, banks, and multinational corporations would pay a premium to lease space in great buildings
designed by world-famous architects. So Hines called in the
likes of Philip Johnson and I. M. Pei and, except in budget,
gave them free creative reign. To keep costs within reason,
he hit upon a scheme for having the Big Name architects do
the initial design, while less expensive local architects supervised the construction. The result, which would have
been startling anywhere, was especially so in a city where
most of the rich seemed to be stuck on French châteaux,
antebellum plantation houses, and other grand styles of the
past.

Hines's buildings—from a silver-skinned abstract rendition of the Empire State Building to a postmodernist rose
granite takeoff of a Gothic cathedral—garnered kudos from
even the most jaded international critics.

By 1989 Gerald Hines had completed 384 projects total-
ing seventy-eight million square feet. But except for a hos-
pital-affiliated office tower in downtown Houston, he'd
stopped building in Texas, at least temporarily. Sixteen percent of the city's office space stood vacant; the situation was
worse in Dallas and Fort Worth and even more desperate in
Austin. From Amarillo to Brownsville and from El Paso to
Beaumont, the whole state was overbuilt. The new construction that bore Gerald Hines's name was in Albuquerque, San
Francisco, New York, Washington, Minneapolis, Boston, Seattle, and Cincinnati. It wasn't in the Oil Patch.

But even in depressed, overbuilt Texas, Hines wasn't
hurting *too* badly. His striking architecture was now prompt-
ing tenants to leave older, less interesting, less prestigious
buildings—especially when Hines tossed in incentives like
a decorating allowance or a year's free rent with a five-year
lease. When the average occupancy rate in Houston had

dropped to 78 percent, the average for Hines's major office towers in the city was still 95 percent.

Other developers weren't so lucky.

"In the first hundred years of Houston's history the city developed ninety million square feet of office space," apartment czar Harold Farb glumly noted in the summer of 1985. "It developed the same amount in the last five years."

That explained why he looked worried. He owned more than a million square feet of that recently built office space, and it wasn't downtown, nor was it in buildings designed by world-class architects.

Harold Farb had other reasons for concern as well. When he'd divorced his blond socialite second wife, Carolyn, in 1983 after six years of marriage, the court had ruled their prenuptial agreement invalid. That contract had limited any potential divorce settlement to $1 million. With it out of the way, she received $20 million, including their River Oaks mansion with its floors copied from those in Versailles, two Rolls-Royces, a Jaguar, and $8 million in cash. To make matters worse, Farb's net worth had been $167 million at the time the court awarded Carolyn Farb the property. Now it was falling fast.

The meteoric rise of Harold and Carolyn Farb on the Houston social scene and the equally rapid and public disintegration of their marriage could almost be an allegory for Houston during the boom. They were ordinary people who rocketed to unbelievable riches and celebrity, but they overreached.

The Farbs never quite seemed to catch on to the way the game was played. And there *were* rules to the game, even in Houston. There was *nouveau riche*—and there was *nouveau nouveau riche*. When they weren't accepted, the Farbs tried harder. They were as diligent and determined as they were audacious. After Carolyn Farb's photograph was relegated to a back page in *Town & Country*'s September 1979 Texas issue, they founded *Ultra*, a glossy life-style magazine intended to appeal to the Texas Big Rich and the advertisers who courted them. Even after four years *Ultra* continued to be a financial drain; in 1985 Farb sold it.

Farb even took on Tony's but lost. At his flashy restau-

rant and nightclub the Carlyle, the prices were high and the
food and service uneven. The overdone red interior was
giddy with chandeliers, mock-classical murals, and massive
floral displays. *Architectural Digest* featured the decor, but
Forbes likened it to a Parisian bordello's. By the time Farb
closed it in 1985, the Carlyle had devoured more than $6.5
million of his fortune.

Harold Farb had put the Carlyle's Red Room on the map
by singing there. Not just "Happy Birthday" to a favorite
patron, but "Singin' in the Rain," "My Funny Valentine,"
"Someone to Watch over Me," and other lounge favorites,
with a full show band for backup. Up onstage he seemed
like a character in a musical—a rich middle-aged man baring
his surprisingly vulnerable heart in song.

"My dad taught me 'Always run your business like
there's a depression going on all around you,' " Farb said,
eyeing the black-and-white photos in his office of his father's
unassuming corner drugstore in Galveston. That advice
stood Harold Farb in good stead—until he forgot it and
started chasing the will-o'-the-wisp of glamour that hovered
somewhere between the actual behavior of the Big Rich and
some Hollywood fantasy.

"I grew up in show business," said Farb, whose father
had also owned movie theaters. "My earliest idol was Bing
Crosby."

After the divorce Carolyn Farb told interviewers that
when she and Harold met, he was just another successful
businessman. "He didn't know a Chloë from a flavor of Bas-
kin-Robbins ice cream," she complained of his ignorance of
haute couture. That was a subject in which Carolyn had certainly became well versed. Three months before the divorce
People magazine featured her closet in a story on world-class
clotheshorses. It measured two thousand square feet—*six
rooms*, a separate one for evening gowns, a separate one for
cocktail dresses, a separate one for bags and shoes. The total
count of the contents? "Easily 1,000 pieces," she told *People.*
The value of that mind-boggling wardrobe? Conservatively,
at least $750,000.

Carolyn Farb wasn't born to that sort of money. She
grew up in a middle-class Houston neighborhood to a some-

what notorious family. Her grandfather was Jakey Friedman, a popular professional gambler who ran Houston's toniest private gaming club. When the authorities stopped winking at his enterprise, he moved on to Las Vegas, where he helped found the Sands Hotel and Casino. When Carolyn visited him during school vacations, she was entranced by the glamorous floor shows—Frank Sinatra, Piper Laurie, all that glitter, all those lights.

Shortly after she and Harold married, Carolyn Farb began turning her husband, and herself, into public figures. He started dressing in fashionable hand-tailored suits and telling people he had majored in art and music—although he'd never been to college. Carolyn, meanwhile, threw herself into volunteer work, where she quickly showed an impressive aptitude for organizing high-ticket fund raisers. Although she was comparatively new on the scene, she was asked to chair two of the city's most prestigious galas—the Houston Ballet Ball and the Museum of Fine Arts Ball.

Both brought her reams of publicity, not all of it uncritical. For the Ballet Ball she took as her theme "Soiree on the Sewanee," the antebellum South, offending those committed to racial equality. And she chose as the location the Houston Country Club, known for having admitted only a handful of Jewish members, most of them spouses of Old Money Gentile members. Carolyn and Harold Farb were Jewish; so were many of the most generous contributors to the Houston Ballet.

Still, the Big Rich came, and they paid. "I was the first to charge ten thousand dollars a table," Ms. Farb said five years later.

Except when it needed her ambition-fueled energy, Houston's *haut monde* seemed, along with the press, to be snickering at her behind its hand. Even at her own Ballet Ball, *Women's Wear Daily* instructed its photographer not to bother shooting Carolyn Farb. Regardless of how well the picture turned out, it wasn't going to use it.

"The Museum of Fine Arts Ball almost drove me up the wall," Harold Farb declared in his divorce deposition. That was the gala based on Renaissance England, the one with fire-eaters and jousting knights at which Farb appeared dressed as Henry VIII. "We had the equivalent of a switchboard in our home with all the phone calls and strange people coming in and out of our home. She did a marvelous job. She told me herself she was going to retire on that ball."

But there were other, bigger social mountains to climb.

Farb complained that his wife had so many outside interests and such a desire for personal glory that he sometimes felt he came last in her attentions. In response, she insisted to *Dallas Morning News* society-watcher Marilyn Schwartz that even though they had servants, she took charge of pampering her husband. "I banished chicken from the house because he hates chicken," she said. "I personally went to the bakery and bought his favorite pineapple pies."

And there was another complaint that came through in Harold Farb's deposition. "There's no satisfying Carolyn," Farb testified, saying that on some occasions, when he'd given her a small ring, necklace, or bracelet as a present, she'd taken it back to the jeweler and traded it in on something more expensive. "A lot of people," he added, "if you buy them something for ten cents, they're happy with it. I mean, it's just the thought."

Had Harold Farb perhaps encouraged her notorious extravagance? "I didn't just turn over a checkbook to her and say, 'Go out and spend all the money you can spend,' " he declared. "From time to time, I wanted to bring Carolyn back into the . . . real world, because there are only so many clothes and so much jewelry that anyone can wear. I do love Carolyn and I would want to have her with all these niceties—I mean, I'm not against them and certainly at that point I felt I could afford it and I would do it, but I didn't want to continue spoiling her to the point where if anything were to happen—I mean a business can fail, you know, anything can happen—that she would be living in a dream world."

Two years after the divorce, sitting in the red-brick white-columned mansion she'd renamed Carolina, Ms. Farb said she was devoting her time to raising money for such odd bedfellows as conservative senatorial candidate Phil Gramm and the Ms. Foundation. (She had declared grandly after winning her huge divorce settlement: "I feel that I have become some sort of heroine to a lot of women—I gave other women hope.")

Her current project was a nonball for Theatre on Wheels, which brought professional dramatic productions to schools. The point was to get people to send money without putting them to the bother and expense of going to a party. The invitation to the "Black and White but Nobody Came Ball" featured a photograph of Carolyn Farb in a romantically ruffled white dress. Beneath it was a dialogue which began: "BOY: 'What a beautiful princess.' GIRL: 'I'm so glad she came to help us or else we may never see the Children's Theatre again.' "

She said of the galas she'd chaired: "I set precedents in the way those things are done." And: "I set a lot of trends. . . . I think my events are art pieces. Each event had something magical, something special." And: "I'm very Renaissance, very involved."

Her unabashed self-praise had a sort of brash naiveté, something sadly fading from Houston in the late 1980's.

Unlike most other cities, Houston doesn't expect its economically privileged to behave better than the less financially fortunate. With disquieting frequency, the Houston rich have gotten involved in murder cases, as victims or suspects. Philanthropist William Marsh Rice, who founded Rice University, was done in by his butler and his attorney. Another butler figured in a case of suspicious death in 1972, when sixty-nine-year-old oilman Collier Hurley's newly estranged wife, Zevonah Faye, a twenty-nine-year-old former exotic dancer stage-named Friday Knight, plummeted from the balcony of their high rise. Mr. Hurley and his servant admitted being on that balcony at the time of the unfortunate Mrs. Hurley's fall, but said they were trying to prevent her from jumping. A grand jury ruled the death accidental.

A Houston society murder that occurred during the 1960's inspired Tommy Thompson's best seller *Blood and Money*. When socialite equestrienne Joan Robinson Hill died mysteriously of food poisoning, supposedly from bacteria-laced French pastries, her father, oilman Ash Robinson, charged that her plastic surgeon husband, Dr. John Hill, was responsible. With superstar defense lawyer Richard "Race-horse" Haynes leading the defense, the courtroom battle ended in a mistrial. While Hill was awaiting retrial, he was mysteriously shot to death by a hired killer. After several inconclusive investigations, Robinson left Houston and subsequently died in Florida.

In 1981 Kathleen Sandiford was tried for shooting her physician husband, Frank Sandiford, second-in-command to world-renowned heart surgeon Michael DeBakey. When Dr. Sandiford met his demise, he was headed up the stairs of their River Oaks home, dressed in his green hospital scrubs, carrying a copy of *Time* in one hand, a bottle of wine and a wineglass in the other. But defense attorney Marian Rosen managed to portray the killing as a virtual act of self-defense —a battered wife desperate to protect herself. Mrs. Sandiford celebrated her probated sentence with a huge barbecue.

Not so fortunate was Markham Duff-Smith, a thirty-four-year-old River Oaks investor. He was sentenced to die by lethal injection for masterminding the murders of his sister, her husband, and their adopted two-year-old son, arranging the crime so that it appeared that his sister had shot her family and then turned the gun on herself. Subsequently Duff-Smith, himself an adopted child, was also convicted of hiring the 1975 killing of his mother, Gertrude Zabolio, in order to inherit five hundred thousand dollars. Harris County Medical Examiner Joseph Jachimczyk had previously ruled the death a suicide, saying Mrs. Zabolio had strangled herself to death with a pair of pantyhose.

Such Big Money murder cases turned several of Houston's criminal defense attorneys into wealthy celebrities. Racehorse Haynes, for example, lived in a large contemporary house in River Oaks, drove a Duesenberg, and cruised the Gulf of Mexico in his sailing yacht *L'Esprit Libre*. "I don't think I'm so much famous as notorious," he said, reflecting on his successes.

In Houston that may be a distinction without a difference.

★

CHAPTER THREE

Joanne Johnson King Herring Davis

Scarlett O'Hara Takes On the World

Texas culture is an amalgam. Certainly the cowboy consciousness is pervasive, but Latin thought and customs flow in across the Rio Grande, and sober midwestern values across the Red River. The tough, crude heritage of Tennessee mountain men and hillbillies pushes through the piney woods along the eastern boundary. The influence of black culture remains strong in the eastern third of the state, where plantations imported slaves. And French Louisiana, from Cajun cooking to zydeco music, flavors the Upper Gulf Coast.

One of the most noticeable of these cultural ingredients, especially in Houston, which lies only one hundred and ten miles west of the Louisiana border, is the Old South. In fancy neighborhoods at least half the mansions seem to sport white-columned porticoes. But examples of pure southernness are rare in Texas. That may be why even Houston had

a tough time figuring out its homegrown southern belle
Joanne Johnson King Herring Davis.

The champagne reception opening the "Treasure
Houses of Britain" exhibit at Washington's National Gallery
was one of the hottest invitations of the fall 1985 social season, for it brought Prince Charles and Princess Di to these
once-colonial shores, and they, in turn, drew more of the
nation's far-flung rich and powerful to Washington than an
inaugural ball.

But despite the crush of celebrities, the image that dominated the front page of the *Washington Post* "Style" section
on Saturday, November 2, was that of Houston's curvaceous
blond honorary consul for Morocco and Pakistan, Joanne
Johnson King Herring Davis—offering her hand and a radiant smile to the worldly-looking prince. Seven years earlier
Sally Quinn—the Boswell of capital society—had introduced
Joanne to the *Washington Post*'s readers as Houston's Scarlett
O'Hara. And like the heroine of *Gone with the Wind*, who tore
down her velvet drapes to make a ball gown, on this more
recent evening Joanne demonstrated her charm and inven-
tiveness. When the dress she'd bought for the occasion didn't
arrive from New York, she decided to wear her grandmother's scoop-necked black evening gown, dating from the turn
of the century, when hourglass figures like Joanne's were
the height of fashion.

She *was* dazzling, with her heart-shaped face, her bow
mouth, her upturned nose, and the contrast between those
warm brown eyes and that tumble of honey-colored curls.
But there were plenty of beautiful, stunningly dressed
women at that party, many of them considerably younger
than Joanne Davis, then in her mid-fifties.

"For some reason, the [*Washington Post*] article focused
a lot on me," she said in an amused tone, shaking her head.
"That was so ridiculous, because I wasn't a stately home,
and I'm not *somebody* in Washington."

Truth be told, Joanne Davis frequently *was* somebody in
Washington, where she entertained the likes of Henry Kissinger and Prince Bandar, the Saudi ambassador to the U.S.,
at the Regent and the Hay-Adams (her favorite capital hotel,

because the ballroom looks across Pennsylvania Avenue at the White House). She was also somebody in New York, in Karachi, in Rabat, in Abu Dhabi—in fact, in much of the world. In Washington they looked down her décolletage. In Muslim countries they addressed her as "sir." After her second husband, Houston Natural Gas Corporation chairman Robert Herring, died in 1981, she continued to function independently and with considerable clout in a milieu where women were virtual nonentities.

Paradoxically, Joanne was effective precisely because she embodied that most feminine of American stereotypes—the southern belle.

"The image I seem to create is so different from what I am that it really leaves me in a state of shock," said Joanne, raising a hand to her rounded bosom and sipping a mixture of iced tea and orange juice.

Far more often than she would like, her image was that of a frivolous socialite.

"I have *never* done anything for social reasons," she insisted to me one afternoon in 1984. She was sitting in the paneled library of her River Oaks château, which she sold half a year later, when she married Lloyd Davis. The ceilings were thirty feet high. Scattered around on antique French end tables were photos of herself with famous people and signed portraits, such as one from the duchess of Paris inscribed "Pour Joanne."

"When I was married to Bob Herring, we entertained for business," she explained. "We tried to mix people who would not necessarily have come in contact with each other. A party is neutral ground. When you go to somebody's office, one person is seated behind a desk. The other is a supplicant, so to speak.

"What happens at a party is that people can come up and talk to each other. Nothing they say is binding. It is totally unofficial. Bob Herring used to do more business at parties in two minutes than he ever did at offices."

Not only was Robert Herring chairman and chief executive of Houston Natural Gas, which sold more natural gas for industrial uses than any other company, he also owned

four thousand miles of pipelines, ninety boats, and assorted
coal mines. He was a very rich man—and a very serious one.

Joanne, on the other hand, was well known for her talent
for making the most serious occasion fun. In her early thirties
she threw the party that established the Houston oil-rich
either as an elite that could laugh at itself or as a clique of
decadent, depraved, self-indulgent hedonists, depending on
whom one asked. The date was 1960. She was married to a
rich real estate developer named Robert King, and he wanted
to give his wife the most creative birthday blowout the Bayou
City had ever seen. It was billed as a Roman Bacchanal. It
turned out to be the ultimate toga party.

"We never *dreamed* it would have such repercussions,"
Joanne said, rolling her eyes to the ceiling. "This is the whole
story of my life, this Roman party."

The Kings invited about fifty of their closest friends—
tout Old Houston—to attend the party and to *participate* in
it. Everyone had to come in costume; everyone had a part
to play. There were even rehearsals. A Ballet Russe cho-
reographer coached the "gladiators" and "slave girls" in appropriate dances.

So much effort went into the soiree that Joan Fleming,
whom Joanne described as *"very* Junior League," suggested
that the Kings invite *Life* to document it for its regular *"Life*
Goes to a Party" department. Even when *Life* accepted, no
one thought the party would actually see the light of print.
National coverage of Houston was usually confined to the
business pages.

Everyone showed up at the Kings' sprawling Tangle-
wood château in costume, ready to play his or her part. The
gladiators danced. The slave girls were auctioned off. Little
Nubian slaves—members of a troop of ten-year-old black Boy
Scouts—refilled the silver goblets raised by reclining revel-
ers. Thanks to cleverly employed fireworks, the burning of
the Christian looked terribly realistic.

"We felt like we were in ancient Rome before it burned
down," one of the guests said later.

Life captured it all, and to everyone's surprise, it published the pictures—Nancy Robbins sitting in a fountain with
her legs exposed; Alfred Glassell lounging on a mattress cov-

ered in black satin; John Blaffer as Bacchus lifting a crystal goblet to lead the revelry; Patrick Nicholson bicycling home at 7:00 A.M. in his toga; Joanne herself being thrown into the pool. Not about to be scooped by the national press, the Houston papers sent uninvited representatives to cover the party and ran the story the next day—on the front page.

"Houston was *so* shocked," Joanne recalled. "They thought it was *the* most decadent, awful, incomprehensible, tasteless affair that anybody had ever had. But it was really just a lot of fun. Nobody even got drunk."

Part of what made Joanne such a celebrated hostess, then and later, was her penchant for getting guests involved in the action. "I was the first person to *move* people at dinners," she boasted. "It got to be such a big thing that *The New York Times* did a write-up on it."

Asking the men to change tables after the soup and again before dessert may be just the thing to enliven a little River Oaks dinner for thirty. But playing musical chairs at a formal Washington banquet, where strict protocol dictates who may sit next to whom?

In 1983, when Saudi Arabia, for the first time, sent a member of the royal family to be ambassador to the United States, Prince Bandar asked Joanne to introduce him to Washington. No sooner did word get out that she was planning a dinner for 116 in the ambassador's honor than she began receiving cautionary advice from powerful friends.

According to Joanne, Senator John Tower phoned the morning of the party to say, "Every Cabinet minister will be there tonight. You've got to behave yourself. I *know* how you like to move people, but you can't do that in Washington. I care about you, and I don't want you talked about tomorrow because you did something that hasn't been done."

Recounting the story two years later, Joanne insisted she had had every intention of following this well-intended counsel, but then, between the fish and the entrée, "Something inside of me said, 'Move them.' " She stepped up to the microphone and announced, "Every man, pick up his wineglass and move two tables to the right."

Her bold party ploy had the desired effect. "It was the biggest success that ever happened," she reported exuberantly. "Everybody said that they'd never had such fun. They *all* got to sit next to Henry Kissinger and Caspar Weinberger and Barbara Walters."

On the other hand, there was the dinner in 1977 for which she converted the party room of her River Oaks house into a seraglio straight out of *The Arabian Nights* to help Jordan's King Hussein and Saudi Arabia's Prince Saud feel at home. King Hussein stayed only fifteen minutes, pleading a dinner engagement with George Bush, and Prince Saud also retired disappointingly early.

Joanne hated being criticized, especially in print, but went ahead and did what she wanted. "Then I'm mad when somebody writes about it and I'm very *unjustifiably* represented," she said. "I think it comes from my father always encouraging me that anything you did that was fun was okay."

Joanne's father was William "Bull" Johnson, who became Texas A&M's first all-American quarterback although he weighed just 155 pounds at the time. Her mother was a Dallas-born southern gentlewoman with Georgia roots. Mrs. Johnson, Joanne says, always believed that there were certain things that ladies *did* and certain things that they *didn't* do and that the distinction was terribly important. "In the South after the Civil War they didn't have anything but manners," Joanne explained. "That's why you never see my mother when she is not *perfectly* dressed. We went to Kenya on safari, and she wore a full-length mink coat."

To hear Joanne describe her childhood, she grew up as the poorest child in River Oaks. Actually she lived in the fifth house built in that exclusive subdivision. One of her mother's ancestors died at the Alamo, earning the family a sizable tract of land. And her father's grandfather had gotten rich by designing the round cotton bale and the Walker Colt ("the gun that won the West"). Still, on those frequent occasions when her grandmother, who restricted herself to two servants, gave seated dinners for eighty, Joanne had to pitch in.

"I set more tables, cooked more cookies," she complained. "Nobody was more of a scullery maid than I was. Then I was expected to dress up and sing for the guests."

To Joanne the deprivation was painful. "I grew up with what you might call the Big Rich of Houston, and I wasn't one of them," she said. "They all had beautiful dresses from Neiman Marcus, and mine came from the local dressmaker. I was *with* the group that made their debut, but my parents decided I didn't need a debut, so I didn't have one."

What she *did* have were a lot of unusual and seemingly contradictory experiences. Her father insisted that she be brave; her mother insisted that she be a lady. When a water moccasin wrapped itself around his ten-year-old daughter's leg, Bull Johnson demanded that she locate an appropriate weapon and dispatch it herself; she did it in with a hoe.

What mattered to Mrs. Johnson was that her daughter had the courage at age twelve to approach such socially prominent party chaperones as Mrs. Morgan Davis, wife of the chairman of Humble Oil, and make polite conversation.

"I grew up where we had artichokes and butter knives at lunch because my mother said, 'This is the way people live,' " Joanne explained. "Once, when I was two years old, I picked up a finger bowl and drank out of it, and I think it left a scar on her."

Joanne Johnson King Herring Davis grew up dyslexic. "I was always considered very dumb," she admitted. "The terrible thing about dyslexia is what the teachers do to you and the students do to you. Then, when I turned thirteen, I became very popular, and it didn't matter if you were dumb," she said with a shrug.

Even as an adult Joanne bridled when people mistook her associative thought patterns and nonlinear logic for stupidity. Yet she persisted in hopping from topic to topic with blithe enthusiasm. That was because her apparent flightiness was effective. It charmed; it disarmed; it got her what she wanted. Like Scarlett O'Hara, Joanne was a survivor.

In 1978 Joanne became the only public official personally appointed by the king of Morocco. "It was a big shock to me," she recalled. After she and Bob Herring had met with the monarch and discussed world affairs for two hours, the king's chief of protocol appeared at their hotel. "He said, 'His Majesty wants *you*—not Bob Herring—to be consul,' " she added, widening her eyes in recollected amazement.

After checking with her existing client, Pakistan (which she pronounced PAW-kees-tan), she accepted.

Joanne first earned the consular plates for her white Cadillac in the early 1970's, when she was appointed honorary consul by Pakistan's President Ali Bhuto. Even after military strong man General Zia ul-Haq staged a successful coup and then executed his predecessor, she continued in her post. In fact, Zia promoted her to honorary consul general in 1980 and she retained that position under Zia's successor.

"I study their history, and I read the Koran," Joanne said. "I try to see the world from *their* standpoint. This is where most Americans make *such* mistakes. They judge everybody by our values. Our values are wonderful, but they're not the values of the rest of the world. We forget that people who have a history of five thousand years have every reason to be proud of their values and they want to be what they are."

Joanne was an unabashed cheerleader for capitalism, the one aspect of Western culture she seemed to have no misgivings about grafting onto the third world.

"I looked at these two countries, and I said, 'What can I give them?' " she asked rhetorically. "I can give them parties in Houston. I can get drunk sailors out of jail. I can send dead bodies home—all of which I do. *Or* I can contribute something that they really need: money. *Where* do they need money? In the poorer sector. I want *badly* to export free enterprise. If we don't export free enterprise, then we can't blame third world countries for listening to other voices."

Her method for exporting free enterprise was to encourage the development of cottage industries, which help the women make money without leaving their homes and thus disrupting social patterns laid down for millennia.

With her storerooms full of fine French antiques and with her smashing *haute couture* wardrobe (Yves Saint Laurent sent her clothes off his runway), Joanne recognized that the market for the quaint, the primitive, the imperfect was limited. "What I wanted to do was find a market which Europe could no longer support because of the price of labor," she explained.

She went around the world asking decorators what they

wanted that they could no longer get. The answer was hand-blocked prints, one of Pakistan's traditional crafts. "But they didn't want minarets, which is what the Pakistanis were doing," she said. "They wanted cabbage roses. So we changed the design and started making cabbage roses."

The first results of this cross between ancient Asian skill and current Euro-American taste were cream-colored cotton scatter rugs emblazoned with hot pink and bright green flowers. One of them covered her dressing-room floor. "The colors aren't quite right," she admitted cheerfully, urging me to remove my shoes and feel for myself. "But isn't it *soft*? It's a hundred percent cotton, and it is *machine-washable*," Joanne added in the same tone she once used to tout the latest household conveniences on Houston noontime television.

She was promoting similar enterprises in Morocco, where the leather was some of the finest in the world but the designs didn't suit the tastes of the Westerners who had the money to buy stylish shoes and handbags. She also encouraged some of the top couturiers in the United States and Europe to utilize Pakistani and Moroccan textiles, beginning with her own wardrobe.

In 1985 Joanne moved into the crisply contemporary, vaguely Moorish house Houston architect Charles Tapley designed for her new husband, Lloyd Davis. Davis's bachelor digs were elegantly spare. The walls were winter white; the floors, gray-veined white marble. His taste in art ran to modern, African primitive (he once owned a large cattle ranch in Rhodesia [now Zimbabwe]), and Art Deco, which he collected. (Joanne admitted Art Deco was the one period she couldn't stand.)

Lloyd Davis was a tall, athletic man with short, thick gray hair and a strong jaw balanced by the laugh lines around his eyes. After selling the communications company he had founded—Fisk Telephone—several years ago, he turned his attention to developing a "smart house"—an electronic system combining security, computer, entertainment, and communications functions. The owner of such an intelligent residence could call up from work to preheat the oven or program the coffeepot and the stereo to start at 6:00 A.M. The cost of the package, marketed under the name High-Tech Homes, would be about ten thousand dollars and could be included in the mortgage for new construction.

At first glance the Davis marriage seemed like a clear case of the attraction of opposites—the crisp-minded Rice engineer and the exuberant southern belle. He liked reggae music; she preferred Peter Duchin. Their living room looked like an exercise in negotiation—her carved and gilded Louis XV antiques asserting themselves next to his low-rise sofas upholstered in off-white Haitian cotton. In August 1988 they sold his Moorish *moderne* house, bought a penthouse next to Ugo di Portanova's in a tony Houston high rise, and announced that they'd be spending much of their time at their house at Lyford Cay, the chic Bahamian resort where their unlikely romance had begun.

Davis had been a friend of Bob Herring's, but he hadn't known Joanne well until he asked her to help him throw an open house at Lyford Cay, where she'd just sold *her* house to the sheikh of Kuwait. Less than a year later they were married.

They honeymooned in a yurt on the Gobi Desert. Davis admitted to me that before he and Joanne became engaged, he'd signed up for the excursion with some friends. "I was a little worried about Joanne's acceptance of the thing," he said, "but she was great. She's one heck of a mountain climber, camper, jock."

Behind Joanne's ultrafeminine exterior was one very game lady. Shortly after Bob Herring died, she was jogging through River Oaks when a dog knocked her down, breaking her leg. Despite a cast that extended from her toes to her hip, she kept up her whirlwind schedule, aided by a pair of Lucite crutches for formal affairs.

And Lloyd Davis himself was more multifaceted than he first appeared. For instance, he loved helping women shop for clothes. Under his guidance, on a trip to New York in the fall of 1985 Joanne headed for the Gallery of Wearable Art in SoHo, where he helped her pick out a one-of-a-kind black crepe cocktail dress with two *very* realistic black serpents curling around the neckline and twining around the waist.

Joanne talked about Lloyd's wanting her to spend more time at home, but so far she hadn't slowed down. "The other night in New York I sat with Vernon Walters on one side and Malcolm Baldrige on the other," she said, her exuberance spilling in giddy waves over the coolly functional living room. "To me, this is pure euphoria—to be with brilliant people who are doing things that mold our world, even if you don't agree with them."

The sparkle in her eyes and the faint peach flush in her cheeks were their own answer. Not even the most rational man could resist the wiles of a true southern belle with the brains to know what she really wanted.

★

CHAPTER FOUR

Josephine Abercrombie

The Pugilists' Pygmalion

Larger than life, red-stenciled supergraphic images of boxers charged across the outside walls of the long, low six-thousand-square-foot gym. Inside the Houston Boxing Association Training Center four young fighters sparred in two rings. Around the periphery three others did warm-up stretches and pummeled punching bags. The air was warm and moist; the smell, pungently masculine.

In the middle of the gym stood a refined, slender, almost delicate woman with aquamarine eyes and softly coiffed frosted blond hair. Wearing a navy blue Adolfo silk with a white collar, she looked as if she might have gotten lost en route to the exclusive shops in the Galleria a mile away. But make no mistake: Josephine Abercrombie belonged here. This was her gym, and these were her fighters.

Josephine Abercrombie's fascination with boxing began in 1938, when she was eleven years old. Her parents traveled by train to New York, where they saw Joe Louis flatten Max Schmeling in the first round. When they returned to Houston, her mother described the slugfest so vividly that little Josephine became an instant fan. Noticing her enthusiasm, her doting father took her to Golden Gloves matches.

By the mid-1980's the name of the heiress to one of Houston's legendary fortunes was appearing almost as often on the sports pages as it did in the society section—and in larger type. In stories short on adjectives and long on punchy verbs, blue-collar staples like the New York *Daily News* heralded her with such headlines as SHE'S CORNERED TOUGHS.

Even in Texas, where a rich woman was likely to be an avid football fan and a crack shot on a dove hunt, her athletic passion sent the social set reeling. Josephine Abercrombie was the most aristocratic boxing impresario since the Marquis of Queensberry. Educated at Pine Manor and Rice University—where she later sat on the Board of Governors —she spoke with a well-modulated finishing-school accent laced with the barest hint of a southern drawl. Her clothes, jewelry, and makeup were elegant and understated. The colors she wore were nothing if not ladylike—blues, pinks, lavenders, grays, and beiges. J. S. Abercrombie Minerals, which she chaired, may have been the only oil company in the world with offices decorated in subtle taupe, rose, and aubergine.

So what was a nice lady like her doing in a sport like this?

The answer was simple. She liked to win. She wanted to produce a world-champion boxer. Founded in January 1983, her Houston Boxing Association had signed twelve promising fighters by 1988, including Olympic gold medalist Frank Tate and U.S. Boxing Association heavyweight champion Tony Tucker. Boxing insiders were beginning to take the country's only female promoter seriously.

"Whatever she does, she does a good job," said boxing impresario Bob Arum of New York. Odds were good Josephine Abercrombie would have a world champion; he explained: "It's just a question of finances."

And finances were no problem for the only child of James S. Abercrombie, who made his fortune in the Oil Patch, first

by finding oil, then by inventing the oil well blowout pre-
venter. As a young wildcatter J. S. Abercrombie (no kin to
the fancy sporting goods clan) had seen a blowout reduce
his single wooden rig to rubble. Inspired by the disaster, he
came up with a device to protect against similar mishaps,
using a stick to sketch the design on the dirt floor of oil field
toolmaker Harry Cameron's cramped little shop. Abercrombie's patented piece of iron made deep drilling possible, and
Cameron Iron Works grew into a publicly held company with
assets of $462 million in 1987—down from $831 million in
1985, but hefty nonetheless. Since the death of her parents
in 1975, Ms. Abercrombie and her family trusts had owned
55 percent of Cameron, plus J. S. Abercrombie Minerals.

Mr. Jim—as his employees called J. S. Abercrombie—
demonstrated an unerring knack for picking up cheap farmland in the direction of Houston's growth. He left his daughter ninety-three acres of prime commercial real estate at one
of the busiest intersections in Houston—Loop 610 and the
Southwest Freeway. He also left her his share in the fifty-
two-hundred-acre Cinco Ranch west of Houston; in 1984 she
and her partners sold it to subdivision developers for a reported $83 million. Then there was Pin Oak Farm in Ver-
sailles, Kentucky, where she raised corn, asparagus, tobacco,
and Thoroughbred racehorses. On top of that, Josephine
Abercrombie owned two Texas cattle ranches—a twenty-
seven-thousand-acre spread sixty miles south of San Antonio
called the 74 and the six-thousand-acre Cannonade on the
Guadalupe River near Gonzales. She transformed a corner
of Cannonade into a boxing retreat, then lent it to the 1984
U.S. Olympic team to train its fighters.

Josephine Abercrombie majored in creative writing in
college. Until she turned thirty-five, her life was "always
having fun." But in 1962, when her father became ill with
atherosclerosis, she started making business decisions, beginning with the farms and ranches. Later, she also ran the
family's oil and real estate ventures. "I started out ten jumps
behind everyone else," she acknowledged. "I felt like an
impostor many, many times. Sometimes I still do."

One place where she always felt on top of things was
Pin Oak Farm, where thirty-two broodmares munched the

dense bluegrass. Over the years the farm produced such top contenders as War and Peace, Roman Patrol, and Make a Play. By 1985 the Houston heiress had five horses racing under her blue-and-gray-striped silks.

She took an almost maternal pride in her Thorough-breds. "For me, the excitement is to watch a horse go from being just a fat little baby to a sleek animal," she explained. "Racehorses get very competitive, just like a fighter does," she said, adding that they also improve once they know they're good. "As they develop and have some wins under their belts, you see their confidence developing."

Mr. Jim gave his daughter her first horse—an old polo pony—when she was four. Two years later she began show-ing horses—and winning.

Josephine Abercrombie remembered her father as a "very loving and kind" man who "spoiled me rotten." Per-haps. But he also believed that athletic competition built char-acter. "When you go into the ring and the gate closes, you're on your own, and nobody can help you," he told her.

It was an invocation of two prime tenets of Cowboy Capitalism—independence and competitiveness. With no sons he determined to foster these virtues in his daughter.

When she was twenty-nine and living in Akron, Ohio, with her third husband, H. B. Robinson, and their two young sons, Josephine Abercrombie trained racehorses. After two years of rising at five each morning to drive to the track in Cleveland, she finally quit. "My children's friends would say, 'Where's your mother?' and my boys would say, 'At the track,' " she recalled. "The time came when I just had to stop it."

Two marriages and three divorces later, Josephine Aber-crombie had resumed her maiden name. She lived alone with a Weimaraner attack dog in posh River Oaks. She ran every day. She played golf. And she remained an avid downhill skier, despite dislocating her shoulder twice on the slopes.

She also loved spectator sports. One evening in 1981 she was at the Summit sports and entertainment complex watch-ing the Holmes-Cooney title fight on closed-circuit television. Because all the seats were taken, Bob Spagnola, a young accountant for Pennzoil, offered her his. She declined but made a counteroffer. "I said I'd love to go to the gyms because I'd never been involved in the activity and I'd always wanted to be," she recalled. "I'd always wanted to own a fighter."

Spagnola said he'd be delighted to take her around. "I could tell from the way she was watching the match that she was a real fight fan," he said four years later. Spagnola went on to head the training and management arm of the Houston Boxing Association, which Texas law requires to be separate from the promotional side, which books the boxers and stages the fights.

For a wealthy socialite, owning a stable of racehorses was one thing. But boxing? Especially for a woman?

At matches Josephine Abercrombie was on her feet, shaking her slender fist in the air and yelling, "Give him an uppercut" one moment, covering her mouth in alarm the next.

From the standpoint of public opinion, Josephine Abercrombie couldn't have picked a worse time to start her venture. On November 13, 1982, lightweight champion Ray "Boom-Boom" Mancini killed South Korean fighter Duk Koo Kim with a knockout punch. The death prompted an outcry against the sport. Even Howard Cosell, who had provided blow-by-blow commentary on the debacle, expressed his disgust with boxing and said he'd never announce another match. In January 1983—the same month the HBA was founded—Dr. George D. Lundberg, editor of the *Journal of the American Medical Association*, cited evidence that 15 percent of all boxers suffer brain damage. He called on all "civilized nations" to outlaw boxing. (Officially the AMA took a milder stand, demanding that all boxing matches be conducted under strict medical supervision.)

In the midst of this fire storm of criticism, on May 13, 1983, Josephine Abercrombie staged a gala charity kickoff match, the first in a twelve-card fight series copromoted with the Houston Sports Association, which operated the Astrodome and owned the Astros' baseball franchise. Ms. Abercrombie appeared in an elegant blue chiffon and sat next to heart surgeon Dr. Denton Cooley. The beneficiary of the evening's entertainment was Cooley's Texas Heart Institute.

Responding to physicians who questioned the propriety of raising money for a medical charity through a boxing bout, Dr. Cooley later told the *Dallas Times Herald* that he'd had "a little misgiving about the thing at the time." But he added that Ms. Abercrombie's "motives and objectives in doing this far overrode any objections. She assumed the sport would continue but that by her involvement in it she could improve it and reduce the hazards of physical injuries."

"I think the furor over boxing is *vastly* overblown," Josephine Abercrombie said later. "Boxing is safer than football," in which players who are injured get sent back into the game, she argued. "We'd *never* do that with a fighter. If one of our fighters got knocked out, he would get a CAT scan immediately, and he wouldn't go back in the gym for a month."

Ms. Abercrombie's boxers receive regular CAT scans and EEGs, plus tests for memory loss and other forms of intellectual impairment. "We hope these tests will be adopted statewide and even nationwide to pinpoint any problems early on," she said.

To minimize the chance of injury during training, Ms. Abercrombie commissioned medical and sports inventor Byron Donzis to design a protective collar and headgear for her fighters. (Donzis developed football pro Dan Pastorini's flak jacket.) The protective devices "reduce the cumulative effect of the pounding the fighters take by at least ninety-five percent," Donzis explained. "That means the boxers will be able to retire with everything intact." He added: "Josephine is really concerned about her fighters as human beings, not just as pieces of meat hung up on a hook and then discarded when you're through with them."

To protect her fighters financially, Josephine Abercrombie put her investment advisers at their disposal. Most of the young men, who ranged in age from eighteen to twenty-five, came from disadvantaged backgrounds where money management was a simple question of meeting next month's rent. They needed help, she believed, holding on to their winnings—as much as twenty-five to fifty thousand dollars a fight. Ms. Abercrombie also invested two million dollars in an entity she called HBA Interests. She held 51 percent,

her fighters 49 percent; their participation was tied to their
completion of their contracts.

"What we're trying to do is take an amateur athlete and
develop him throughout his professional career and avoid
the rags-to-riches-to-rags syndrome," said Bob Spagnola. By
1987 HBA Interests owned a paper-recycling company, a
drilling-mud supplier, a few tracts of commercial real estate,
and the apartment complex where the boxers lived.

To make sure her sluggers would get at least one nutritious meal a day, Ms. Abercrombie sent a cook over to
serve them broiled meat and fresh fruit and vegetables in the
communal dining room. She also invited her "baby beeves,"
as she called them, to her house for dinner and maternal
chats. And every couple of weeks, as a special treat, Josephine Abercrombie paraded her pugilists through one of the
ritzy hangouts of Houston's smart set—Tony's, Maxim's, or
The Palm.

"It gets a lot of eyes and a lot of heads turning because
here she is—a *very* pretty and *very* well-dressed woman—
with all these sort of tough-looking, physically fit young
guys," noted Tony's proprietor, Tony Vallone. "They handle
themselves very well at the table," he added approvingly.
"They order veal, fish, pheasant. It's not 'Gimme the biggest
rare steak in the house.' "

Josephine Abercrombie played her Pygmalion role to the
hilt. After a few months around her the boxers developed
almost courtly manners. Even in the middle of a workout at
the HBA Training Center, one of her fighters introduced
himself politely and removed his right glove to shake hands.

The long-range question was, Would Josephine Abercrombie be able to reform professional boxing by force of her
example, or would the HBA's physically—and fiscally—nurturing approach prove impractical for other operators who
had to make money?

The things the HBA introduced to boxing—from profit
sharing to neurological testing—were things "no one else
has attempted or probably will ever attempt because they're
not cost-effective," Spagnola admitted. "I don't have to make
a living doing this," Josephine Abercrombie noted. Other
managers and promoters—even biggies Bob Arum and Don
King—did.

Whatever she got from boxing—from the vicarious thrill of raw, aggressive competition to the satisfaction of transforming uncouth kids into poised professional athletes—Josephine Abercrombie worked hard for it.

"I'm working on this thing eighty percent of the time," she said. "I see title fights in Houston. I see some of our fighters being world champions. I see the public getting behind this because we'll have some winners here."

If rock star Cyndi Lauper could make wrestling trendy, socialite Josephine Abercrombie might yet make boxing chic.

★

CHAPTER FIVE

Walter Mischer

The Kingmaker

Back in the thirties and forties, when "Mr. Jim" Abercrombie was building his oil tool and real estate empire, Texas was run, by and large, from a hotel suite in downtown Houston. Every afternoon a cadre of wealthy middle-aged men would gather in Suite 8F of the since-demolished Lamar Hotel to play poker, drink whiskey, and determine the fate of the state. Thanks to their tight connections in New Deal Washington, they also influenced the course of the nation. They had the ear of fellow Texan and Speaker of the House Sam Rayburn; a young congressman named Lyndon Johnson often tended bar during their games.

At the close of World War II a young man came to Houston and caught the 8F Crowd's attention. Walter Mischer was a twenty-three-year-old oil refinery worker from Gillett, a little brush-country town in Karnes County in South Texas, where he was born on the Fourth of July 1922. Soft-spoken and less than five and a half feet tall, Mischer was singularly unprepossessing; he sometimes stammered or lisped. But the 8F Crowd recognized a formidable ambition beneath that surface, and made him its youngest member. More than forty years later, even in the wake of the oil crash, Houston—with its giant law firms, multinational corporations, bank holding companies, and international port—was still the seat of the state's power. And Walter Mischer was still one of the most powerful men in the Lone Star State and one of the nation's kingmakers.

After his father's death in 1934 Mischer had watched the creditors move in on his family's ranch, whittling the property down from thirteen thousand acres to fewer than four hundred. He'd seen his mother forced to return to teaching school to support him and his two younger sisters. He'd had to finance his two years at Texas Arts and Industries College in Kingsville by stringing fence on the King Ranch. He arrived in Houston determined to put a lot of money and clout between himself and the humiliation of those lean years. And he did.

By his middle fifties Mischer was a behind-the-scenes power broker capable of making and breaking political careers on both sides of the aisle. His backing helped propel Democrat Barbara Jordan, a black state representative from Houston's Fourth Ward, into the U.S. Congress, where her ringing rhetoric mesmerized television audiences during the Watergate hearings. He aided a more conservative Democrat, Lloyd Bentsen, Jr., in keeping his Senate seat term after term. Yet Mischer was one of the key players in delivering traditionally Democratic Texas to Ronald Reagan in 1980 and 1984.

Mischer's power and wealth grew simultaneously. He became the fourth-largest private landowner in Texas (in addition to his mahogany, teak, and rosewood plantation in Belize) and the chairman of the state's sixth-biggest bank holding company, $9.15 billion Allied Bancshares, which merged with $52.1 billion First Interstate of Los Angeles in 1987. Mischer's office was on the seventh floor of Allied's headquarters, a seventy-one-story postmodern skyscraper on the western edge of downtown Houston. Sheathed in emerald green glass, the building consisted of two offset hemicylinders; from the air it resembled the mirror image of a dollar sign. Inside, marble the color of freshly minted money was everywhere, covering the walls in the lobby, even surrounding the sinks in the rest rooms.

Despite its normally laissez-faire attitude toward most business, Texas had always been suspicious of Big Banking, seeking to hobble it with arcane restrictions. The Republic of Texas outlawed banking altogether; financiers had to call themselves cotton factors to get around the prohibition. Later, fearing that the state would come to be dominated by a few big banks, which would muscle out competition from small independents, the legislature put the kibosh on branch banking and kept it there until 1987.

In 1961 Mischer and developer Howard Terry, his some-time partner in real estate ventures, bought suburban Continental Bank. Within the next fifteen years Mischer had picked up several other medium-size banks around the state. Then, as soon as Texas bank holding companies were made legal in 1977, he merged them into Allied Bancshares. Walter Mischer was learning how to manipulate money.

The Texas oil and real estate crash caused a bank a week to fold in the state during the first half of 1987. Allied Banc-shares managed to limp on. One reason was that its portfolio was lighter on energy and real estate loans than the holdings of most other Oil Patch banks, and it had resisted the temptation to participate in foreign loans. Another was that the company had always sought as clients middle-ground businesses doing three hundred thousand to ten million dollars a year. For a bank that wanted to grow, Mischer said, they made much better customers than large multinational corporations. He explained: "If you have a line of credit with Exxon, for instance, you might have a line of ten million dollars and you'd have ten million dollars the next year and ten million dollars the year after that. We'd just as soon put our money with people that were growing."

Wearing a gold Rolex President watch (known around these parts as a Texas Timex) and an expensive but rumpled navy blue suit with a faint pinstripe, Walter Mischer sat in the conservatively masculine meeting room next to his office. Along one wall was a glass case four feet long containing a lifelike arrangement of dried brush, a sun-bleached cattle skull, and four mounted blue quail, native to the desert of West Texas.

Speaking so softly that I had to lean forward to hear, the man who had raised more money than anyone else in the country for Ronald Reagan in 1980—$3.2 million—said: "Houston has always been a very entrepreneurial city, an open city. There was no establishment that anybody had to check with. You could do anything you were big enough to do in Houston, and most people would help you."

In truth, there *was* an establishment. But that establishment was the 8F Crowd, and Walter Mischer was its darling.

Mischer made his first millions off the Veterans Administration–financed construction boom that followed World War II. Once he'd saved almost twenty-five thousand dollars working as equipment supervisor for a refinery contractor, he quit, taking concrete foreman Emil Harris with him. Together they developed thousands of acres of farmland surrounding Houston into middle-class subdivisions. Mischer didn't build the three-bedroom ranch houses; he prepared the tracts for builders, clearing land, paving streets, and putting in storm sewers. That way he didn't have to wait for the houses to sell to turn a profit. But many of those houses sported air conditioning and kitchen cabinets supplied by subsidiaries of the Mischer Corporation. In 1954 he dissolved his partnership with Harris and founded the Walter Mischer Corporation, by 1987 a publicly traded company with more than eighty million dollars in annual revenues and his son, Walter, Jr., as president.

The company's growth was due partly to innovative thinking. For example, in 1964 Walter Mischer built a thousand-acre town house project—then the world's largest—at a time when few people in Houston knew what a town house was. But more important to his success was the political savvy he learned at the feet of the 8F boys.

Traditionally Texas had bent over backward to make business comfortable, and Walter Mischer wanted it to continue bending. For instance, Texas had no personal or corporate income tax. It was also a right-to-work state, which limited the potential power of labor unions by outlawing closed shops.

"I think it's important for businessmen to be sensitive

to state politics and to keep our business climate good," Mischer said.

But Walter Mischer, kingmaker, went a long way beyond being sensitive. He used his influence to see that other businessmen anted up in the great poker game of politics.

Mischer was a political pragmatist. He didn't demand ideological purity of the candidates he supported, just a leaning in favor of growth and against restrictions on free enterprise. In 1986, the man who had raised all that money for Ronald Reagan passed the hat for incumbent Governor Mark White, a Democratic lawyer who lost to Dallas oilman Bill Clements. Besides being a fellow Houstonian, White had put a lot of money into highway improvements, so dear to the construction industry's heart, and had instituted sweeping educational reforms.

"I thought that White showed a lot of courage and a lot of insight by doing what he did for education and highways," Mischer explained three years later. "And I think a guy should be rewarded for what he does and not for any political affiliations he might have."

Mischer sometimes contributed to *both* candidates—one before and one after the election. He was credited with coining the Texas political adage "There's always time to buy a ticket on the late train." He did just that in Houston's 1981 mayoral race. Initially Mischer had backed the incumbent, Jim McConn, a good ol' boy with a fondness for Las Vegas junkets. A thirty-five-year-old CPA named Kathy Whitmire —young, short, blond, and female to boot—won, proving that the wielding of power in Houston was no longer a simple thing. Instead of bemoaning the shift in the landscape, Walter Mischer contributed five thousand dollars to Whitmire's campaign on January 18, 1982—more than two weeks after her inauguration.

Like so many rich Texans, as soon as Walter Mischer began to get successful, he went out and bought a ranch. Only he didn't stop with just one. He accumulated 327,000 acres, most of it in the mountainous desert west of the Pecos River. He bought this Trans-Pecos property not to develop and sell, as he'd done with land around Houston, but because he liked it. "It's hard to explain why," he said, sitting in his suite in the Allied tower overlooking the green curve of Buffalo Bayou. "It's just big country. It's very tranquil. It's so quiet sometimes it's eerie."

Mischer began stockpiling desert in 1952 when he bought 26,000 acres of ocotillo, creosote bush, and cactus at Lajitas. They lay in the middle of nowhere, 430 miles west of San Antonio, 300 miles southeast of El Paso, more than 600 miles from Houston—and in the middle of the Chihuahuan Desert, the driest stretch of real estate in the United States.

Lajitas, which means "flagstones," sits at the bottom of the abrupt swing to the northeast that the Rio Grande makes as it slices between Mexico's high sierras and the seventy-eight-hundred foot Chisos Mountains in Texas, winding through narrow canyons with sheer walls as high as fifteen hundred feet. Without topsoil and trees to cloak their form, the ivory and ocher cliffs, rose and peach mesas, and wind-chiseled lavender rocks look like the jumbled bones of Creation.

The southwestern scenery visible from Lajitas has few rivals short of the Grand Canyon. But along with the dramatic landscape, heat molds life in the Big Bend. During the searing summer the ground temperature can reach 180 degrees Fahrenheit—hot enough to kill a rattlesnake if it doesn't find shade within a few minutes.

In many ways the Big Bend is still the frontier. Cougars and bears prowl its mountains. Despite the advent of paved roads and automobiles, this country was more sparsely populated in the late 1980's than it was seventy-five years earlier, when flourishing mercury mines brought workers down from the rest of the United States and up from Mexico. By 1950 the mines had largely played out and the adobe houses had crumbled into weathered ruins.

In the late seventies a couple of dozen artists, writers, and river guides, most from Houston and Austin, began fixing up some of the ruins and turning the ghost towns into posthippie communities. But when Mischer came to Lajitas in 1952, it was nothing but a trading post on the banks of the Rio Grande overlooked by the ruins of a cavalry post last

occupied by General John "Black Jack" Pershing and his
troops when they fought Pancho Villa in 1916 and 1917.

With its two-foot-thick adobe walls still bearing the
marks of the *villistas'* bullets, the trading post continued to
function as both general store and community center thirty-
seven years after Mischer first saw this harsh and striking
country. Inside, the trading post was dark and cool, even
without air conditioning. Shovels, picks, hoes, iron skillets,
and pots and pans hung from the walls. Canned goods,
agates, cereal boxes, fishing line, gimme caps, patent med-
icines, and electric irons lined the shelves. Outside, five goats
milled around a pen. The larger of the two billy goats, Clay
Henry—a shaggy 130-pound black beast with an impressive
set of backswept horns—guzzled beer to the delight of onlookers.

Gradually, as Walter Mischer picked up land in the Big
Bend, an idea began to develop. If he loved the country so
much, there had to be other rich Texans who'd love it, too
—and maybe even well-heeled midwesterners eager to escape cold winters. He decided to try to make Lajitas, Texas
—home of Clay Henry, the beer-guzzling goat—the next
Palm Springs. After all, the Big Bend's air was similar in
temperature but drier and less polluted. Never mind that
Palm Springs was two hours by car from Los Angeles, while
Lajitas was seven and a half hours from San Antonio and
five hours from the nearest commercial airport—Midland/
Odessa. Never mind that despite its dramatic scenery and
385 species of birds, Big Bend National Park—the least visited
national park for its size—attracted only five hundred thousand visitors a year simply because it was so far from the
family vacation circuit. The people Mischer was after could
afford to charter planes or fly their own.

"The good news and the bad news about Lajitas is it's
remote," he said good-naturedly.

In 1974, with local land values up to a hundred dollars
an acre, Mischer bought thirty thousand acres from Rex Ivey,
a pioneer desert rat who'd come to the region in the twenties.
By 1978 Mischer was putting in roads, utilities, and an airstrip. When he could take a few days away from Allied Banc-
shares, he liked to fly out and operate the earth-moving
equipment himself. He split his time in the Big Bend between

Lajitas and his neighboring ranches, where he rode around in a Jeep or on horseback, looking at his cattle when he wasn't running more heavy equipment.

"That's kind of my first love," he admitted. "I've got a couple of dozers out there that I keep busy most of the time, trying to cut down on erosion."

Somehow holding on to the agricultural water allowance that came with the land, Mischer turned the irrigated alfalfa field into a nine-hole golf course, the only patch of lawn in the area. On the site of General Pershing's old cavalry post he built a motel, complete with swimming pool, and a cluster of ninety-dollar-a-night condominiums across the street. He established the Lajitas Museum and Desert Garden—a nature walk with the plants labeled. He even put up a false-fronted wooden strip shopping center, which looked like a hastily erected western movie set. No one in this virtually treeless part of the Old West would have dreamed of using clapboard construction, but the tourists liked it. The rickety wood siding concealed a laundromat, a modern drugstore, an outfitter specializing in raft trips through the Rio Grande canyons, and a boutique stocking ostrich-skin boots, Ultrasuede skirts, and hand-knit sweaters. More than half the space was devoted to the Badlands Hotel, with ersatz Victorian decor and a huge bar, called, of course, the Saloon. It sat on a rise just above that authentic western landmark the Lajitas Trading Post, which Mischer bought but leased back to Rex Ivey and his son Bill.

Lajitas was still a far cry from becoming another Palm Springs. By early 1987 only some forty people had built houses or bought condominiums. Most of the fancy houses belonged to executives with the Mischer Corporation. But Mischer was still predicting that Lajitas on the Rio Grande would eventually become a popular winter resort. "I think there'll probably be twenty-five hundred or three thousand people there by the turn of the century," he said with a slightly wistful smile. And even if Lajitas never took off, Walter Mischer was rich enough to absorb the five million dollars or so he'd invested in the resort. He may even have felt a bit ambivalent about having thousands of snow dodgers disrupting the eerie emptiness of the Big Bend.

CHAPTER SIX

★

Chasing the Cowboy Mystique

By the mid-1980's ranching, which gave Texas its first wealth and its lasting mythos, was headed for the last roundup, despite the powerful appeal the cowboy fantasy held for the Texas Rich. Cattle and horses may have been a big part of what made Texas Texas, but it had been almost a century since they were a big part of what made Texas rich.

When I met them in 1984, Conley and Polly Brooks had three ranches, two near Fort Stockton, the other 75 miles to the southwest near Marfa, where *Giant* was filmed in 1956. The Brookses owned over a hundred sections, each a square mile or 640 acres. They raised Hereford cattle and Rambouillet sheep, plus some wine grapes and pecans.

Although much of their land was worth more than a hundred dollars an acre, the Brookses didn't fit the stereotype of the rich Texas rancher, driving around in a Cadillac with steer horns bolted to the grille. They lived modestly and considered themselves prosperous, rather than wealthy. By that time even a large, well-run ranch was a break-even proposition. The one cost that didn't rise much with the inflation of the seventies was the price of beef.

"Conley compares a ranch to a piece of fine jewelry," said Polly Brooks. "It's beautiful, but it doesn't pay for itself."

During the oil boom the price of ranchland stampeded, particularly in the scenic mountains of the Trans-Pecos. New petromillionaires weren't looking for profits on the hoof; what they wanted were places to shelter their taxes and to hunt. When they got tired of being predatory in the Oil Patch, these nimrods could excuse themselves from boring Houston or Midland charity benefits with a casual "Gotta get up early. We're culling tomorrow out at the ranch. . . . Just a little spread over by Marathon. Why don't you fly out with us next weekend and we'll bag us some antelope?"

Oilmen pushed the prices up as high as $250 an acre for large parcels of land in country so rugged it would support only eighty cows a section in a wet year; smaller acreage, intended to be subdivided into five-acre "ranchettes," went for $350 an acre or more. Those real estate values were a boon for owners who wanted to get out of ranching and retire to San Antonio, but they also broke up family ranches. To get through tough times, ranchers borrowed on the inflated value of the land; the interest ate their profits, and then the only way they could pay the principal was to sell off land.

If keeping an inherited ranch alive became difficult, buying a ranch and running it at a profit became next to impossible. "You can't pay even ten dollars an acre for land and ranch it and make any money," said Conley Brooks, sitting in the den of his far-from-palatial one-story brick house in Fort Stockton. "To pay for it, you have to stock it with seismograph crews. It's hard to do it with cattle and sheep."

"My father always told me, 'Whatever you do, don't part with your mineral rights,' " said Mrs. Brooks. Even at twenty dollars a barrel, West Texas intermediate crude could pay for a lot of irrigation water and improvements.

Dr. D. J. Sibley didn't part with his minerals, and they made him far richer than his Fort Stockton medical practice

ever could have. They also enabled him to become a professional student of the Chihuahuan Desert, particularly its
thorny, efficient plant life. Compared with the rough-hewn
West Texas oilmen around him, D. J. Sibley had the air of a
nineteenth-century English gentleman naturalist. His thick
white hair, his bushy, upturned moustache, and the limp
resulting from three hip replacements reinforced that impression, as did his habit of wearing multiple strands of Navajo
coral or turquoise hishi beads in lieu of a tie. Yet his wealth
blew in on a mixture of luck and violence that matched any
in the Oil Patch.

Like most of the well-educated people who ended up in
West Texas in the early twentieth century, D. J. Sibley's father, Central Texas dentist D. Jacobus Sibley, had come to
the Trans-Pecos in hopes that the desert air would cure his
tuberculosis. "That was a common misconception at the
time," Dr. Sibley explained. "There's about as much respiratory disease in arid climates as there is anywhere else. But
he came out here and went to bed for six months. That was
what helped."

After recovering from his ailment, the young dentist set
up a thriving practice in Fort Stockton and began buying
land. At his father's urging, D.J. earned a medical degree,
hung out his shingle in the same town, and acquired more
ranchland. In the wake of World War II and his own battle
with TB, he decided that he couldn't ranch and practice medicine at the same time, so he sold his herd and hired out the
land to other cattlemen.

D. J. Sibley sold the surface of his flat, mesquite-riddled
ranch at Coyanosa, between Monahans and Fort Stockton,
but held on to the mineral rights and leased them to Humble,
which subcontracted the drilling to Mobil. At first these sections of Chihuahuan Desert range were disappointing. By
early September 1961 Mobil had sunk forty dry holes looking
for oil or natural gas, and the crew was cutting corners, using
drilling pipe only on the five hundred feet closest to the
surface, as required by law, and leaving the rest open hole
—bare rock. That made the job cheaper but harder to control.

Mobil's geologists reckoned that the forty-first well, if it
struck anything, would strike gas at ninety-six hundred feet.

Instead, it hit a powerful pocket of gas at five thousand. In an attempt to slow the new well, Mobil brought in dozens of Mexican braceros—Mexican laborers with green cards—who poured bucket after bucket of drilling mud down the hole. It didn't work. Five days after the well came in, it blew out and blew up, killing the five men on the drilling platform floor and injuring scores more. The fire was so intense that only three bodies were found; the other two had been incinerated. It took legendary Houston oil well fire fighter Red Adair to quell the blaze on the Potts Sibley One.

Once the well was brought under control, the Sibley field proved one of the richest gas plays in West Texas. It made it financially feasible for D. J. Sibley to retire from medicine, where his new wealth made him an attractive target for malpractice suits. He accepted a position with the Balcones Research Center in Austin, studying the medicinal and otherwise useful compounds produced by Chihuahuan Desert plants. The Apache and Comanche Indians had used teas and powders made from the creosote bush, sotol, and various cacti to treat everything from colds to cancer; maybe these flora could be refined into pharmaceuticals. Dr. Sibley isolated several substances already being derived from other sources, but the funding ran out before he completed his work.

In Austin D. J. Sibley and his wife, Jane, were the unofficial but undisputed ambassadors from the Trans-Pecos. They decorated their rambling white stucco and red tile-roofed Mediterranean Revival house with the pelts of bobcats, cougars, and other predators shot on their Glass Mountain Ranch. Looking like a prehistoric tree, the ten-foot-tall dried bloom stalk of a giant maguey guarded their entry hall. A stylized painting of a buzzard adorned each side of the chimney.

"Buzzards are the most maligned, least appreciated creatures on earth," Jane Sibley declared. "Think what our West Texas highways would look like without them."

A slender woman with a striking and possibly conscious resemblance to Georgia O'Keeffe, Mrs. Sibley wore her brown hair, with its single dramatic white streak, in a low bun punctuated with a gray buzzard feather—even with cou-

ture gowns on the dressiest occasions. She revived the Austin
Symphony by pumping up financial support from the community's business leaders. She also initiated the high-tone
yet down-home social craze that swept Texas during the early
1980's—the black-tie and boots party, to which men wore
black cowboy boots with their tuxedos. Rich ranchers had
been doing just that, more or less on the sly, for decades,
but it took Mrs. Sibley to make it chic rather than merely
excusable.

Jane Sibley was a Fort Stockton native eleven years her
husband's junior. She knew the Comanche method for making medicinal greasewood tea, and she claimed to be able to
find water with a divining rod. She was proud of her pioneer
forebears, particularly her mother, who had emigrated to the
Trans-Pecos as a young girl.

"Mother was sixteen years old, and she was coming
down the mountain driving a wagon, and she couldn't see
where she was going because the tears were streaming out
of her eyes in terror," Mrs. Sibley recounted, fishing around
in a huge double-door refrigerator for caviar and sour cream
to serve with the artichokes their servant Arturo had prepared for lunch.

Jane Sibley was holding court one May weekend in 1989
at El Castillo—the Castle, the hideaway she and her husband
had built twenty years earlier on their Glass Mountain Ranch.
Rising from a grove of piñon pines atop a five-thousand-foot
mountain eighteen miles down a dirt road, the house was
hexagonal, its main walls sheer plates of glass anchored by
six turrets made of limestone picked up on what the Sibleys
called "our country." Atop each of those towers flapped one
of the six flags that had flown over Texas.

On a clear day you could see more than sixty miles from
the Castle's flat roof. In one direction were the Glass
Mountains—once a submerged reef in a Permian sea. In
another was a series of flat-topped mesas. Scattered across
the landscape were features that appeared on geodetic survey
maps with the names D. J. Sibley had given them as a twelve-
year-old boy, when he'd camped out on his father's land
with a pair of young government geologists. "It's not important, except it gives me a kick," Dr. Sibley declared.

Over here was Panther Mesa; yonder was Cave Mesa, where cowboys, upon discovering a large dirt-blocked hole just below the cap rock, had hoped to find gold buried by the Spanish conquistadors; instead, they unearthed a few hundred pairs of Indian sandals fashioned from sotol fiber. Closer to the Castle were other Sibley-nyms that didn't appear on official maps, among them Son-of-a-Bitch Road and Impossible Ridge. Buzzards drifted gracefully on the warm updrafts. Below, the desert mountainside was ablaze with fuchsia-flowered cholla, lemon-blossomed prickly pear, and the V-shaped red blooms that settle atop the spindly, otherwise dead-looking ocotillo like scarlet butterflies perched on thorny gray walking sticks.

"Out here your position in the universe changes completely," Jane Sibley said. "You know you're not the center. The universe is just tolerating you."

The most famous ranch in Texas survived relatively intact into the late twentieth century because of its oil and gas. But that very mineral wealth divided the insular South Texas dynasty that owned it.

Originally the King Ranch wasn't the biggest spread in Texas. The XIT stretched across three million acres of the Panhandle; the Matador Land and Cattle Company covered two million acres in the High Plains. The King never measured more than 1.2 million acres, a bit bigger than the state of Delaware. But by 1989 the XIT and the Matador were long gone, and the King Ranch still sprawled across 825,000 acres—smaller than Delaware but bigger than Rhode Island or, as Robert Reinhold of *The New York Times* put it, "the size of 982 Central Parks."

Starting south of Corpus Christi and ending just shy of the Rio Grande, the King hopscotched over six counties. The distance from ranch headquarters near Kingsville to the southernmost fence post was ninety-three miles. This was the flat, brush-choked coastal plain, once called the Wild Horse Desert, where everything from the prickly-pear cactus to the huisache and mesquite had thorns. To save the hides of horses and cowboys, the ranch used helicopters to round up reluctant cattle.

Captain Richard King founded the King Ranch in 1853; nearly a century and a half later it remained in the hands of his descendants. The son of Irish immigrants, King gave up his trade as a jeweler's apprentice in New York and made his way down to Texas, where he ran an army steamboat on the Rio Grande during the War with Mexico. After the war he bought a military surplus steamboat and went into business for himself, mostly smuggling but occasionally carrying passengers and legitimate freight. His friend Robert E. Lee told him, "Buy land and never sell." With the profits from his steamboating, Captain King did just that.

The land King picked up, often for pennies an acre, lay south of the Nueces River, which many historians suggest makes a more natural border between the United States and Mexico than the Rio Grande. (In this part of Texas Spanish still is spoken more often than English.) Captain King set up his ranch on the Mexican *patrón* system, under which the landowner provides security and often housing and medical care in exchange for generations of loyalty and hard work. To help run his spread, he went south of the Rio Grande and persuaded an entire Mexican village to relocate. Their descendants still call themselves *kiñenos*—"King's men.".

Before 1867 Richard King had little market for his cattle. With no practical way to get the animals to the people with the money to buy beef, he got by on selling the hides and tallow and dumping the carcasses in the Gulf. But when the railroad reached Abilene, Kansas, King began making real money driving thousands of cantankerous longhorns up the Chisholm Trail. The era of the big trail drives lasted only eighteen years, but it left an indelible mark on the American imagination and built Richard King's fortune. He herded more than a hundred thousand cattle to market; one year he made four hundred thousand dollars.

When Richard King's widow, Henrietta, died in 1925, three quarters of the 1.2 million acres of ranchland went to her daughter, Alice Kleberg, whose husband, Robert, had managed the ranch since Captain King's death in 1885. In 1934, to protect the ranch from being whittled away by inheritance taxes, the Klebergs and their five children incorporated. By 1988 more than sixty Kleberg heirs owned shares in the King Ranch.

Starting in 1916, Robert Kleberg's son Robert, Jr., took over the reins. From then until his death in 1974, Bob Kleberg was the King Ranch *jefe*. He was a charismatic character full of energy and ideas. On the range he went in for a beat-up cowboy hat. When he finally had to buy a new one, he had one of his *kiñenos* wear the replacement for at least six months, until it looked disreputable enough to suit his taste.

Kleberg developed the first American breed of cattle— and the first new breed introduced anywhere in more than a century. Longhorns were well adapted to South Texas, but the docile breeds that produced the most tender beef and gained weight the quickest thrived in cooler, lusher climates. Introduced to the King Ranch, with its scorching summers, sparse rainfall, and dense chaparral, English shorthorns and Angus got thin and sickly and lost interest in sex. The one breed that steamy summers couldn't faze was the Indian zebu, also called Brahmas. *Their* main problems were low fertility and intractable attitude. Determined to capture the best of both, Bob Kleberg crossed Brahmas with shorthorns, an experiment his father had begun in 1910. He called his three eighths five eighths cross Santa Gertrudis, after the creek running through the first ranch Captain King had bought. By 1940 his strain of heat-resistant animals with manageable dispositions was breeding true.

Kleberg also invented the cattle prod, which he based on an electric fly killer he had been tinkering with. And he got the ranch into farming, raising cotton for sale and milo to fatten the cattle in its own feedlots.

For years Kleberg had rebuffed interest from oil companies wanting to drill on his land. The Klebergs were cattle ranchers, not oil people. And they wanted to keep their kingdom private.

Despite all his ingenuity, the King Ranch fell on hard times during the early 1930's. The devastating drought that caused the Dust Bowl hit South Texas, forcing the ranch into debt. In 1933 Bob Kleberg signed an oil lease with Humble, the company that evolved into Exxon. Covering a million acres, including some belonging to his cousins, it was the largest oil deal in history. It brought in the three million dollars needed to pay the ranch's debt, with plenty to spare. Kleberg negotiated a shrewd royalty arrangement; instead of

the usual one eighth of the income from oil and gas production, the King Ranch would get one sixth.

For more than a decade those royalties amounted to a
sixth of nothing. Then, in 1945, a huge field came in, and
by 1953 there were 650 oil and gas wells on the ranch. By
1969 the King Ranch was producing $120 million a year in
oil and gas, netting annual royalties of $20 million—fifteen
times the profit from ranching.

Bob Kleberg plowed that enormous wealth into more
land—land in Montana, Florida, Virginia, and Pennsylvania,
land in Venezuela, Argentina, pre-Castro Cuba, Spain, Morocco, and the Australian outback. Shortly before his death
he had his eye on the Amazon jungle.

With some of the rest of those royalties, Kleberg developed a top line of agile quarter horses and raised some of
the fastest Thoroughbreds of the century. Middleground and
Bold Venture won the Kentucky Derby wearing the King
Ranch brown and white silks and running W brand. Assault
took the Triple Crown in 1946.

When Bob Kleberg died in 1974, he left boots that were
next to impossible to fill. For fifty-six years he'd been the
dynasty's undisputed leader. Many had assumed that his
power would pass to one of his late sister's sons, either B. K.
Johnson or Bobby Shelton, orphaned in childhood. Kleberg
and his wife, who had only a daughter, had reared his nephews as their own. But it wasn't up to him to name his successor. That was up to the corporation, and it chose James
Clement, an in-law in his sixties.

In the wake of the decision, both Johnson and Shelton
left the family corporation. Buying them out cost the King
Ranch plenty. The corporation liquidated its property in
Pennsylvania, Spain, Venezuela, and Argentina and cut back
on its operations in Australia. In 1977 it also took another
expensive step: It decided that 75 percent of its oil and gas
royalties should go directly to the shareholders. That left only
25 percent to cushion the ranch against reverses in its agri-
business enterprises. By 1986 the energy crash had cut the
total to $40.3 million. That same year an experiment with
shrimp aquaculture, an attempt to find a productive use for
the swampland along Baffin Bay, turned out to be an ex-

pensive failure. James Clement stepped down in June 1987, and another Kleberg in-law, John B. Armstrong, a world-class polo player, then sixty-eight, took over as president. The following month *The New York Times* reported that the King Ranch was said to be looking for an outside corporate type to head the company. It chose Darwin Smith, CEO of Kimberly-Clark.

In 1983 the spread had employed seven hundred people, many of them fifth-generation *kiñenos*. By July 1987 the payroll was down to three hundred. Cowboys who thought they had their jobs not just for life but for their descendants as well were laid off abruptly.

Severed though he was from the King Ranch Corporation, Bobby Shelton had a chance at being its salvation. With the help of monumentally persuasive Houston personal injury lawyer Joe Jamail, who won the $11 billion settlement for Pennzoil against Texaco, Shelton sued Exxon, claiming the energy giant had underpaid its leases to the ranch from 1973 on. Of the $250 million the blond, curly-haired, almost baby-faced land baron was seeking, $155 million would be for himself, the rest for the ranch. To complicate matters, Shelton named the King Ranch as both coplaintiff and codefendant, charging that the family corporation had failed to protect his interests. This was the stuff of which prime-time soap operas were made.

Shelton claimed that Exxon's way of figuring the market price for King Ranch natural gas kept it artificially low, defrauding the shareholders of their rightful royalties. Back in 1972 Exxon set a fixed price of 19.25 cents per thousand cubic feet for gas discovered prior to that date. Only gas reserves found after that would be subject to market forces. By Exxon's reckoning, 94 percent of the King Ranch field, which produced nine *trillion* cubic feet of gas between World War II and 1987, was old gas. So when the price of natural gas jumped to more than three dollars per thousand in the late 1970's, it had almost no effect on the ranch's royalties.

One reason Shelton split with the King Ranch was that his relatives refused to support his intention of suing Exxon. Instead, when the lease came up for renewal in 1980, they allowed the company to settle their claims to date out of court for a hundred million dollars. But Shelton refused to accept the seven million dollars that would have been his share.

A decade after he left the King Ranch, Bobby Shelton rode mighty tall in the saddle, even though he measured a compact five feet eight inches. He owned five ranches—four in Texas and one in Montana—plus a seventeen-thousand-acre farm in Florida's Everglades. He had his own fleet of aircraft parked at his own tastefully landscaped hangar, and his oil and gas wells were pumping in money from North Dakota to California.

With four hundred broodmares, his Kerrville quarter horse operation, Comanche Trace, brought in two million dollars in 1984. He showed off his stock in his enclosed thirty-six-thousand-square-foot arena, his vets used closed-circuit television to monitor mares in labor, and he kept track of his breeding program on an IBM System 38, the same computer large banks used.

With oilmen and big-city doctors eager to get into ranching and Texas chic blossoming in the East, Bobby Shelton hit on some inventive ways to make money off his quarter horse operation. He sold leases in his pregnant mares and shares of foals in utero. Rich investors in California, Pennsylvania, and Florida, some of whom had never seen a horse before, flew down to Kerrville, donned boots and cowboy hats, downed catered barbecue, and admired "their" quarter horses.

"You can pet a horse," Shelton observed, explaining the emotional appeal of the investment. "You can't pet a building."

When he wasn't inventing new ways to make money or hunting wild game on African safaris, Shelton spent much of the boom on horseback. He and his mare Barlon's Toni made it to the National Cutting Horse Association finals two years in a row.

Cutting horse competition began as ranch recreation. Cowboys from two neighboring outfits would see which working cow pony and rider could do the best, fastest, showiest job of cutting calves—separating yearlings from their mothers so that they could be roped and branded. Frequently the hands placed a little money on the outcome. By 1985 the sport had been formalized into a favorite pastime of the Texas Big Rich, with prize money in the millions.

Although cutting was one of the essential tasks of every roundup, the way a given horse handled himself could be anything but routine. A good cutting horse could hop, pivot, and spread his forelegs so wide that his chest almost touched the ground, putting him on eye level with a baffled calf. Cutting horse quality was a matter of talent, not looks, speed, or flawless lineage.

"A cow-smart horse wants to play with the cow much like a cat plays with a mouse," Shelton explained. He also compared the 2.5-minute event with ballet. "It's a pas de deux on horseback," he said.

Bobby Shelton bet that his high tech horse operation would keep bringing in more and more money, but he bet wrong. As with all registered animals, the value of a quarter horse was based on the assumption that his offspring collectively would be worth more. That happened pretty regularly when the hills were thick with New Money looking for tax shelters with sex appeal. It stopped when energy prices tumbled, kicking the artificial props out from under the state's ranching business.

Remarkably, a few ranches without a spot of oil, gas, or anything else valuable underground managed to turn a healthy profit. Claytie Williams did it by using his Aggie ingenuity to alter the environment. His neighbor Chris Lacy did it the way his great-grandfather had.

Chris Lacy lived what the rest of Texas dreamed. He was boss and heir apparent of the 06. At 141,000 acres, only a sixth of the size of the King Ranch, it was nonetheless one of the largest ranches in Texas and without doubt the most scenic of the big spreads. The 06 wrapped around Williams's Happy Cove like a giant horseshoe. It straddled the Davis Mountains, covering most of the 24 miles between Alpine and Fort Davis, a little town at 5,050 feet. This was the red rock country, a land of towering cliffs and volcanic peaks. The 06 had the highest concentration of eagles in the United

States, and pronghorn antelope grazed among the russet-coated, white-faced highland Herefords.

The 06 looked exactly like what it was—an old-fashioned working ranch. With his curly blond hair, square jaw, and white Stetson, Lacy himself could have walked right off the set of *Oklahoma!*, as could his wife and children. Diane Lacy was a naturally pretty woman with long, straight light brown hair and a fondness for prairie-style skirts. Their teenage son and daughter were golden-haired, good-looking, and unnervingly polite. They were being reared to be ranchers; the question was whether they, and their children in turn, would be able to be.

Sitting with me in Sutler's Boarding House, the fanciest of the three restaurants in Fort Davis (it featured a salad bar in a claw-footed iron bathtub), Chris Lacy talked tentatively about incorporating, as the King Ranch had done in the thirties, to keep the 06 together for future generations and provide some relief from inheritance taxes. At the size it was then, in 1986, the 06 could still operate at a profit, he said, but families that had seen their land whittled down generation by generation to fifteen-thousand-acre chunks no longer could support themselves by ranching. "They'd be working at the post office or they'd be lawyers or they'd be working at the bank," he explained. The ranch would be a sideline.

Chris Lacy ran the 06 for his grandfather, H. L. Kokernot, Jr. Descended from French Huguenots who fled to Holland to avoid religious persecution, the Kokernots had Texas roots dating back to 1828, when Chris Lacy's great-great-grandfather, a ship's pilot, landed in Galveston. After fighting in the Texas Revolution, David Kokernot began ranching around Gonzales near the Gulf Coast, registering his 06 brand in 1838.

When Lee M. Kokernot, stepped off the train in 1883 in what is now Alpine, he found nothing but a boxcar and a watering tank. He opened a store; his son, Herbert L. Kokernot, Sr., went on to start the community's first bank and eventually the National Finance Credit Corporation, which lent farmers and ranchers money on their crops and livestock. Not all the ranchers in the area were good businessmen, and droughts and other natural calamities made times tough even for astute managers. Herbert Kokernot had plenty of opportunities to buy small ranches at distressed prices, which is how the 06 grew.

H. L. Kokernot, Jr., held doggedly to the same philosophy of ranching that his father had before him: Even in good years, run only as many cattle as the land can support in a drought; that way you avoid feed bills that eat up profits. And fence the perimeter of the land but not the individual pastures; cattle are territorial and thrive best when they're allowed to roam freely and return to the meadows where they were born.

Kokernot still lived on the ranch and made many of the major decisions, but Chris Lacy had been foreman since 1973. The 06 was what was called a cow-calf operation. It raised beef for the table, not fancy registered stock. In the late 1980's the ranch ran about two thousand mother cows—about one cow and one calf for every seventy acres. In normal to wet years the ranch *could* support twice as many animals, but that would have meant either feeding the cattle during dry spells or thinning the herd at distressed prices. And it would have been hard on the land.

"We're raising grass, not cattle," said Diane Lacy. "We try to be conservative and see it as a responsibility to nature."

Combined with the rugged landscape, this approach necessitated old-fashioned roundups. Twice a year—for a month in the spring, when the cattle were branded and vaccinated, and a month in the fall, when the calves were separated from their mothers and shipped for sale—Chris and Diane Lacy and their two children took sixteen cowboys, a chuck wagon, and a remuda, or working string, of 110 horses up into the high pastures to gather the herd. Cowboys came from as far away as Montana for the now-rare opportunity to participate in the ranching ritual.

As traditional as an 06 roundup was, Chris Lacy didn't do it that way just for the nostalgia and romance of the Old West. He did it because it worked as a business. The 06 had turned a profit every year since it was founded. Yet Lacy saw profit not as an end in itself but as a way to keep ranching in an era when interest rates and inheritance taxes made family agricultural enterprises more and more difficult.

Real estate agents in Alpine estimated that the scenic

value of the 06 Ranch would bring $350 an acre, were the Kokernots to sell it in ten-thousand- or twenty-thousand-acre parcels to resort developers. The prospect of subdividing the ranch, selling it, and putting millions of dollars in the bank and living off the interest might have tempted some, but not Chris Lacy. Ranchers who do that "have CDs, but they don't have a ranch anymore," he said. "All the power and all the money in the world won't give you that stability. And they'll always want more, because money isn't stable anyway."

He added: "*Nobody* can feel like they own land. It's been here for so long. You're just paying for the privilege of using it. I'd hate to see this ranch under *any* kind of development. I'd like to see it stay this way forever. Everybody who writes about us always uses a title like 'The Last Cowboys' or 'The Last Roundup,' as if it were over. If we have *our* way, it's going to continue like this for a long time."

When it came to keeping *his* fifty-thousand-acre ranch in the family, Charles Schreiner III, known as Charlie Three or simply Three, was no purist. He gave his antic imagination and flare for self-promotion free rein. He established a summer camp, helped bring the once-reviled Texas longhorn back into vogue, and built a cowboy-chic hotel with chandeliers made of branding irons—probably the only Hilton with a towering mounted grizzly bear dominating the lobby. Most startling, Three turned his YO Ranch into a Hill Country version of Kenya. Giraffes nibbled the treetops, emus grazed with native whitetail deer, and ostriches galloped stiff-legged across the pasture. In all, thirty different exotic species mingled with the native mountain lions, wild turkeys, javelinas, and armadillos. The late shah of Iran hunted here; so did astronaut Neil Armstrong and former Governor and Secretary of the Treasury John Connally. Even a Zulu chieftain hunted on the YO and pronounced it just like Thika. "If you were to blindfold me and turn me around three times, I'd look for my house," Charlie Three said the African tribal leader told him.

The YO was thirty miles northwest of Kerrville, home of Schreiner College, the Schreiner National Bank, Schreiner's Department Store, and the YO Ranch Hilton, dubbed the Yo-Yo Hilton by local wags. But the days when the Schreiners could buy and sell Kerrville were gone. By 1987 this town of 15,276 boasted more than 40 multimillionaires who weren't Schreiners. Virtually all of them had made their fortunes elsewhere; many had come there to get away from Houston or Dallas. Kerrville was a sort of Texas Aspen without snow.

Among its other attractions, Kerrville was the home of the Cowboy Artists Museum. All the bronzes and paintings displayed in these galleries were produced by members of the Cowboy Artists of America, who worked "in the tradition of Frederic Remington and Charles Russell," as the museum's brochure explained. The difference was that Remington and Russell documented what were then contemporary or at least recent scenes of the Old West, while these cowboy artists painted visions of a West they only imagined, one that had vanished generations before they were born.

The countryside around Kerrville was hilly rather than mountainous, with maximum elevations of twenty-five hundred feet. But it still looked plenty western. The YO sat on the Edwards Plateau, the first giant step the Texas landscape made on its way from the Gulf Coast to the Rocky Mountains. The hills were white limestone spotted with stubby gray-green mesquite and juniper, yellow-flowered huisache trees, prickly-pear cactus, and spiny yucca. Except along spring-fed stream beds, nothing grew much over ten feet tall, so the vistas were long and rolling.

The first Charles Schreiner came to Texas from Alsace-Lorraine in 1852 at the age of fourteen. Orphaned two years later, he joined the Texas Rangers as a scout, quitting when he found a quarter section (160 acres) of land he wanted to homestead near Kerrville. During the Civil War he rose to the rank of sergeant. After Lee's surrender he walked back to the Hill Country with nothing but a five-dollar gold piece in his pocket, but he soon started a store and began buying up longhorn cattle and homesteading more land. Schreiner became one of the biggest cattlemen in Texas. He drove more than three hundred thousand head up the Western Trail to Dodge City, Kansas. By the time the trail drive era ended in

1890, he'd rounded up more than half a million acres under the YO brand.

Compared with the Davis Mountains, the Hill Country is relatively lush, with plentiful grass and about thirty-one inches of rainfall a year. But during the fifties Texas was hit by a devastating seven-year drought. The grass shriveled up. Some ranchers who couldn't afford to feed their cattle drove them into ravines and shot them; others sold out cheap or went bankrupt. Charlie Three, however, diversified.

Since 1938 the Schreiners had leased out hunting rights to city folks eager to bag the small but prolific whitetail deer. Faced with the drought and not "a nickel's worth of grass," Charlie Three began stocking sheep, antelope, and deer not indigenous to North America, then charging people to come shoot them. To Charles Schreiner III big-game hunting was almost as good as striking oil.

"We don't have any oil wells out here," Charlie Three said. "We had seven or eight wells drilled, but they all came up dry holes."

He was in the gun room of his hilltop ranch house, sitting on one of two long sofas upholstered in the speckled brown-and-white hides of YO longhorns. Behind him was a huge lighted glass case filled with his collection of antique firearms, which included a gun belonging to Texas Ranger Frank Hamer, who killed Bonnie and Clyde.

Asked if hunting Asian and African wildlife on the YO wasn't a bit like catching trout at a fish farm, Schreiner was quick to point out the difficulties and rigors of the chase. The ranch was big; the animals were free-roaming. It typically took a week of camping out in the mesquite to track down and kill an aoudad, a wily, big-horned sheep with a taste for rocky terrain and an impressive ability to do without water.

In 1989 bagging a YO aoudad cost fifteen hundred dollars, plus two hundred dollars a day for meals, lodging, and the services of a guide. The cheapest of the exotic animals was the wild Spanish goat, with a comparatively modest $450 price on its head. And since there were no seasonal restrictions on the imported species, the ranch pulled in that income year-round.

"We don't guarantee you anything," Charlie Three explained. "It's just that we don't charge you except for the per diem unless you get your animal."

Like many hunters, Schreiner considered himself a conservationist. In fact, although he raised thirteen species of exotic grazers to be shot, he also bred twenty others for sale to zoos and for the enjoyment of guests who preferred to shoot animals with a 35 mm camera rather than a rifle. Bison, zebras, giraffes, and emus grazed and browsed without fear of predators. The most dangerous animals on the entire spread were the male ostriches, which occasionally attacked the photo safari tour vans, denting the doors with powerful kicks.

With ten thousand animals roaming its pastures, about half the YO's income came from hunting, summer camps, and sales to zoos at two hundred to two thousand dollars a head; the other half came from its domestic cattle, quarter horses, sheep, and goats. With a keen nose for market trends, Charlie Three was even raising deer for slaughter, to supply chichi restaurants specializing in New Southwestern Cuisine—things like Mu Shu venison and tenderloin of javelina in wild prickly pear sauce. His success with exotics spawned a trend of its own. About three thousand ranchers in Texas had taken to stocking nonindigenous animals and charging people to hunt or photograph them. One South Texas rancher, Calvin Bentsen, even raised rhinos.

Charlie Three was also largely responsible for another trend: the rehabilitation of the Texas longhorn. Some of the cattle the Spanish first brought to the New World ran off; some became wild after Indians killed their owners. Those that survived in the semiarid rangeland of northern Mexico and South Texas did so because they were wily and sturdy. After a few hundred years they developed the characteristics of a separate breed, with big, curving horns and piebald coats. They were lean, cantankerous, and by most standards pretty peculiar-looking. By the 1950's breeds with fattier, more tender meat and more docile dispositions had replaced them as commercial livestock. The few longhorns left were kept for nostalgia.

Around 1960 Charlie Three started breeding longhorns and talking them up to other ranchers. In 1964 he and a handful of other cattlemen founded the Texas Longhorn Breeders Association and began registering animals that had theretofore been accorded about as much genetic respect as alley cats. By 1989 a thousand Texas longhorns were roaming the YO. "We have the best longhorn herd in the country," Schreiner said, noting that the breed was becoming better domesticated than it had been thirty years earlier.

Longhorns were also becoming more profitable. As the price of feed and veterinary care rose while the price of beef stayed the same, ranchers developed a new admiration for a naturally disease-resistant animal, adapted to the local climate, that could fend for itself—what the cattle industry called easy keepers. At the same time Americans began asking for leaner beef, rather than steaks marbled with fat.

"When I started in the longhorn business, a bull would bring five hundred dollars, and we thought that was wonderful," Schreiner said in 1984. "Now a bull goes for one million dollars. That's a lot of money."

During the seventies and early eighties there were plenty of oilmen eager to spend their windfall profits tax-deductibly on registered longhorn cattle. But after the oil crash that source of new buyers dwindled, and the demand for fancy hunting fell off. The YO Ranch found itself once more in need of a cash infusion. About the only source left was the land itself. Hoping to raise at least ten million dollars, Schreiner and his four sons subdivided seventy-five hundred acres in the northwest corner of the YO into hundred-acre parcels selling for roughly two hundred thousand dollars apiece. Charlie Three had put a price tag on a Texas legend, but it wasn't cheap. He'd stocked the ranch with just about everything else; now it was time to try stocking it with Dallas millionaires.

Charles Schreiner III may have brought back the Texas longhorn, but Billy J. "Red" McCombs transformed it from a romantic anachronism into a hot investment. He even invented his own breed of cattle, Gelorn—a cross between longhorns and hefty German Gelbrieh—developed to produce beef appealing to health-conscious yuppies.

Leaning back in a plain wooden chair and propping his cowboy boots on the unfinished pine table that served as his desk, McCombs said in a mellow West Texas drawl, "The first thing that's great about Texas longhorns is that they're profitable, which is hard to come by in the cattle industry." The reason they were profitable, he added, was "supply and demand."

Longhorns were in demand because they were profitable. And they were profitable because they were in demand. From anyone else that would sound like circular reasoning, but accompanied by McCombs's direct, almost hypnotic gaze and his tone of barely contained enthusiasm, it was pretty damn convincing, as if he were working some rare brand of mercantile magic. Red McCombs may have been a cattle breeder, but he was first of all a consummate salesman. He gave the impression of being utterly persuaded that whatever he was selling had considerable potential, as yet unrecognized. Although his once-bright red hair had faded to auburn, his square-jawed face lit up with youthful eagerness when he contemplated fresh business worlds to be conquered. His favorite expression was "It seems like a great opportunity."

Red McCombs was born in 1928, the son of a mechanic in Spur, Texas, a little town on the High Plains between Lubbock and Abilene. After graduating from the University of Texas with a bachelor's degree in business, McCombs spent a year and a half at UT Law School, which he quit in 1950 to get on with his childhood ambition: becoming rich.

For three years he sold new cars in Corpus Christi. When the dealership refused to give him a management position, he left to start his own used-car business. In 1958 Ford not only granted McCombs a dealership in San Antonio but flew him out to Los Angeles to teach a sales seminar for his California counterparts. Two years later, by the age of thirty-two, the lanky six-foot-three-inch transplanted country boy had chalked up his first million. By 1983 Red McCombs was one of the richest and most powerful men in San Antonio. *Forbes* estimated his wealth at seventy-five million dollars and growing. McCombs was San Antonio's one-man conglomerate: In 1989 his businesses spread from the San Antonio Spurs NBA basketball franchise to twenty-three automobile dealerships to the film investment company that helped bankroll *The Verdict* and *Poltergeist*. He was a partner in twelve radio stations, and he was expanding into breeding Thoroughbred racehorses.

Since his holdings included some of the city's prime commercial property, McCombs could have had an office on the top floor of a high-rise glass tower with the city at his feet. Instead, he worked out of a modest back room at his car dealership, where he could wear open-collar western shirts with pearl snaps. In one corner a silver-dappled black saddle straddled a sawhorse. Nine paintings depicting cowboys at work ranged across the walls, along with an oil portrait of a pretty blonde in an evening dress—his wife, Charline. Country music moseyed out of his radio, and a longhorn hide spread across the wood floor.

"The reason Red keeps his office at his dealership is so that if he hasn't made another trade by ten-thirty in the morning, he can go down and trade a car to keep in practice," said L. D. Brinkman, founder of Brinks Brangus, a registered cattle operation. "If he had a hundred businesses, if he hadn't made a deal in thirty minutes, he wouldn't be happy."

Once, Brinkman added, McCombs took a vacation to a part of Northern California where he'd never been before and came back with the title to a ranch, just because the property was available at a good price. "He'll trade you out of your boots," Brinkman continued. "That guy would rather trade than eat."

What McCombs liked best about raising registered cattle was the sale. He didn't bring in country and western recording stars or shoot off fireworks the way Claytie Williams did, but he did gin up an entertaining sales spiel for each cow, often slipping into car-lot vernacular. "This little heifer," he announced at his Seventh Annual Fiesta Texas Longhorn Sale and Heifer Futurity in 1985, "is a 1983 model with a lot of miles left on her. Isn't she a beauty?"

During the early 1980's McCombs's pitches brought an average of five to six thousand dollars for good bulls and top heifers. And that didn't include Classic—a rugged, well-formed animal crowned with the breed's longest horns, sixty-one inches from tip to tip. In 1982 McCombs and coowner Blackie Graves syndicated Classic's semen for a cool one million dollars. Not bad for a relic of the Old West. Members of the Classic syndicate received straws filled with the bull's

reproductive fluid, used to inseminate their best cows artificially, while McCombs and Graves retained the rights to
the bull himself.

What made a bull worth that much was genetics. If the
offspring of Bull A tended to get heftier quicker on less feed
than the offspring of Bull B, that made Bull A more valuable.
But in reality, such practical considerations were overshadowed by aesthetics. Breeders rhapsodized about the size of
an animal's horns or the distinctive way they curved up and
then back. The more a longhorn *looked* like a longhorn, the
higher price he brought.

Red McCombs took an active part in the breed's appreciation. In 1983 he and Charlie Three founded the annual
Texas Legacy Show and Sale, to which longhorn breeders
from all over the West consigned their top animals. "That's
the World Series," McCombs explained.

But the oil crash hit the registered cattle business hard.
Auction bids dropped by 40 percent; so did the number of
sales. The reason was that a bull or cow was worth a phenomenal amount only if its offspring were potentially worth
a lot as well. True, a commercial rancher might buy a ten-
thousand-dollar bull in the hopes of putting five percent
more meat on his herd down the road. But most registered
cattle were sold to registered cattle breeders. A lot of what's
called brother-in-lawing went on: I'll go to your sale and bid
up your stock with the understanding that you'll go to mine
and do the same.

The new breeders got caught up in the high-rolling competitive frenzy. Flush with profits they sought to shelter from
taxes, they stocked their ranches with the best bloodlines,
sold to each other, and bragged a lot. But when their primary
source of income dried up, they stopped buying. If the bull
they had could still function, they could wait awhile before
replacing him with a newer, more expensive model.

"It's like your car," Red McCombs explained philosophically. "You may want to replace it every three years, but
you don't *have* to get a new one that often."

In June 1987 McCombs got out of Brangus, the priciest
of all registered cattle, and put that money on Thoroughbreds
and Gelorns. He also began test-marketing the lean meat of
his new breed—raised without steroids, antibiotics, or other

chemicals—at Sun Harvest, a chain of health-conscious food
stores in San Antonio. Despite costing 30 percent more per
pound than ordinary U.S. Choice, the Gelorn steaks disappeared from the cooler as fast as McCombs could stock it.

Cattlemen were always looking for cows that would produce a calf every year for more years and for calves that
would gain more weight on less grass and water. During the
early 1940's Oklahoma ranchers Raymond Pope and Frank
Buttram decided that they could go the King Ranch one better. They began crossing Brahmas with even beefier Angus
and came up with Brangus.

Producing a new bovine breed wasn't simple. Since
Brangus were three eighths Brahma and five eighths Angus,
it took a couple of generations to get the proportions right.
Not only that, but the crossed cattle had to breed true. Two
coal black Brangus had to produce offspring that looked like
them, not like Angus or Brahma throwbacks.

The new breeds did serve their intended functions pretty
well, but eventually the kind of competitive hype that afflicts
the breeding of all registered domestic animals took over,
turning cattle into grass-chomping status symbols. Ranchers
started talking about color and conformation. The most
prized Brangus, for example, were those with big, airfoil
Brahma ears and no Brahma hump. "She's got a lotta ear on
her," a breeder would say, admiring a heifer.

Some of those females sold for as much as $150,000 be-
cause new technology made them capable of producing more
offspring. Pumped full of fertility drugs, those top heifers
could be made to produce dozens of embryos a year, each
of which was transferred, through a technique called an embryo flush, to the uterus of a less valuable animal, usually a
dairy cow.

The fanciest registered cattle sales were thrown in the
mid-eighties. By 1987 some of the best breeders, like Brinkman, were holding their auctions in Kansas, away from the
blighted Oil Patch. But in 1985 they were still telling each
other that the registered cattle business was great and bound
to get better.

For sheer style and ostentatious display, no other Brangus breeder could touch I. David Porras. Porras was a flamboyant Midland interior designer specializing in creating for the Oil Rich his own witty, worldly version of the Texas Look—antelope antlers hung on forest green suede walls; steer hides arranged elegantly on bleached oak floors. He commuted to his Pyramid Land and Cattle Company—the only ranch in Texas with a date palm in its brand—in two Bell JetRanger helicopters painted black to match his cattle ("They just think the helicopters are flying cows," he explained), with gold and silver racing stripes for added drama. The interiors were red Hermès leather.

Why two helicopters, especially ones that start at $250,000 apiece sans Hermès? "Why only one?" he replied. "If one is good, two are better. They're not very big, and I wouldn't want to be flying around in one with all the luggage." He added: "I've got a Learjet, too, but you've got to find an airport for one of those."

Despite his preference for silk ascots over string ties, Porras earned the respect of other breeders. From the day he started his herd in 1970, he spent whatever it took to buy the most prized bloodlines and then made the most of them with the latest breeding techniques. Weeks before his annual March heifer sales, Brangus breeders all over North America received Pyramid's catalog, with its embossed cover and heavy, glossy paper bearing four-color photos of the cows to be auctioned. It was a presentation worthy of Sotheby's luring bidders for the venerable treasures of a famous estate. The sale even had a highfalutin' name, Genetic Momentum.

Potential buyers joined the merely curious flying Cessnas and driving Mercedes and Suburbans to the ranch eighty miles south of Dallas. The land here was green, rolling, and woodsy, very different from Midland. A few hundred yards from the 4,750-foot airstrip, capable of handling Learjets and Gulfstreams, was the permanent sales arena with black metal theater seats upholstered in red hopsacking. The cattle to be auctioned munched hay in individual corrals built of shiny red pipe. Across the road, banners bearing the names of Pyramid's top cattle—Captain Nemo, Nefertiti, Cleopatra, Marcus Aurelius—hung from the ceiling of another pavilion twice the size of a basketball court. On the stage at one end, a country and western band deployed its equipment; at the other, earnest-looking young ranchers listened intently as a pretty young blonde in tight jeans used a flip chart to explain why it wasn't crazy for a commercial cattle breeder to pay forty or fifty thousand dollars for forty straws filled with semen from a registered bull.

In 1985 the late March weather was freakishly wet and chilly, and by 10:00 A.M., men and women in ostrich-skin boots and hand-embroidered western shirts crowded the white tent where San Antonio society caterer Don Strange, who did most of the best cattle sales, was dispensing fried oysters and shots of vodka. Nearby, Neiman Marcus had set up business in two white cabanas. The one selling the sixty-thousand-dollar emerald-and-diamond ring and other fine jewelry was almost empty. But the one with ninety-two furs, including a hundred-thousand-dollar full-length sable coat, was jammed. "I can always return this Monday if I decide I don't really want it," drawled a shivering brunette as she whipped out her charge card to pay for an appropriately *sportif* thirty-five-hundred-dollar mink jacket.

Given shrimp, steak, and live music for lunch and four bars dispensing whiskey, beer, and Perrier, the auction itself was almost an anticlimax. But auctioneer Ruben Reyes, a fixture at fancy cattle sales, pumped up the bidding, bringing $115,000 for one handsome heifer named Miss BB Cloud 193M6. Still, the crowd was busy speculating about the after-the-auction entertainment surprise. That's what most of them had braved the blustery weather for. I. David Porras was known for bringing in famous performers but keeping their identities a secret. In 1984 it was Donna Fargo. For 1985, rumor had it, Porras had signed someone completely different.

But when Fats Domino stepped out of his black limousine, he took one look at the open-sided stage, with the wind blowing cold rain across the piano, and eased his bulk back into the car. "I thought you wanted me to play *inside*," he said. Porras screamed at the rhythm and blues great to get off his land, adding that Donna Fargo or Janie Fricke or any number of other stars would have been glad to honor their contracts, whatever the weather.

The chill rain and Fats Domino's defection were omens. For the registered Brangus business, the party was over.

★

CHAPTER SEVEN

John Connally

Mr. Texas Goes Bust

As well-larded with extrava-gant hoopla and downright silliness as the Pyramid Land and Cattle Company's auctions were, at least they were held on a ranch and most prospective buyers wore boots and jeans. At the Western Heritage Sale, ranchers in tuxedos and their wives in evening dresses bid on Santa Gertrudis cattle and registered quarter horses paraded beneath the glittering chandeliers of the Shamrock Hilton's Emerald Room.

Along with ranchers Louis Pearce and Joe Marchman, John Connally, former governor of Texas, cooked up this annual black-tie consignment sale of cattle, horses, and west-ern genre art in 1976, billing it as a bicentennial salute to America's ranching tradition. In truth, it was the ultimate self-congratulatory expression of Cowboy Capitalism.

Some of the most aggressive bidding at the 1979 Western Heritage Sale arose over a mare named Doc's Royal Jassy. The horse had been consigned by Connally, who had just announced his intention to seek the Republican nomination for President of the United States. (He'd tried twice before: for the Democratic ticket in 1968 and for the Republican ticket in 1976.) The bidding climbed quickly from ten thousand to fifty thousand and finally to eighty-six thousand dollars— almost three times as much as the top horse had taken the year before. Sitting at a table off to the side of the main action was a Missouri breeder who owned the mare's sire. "I'd say that's a sixteen-thousand-dollar horse and a seventy-thou-sand-dollar campaign contribution," he opined.

That campaign proved disastrous. Connally spent twelve million dollars and still got only one delegate.

In 1985, with his real estate empire cracking at the seams, Connally announced that that April's Western Heritage Sale would be the last. Despite sliding oil prices, the sale grossed $3,307,050—down from its record $4,539,400 in 1981, but about the same as it had made in 1982, 1983, and 1984.

"Most people assume politics was my career objective, but it wasn't at all," Connally said on January 22, 1988. Wear-ing a finely tailored blue suit with an almost invisible pin-stripe, he sat in the back office at Houston's Hart Galleries, the auction house where two days later the contents of three of his five households were to go on the block. The bank-ruptcy sale was to help pay a fraction of the unsecured debt that he pegged at $41 million but that some of his creditors claimed was as high as $128 million.

"I really wanted to practice law, but I was frustrated for so many years of my life," he continued. "I didn't *ask* to be secretary of the navy. That came about because of Sam Ray-burn. I didn't *ask* to be secretary of the treasury. That was President Nixon's idea."

Reared in the hardscrabble brush country south of San Antonio, Big John Connally was one of seven children born to a man who worked as a barber, a butcher, a bricklayer, a bus driver, and a tenant farmer. When Connally was a soph-omore at the University of Texas, his jack-of-all-trades daddy ran successfully for county clerk on the reform ticket. The door-to-door campaigning gave young John a taste for poli-tics; two years later he became president of the UT student body—a first step for a surprising number of Texas politicians. More important, that campaign introduced Connally to some of the most powerful South Texans, among them Congressman Richard Kleberg, the political member of the King Ranch dynasty. Kleberg's former secretary Lyndon Baines Johnson was state administrator of the National Youth Administration, a New Deal program. To help defray Connally's college expenses, Johnson gave him an NYA job working in the State Supreme Court library at seventeen cents an hour. As Johnson rose to Congress, then the Senate, and finally the White House, Connally rose with him. The two maintained their friendship until Johnson's death in 1973.

When John Kennedy took office in 1961, he named Connally secretary of the navy. Kennedy and Connally were two very different breeds of Democrat—one a Yankee liberal, the other a southern conservative. But both were committed to keeping their party in power in Texas. The long-standing antipathy toward the Republican party expressed by Texas Boll Weevils, as right-wing southern Democrats were called, had its roots in the Reconstruction, but by the 1960's it had a more practical purpose: By keeping conservatives of all economic stripes Democrats, the state's establishment could prevent labor, minorities, and liberal intellectuals from taking control of the party and using it to legislate change. Texas could remain a right-to-work state; it could continue to rank among the stingiest in welfare, mental health, and education. The conservatives figured a viable Republican party would threaten their control rather than enhance it.

So when, in 1961, the voters elected John Tower—the first Republican Texas had sent to the Senate in eighty-four years—to fill Lyndon Johnson's unexpired term, John Connally resigned as secretary of the navy and headed home to run for governor. He won the election, but not by a landslide, and although he had the blessings of both wings of his party, he didn't keep them for long. Conservatives didn't trust him because they associated him with a liberal administration; liberals, led by Texas's senior senator, Ralph Yarborough, a staunch supporter of JFK's New Frontier social programs, didn't like him because he came out against repeal of the poll tax. With or without Connally, the Texas Democratic party was about to rupture. It needed some grand public event to bind it together, especially with Yarborough coming up for reelection in 1964. Governor Connally and his mentor, Vice President Lyndon Johnson, had the answer: a presidential visit.

It had been two years since John Kennedy had made his last official trip to a state, but in the summer of 1963 he agreed to come to Texas in late November. The two-day tour would take him to five cities—San Antonio and Houston on Thursday, November 21, and Fort Worth, Dallas, and Austin the following day. He planned to spend the night of November 22, 1963, at the LBJ Ranch west of the state capital. Thursday afternoon the *Houston Chronicle* announced the results of its latest poll: If a gubernatorial election were held that day, John Connally would have no more than a fifty-fifty chance at reelection.

Kennedy left the details of his itinerary up to Connally, who selected the Dallas Trade Mart for the President's lunch-hour address. It was a fateful choice. Since there was only one logical way to get from Love Field to the site, anyone who knew the city could figure out the route the motorcade would take. In fact, Connally's office naively distributed a press release describing it. Then, shortly after noon on November 22, as the open presidential limousine swung from Elm Street toward the entrance to the Stemmons Expressway, the shots rang out that would kill John Kennedy and salvage the political career of the man beside him.

Reared in South Texas, where deer hunting is a popular pastime, Connally immediately recognized the first shot as high-caliber rifle fire and looked over his right shoulder in the direction of the sound—toward the Texas School Book Depository. Because Connally was turned, the second shot hit below his right shoulder blade; the bullet pierced his right lung, shattered a rib, broke his right wrist, and lodged in his thigh. If he'd been staring straight ahead, it would have passed through his heart.

The way John and Nellie Connally reacted in the seconds after the shooting helped transform him from a deft politician into a legendary figure. While others in the car appeared to panic, Mrs. Connally pulled her husband down protectively

into her lap, then kept repeating gently that he was going
to be all right. And he instinctively wrapped his right arm
around the exit wound in his chest, a move that kept his left
lung from collapsing. Fortunately Parkland Memorial Hospital, Dallas's main trauma center, was only five minutes
away.

Governor Connally easily won a second term in 1964.

Despite Connally's party affiliation, Richard Nixon made
him his treasury secretary in 1970. Connally did become a
Republican, but he waited until May 1, 1973, three months
after Lyndon Johnson's death. He also became a partner in
Vinson & Elkins, the state's largest law firm.

But in 1972, while serving as secretary of the treasury,
Connally was accused of accepting a ten-thousand-dollar
bribe in exchange for urging the President to raise milk price
supports. Largely thanks to such eloquent character witnesses as Barbara Jordan, the black, Democratic Houston
congresswoman, Connally was acquitted, but a shadow lin-
gered over his otherwise brilliant political career.

After his 1980 presidential campaign debacle Connally
declared that he was leaving public life. He was going into
business to do something he couldn't do, he said, as an
elected or appointed official: make a lot of money.

Later he was to tell the scores of newspaper, magazine,
and television reporters covering his bankruptcy auction that
money hadn't been his motive after all. "It was more the
challenge to do something and build something," he said.
"I can't sit idle."

Yet at the time he sat on the board of directors of the
Ford Motor Company as well as First City Bancorporation,
the fourth-largest bank holding company in Texas, and was
already a millionaire several times over.

The problem was that ever since 1942, when he became
a lawyer for Fort Worth wildcatter Sid Richardson, John Connally had run with the Big Rich, people with ten times his
wealth and more. He had his own plane. He had four residences, including a romantic adobe in Santa Fe and a million-
dollar Washington *pied-à-terre* he and Nellie had bought from
the sister of the late shah of Iran. That was a standard of
living anyone with his mere six million dollars would be hard

pressed to support. The urge to go out, while he still had his vigor and charisma, and found one of the state's legendary fortunes must have been close to irresistible.

So, at age sixty-six, in partnership with his former political protégé Ben Barnes—once Texas's youngest state legislator, later its lieutenant governor—Connally proceeded to get *really* rich. The pair bought an air charter service, purchased the *Austin Business Journal*, and even invested in a catering company that provided meals to offshore oil rigs. Since 1975 Connally had held a substantial position in Chapman Energy, a small oil and gas company. In 1981, at the height of the boom, its assets were a lackluster three million dollars. Then, as oil prices began to drift south, Connally hit on a new strategy: grabbing up failing oil companies. He figured it was cheaper and surer to find oil by buying up others' proven reserves than by sinking wildcat wells. In its 1985 annual report Chapman listed its assets at eighty-two million dollars.

Mostly, Barnes and Connally got into real estate development. By 1986 they had three hundred million dollars in real estate projects under way, and Connally's net worth had soared to twenty-eight million dollars. Connally later said that Barnes "talked to me about becoming involved in one or two projects, and that quickly expanded into more. It's kind of like Topsy. The whole thing just grew until it became rather huge."

The partnership didn't have to put up its own money. Lenders were so flattered to be asked to do business with the man Texans still called Governor that they didn't ask Connally and Barnes to ante up the usual 20 percent. Their signatures alone were considered enough to secure multimillion-dollar deals. The catch was that those were personal signatures. In order to operate with no money down, the two erstwhile bright political lights had to step out from behind corporate protection and put their personal fortunes at risk. It was an audacious gamble, and they lost. They broke ground on their first real estate project in 1982, at the crest of the oil boom, and were wiped out in the crash.

"Looking back on it, we probably did try to do too much too quickly," Connally said two days before his bankruptcy auction. "But I don't think it would've made a whole lot of difference. Our principal difficulty was timing. No one really could foresee the precipitous decline of this economy and the depth of it. I certainly didn't."

On top of the oil crash, Sunchase IV, their $21.5-million condo tower at the beach on South Padre Island near the Mexican border opened just as Mexico's peso collapsed, eliminating a major part of the market for the $240,000 units. But timing wasn't the only problem. Triple Crown, their $15.5-million 104-unit condominium project next to New Mexico's Ruidoso Downs racetrack, a popular gaming spot for the Texas Rich, was set on an unattractive site in the wrong part of town downwind from the horses. The partners' attempts to sell offices on the condominium plan failed; Shepherd Place, their office tower three miles west of downtown Houston, hit the overbuilt market. And in trying to turn a 1,480-acre ranch on an ecologically sensitive West Austin watershed into an exclusive neighborhood, with $65,000 lots and a comparably pricey country club and conference center, Barnes and Connally misjudged the community; the Estates of Barton Creek was a $105 million error.

Yet Connally remained upbeat about the state's economic prospects, even when the weather vane pointed in the opposite direction. In 1983 the slick monthly *Texas Business* chose him for its August cover. Inside, it quoted Connally as saying, "We're beginning an era of prosperity like America hasn't dreamed of, and Texas will be at the forefront of it."

As the eighties wore on, John and Nellie Connally kept up a rich front. With the help of an interior design firm, Nellie added $250,000 in furnishings, fixtures, and other improvements to their personal penthouse atop Sunchase IV on South Padre Island. The condo measured 3,845 square feet, with an additional 3,405 square feet of tiled balconies. In October 1984 the Connallys hosted a barbecue for Princess Margaret and her entourage at Picosa Ranch, headquarters of their 10,000-acre Santa Gertrudis and quarter horse operation in Floresville. Fifty wealthy and influential Texans flew in for the occasion.

The following February First City sued Connally for defaulting on a $4.05 million loan he'd cosigned for his 1980 campaign aide Bryan Lewis, who had used the money to purchase and renovate a house in River Oaks. Because of sliding real estate values, the house was now worth $2.2 million less than the $4 million balance due. That April Connally stepped down from the First City Bancorporation board of directors, which he'd joined in 1972. Plagued with additional problem loans, including two to other members of its board—one for $20 million, another for $25 million—First City skidded to the brink of failure. (Remarkably, a resuscitated and reorganized First City Bancorporation hired Connally as a consultant in 1989.)

In March 1985 Connally resigned from Vinson & Elkins, declaring that both he and the firm had agreed that he was too busy with other business interests. By the spring of 1986 rumors were circulating that the Barnes-Connally partnership might be close to cratering. By late summer their Austin headquarters was posted for foreclosure, as were Triple Crown and the Houston condo office tower. The lender had taken over management of the Estates at Barton Creek. Other creditors had filed suit to collect millions in unpaid debts. Even Chapman Energy was coming unglued. The company lost $43 million in 1986 and was in default on $22.5 million in bank loans.

In November 1986 Connally auctioned off 126 of his prize racehorses, but the five hundred thousand dollars he brought in wasn't enough to keep his creditors at bay for long. On July 31, 1987, the Barnes-Connally partnership filed for liquidation under Chapter 7 of the Federal Bankruptcy Code, and Connally filed Chapter 11 to protect his assets while he reorganized his personal finances.

The debts of the partnership plus twenty related companies totaled more than $170 million. Connally listed his personal debts as $93 million, $49 million of them unsecured. They ranged from a $17.2 million loan balance with San Antonio Savings Association to $26.91 owed the *Austin American-Statesman* for a newspaper subscription. He also owed $12,500 to a dry cleaning establishment, $5,857.55 to the electric company, and $9,600 to Domino's Pizza. His assets amounted to about $13 million, including his antiques, his western art, his collection of cuff links, and four thousand uncirculated one dollar bills bearing his signature as secretary of the treasury. Except for two hundred acres (including the house, swimming pool, and tennis court) of his thirty-four-hundred-acre Picosa Ranch and $30,000 in personal effects the Connallys were allowed to keep under the Texas Property Code, everything had to go on the block to pay creditors.

"I've never viewed myself as a rich Texan," the former governor told the Associated Press two days after he'd filed for bankruptcy. "Nellie and I have accumulated things over our lives. We've been frugal. We've never been extravagant. We've taken great pride in what we've been able to acquire and it's not pleasant now to consider the prospects of giving it up. But we're going to do it."

Even as he slid under, Big John Connally wrapped himself in the Texas flag, comparing himself with the state's martyred heroes. "The people who came to Goliad and who came to the Alamo took a few risks, and for what?" he said to the *Houston Chronicle*. "For what they thought was right. I'll never quit taking risks."

For his auction house, Connally picked Hart Galleries of Houston. One reason was that Hart, while a major regional auctioneer, accepted everything, down to the Santa Claus cookie jar and the 1978 Westinghouse washer and dryer. International auction houses like Sotheby's and Christie's would have skimmed the cream—the most valuable paintings, the pair of exquisite Persian rugs that had graced the Saudi royal palace, some of the rarer guns—and rejected the rest. Another reason was that many of Connally's political memorabilia and much of his Texana were bound to bring more in Houston than New York.

During their fifty years in the business the Harts had auctioned off the estates of some of the most celebrated Texans, but never had this venerable establishment operated under a brighter spotlight. Jerry Hart had spent seventy thousand dollars on a four-color catalog, with the lots cleverly orchestrated to prevent boredom and maximize bidding. Rather than list in a row dozens of Chinese ginger jars (worth one hundred to two hundred dollars apiece if they hadn't belonged to a celebrity), he peppered them among the tooled leather saddles and Queen Anne chairs. When Hart's five

moving vans and flatbed truck pulled up to Connally's Flo-
resville ranch house, the national media were there. For days
the sale dominated the front pages of papers across Texas.
On opening day it made page one of the *Wall Street Journal*.
It generated two full hours of television coverage, including
Governor Connally's live appearance on *Nightline*. The first
night The *New York Times*, the *Miami Herald*, the *Boston Globe*,
and *People* all were there. Even the foreign press showed up.

Inside Hart Galleries that evening 2,150 people jockeyed
for 1,650 chairs or milled around sizing up the more than
eleven hundred auction lots and each other. *Grandes dames*
smiled serenely at their admirers. Ready to do some serious
competitive bidding, Houston Oilers owner Bud Adams and
his wife, Nancy, staked out chairs squarely in the middle,
with a good view of one of the seven television monitors
rigged to show details of items on the block. The hungry
compared notes on the refreshments. Cheese, wine, and coffee were free, but Demeris Barbecue was doing a brisk business in brisket sandwiches ($2.50), Cokes (75 cents), and
candy bars (75 cents).

Some people, like Hermann Hospital Life Flight director
and television personality Dr. Red Duke, were in jeans. (As
a young medical resident he'd helped patch Governor Connally's bullet wounds in 1963.) Some were dressed just short
of black tie. Others were duded up in high-style cowboy
gear—fancy fringed leathers and bola ties with diamond
slides. Strip-center tycoon Jerry J. Moore, whose net worth
Forbes pegged at six hundred million dollars in 1988, flaunted
his polyester—a white shirt with long collar points paired
with a sports coat and pants of unmatched navy. But most
wore the sort of expensive casual wear favored for relaxed
little dinners. Socialite Carolyn Farb turned heads in a black
leather pantsuit, a black cashmere turtleneck, and a necklace
and earrings of serious diamonds and emeralds. Lawyer and
Texana collector Don Thiel sported a gray business suit, a
Texas sesquicentennial-edition gold Rolex with the state seal
as its face, and a maroon tie emblazoned with a likeness of
the San Jacinto Monument, commemorating Sam Houston's
defeat of Mexico's General Antonio López de Santa Anna.

That evening's turnout demonstrated that anything can
become trendy if enough of the right people are doing it.

And lately in Texas a number of the most high-profile multi-millionaires had declared personal or corporate bankruptcy. Two of the state's most prominent and popular Chapter 11's—Bobby Sakowitz, whose family's specialty stores were now controlled by an Australian conglomerate, and heart surgeon Denton Cooley, whose real estate ventures had run amok—were there with their wives, smiling gamely but not bidding. If bankruptcy hadn't exactly become chic, at least it had lost its stigma.

The Connallys were at the auction every day, sitting in the center of the second row, smiling bravely and flanked by their children and grandchildren. Occasionally, when the bidding slowed on a particular item, Governor Connally would take the microphone from Jerry Hart and describe how he and Nellie had come to possess the item under consideration; after his anecdotes the prices invariably leapfrogged. At other times he strolled back toward the Hart offices, carrying a stack of those uncirculated dollar bills bearing his signature as secretary of the treasury; autographed, they brought twenty dollars apiece.

Each day of the auction had its own distinctive flavor. Saturday drew ranchers eager to bid on the ex-governor's gun collection. Sunday brought out the art and rug collectors and found auctioneer Jerry Hart hoarse. ("I got too emotionally involved," Hart admitted later, "shouting to reach the last row.") On Tuesday, when most of the linens and ordinary household items came up, tight flocks of well-dressed dowagers circled the room as a pair of ashtrays went for $70 each, a ten-year-old refrigerator for $475, a Lucite egg timer for $850. One woman bid $5,500 for a Buck knife—worth $50 new if it hadn't said "John B. Connally" on the side.

Connally's art collection included eleven paintings by the late forger Elmyr de Hory. De Hory, who sold $150 million in fakes during his lifetime, was unmasked in 1976, after Dallas philanthropist Algur Meadows invited two art dealers—one from New York, the other from Los Angeles—to admire his French Impressionists over lunch; the guests sadly informed their host that forty-nine of his fifty-three paintings were frauds.

Possessed of an astounding ability to paint in dozens of

styles, De Hory had fooled the art world for decades with uncanny knock-offs of the most famous French Impressionists. Desperate for cash to support his lavish life-style, during the mid-1970's De Hory had sold hundreds of his paintings to a London bookie named Talbott.

Connally learned about De Hory two years after the faker's apparent suicide. Together with his friend Dr. Horace Finn, a Santa Fe art collector, Connally knowingly bought a hundred of the forgeries from Talbott for a few thousand dollars apiece.

When they came up for auction, Connally defended his purchase. "I like the quality of the paintings," he declared. "This fellow, even though he was a faker, was a really superb artist."

"This is Elmyr de Hory doing his interpretation of Vincent van Gogh," auctioneer Jerry Hart announced, displaying "In the Boudoir," a sensual work signed "Vincent" on the front, "Elmyr" on the back. "Those of you who read the papers know that two Van Goghs sold recently for twenty-two million dollars and fifty-five million dollars. Who'll bid a tenth of that for this great fake?"

"In the Boudoir" went for $17,500. The top De Hory, a lovely ersatz Modigliani, "Woman in a Hat," went for $22,500.

When the last lot had sold, the take totaled $2.75 million—about eight cents on the dollar for Connally's creditors, but more than twice the $1.2 million Jerry Hart reckoned the merchandise would have been worth if disposed of anonymously. "This wasn't an auction to find a bargain," Hart observed. "This was an auction to attend to say, 'I bought a piece of Texas history.' "

Having the Connallys present at the auction added substantially to the money their belongings brought, as did the letter of authenticity, signed by John Connally, that accompanied each item. But the personal cost of doing it all so publicly must have been considerable. Nellie Connally had been a drama major at the University of Texas, and both she and her husband seemed to recognize this as one of their most important roles—symbols of Texas in hard times, just as they'd been in good. "This is a big part of our life that will be passing by," Nellie Connally said the Wednesday before the auction, "and we're going to be right there to watch it go. It never occurred to us not to be there."

Like other rich Texans who file bankruptcy, the Connallys emerged far from penniless. In addition to his homestead, John Connally was entitled to his pensions as former governor, secretary of the navy, and secretary of the treasury. With his salaries for serving on corporate boards, his income from sources not affected by his bankruptcy came to more than three hundred thousand dollars a year. He declared he'd retire to his ranch and write his memoirs, adding that he planned to turn Picosa into a Thoroughbred horse farm. The state legislature had legalized parimutuel betting in 1987; Picosa was forty miles from the site selected for one of the first tracks. And because Nellie Connally wasn't personally bankrupt, she held on to her separate property—her jewelry, furs, and inheritances and gifts, which included a Monet and a Van Gogh.

John Connally was even getting into commercials. Less than a week after the auction Houston-based University Savings announced that the man who'd defaulted on so many loans from hapless financial institutions had agreed to be its spokesman. Holding television viewers and newspaper readers with a direct and sober gaze, he proclaimed: "Nellie and I worked hard all our lives to make sure our future would be financially secure. Well, the future is here, and things haven't quite worked out like we'd planned. But that's all right because there's no better place than Texas to start over and to save a little something."

Two years later, University Savings joined the swelling list of failed Texas savings and loans.

To the Connallys' embarrassment, many people in far worse circumstances read about their plight and offered to help. "The mail comes from all over the United States, even from foreign countries," Nellie Connally said, looking elegantly prosperous in a subdued red silk dress. "They send in little contributions—five dollars, fifteen dollars. Could they please pay a bill under fifty dollars? Of course, we send all that back. Many say, 'We don't have anything. We can't help you except with our prayers.' There's a real religious overtone to much of this mail. Everybody has been so wonderful that sometimes it's hard to remember that we did this to ourselves, that nobody did this to us."

Since weeks before the auction rumors had been circulating that friends and admirers planned to buy items to return to the Connallys after the bankruptcy was resolved. Houston socialite Dody Resnick's daughter Sallie Gonzales, for example, paid nine hundred dollars for a chemin de fer shoe to which she'd heard Connally had a sentimental attachment. But most who bought with that in mind weren't telling. People had pestered the couple to name the things that mattered to them most, but, Connally explained before the auction, "We have not encouraged that. If we suggested to someone that they buy something back for us and it went for more than they were prepared to pay, I would feel extremely bad about it." Consider the nineteenth-century Khyber rifle Dr. Red Duke had intended to win back for Connally but finally lost to Bud Adams for six thousand dollars. Sixteen years earlier Duke had helped Connally find that gun in Afghanistan. As he shook his head no to the spotter, the flamboyant physician's face sagged in disappointment.

There was a different sort of sadness on Nellie Connally's countenance as she paused the last afternoon of the auction to give a fond pat to a marble statue of Michelangelo as a child chipping precociously at a rock. The intricately carved and unabashedly sentimental piece had gone Friday night for $15,500.

Yet a few days earlier, she'd talked of redecorating the ranch house, using bright fabrics and pickling the dark paneling. "I'm totally free of things that have probably controlled a lot of my life," she said. "I don't think we'll ever try to amass possessions in the amounts we are auctioning off. When you grow up with nothing and suddenly are exposed to all these wonderful things, you just sort of want to have them for yourself and your family. I think we had too many."

CHAPTER EIGHT

★

Dallas

Glitz and Glitter on the Prairie

Along a narrow, rural stretch of Highway 114 well northwest of Dallas/Fort Worth Regional Airport, a traffic jam of Jaguars, Mercedes, and an occasional Rolls waited to turn into the entrance to the Circle T Ranch. On this particular warm June evening in 1984, thirteen hundred people were paying six hundred dollars a couple (twice that for the five hundred sponsors) to drive through those white wooden gates and into a fantasy. Nelson Bunker Hunt's spread had been transformed for the occasion into a fake frontier outpost straight out of a 1950's western movie. Dressed as cavalrymen, caterer Don Strange's crew dished out sautéed oysters and sizzling shish kabobs instead of chili and beans.

The event was the highpoint of Dallas's summer social season, the Cattle Barons' Ball. Held at a different ranch each year, this most Texan of fund raisers netted, in good times and bad, more than half a million dollars annually for cancer research in Dallas County, making it the biggest cancer gala in the world. It also provided an excuse for the fashion-obsessed and much solicited Dallas gentry to don purple ostrich-skin cowboy boots and squash-blossom necklaces heavy with turquoise.

Decked in fringed and beaded leather, real Kiowa Indians (most of them moonlighting from white-collar jobs in Dallas offices) danced around genuine tepees. Socialite volunteers looked brassy and believable as saloon hussies. But they had nothing on the partygoers. One man sported a red snakeskin Stetson. A middle-aged blonde wore a black satin rodeo shirt, black jeans, and a black sequined cowboy hat. A buxom young woman flaunted the ultimate Indian princess dress—velvet-soft ivory deerskin trimmed in ermine. An oilman flashed a solid gold belt buckle etched with a Texas map with diamonds denoting Houston, Dallas, and Midland.

As the sun hunkered down toward the horizon, hundreds of duded-up Dallasites crowded around the portable stage from which *Dallas* star Larry Hagman, in his best J. R. Ewing style, was tossing fake hundred-dollar bills with his picture where Ben Franklin's should have been. When America's favorite antihero had everyone's attention, he started auctioning off a mixed bag of donated merchandise —everything from jewelry, furs, and a full-page ad in the *Dallas Times Herald* to livestock and a four-wheel-drive Land Cruiser modified for hunting by the addition of camouflage paint, a shooting platform, three telephones, a bar, and a top-of-the-line stereo system. Of more questionable utility were a Waterford cut crystal cowboy hat—made in Ireland —which brought $11,500, and Resistol's wearable white ermine version of the same headgear, which landed $3,500.

Inside a stockade fashioned from weathered two-by-fours accented with twinkling Tivoli lights, guests staked their claims to round tables with centerpieces of crossed carbines pointing skyward over ammunition boxes planted with daisies. Even those who held sponsors' tickets had to line up at barbecue pits for their steaks, baked potatoes, and avocado salads.

Once everyone was fed, horse opera celebrities took their

turns addressing the crowd. Chief Iron Eyes Cody, star of the "Keep America Beautiful" public service television spot, recited an Indian prayer simultaneously in English and sign language. John Crawford, who had acted the part of the Rifleman's son, demonstrated fancy roping. Ken Curtis of *Gunsmoke* and Will Hutchins of *Sugarfoot* were followed by a stream of faces from late-night movies and reruns. Even Clint Walker and Jane Russell were there, but they were upstaged by a specially made surprise videotape featuring the former host of *Death Valley Days* himself, Ronald Reagan.

Dressed in a conservative dark suit and gazing into the camera with a look of utmost sincerity, President Reagan apologized for not being present in person, praised George and Barbara Bush, and talked about the crisis in Central America. After five minutes someone stopped the tape, recognizing that it had been intended not for the Cattle Barons' Ball but for the Washington Charity Dinner, hosted by the Bushes and benefiting humanitarian efforts in Central America. That same evening in the nation's capital, impeccably attired diplomats and their wives probably sat baffled as they watched a tape of the President in cowboy garb lauding Dallas for its generosity and recalling his days in westerns.

Six months later Southfork Ranch, the location for the *Dallas* television series, hosted a gilt-edged cattle sale that took in $11.7 million—enough to rock the most high-rolling Brangus and Santa Gertrudis breeders back on their alligator heels. Only those weren't beeves on the auction stage. They were dairy cows—even though Southfork had never had anything to do with the dairy industry, either fictionally or in reality. The forty cows to be auctioned off were the cream of the cream-milk-and-butter crop, and Price's Dairies of El Paso, which was sponsoring the sale, figured that Dallas style would attract investors with the deepest pockets. Price's screened them before sending out invitations, checking financial statements to make sure each of the six hundred potential bidders could ante up at least $250,000. Destined for transplant into less pricey cows, the embryos of the best bossies could bring $100,000 apiece.

Investors munched salmon mousse, barbecued shrimp,

Texas-shaped nachos, and petits fours. Leggy models dressed in skimpy blue shorts and clear plastic chaps distributed drinks. For those who wanted to keep clear heads, milk gurgled from a silver fountain.

With the theme from *2001: A Space Odyssey* for a fanfare, Stephanie, the top diary cow in America, producer of fifty-one thousand pounds of milk a year, strolled into the pink spotlight. She sold for $1.1 million, more than any of her rivals in the sale.

Buyers and consignors came to Southfork from as far afield as California, Michigan, and New York. "Some of these people have never seen a cow," Gregg Feinberg, a lawyer for a Pennsylvania car dealer investing in diary cattle, told the *Dallas Times Herald*. "They wouldn't know a cow from an oil well."

Dallas had always exuded a sense of theatrical style, sometimes outrageous, sometimes obsessively elegant, but always bigger than life. In its eagerness for the world to take it seriously as a sophisticated metropolis, Dallas hung up its spurs over a generation ago. More than any other city in Texas, it downplayed the cowboy mystique. "The Cattle Barons' Ball isn't the *real* Dallas," rich Dallasites protested defensively. "That's just a costume party. Now, take the Crystal Charity Ball. That's the *real* Dallas," they added, referring to the fall fund raiser that served as a showcase for $10,000 couture gowns and $250,000 diamond necklaces.

The way the Dallas rich liked to see themselves portrayed was the way they appeared on their namesake television series. Never mind that J. R. Ewing was greedy and amoral. He played for high stakes, and he won. He was also polished and charming. Besides, he and the other characters dressed so well.

November 22, 1963, was a watershed for Dallas. The Kennedy assassination forced the city to confront its somewhat undeserved reputation for combining the worst elements of the Old South and the Wild West. In the wake of the tragedy, Dallas replanned its downtown and laid out the D/FW Regional Airport, which put it in touch with the world's capitals.

From the beginning Dallas had represented the triumph of unbridled optimism, naive ambition, and sheer determination over sober reality. Stuck out on the flat Northeast Texas prairie, it had no geographical raison d'être. Dallas wasn't here because of a port. It wasn't even here because of oil; the nearest field was more than a hundred miles away. It was here because its first citizen, an Arkansas merchant named John Neely Bryan, was a wizard at land promotion. Ever since Bryan established his trading post on a bend in the Trinity River in 1841, this had been a city of promoters, of merchants and bankers. In 1932 Republic Bank of Dallas became the first bank in the world to lend money on proven oil reserves, but none of its officers got his hands dirty in the process.

Despite a population in the late 1980's of close to a million, not counting the surrounding suburbs, Dallas remained the most politically conservative city in Texas—and that was saying something. Republican candidates pulled majority votes here back when the rest of Texas considered itself a one-party state. And some of the Republicans Dallas spawned would make the average Republican look like a left-wing radical. Take late Congressman Jim Collins. During the 1973–74 Arab oil embargo, he suggested that Texas secede from the Union and join OPEC.

Dallas was enormously proud of landing the 1984 Republican National Convention and of raising from the private sector the entire nine million dollars to stage it.

"Just let us alone and we'll get the job done," said Republican Paul Eggers, who lost the governor's race in 1968 and 1970. "It's still the old idea that this country grew great from private capital and private labor, and if you'll keep government out of our hair, we'll make this a great city."

That didn't mean that all was laissez-faire. Far from it. Firmly lodged at the civic helm was the Dallas Citizens Council, a body of two hundred corporate presidents, chairmen of the board, major independent businessmen, and attorneys. Once this power elite was all male and all white. By 1989 it included some women, blacks, and Hispanics. But it remained the permanent establishment, above the whim of voters and invulnerable even to tremors in the oil market.

Very little happened on a major scale that didn't meet with the approval of the Dallas Citizens Council.

Dallas was the ultimate consumerist culture. Nowhere did people care more about how they spent their money than they did here. Among the Dallas rich and the upper middle class, appearances were terribly important. Even women on limited budgets looked perfectly turned out, and men in the city's power elite showed up for business confabs in exquisite European tailoring, flawless down to their French cuffs.

"Everything goes together," said Loretta Blum, proprietor of one of the most expensive and *au courant* boutiques in town. "Even the soap in their bathrooms is the right color and the right fragrance for the season."

Fashion was one of the linchpins of the local economy. Dallas was the home of Victor Costa, who knocked off Oscar de la Renta and other couturiers for those whose pocketbooks ran to five hundred rather than five thousand dollars an evening gown. Trammell Crow's 7.5-million-square-foot green and white Dallas Market Center sprawled across what was once the Trinity River floodplane. Its nine annual apparel markets drew manufacturers from all over the country and buyers from stores throughout the the United States and Latin America.

But fashion was more than big business in Dallas; it was a way of life. To be considered socially appropriate, Dallas women needed a lot of clothes. "They change outfits six times a day," Ms. Blum explained. "They wear one thing to exercise class, one to car pool, one for lunch, one for tennis, one for a committee meeting, one for dinner."

With the possible exception of San Francisco, Dallas was the dressiest city in the country. Ms. Blum said that after moving from New York, where she was a buyer for Bergdorf Goodman, she "learned right away that 'casual' in Dallas doesn't mean casual for women." What it meant, she observed, was short silk dresses, "little colorful things done with V necks so the jewelry shows."

And what baubles those were. Carla Francis, who had the jewelry concession at Loretta Blum, sold Brobdingnagian stones: a ring consisting of a nile green indicolite an inch and a half across, surrounded by diamonds ($36,500), another a twenty-nine-carat acid green peridot ($18,500) so heavy its owner would have to do finger flexes for a week to prepare to wear it. Anyplace else stones this size would be assumed to be fakes, but not in Dallas.

The one entity most responsible for imparting style and taste to that competitive display of wealth was Neiman Marcus, the department store that was practically synonymous with Dallas money. Neiman Marcus began in 1907 with a flawed business judgment. Brothers-in-law Herbert Marcus and Al Neiman were given the choice of accepting the Missouri franchise for a newfangled temperance tonic called Coca-Cola or opening the store. Had they done the former, the family would have been considerably richer but not nearly so influential. When Herbert's son Stanley Marcus, by the 1980's chairman emeritus of the board of directors, entered Harvard in 1921, he was surprised that no one seemed to have heard of his family's store or even to know where Dallas was. "I made up my mind that when I grew up, I was going to put Neiman Marcus and Dallas on the map," he recalled in 1984.

Preaching a doctrine of less is more elegance that still allowed extravagant display—not layers of jewelry but one breathtaking pair of forty-thousand-dollar cabochon emerald earrings—Mr. Stanley, as he was known in Texas, transformed his oil-rich customers from country bumpkins into fashion plates who could more than hold their own in New York or Paris. For generations, women from all over Texas flocked to the 451,000-square-foot store at Commerce and Ervay in downtown Dallas. Limousines ferried favored customers from their private planes to the Art Deco front door. Neiman's had twenty branches, as far-flung as Boston, Bal Harbour, and Beverly Hills, but none of them embodied the sense of legendary luxury that seemed to seep from the walls at that original location. For the Big Rich, Neiman's came to them. Every year the store sent two bobtail trucks—one loaded with furs, the other with ball gowns and daytime couture—327 miles south to Beeville, an unassuming oil town of 14,574 distinguished mainly by its profusion of frozen custard establishments.

By 1960 Neiman's international reputation was so secure

that it could afford to make Texas excess chic. That year's thick, glossy Christmas catalog included a novel gift idea—his and her Beechcraft airplanes. It wasn't just a gimmick; they sold. In subsequent years Mr. Stanley followed with his and her submarines, his and her camels ("for people who have been promising themselves to slow down"), his and her mummy cases ("richly adorned, but gratefully vacant"), and his and her natural safety-deposit boxes, hidden inside a nine-thousand-foot mountain in Utah's Wasatch Range.

As one of the rare avowed liberals in Dallas's establishment, Stanley Marcus also turned his attention to more meaningful issues. During the late 1950's he championed desegregation of Dallas's stores, which had, until that time, forbidden blacks in dressing rooms. "We had only one customer close her account," he said.

In 1969 the Marcuses sold out to Carter Hawley Hale, the retailing giant that owned Bergdorf Goodman, Walden bookstores, and the Canadian specialty chain Holt, Renfrow and Company. Although the family continued to maintain considerable control over the enterprise, the merger was mourned throughout the state much like the decision of the Republic of Texas to join the Union. Texas had given up one more measure of its independence.

"We saw the need for expansion, and we wouldn't have been able to expand without additional capital," explained Mr. Stanley, who became a member of Carter Hawley Hale's board of directors and whose son, Richard, was chairman and chief executive officer of Neiman Marcus. "We figured we might as well go out and marry a rich girl and get it over with."

One reason the Dallas rich went in for such a conspicuous display of wealth was that the elite here was so new—even newer than Houston's. Many of the founders of the city's great fortunes were still alive, and dynasties in their second or third generation of wealth were considered Old Money.

"Mother and Dad came to Dallas on their honeymoon, and now we're an old, old family," said Ruth Collins Sharp, past president of both the Junior League and the Dallas Women's Club, the closest the city had to a bastion of the old guard. Her father moved to Dallas from East Texas during the 1930's and founded the Fidelity Life Insurance Company.

What passed for Old Money in Dallas lived in the Park Cities—Highland Park and University Park. These enclaves of wealth were so close to downtown that for most purposes, except for their separate public school systems, they functioned as neighborhoods rather than as distinct suburbs. Highland Park was less homogeneously grand than Houston's River Oaks, but the most modest houses carried hefty price tags, thanks to their ZIP code. Even in the wake of the oil collapse, a fifty-by-fifty-foot lot sold for $240,000, down from $300,000 in 1984, and a three-bedroom, two-bath "tacky teardown" on a not especially chic street was $600,000.

The Dallas rich could educate their young from kindergarten right through graduate school without subjecting them to any unsavory influences outside the Park Cities. Set next door in somewhat less pricey University Park was Southern Methodist University. With tuition, room, and board for 1989–90 of $12,000 a year, SMU was one of the most expensive colleges in the country. Yet academically it ranked well behind Texas's two other well-known private universities, Rice in Houston and Trinity in San Antonio, as well as behind both the University of Texas and Texas A&M, where annual tuition and fees ran an accessible $870. For many families who sent their children to SMU, the point was social rather than intellectual.

"There are a lot of people who grew up in Highland Park, went to SMU, married people in Highland Park, and never moved," said Marilyn Schwartz, who tracked the doings and undoings of the rich for the *Dallas Morning News*. "It's like a little Camelot. Kids there take drugs and have nervous breakdowns, but you never know it."

A University Park drugstore set one of the richest men in Dallas on his road to wealth. In 1961, when he was twenty-nine, Harold Simmons, the son of two schoolteachers from the East Texas town of Golden (population two hundred), bought a drugstore across the street from Southern Methodist University. He paid five thousand dollars down and signed a ninety-five-thousand-dollar note. Using his profits to pick up other family-owned pharmacies across Texas, he built a hundred-store chain, which he sold in 1973 to the Jack Eckerd Corporation for fifty million dollars in stock.

With the money his stock brought in, Simmons launched a series of hostile takeovers. Some of his early forays, most against insurance companies, were failures. But analysts estimated that he averaged a 90 percent profit on everything he bought and sold between 1977 and February 1989, when wealth watchers pegged his net worth at $1.5 billion.

With all that money made in corporate raids, Harold Simmons naturally aroused the suspicion of the Securities and Exchange Commission—especially when the Young Turk who helped put some of his deals together, junk bond genius Michael Milken of Drexel Burnham Lambert, became embroiled in an insider trading scandal. But even under close regulatory scrutiny, Simmons came up clean. He insisted that in picking takeover targets, he relied not on privileged information but on annual reports mailed to shareholders and on financial statements submitted to the SEC. Simmons seemed to have an uncanny ability to see things others overlooked.

In part that was because Harold Simmons was bright. Despite playing a lot of tennis and belonging to the 1951 University of Texas basketball team that won the Southwest Conference championship, he was Phi Beta Kappa at UT, where he went on to earn a master's degree in economics. The only thing that slowed Simmons down was a form of arthritis that caused him severe back pain. In 1985 he anted up ten million dollars to establish an arthritis research center in Dallas. Three years later he gave the University of Texas Southwestern Medical Center forty-one million dollars to study arthritis and cancer.

By Texas tycoon standards, Simmons wasn't flamboyant, but neither was he shy about his success. When *Forbes* left him off its summer 1988 list of the world's billionaires, he wrote a letter correcting it. He even handed out business cards, ordered for him by a friend as a gag gift, that introduced him as "Harold Simmons, M.A., Phi Beta Kappa, Billionaire, Dallas."

* * *

Perhaps because it *was* so recent, Dallas high society took its institutions very seriously. It had the longest and most demanding debutante season in the country. Four separate social clubs presented the girls, who often took a semester off from college in order to deal with the breathless round of parties—more than two hundred in three and a half months. The season opened with the Idlewild Ball in late October and closed with the Terpsichorean Ball (called Terps) in mid-January. In between were the Dervish in November, the Calyx in December, and scores of teas and receptions thrown in the girls' honor by indulgent aunts and friends of the family. Then there were the private balls given each girl by her parents. Some Dallas debs did make their bows in flower-filled ballrooms of country clubs, like daughters of the gentry in more subdued locales. But many of the Dallas rich deemed such traditional affairs an inadequate demonstration of the pride a man ought to take in the young woman he had produced and the wealth he had accumulated. To them, a Dallas deb party had to have a creative theme, one or more bands with national recording contracts, and a price tag of at least fifty thousand dollars. Corporate lawyer Henry Stoellenwerck staged a three-ring circus, complete with elephants, for his daughter, Brooke. But no one managed to top the Dallas tycoon who flew his daughter's entire deb party down to Acapulco in a chartered 747.

By the late 1970's inventive extravagance had flowed far beyond debutante parties. To celebrate the engagement of two friends, Mary Murchison Kehoe tossed a Middle Eastern couscous party, complete with belly dancer. Guests reclined on huge, exotically embroidered pillows scattered around the pool and sampled the twenty unfamiliar courses set in front of them in individual bowls. For another major bash, Mrs. Kehoe went Caribbean, importing a genuine West Indian band that belted out everything from calypso to reggae. "The music made that party," Mrs. Kehoe said. "People really *danced.*"

For a price Wendy Moss, daughter of Dallas oilman Bill Moss and actress Jane Withers, helped Mary Kehoe and other Dallas hostesses handle the headaches such elaborate parties entailed. Ms. Moss knew where to find on short notice a giraffe that wouldn't stampede through the shrubbery, an actor who could pull off an eerily accurate imitation of Humphrey Bogart, or a chef adept at authentic Nepalese cuisine.

Wendy Moss started her company, An Affair to Remember, in 1979, just as Dallas's most privileged baby boomers were coming into their inheritances and newly arrived Young Turks were making fortunes in real estate speculation. Her first party, held at the Bent Tree Country Club, was entitled "Murder in Marrakesh." It revolved around a mystery she'd written for the occasion, incorporating props she'd picked up on a recent trip to Morocco and actors and models playing characters from *Casablanca*. She transmogrified the clubhouse foyer into a makeshift souk. "We had all the rugs and carpets and live chickens—everything you would find there," said Ms. Moss. The guests had roles to play.

Some Dallas parties got so creative that they careened right to the borders of good taste. Take the combat chic affair Bradley and Twinkle Underwood Bayoud threw during the 1984 Dallas Film Festival to honor the premiere of *Purple Hearts*, a Vietnam War flick starring Ken Wahl and Cheryl Ladd. Given four days' notice, Twinkle converted her father's Georgian mansion into a jungle, with towering tropical potted plants and camouflage tablecloths. "MPs" parked cars; "army nurses" dispensed hors d'oeuvres. Fake napalm lit the dance floor while the band played hits from the late sixties, interspersed with frequent reprises of the theme from *Entertainment Tonight*, which was covering the sanguinary scene.

Young, rich, trendy, and gifted with a genius for self-promotion, Twinkle stood a petite five feet three inches, with long blond hair, chocolate brown eyes, and the kind of figure—tiny waist, narrow hips, high bust—many women would sell their souls for. She was born in 1957 as Norma Carol Underwood, but what stuck was the nickname bestowed by her father, who made his fortune developing the family ranch into the North Dallas suburb of Carrollton. For her sixteenth birthday her daddy gave her a Mercedes. But from an early age, she insisted, her parents strove to teach her how to make her own money.

"It's unhealthy to sit around and wait for someone to die so your trust fund will kick in," she told Skip Hollandsworth in 1984 for *Dallas Life*, the Sunday magazine of the *Dallas Morning News*.

At fourteen Twinkle made her first investment; she borrowed seven thousand dollars on a note cosigned by her father and bought a herd of Hereford and Charolais cattle. "It's *amazing* how successful it was," she said on December 30, 1986, sitting in the sunny coffee shop of Dallas's most opulent hotel, the Mansion on Turtle Creek, and wearing a tailored long-sleeved silk dress, her only jewelry a simple gold watch and a pair of awe-inspiring David Webb earrings—black jet and diamond pavé chevrons topping thumbnail-size cabochon emeralds. "I paid for all the feed, all the overhead, paid the interest, paid my note off really quick," she added. "It was my father's way of teaching me the value of investment and the value of a dollar. I couldn't balance my checkbook at the time."

In 1983, once more with Daddy's help, this time a fifty-thousand-dollar loan, Twinkle opened her own real estate office, Bayoud & Bayoud. Twinkle didn't have a license, but her husband, Bradley, did, so he could put the official imprimatur on all the deals. Twinkle had something more important than a license; she had an audacious marketing plan, pure Dallas rich. While Bradley pursued his postmodern development dream—Planets, a shopping center cum architectural sculpture garden five minutes south of D/FW Airport—Twinkle launched herself like the Fourth of July.

She inaugurated the firm in August 1983 with a fifty-five-thousand-dollar party at the Mansion. *Tout* Dallas came. Twinkle upstaged them all in the Dress, a Karl Lagerfeld Bradley had given her on her birthday. From the front it was a simple black number. But the back, bare to the waist, bore the black-and-white-beaded likeness of an electric guitar, with the frets reaching up to the left shoulder and the sounding box forming the seat.

For her sales force Twinkle hired debutantes, most of them fresh out of college. "I believe in success and youth," she explained three and a half years later. Success, youth, and connections, that is. The Bayoud & Bayoud debs knew plenty of rich people ready to sell and buy million-dollar-plus homes.

The first year out, Twinkle sold $13 million in properties. She was twenty-six. Some of Bayoud & Bayoud's listings were relatively modest—$150,000 and $200,000, considered starter houses among the Park Cities set. But other listings, billed as "select second homes"—were strictly from Fantasyland: a $2 million castle in Italy, built in 1492 and belonging to the Borghesis; a villa overlooking the Mediterranean and owned by the mayor of Nice, with a shooting range in the basement and a lush olive orchard; a sixteenth-century Belgian château—a steal at $1.75 million—with eighteen bedrooms, a dining room seating sixty, a cozy library with shelf space for four thousand books, a dear little chapel, and nine guest cottages.

Meanwhile, Twinkle got enough ink to float the *QE 2*. *Australian Vogue* featured her in September 1983. New York's empress of fashion, late *Vogue* editor Diana Vreeland, threw a dinner for her in August 1984. *Madame Figaro* called her more astonishing than the women on *Dallas* in July 1985. In between there were items in the *Hollywood Reporter*, tidbits in Suzy's column, a feature in *Interview*.

For Twinkle, anything was possible. "Positive breeds positive; negative breeds negative," she explained. "I'm a firm believer in that. If you visualize what you want, it comes to you. If you do get stuck in a slump, any decision is a move forward. You make those little decisions, and all of a sudden you're deciding to merge with GM or something."

In November 1985, just as the Dallas real estate market was beginning to turn seriously sour, Twinkle and Bradley sold Bayoud & Bayoud and rented an apartment in New York, where they both took acting lessons. Twinkle landed a few bit parts—one in *Texas Chainsaw Massacre, Part Two*, another in the low-budget *Club Sandwich*, about a cut-rate version of Club Med—and she was an extra in David Byrne's deft New Wave comedy *True Stories*. But nothing she did on film approached the real-life celebrity she'd built for herself.

The glare of that spotlight could be painful. In March

1986 Twinkle and Bradley Bayoud appeared on the cover of *Texas Monthly,* she kicking up her heels in a short, shimmering gown pavé in silver and black bugle beads, he jumping for joy in a double-breasted tuxedo. The cover line read: "Doin' the Social Climb: How Dallas Realtors Twinkle and Bradley Bayoud Twirled Their Way into the International Jet Set." Inside, Mark Seal described their enviable life-style: the parties; the press; the clothes; the house. But within a few months after that issue flashed across Texas, Twinkle and Bradley Bayoud, Dallas's golden couple, were on their way to the divorce court.

By the end of 1986 Twinkle Underwood had made another shift in her persona. "I haven't been granting any interviews at all," she said, glancing at the tape recorder pointing across the crisp linen tablecloth at the Mansion. "I've been trying to stay out of the press."

She'd also given up on show biz, at least temporarily.

"I'm no longer pursuing the entertainment industry," she said. "I loved studying acting, and I loved the personal expression it gave me; but it's not my kind of business. I don't have enough control. I just don't like the business as a business."

She'd put her trend-splendid house on the market and was now even cool on postmodern design. "My style is changing," she said. "I'm a cowgirl at heart. Personally I'd be just happy with plain old wood furniture and a horse in the yard."

Even her business interests had turned down-home. She'd bought a strip shopping center in Richardson, a middle-income Dallas suburb. "My anchor tenant's Tom Thumb," she said, "so I'm really dealing now in more mom-and-pop, and I love it. I'm learning a lot about the gas station business."

She was also toning down her social life, although a toned-down social life for Twinkle would be the dizzying heights of glamour for most people. "I don't like to club it," she said. "I don't like to go out that much at night." Except, of course, when she had guests from out of town; then she showed them the Starck Club, the slick night spot designed by Parisian architect Philippe Starck, or the Rio Room, with its etched glass mural of a fish-filled Rio Grande. Twinkle confided: "I went there with what's her name—Princess Stephanie—and her boyfriend what's his name—Rob Lowe."

The statewide depression had changed the way the Dallas social game was played. Take asking someone you met at a party, "What do you do?" "It's like the worst question to ask anybody," Twinkle said. "Nobody wants to say what they do. The moment somebody asks you what you do, you don't speak to them again for the rest of the night. I asked one man, 'What do you do?' He went, 'I'm broke.' I loved it. It was just the best. Then somebody else said they were in real estate, and I said, 'Oh, you must spend a lot of time on the golf course.' "

There was nothing like drastically altered economic fortunes among social equals to dampen the party spirit. "There's been so much negative energy," Twinkle said. "A lot of the parties I've been to, I think people have felt like 'I'm spending too much money on this party' or 'I shouldn't be here; I just bankrupted the person next to me.' "

When *she* threw a bash during the bust, Twinkle tried to distract her guests from such gloomy thoughts. First, she didn't limit her guest list to present and former rich. She was fond of combining "heavyweights socially with penniless actors, hairdressers, Europeans and then making people get down on their hands and knees and chase armadillos. It works."

In her campaign to promote positive thinking, Twinkle filled her swimming pool with oil barrels with "$55" painted on their sides for a party she tossed for three hundred in November 1986. The invitations were chocolate chip cookies in little bamboo boxes. Each guest received a T-shirt designed by Dallas Texas-funk artist Bob Wade, who did the iguana sculpture that sat atop the Lone Star Café in New York. Twinkle served Mexican food, barbecue, and rattlesnake— "all my favorite things"—and, because it was a Tuesday night, "little drinks"—shots of vodka in which jalapeños had been marinated. "I had chickens with bandannas on their necks dancing," she said. "It was real up, real Texas. The energy was real positive."

But even Twinkle found the crash sobering. "Besides oil going down, there was a false real estate market created with false prices," she said. "And the last-fool theory was bound to happen because too many people were just dumping money. They weren't letting our capitalistic society work the way it should."

She continued: "I still think there's going to be a real Texan breed in the state. Because we're having a bad market, people from other places with the money are coming in, and that's going to influence our culture. But I think there still is a good ol' boy philosophy. I just don't think you're going to have as many *nouveau riche* oil people, that kind of rags to riches overnight, gold Rolexes with shiny little diamonds."

Twinkle was something of a Texas chauvinist. "Texans are better than other people," she declared matter-of-factly. "It's not growing up in buildings, in high rises. The dirt underneath our feet keeps our feet on the ground. I think Texans are solid. I think everybody loves Texans, real Texans. . . . That doesn't sound racist or something, does it?"

One of the most interesting real estate deals Twinkle Underwood worked on was the sale of Spanish Cay, a private island in the Bahamas. The seller was troubled Dallas tycoon Clint W. Murchison, Jr. The prospective buyer was billionaire Arab arms dealer Adnan Khashoggi. "Murchison didn't want to sell to Khashoggi, and Khashoggi didn't want Murchison to know it was him," Twinkle confided. "It was before Clint realized how deep in trouble he was. They were only about five million dollars apart, which for that price range is not too bad. I worked on it for about a week; then the bankruptcy papers hit, and it was impossible. Whoever handles bankruptcies was not about to let him sell anything."

Murchison's bankruptcy was one of the first and in many ways the saddest of the big Texas tumbles. Sporting a gray crew cut and short-sleeved white shirt, even in winter, Clint Murchison (pronounced MUR-ka-son), Jr., was one of the most likable multimillionaires in the state—decent, philanthropic (especially to youth-oriented charities like Boys Clubs, Inc.), and down-to-earth, with a keen sense of humor that sometimes ran to jokes at his own expense. He was exceptionally well educated; he held a Phi Beta Kappa key in electrical engineering from Duke and a master's degree in mathematics from MIT. And he made himself a local hero by founding the Dallas Cowboys and nurturing them into America's Team.

Most tragically, Murchison's financial decline coincided with the onset of an incurable and eventually fatal genetic nerve disorder, cerebellar degenerative disease, which affected the part of his brain controlling balance and motor functions. Although his mind remained sharp, he found it increasingly difficult to walk and speak. His signature was reduced to a spidery C.

Founded on the oil boom of the 1920's and 1930's, the Murchison money was one of the state's great dynastic fortunes. Clint Murchison, Sr., known as Big Clint, began by trading oil leases. Then, using borrowed money, he started sinking his own wildcat oil and gas wells. By 1927, at the age of thirty-two, he'd made between five million and six million dollars in the Oil Patch. He eventually leveraged himself into ownership of 115 companies, from oil pipelines to movies. He called his method of doing business "financin' by finaglin'."

In 1953 *Fortune* pegged Big Clint's worth at three hundred million dollars, saying he owned 103 companies, including Martha Washington Candy and *Field and Stream* magazine. The following year *Time* placed him on the cover in a cowboy hat with the caption "Clint Murchison: Big Wheeler Dealer."

Clint Murchison, Sr., died on his ranch outside Athens, Texas, in 1969 at age seventy-four, succumbing to the same disease that was to strike Clint, Jr. He left his two sons— Clint and his brother, John, two years older—seventy-five million dollars and his fiscal philosophy. "Money is like manure," he said. "If you pile it up in one place, it stinks like hell, but if you spread it around, it does a lot of good."

Big Clint's sons already had made themselves millions of their own in their "odd couple" holding company partnership, Murchison Brothers. John Murchison preferred safe, stable investments, while Clint, Jr., was an uncanny image of his gambler father, both physically and temperamentally. To suit John's tastes, the two acquired more than twelve banks and a data processing company; to suit Clint's, they bought a Mexican silver mine and sank ten million dollars into an Oklahoma project to convert cow manure into a substitute for natural gas. (When it couldn't be made to work economically, they converted the process to produce a cattle feed supplement.)

The brothers held each of their ventures jointly, but Clint had the higher profile. He liked his investments risky and complicated. He chose his executives by playing poker with them; if they passed his scrutiny over the green baize, he hired them and gave them free rein.

Of all the businesses Clint Murchison, Jr., owned, his delight was the Dallas Cowboys. He'd played football as a linebacker for Lawrenceville, his prep school, even though he'd been a scrawny five feet seven inches and 120 pounds at the time. Murchison founded the Cowboys in 1960, paying $50,000 for the National Football League franchise and $550,000 for players from other teams.

The Cowboys didn't win a single game their inaugural season. For the first few years they played atrocious football and lost the Murchisons four million dollars. But rather than fire the coach, Tom Landry, Clint Murchison signed him to a ten-year contract in 1964. And Murchison's confidence paid off. Between 1969 and 1979, with Roger Staubach as quarterback, the Cowboys made it to the Super Bowl five times, winning twice. They also brought in annual profits of three million dollars. Clint Murchison visited the locker room after every game to offer congratulations or condolences, but he let Tom Landry and the general manager, Tex Schramm, run the team.

The Murchisons were always very secretive about their money, holding all their businesses privately. But Clint Murchison lived very well. Besides the private island in the Bahamas and a penthouse in New York, he and his wife, Anne, built a forty-three-thousand-square-foot house on a twenty-six-acre wooded estate off Forest Lane in North Dallas. Constructed all on one level, the house covered a full acre.

In 1979 John Murchison died in a car crash. The terms of the Murchison Brothers partnership stipulated that on the death of one brother, the survivor would liquidate all jointly held assets. But that was no simple matter. The holding company encompassed around a hundred businesses. Over and over the Murchisons had used one company as collateral to borrow money for another. Because of this cross collateralization, it was impossible to sell off one entity without paying off the note for something else. And Clint Murchison, like his father before him, didn't believe in keeping a lot of cash lying around; those who were cash-heavy, he predicted, would find their fortunes whittled away by inflation.

Clint Murchison began untangling the partnership's affairs so carefully and quietly that the first hint the outside world had that anything might be amiss was in 1981, when his nephew John Murchison, Jr., filed suit against him. Before he died, Big Clint had established separate trusts for his grandchildren; now John, Jr., claimed that his uncle had encumbered those trusts' assets improperly by using them as collateral for loans. Two years later the suit was settled out of court, reportedly for between twenty million and thirty million dollars, and the records were sealed.

In the eyes of most of the Dallas rich, that was just another regrettable family squabble, not a sign that the Murchison empire was coming unraveled. But when Clint Murchison put the Dallas Cowboys on the block in late 1983, everyone knew he was in trouble. He loved that team; he was its number one fan. He would put it on the block only if he were desperate.

And he was.

Clint Murchison had always relied on borrowed money and had personally guaranteed many of his loans. During the late seventies and early eighties he'd gotten heavily into real estate and building, buying a construction company in Hawaii, starting a resort in the Florida Keys, and erecting condominiums in California and Washington, D.C. Soaring interest rates hit just as his moderately priced units in Richmond, California, and his luxury town houses across the street from Georgetown University in Washington were about to come on the market. At the same time, his oil and gas holdings in Texas and Oklahoma were losing value.

In February 1984, six months after Clint Murchison had

put America's Team on the block, he sold it to a limited partnership led by Dallas financier H. R. "Bum" Bright for sixty million dollars; the lucrative rights to Texas Stadium went to Bright alone for an additional twenty million. Considering that the team had cost Murchison six hundred thousand dollars twenty-four years earlier, that was a phenomenal profit, but he didn't see a penny of it. The first thirty million went to his brother's estate; the rest went to Continental Illinois National Bank and other creditors. Worse, the sale of the Cowboys combined with fears of more family infighting and concern about Clint Murchison's obviously failing health sent a nervous tremor through his other creditors, who got in line with more than thirty lawsuits for $175 million in delinquent loans.

For its 1984 Rich List, *Forbes* pegged Clint Murchison's wealth at $250 million, down from $350 million in 1983. A statement of his financial condition that he circulated to his creditors in late 1984 was more modest, indicating that his net worth, after settling all his obligations, would be a still very respectable thirty-nine million dollars; but that assumed his assets would be sold off in an orderly manner, not at fire-sale prices. Long after most other wealthy men would have sought shelter under Chapter 11, Murchison put off filing bankruptcy. He insisted that he intended to pay all his obligations in full.

His peers in Texas believed him. Clint Murchison was known as a man whose handshake was as good as a signature, even after both had become shaky. His bankers, spread across North America and Western Europe, were less confident. Had he been physically vigorous and able to communicate his ideas, they might have reacted differently; as it was, they were preparing what the ailing tycoon's friends described as "a run on the Murchison bank." As 1984 drew to an uneasy close, the Big Money boys in Dallas speculated about how long Clint Murchison could hold back the creditor stampede.

The first week in December 1984 InterWest Savings of Fort Worth announced that it was putting Murchison's twenty-five-acre estate up for auction to satisfy $9.8 million in delinquent debts. Under Texas homestead law, Murchison

was entitled to keep his house and an acre of land—along
with some seed corn, a rifle, and a mule. (The two hundred
acres allowed John Connally applied only to *rural* home-
steads.) But Murchison's house covered an entire acre, so
that even the driveway lay on the land InterWest sought to
seize. On top of that, fifteen other creditors had claims
against the property. The court halted the auction.

On February 1, 1985, Murchison met with his creditors
and announced that he planned to liquidate virtually all his
assets to pay his debts. But a week later three creditors—
Citicorp Real Estate, Toronto Dominion Bank, and Kona-
Post—petitioned to put him into involuntary bankruptcy.
Within the fifteen-day grace period allowed by federal bankruptcy statutes, he filed Chapter 11.

Even with the court now approving his plans for liquidation, creditors remained spooked by Clint Murchison's faltering health. They complained that they couldn't
understand him over a telephone. In July 1985 they petitioned unsuccessfully to have a trustee appointed to liquidate
his estate—a measure normally granted only when there is
evidence of fraud, mismanagement, or inability to formulate
a reorganization plan. By the end of that month the *Dallas
Times Herald* estimated his total debts at four hundred million
dollars—more than double the original figure. In 1986 Murchison sold the land around his house and auctioned off his
art and antiques. On March 31, 1987, he died at sixty-three,
succumbing to the disease that had ravaged his health and
helped destroy his fortune.

The scores of civic leaders who attended his funeral
seemed genuinely moved.

CHAPTER NINE

★

H. R. "Bum" Bright

Cowboys and Capitalism

When Clint Murchison sold the Dallas Cowboys in 1984, the man who bought America's Team was a low-key petroleum engineer who had quietly amassed an empire spreading from oil to real estate to trucking to banking, one *Forbes* estimated was worth six hundred million dollars by 1987. But by 1989 that empire was in disarray. Fierce competitiveness, bulldog tenacity, and vaulting self-confidence—qualities that had helped H. R. "Bum" Bright build his fortune—ultimately devastated it. He was one of the most frugal, crafty, hardworking entrepreneurs in Texas, yet even he failed to foresee that if oil fell, real estate and banking would topple along with it.

Before he bought the Cowboys, Bum Bright wasn't a Texas legend, but only because he'd avoided the public eye. In addition to his vast wealth and his paradoxical name, his life had all the mythic ingredients: modest beginnings, a brief career as an oil field roughneck, a passion for hard work, a hatred of losing, and a reputation as one of the toughest and most creative deal makers since H. L. Hunt. Add to that a string of personal eccentricities: He always put his right shoe on first and sorted his pocket money by Federal Reserve Bank number. He cast lead soldiers as a hobby and recited pages of Kipling by heart. And he named some of his 120 companies after minerals (Antimony, Beryl, Chalcopyrite), Indonesian islands (Sulu, Java, Surinam), and Italian food (Manicotti, Fettucini, Scallopini).

Figuring that the money the Cowboys would bring in would barely pay the carrying costs on the sixty-million-dollar sale price, Bright twice declined. But just before the team's general manager, Tex Schramm, approached him a third time, Bum Bright got a call from Charles Pistor, chairman of RepublicBank Dallas, where Bright sat on the board of directors and held 3.7 percent of the stock.

A year and a half later Bright recounted Pistor's words: "When I go to Singapore or I go to Tokyo or Mexico City or Paris or London and I introduce myself as Charlie Pistor, chairman of the board of Republic National Bank, everybody just looks at me with a blank look. But then I say, 'Dallas,' and they say, 'Oh, Dallas Cowboys! I'm a Cowboys fan.' If we could be the bank of record for the Cowboys, it would be of great benefit to the bank. You're our largest shareholder, and it ought to be of interest to you. Why don't you buy the Cowboys?"

To sweeten the deal, Bright said, the bank chairman offered to lend him the money to make the purchase at an attractive rate. With this new information, Bright went back and "conceptualized." He figured there was money to be made through creative employment of the tax laws by buying the assets of the corporation—players' and coaches' contracts, television deals, helmets, the works—rather than the corporation as a whole and then depreciating those assets. Since even he couldn't use the entire estimated ten million dollars a year in tax credits, he put together a limited partnership.

Sitting in his wood-paneled office in July 1985, Bum Bright explained how he had closed the Cowboys deal. Behind him was a large tapestry, custom-woven in England, depicting his favorite scenes from the tales of King Arthur and the Knights of the Round Table, but the tale he told had nothing to do with chivalry.

One bargaining session began at 9:00 A.M. Sunday and ran until 4:00 A.M. Monday. As the hours wore on, Jack O'Connell, negotiating on behalf of the Murchison family, got hungry. Bright, who'd discovered a box of Girl Scout cookies in his lawyer's office and partially consumed it, sold O'Connell the remainder for ten dollars. When O'Connell ran out of cigarettes, Bright charged him a dollar each for his. Toward the end, when they were quibbling about a hundred thousand dollars, Bright flipped a quarter to settle the matter. Then, winning the toss, he kept the quarter. Invigorated by his success, he went home at 4:00 A.M., showered and shaved, ate breakfast, and was at his office by his habitual 7:00 A.M.

"It eventually all came out our way just because they wore out," Bright said, wrinkling his nose and turning up his cherubic bow mouth in a self-congratulatory smile, his bushy brows rising like wings above his tortoiseshell glasses. "They didn't have the stamina."

Appropriately, Bum Bright was fond of quoting a particular verse by Rudyard Kipling: "If he being young and unskillful/ Play for sheckels of silver and gold,/ Take his money, my son, praising Allah,/ For the kid was ordained to be sold."

Born in Muskogee, Oklahoma, on October 6, 1920, Harvey Roberts Bright got his nickname when his father, a salesman for Johnson & Johnson, observed that the baby wrapped in blankets with his face reddened by the cool fall air looked like a little railroad bum. Bright was in the third grade before he found out Bum wasn't his given name.

When Bright was four, the family moved to Dallas, where his father bought the University Park Pharmacy. Bright's mother, a former schoolteacher, taught both Bright and his sister to read before they entered school and encouraged them to memorize poems she considered uplifting.

To his parents' disappointment, rather than enter college after Highland Park High School, Bright went to work as a

roughneck in the Oklahoma oil fields. One day, noticing a
petroleum engineer dressed in gabardine slacks and a sports
shirt, he decided that he'd rather make his living with his
head than with his back. He enrolled in Texas A&M, where
the rigorous discipline helped him develop the habit of getting up early and attending to details. He graduated in 1943,
married his high school sweetheart, Mary Frances Smith (she
died of cancer in 1971), and promptly enlisted in the Army
Corps of Engineers.

After the war Bum Bright went to work for the Sun
Company, where he rose through the ranks to field engineer
in less than a year. With the sixty-five hundred dollars he'd
saved from his Army pay, Bright decided to quit before he
was encumbered by children or a mortgage.

With his college roommate, Herbert Schiff (whom he
bought out in 1977), Bright began trading oil leases. On his
twenty-seventh birthday he was down to $12.76 in his check-
ing account. Three years later he and Schiff sold half their
holdings for five hundred thousand dollars and bankrolled
their own exploration and production company.

In the late fifties, when the major oil companies with
which they were competing began getting tax breaks for drilling overseas, Bright and Schiff moved into real estate. Then
came trucking. Then financial services.

"I decided that we ought to get into the money-changing
business," Bright explained. "The volume of money has increased, but if you're in the money-changing business, you
maintain the spread. This was the best hedge against inflation I could conceptualize."

That "money-changing business" became the second-
largest savings and loan in Texas, five-billion-dollar
BrightBanc, which Bright vowed to turn into a "nationwide
financial services juggernaut" by 1990. BrightBanc was an
amalgam of several separate thrifts, all assembled with Bum
Bright's particular brand of persistence. It took him almost
three months to acquire $2.2-billion Dallas Federal. At one
point he even leveled a lawsuit against Albritton Development, the "white knight" called in as an alternate purchaser.
Bright wound up raising his original offer from $98.6 million
to $109 million—thirty-three dollars a share, or 1.6 times
book value.

He won the bidding battle, but the victory proved Pyrrhic. Among the assets Bright used to finance his ambitious S&L was his stock in the RepublicBank Corporation. When bad energy and real estate loans knocked the giant holding company off-balance, Bum Bright "conceptualized" a solution: Republic would merge with its hometown rival, InterFirst Corporation, which was stricken with more than three hundred million dollars of its own losses. After cutting staff and consolidating functions, the two reeling giants would be one lean, healthy institution. But the strategy failed. RepublicBank and InterFirst pulled each other under. Bright, who owned substantial shares of both institutions, suffered thirty million dollars in lost stock value. NCNB Corporation—a superbank from North Carolina—stepped in and picked up what had been the two pillars of the Dallas financial services industry.

When it came to its loan portfolio, NCNB Texas was so conservative that businessmen around the state joked that its initials stood for "No Cash for NoBody." It insisted that Bright begin repaying the interest on the fifty-seven million dollars he'd borrowed to buy the Cowboys. Instead, in February 1989 he sold the team to Little Rock oilman and former University of Arkansas football player Jerry Jones. The first thing Jones did was fire the head coach, Tom Landry, the granite-faced man who'd been synonymous with the Cowboys from the start, and replace him with the Miami Hurricanes coach, Jimmy Johnson.

Even at the height of his wealth, Bright had a very real fear of going broke. A bronze bust of Napoleon stared over his right shoulder as he sat at his desk. He'd bought that bust in the early fifties, he explained, from a neighbor who had made a fortune and then lost it as a result of drink and a general lack of attention to business.

To keep a similar fate at bay, Bright put in five eleven-hour workdays a week. In good times and bad, he rose at 5:00 every morning and was in his office by 7:00 A.M., maintaining logs on test wells, checking vacancy rates on his apartments, keeping tabs on Bright and Company (his oil company), BrightBanc, and his other holdings and on the smaller real estate trusts set up for his four children and twelve grandchildren. In the cramped room just off his office, ledgers lined the gray metal shelves. Each ledger was filled with figures entered in Bum Bright's own compact, precise hand.

Often he went in to work on Saturday mornings, too. On Sunday mornings he got a haircut at the Dallas Country Club, then played golf with a longtime buddy. After that game Bright's children and grandchildren—all of whom lived within a six-block radius—came over to his house for dinner, and Bright got down on the floor with the kids. Sometimes they went upstairs to his den and watched him operate his model railroad set, with scenery he made by hand. At Christmas Bright set up a larger electric train, big enough for the children to ride on, that circled his living room, dining room, and music room.

Bum Bright's pleasures were few and simple. He limited himself to ten or fifteen alcoholic drinks a year, preferring vanilla malts. He kept himself on a two-hundred-thousand-dollar annual budget—modest considering his means. Since 1955 he'd lived in the same house, a red-roofed Mediterranean Revival stucco structure in Highland Park. His manners were courtly, and cultivated diction softened his southern drawl. Yet he and his second wife, Peggy, weren't part of Dallas's glittering social set. He sat on the boards of the Texas State Fair, the powerful Dallas Citizens Council, and several corporations, and he was chairman of the Children's Medical Center of Dallas, but none of those commitments entailed a lot of formal socializing.

"While I do own a tuxedo, it makes my eyeballs pop to get in it, and I don't like to wear it," he admitted.

The romantic notions embodied in the Arthurian legends influenced more than his office decor. His attitude toward women was chivalrous but decidedly preliberation.

"On my floor I want all my ladies to wear dresses," he said. "I expect them to look like ladies, act like ladies, and they can expect to be treated like ladies." That meant that the last man in an office couldn't leave until he'd seen the last woman to her car. It also meant a ban on swearing and "untoward activity."

Bright's protective yet restrictive attitude raised the ire of feminists when, as chairman of the Texas A&M board of regents, he fought the admission of women to the Aggie Band and the Corps of Cadets. The embossed A&M seal adorned the high back of the red leather armchair behind Bright's desk, and his blood ran so maroon that he threw a fund raiser for Garry Mauro, the successful candidate for Texas land commissioner. Although Mauro was a liberal Democrat and Bright described himself as a conservative independent, Mauro was an Aggie, and that was the important thing.

Beneath Bright's courtly manner lay a well of atavistic aggressive energy that could make the toughest Aggie quarterback quail. When he was thwarted in business, Bum Bright could be an awesome opponent. Back in 1967, Bright owned East Texas Motor Freight and another line that served Oregon and Washington. He needed a California trucking company to unite the two, so he went after one based in Los Angeles. Half the company was owned by a wily septuagenarian. Bright approached the half-owner and spent every weekend for six months flying out to California armed with cross-referenced copies of contracts on every deal the half-owner had made before. At one point, fearful that the old man might slip out a window, Bright even followed him into the bathroom of his apartment. Still, the obstinate owner wouldn't sell.

Finally, Bright tried an end run. He went to the two other partners in the motor freight line and offered them three million dollars for 25 percent, seven million dollars for 50 percent, or seventeen million dollars for 100 percent. When the half-owner heard about the move, he tried to borrow seven million dollars from Valley National Bank in Phoenix to buy out his partners. Not having that kind of cash on hand, the bank asked RepublicBank in Dallas to participate in the deal. Republic's directors, who included Bum Bright, declined.

Eighteen years later Bright recounted the conflict with relish, acting out both sides of the conversation. His antagonist had been livid. "He said, 'By God, I'll have a shiv stuck in your back and leave you lying in the gutter.' " Bright imitated him. " 'You're in my territory here in Los Angeles. You go to my partners behind my back, by God, I'll have you thrown in the ocean tied up, and the crabs will pick your bones, and your bones will wash up on the Mexican shore and no one will ever see or hear from you again. You get out of here. You ain't *never* gonna buy this freight line.' "

Bright countered that no matter how much his adversary offered the other two partners, Bright would offer them more. "You hock everything you've got and offer them eight and a half million; I'll offer them nine," he recalled saying. "Eleven and a half for you? I'll offer them twelve. Because when I own that half interest, there is only *one* market for your half interest, and that's me. I've got twenty-five years on you, and I'll drive you to your goddamned grave, and I'll stand on your grave and buy your fifty percent from your executors if I have to. And I'll buy it for the difference between what I have to pay your partners and seventeen million dollars."

Eventually the old man split the seventeen million with his partners. In 1982 Bum Bright sold East Texas Motor Freight, which by then stretched from Seattle to Jacksonville, for $250 million.

By our 1985 interview, Bright was at the stage where he took his own mortality into account when making business decisions, but he had no plans to retire. With his affection for poetic metaphor, he likened himself to a bull elk with a herd of cows. The bull elk, he said, went where the grass was greenest and the water sweetest, ran off all challengers, and sired a strong herd. But after being hooked and lamed season after season, the old bull would look for a pasture in a V-shaped draw, where the grass might be sparse and the water sour, but where he didn't have to watch his back.

"When you find yourself looking for shelter rather than looking for the long grass and the sweet water, that's the point where you should start to back out," he said. "But now I'm still looking for the sweet water and the high green grass."

Maybe Bum Bright was just too stubborn to know when he'd been hooked. The weaker his enterprises got, the harder and more inventively he fought to prop them up. By early 1986 BrightBanc, like other Texas savings and loans, was awash in repossessed real estate—$300 million worth. In an attempt to wipe those losers off the books, Bright tried to transfer them to a separate entity he'd set up with $2.3 million of his own money. With typical candor, he called the new company Vulture Fund. Federal regulators quickly shut it down.

BrightBanc's fall 1988 report announced that the thrift had slid into the red. Liabilities outweighed assets by $242 million. Despite Bum Bright's active support of the Republican administration (he'd hosted a 1987 fund raiser at his mansion for George Bush), the Federal Home Loan Bank Board refused to advance him the $350 million he needed to retain control. In March 1989 savings and loan regulators seized BrightBanc and moved into the offices of what Bum Bright had once envisioned as his nationwide financial services juggernaut.

But the tough little Texas bulldog wasn't letting go. He showed up at those same offices every morning at seven, put in a full day's work, and signed the payroll checks. The bust of Napoleon still stared over his shoulder. Bum Bright was no longer a semibillionaire, but he was a long way from being broke.

★

CHAPTER TEN

The Hunts

Daddy's Money

Among all the Cowboy Capitalists in the history of Texas, H. L. Hunt was the quintessence of the breed. His was the ultimate wildcat success story. He started out as a professional gambler, brought in a gusher with his first oil well. By the close of World War II his income was a million dollars a week; from then until his death in 1974 at the age of eighty-five, he was considered the richest man in the world.

Hunt's personal eccentricities were as legendary as his wealth. He was a bigamist who fathered three overlapping families. He didn't believe in contributing to charity, and his politics were so reactionary he could have made Jack Kemp look liberal. Although he could afford every conceivable luxury, Hunt brought a sack lunch to work and drove a nondescript old car. In 1948 he told Frank X. Tolbert of the *Dallas Morning News*, "Money as money is nothing. It's just something to make bookkeeping convenient."

Despite his disdain for money, H. L. Hunt established one of the greatest family fortunes of all time. Of the six sons and daughters borne to him by his first wife, all were billionaires or close to it by the early 1980's.

Yet by September 1987 a substantial part of that fortune—that held by his sons Bunker, Herbert, and Lamar—was in disarray. The liquidation value of their assets had fallen to $1.48 billion, while their debts totaled $2.43 billion. One of their companies, Placid Oil, was in bankruptcy; so were three of their family trusts. Creditors were seeking to attach their personal assets.

The billion-dollar shortfall was due partly to tumbling prices in the Oil Patch and in Texas real estate and partly to the brothers' love of high-risk, high-payoff ventures. It was also due to a flawed focus: a drive to protect and expand their wealth without apparent regard for the social costs. By 1988 their half brother Ray Hunt, who started out with far less, was far richer than they. He'd used his money to found stable companies, creating true wealth rather than speculative profits.

But Bunker, Herbert, and Lamar were far from finished. They filed two countersuits against their creditors, one claiming lending fraud, the other alleging that twenty-three U.S. and foreign banks were conspiring to take over the world's offshore drilling business. To make the suits credible, the Hunts' attorneys, who brought in half a million dollars a month in legal fees, hoped to show that three men who had a combined net worth of between seven billion and eight billion dollars in 1980 were ordinary people who were taken in by those slick bankers.

"Everyone assumes the Hunts are sophisticated businessmen," Stephen D. Susman, the Hunts' chief litigator, told *The New York Times Magazine* for its September 27, 1987, issue. "They are not. They aren't rubes and hayseeds, but unlike other wealthy families who found top executives, paid them half a million dollars a year, and gave them a piece of the business, there is no one you will meet around here who is a financial genius."

Shortly before his death H. L. Hunt appeared with his family on *60 Minutes*. During the quarter hour segment he led his children and grandchildren in one of his favorite songs. It went: "We're just plain folks,/ Your mother and me./ We're just plain folks,/ Like our own folks used to be."

By all reports, Haroldson Lafayette Hunt never seriously considered himself ordinary. Born near Vandalia, Illinois, in 1889, he was a child prodigy. He read the newspaper by the age of three, showed a great gift for numbers, and was a crackerjack cardplayer, able to memorize the order in which cards appeared in a deck.

Hunt was the youngest of ten children. His father was a banker, his mother a college-educated schoolteacher who taught him at home and allowed him to continue nursing until well past his seventh birthday. With all that special attention, H. L. Hunt grew up suspecting that he carried a gene for genius and acted throughout most of his life as if he didn't have to play by the same rules that restricted everyone else.

After inheriting eighty acres of land and five thousand dollars from his father's estate in his early twenties, Hunt became a professional gambler in Arkansas. It was a small step from the poker table to the high-risk, high-stakes game of wildcat drilling in the East Texas oil fields. Hunt didn't base his drilling on fancy seismic reports; in fact, he hired his first geologist in 1945, after his own unaided discoveries had made him the world's richest man. Using a system he called creekology, he studied surface features of the land— the roll of hills, the shape of valleys, the way streams flowed—and decided whether a given piece of woods or pasture looked as if there were oil underneath. That method has been largely discredited by modern geologists as little better than the variations on water witching and similar practices common in the early days of the East Texas oil boom. (One woman would dance around the Spindletop field until her drawers fell down, indicating the spot to drill.) Hills and valleys offer little or no information on what may be lurking twenty-five hundred feet underground. But even if it was nothing but pure intuition, creekology worked for Hunt. With incredible luck, he struck oil on his first well, and he enjoyed a phenomenally high ratio of producing wells from then on.

Hunt's biggest single success was the Dad Joiner deal, struck in 1930. Joiner was an aging wildcatter with a promising but unproven East Texas oil lease and no money to drill. Hunt was convinced that the field would become a big producer and wanted the rights to the land at the lowest possible price. He cornered Joiner in Suite 1553 of the Baker Hotel in Dallas while they haggled over terms. At the end of thirty six hours Hunt emerged with a lease on 4,580 acres that was to turn into one of the most petroleum-rich pieces of property in the history of the Oil Patch. It cost him $75,000 in cash—$30,000 to Joiner, $45,000 to intermediaries—plus an additional $1.3 million Joiner was to get in future royalties.

While the two men were locked away talking terms, one of Joiner's wildcat wells blew in, potentially generating more than enough money for the wizened driller to develop his field. Detractors later claimed that Hunt, who had his own scouts at the well site, controlled all the information coming into Suite 1553 and kept Joiner from learning of the gusher until after they'd signed the deal. Some even suggested that Hunt had provided Joiner with female companionship to put him in a more conciliatory mood. Years later Joiner sued Hunt, alleging he'd been hoodwinked, then dropped the suit suddenly and mysteriously.

"He was about the smartest businessman I ever saw," Bunker Hunt said of his father in 1985, "and he had a great ability to make the right moves at the right time."

As rich as he was, H. L. Hunt showed a Scrooge-like reluctance to spread any of his wealth around. He considered charities an extension of the public dole, sapping the will to succeed, and he refused to contribute to them. Hunt's largess was limited to archconservative political causes and, later in life, fundamentalist religious groups.

When it came to right-wing politics, Hunt did more than send money. He wrote and self-published a novel entitled *Alpaca*, which described a fictional utopia where votes were apportioned according to how much a citizen paid in taxes. He also bankrolled two reactionary radio programs: first *Facts Forum* and then *Life Line*. Christian fundamentalism occupied part of each fifteen-minute *Life Line* program, but the commentator always devoted at least half the time to attacks on

Hunt's favorite political targets—such as communism, unions, the UN, and the Supreme Court—or to support of the oil depletion allowance.

Hunt's extreme attitudes extended to health as well. The richest man in the world carried a brown-bag lunch to work not because he was too cheap or too busy to eat out but because he thought certain foods, like apricots, had special health-enhancing properties, while others, such as white sugar and white flour, sapped vitality. This habit predated widespread interest in organic and whole foods by more than a decade. Hunt produced his own brand of HLH health foods and aloe vera products, but they were grown the usual way, with chemical fertilizers and pesticides. Toward the end of his life Hunt also came to believe that crawling on all fours would keep senility at bay by reconstructing damaged neural pathways. But when Hunt demonstrated his "creepology" for startled reporters, intending to show them how he maintained his mental acuity, he often had the opposite of his desired effect.

Throughout his life H. L. Hunt was a Social Darwinist. He believed that economic inequities reflected the law of the survival of the fittest; thus he and the other rich had a right to accumulate a vastly disproportionate amount of the world's wealth if they could. That philosophy still is held by many more rich Texans than would care to admit it, but Hunt carried it a step farther than his peers: To spread his superior genes around, he fathered three simultaneous families, siring fifteen children.

In 1914, while he still lived in Arkansas, Hunt married Lyda Bunker, a schoolteacher with striking similarities to his indulgent mother. She bore him seven children. The first, Lyda, died in infancy. Another, H. L. III ("Hassie") suffered from incapacitating emotional problems. The other five— Margaret Hunt Hill, Nelson Bunker Hunt, Caroline Rose Hunt, William Herbert Hunt, and Lamar Hunt—constituted what Texans called the First Family.

Eleven years after he married Lyda, H. L. Hunt met a pretty young woman named Frania Tye. She was selling Florida real estate, and he was buying—under the name of Major Franklin Hunt. After a whirlwind courtship they were married, she later claimed, by a justice of the peace. Rather than divorce Lyda, Hunt moved Frania to Texas and commuted between the two households. Neither wife knew about the other until Frania learned Hunt's true identity and marital status in 1934. Meanwhile, she bore him four children.

Faced with Frania's discovery, Hunt first tried to persuade her to move to Utah; he was under the mistaken impression that polygamy still was legal there. When that gambit failed, he bought her off for a million dollars and two thousand dollars a month in support. Frania moved to Louisiana, where she married a Hunt Oil employee with no previous wife.

During World War II Hunt became involved with Ruth Ray, a young Hunt Oil secretary. Again, this was no casual affair. He set out to create another family. Ruth bore him a son and three daughters, but this time there was no bigamous ceremony. Hunt waited to marry her and officially adopt her children until 1957, two years after Lyda had died.

Chronologically Hunt's union with Ruth Ray produced his third set of offspring, but because this household was open knowledge, Dallas called it the Second Family. Although the two sets of Hunts were a generation apart in age and never close socially, after the old man had died in 1974, they united to fight claims against Hunt's estate made by Frania Tye and her children. Over the years Hunt had already transferred hundreds of millions of dollars to trusts held by the First Family, trusts that invested in oil-related companies with names like Placid Oil, Penrod Drilling, and Planet Investments. (H.L. had always considered six-letter words beginning with P lucky.) In his will he left the bulk of his remaining estate, including his house—a mansion modeled after Mount Vernon—and all his stock to his widow, Ruth, and named her son, thirty-one-year-old Ray Hunt, his executor. He also split a minor part of his assets, some oil leases in Louisiana, equally among all fourteen children.

Although Frania Tye Lee's offspring received four fourteenths of Hunt's Louisiana holdings, those shares were worth only a few hundred thousand dollars apiece. To make matters worse, Hunt's will didn't acknowledge the Third Family by name. The bequest went to Reliance Trusts, the

entity he'd established for Frania's children forty years earlier. Displeased with the double slight, Frania sued in 1975,
bringing into the open for the first time the existence of three
overlapping Hunt households. In 1978 the First and Second
families settled with the Third out of court for $7.5 million.
Shortly thereafter Ray Hunt bought out the First Family's 18
percent interest in then struggling Hunt Oil.

Born in 1943, Ray Hunt was fourteen when his parents
married. But being sired out of wedlock didn't keep him from
being accepted by Dallas society. As a young man Ray belonged to all four of the exclusive clubs that presented the
city's debutantes—Idlewild, Terpsichorean, Calyx, and Dervish. In 1975, at the age of thirty-two, he became the youngest
president in the history of the Dallas Petroleum Club. And
he sat on the socially prestigious board of the Dallas Museum
of Fine Arts.

Ray Hunt fitted into the Dallas establishment as his father and older half brothers never did. He contributed time
and money to civic causes, his politics were mainstream
George Bush-Republican, and he and his wife were low-key
but relatively social. He also invested in the city by founding
D Magazine, a glossy monthly, and developing Reunion Center, a sports and hotel complex that revitalized the once-
shabby east side of downtown. Some critics derided Reunion's shimmering silver glass skin and the revolving lighted
ball hoisted atop the complex, but in Dallas flashiness was
no crime.

Under Ray Hunt's direction, Hunt Oil expanded steadily
and healthily, aided by a major strike in the North Sea during
the late 1970's and another big play in North Yemen in 1984.
In 1989 *Forbes* pegged the value of the Second Family companies Ray directed at $1.4 billion, and Standard & Poors
gave Hunt Oil an A rating. Ray Hunt's major business
problem was letting the world know that his enterprises
were totally separate from those of the First Family. In 1985
he began running notices in the local papers saying he
wasn't involved in the exploits of Bunker, Herbert, and
Lamar—what wags called his "I'm not heavy; they're my
brothers" ads.

* * *

H. L. Hunt's two First Family daughters, Margaret Hunt Hill and Caroline Rose Hunt, were also doing their best to disassociate their business dealings from those of their beleaguered siblings. In their case, however, the issue was cloudier than it was in Ray's.

Although neither Margaret nor Caroline participated in their brothers' speculative commodity schemes, they did own part of Placid Oil, and they did permit Bunker, Herbert, and Lamar to pledge assets of that family-held company as collateral for the 1980 $1.1 billion loan that allowed the three to cover their margin accounts when silver prices crashed. Reportedly, strong-minded Margaret insisted, as part of the deal, that her siblings put up some of their personal possessions as well. And when banks foreclosed on some of their North Dallas real estate, she scooped it up off the auction block. The sisters and Hassie, the incapacitated eldest brother, whose assets Margaret controlled, withdrew their shares from Placid Oil in 1983 but were still named in a number of suits filed by creditors. The 1989 *Forbes* Rich List estimated Margaret and Hassie's combined worth as $1.2 billion and Caroline's as $800 million, making them two of the richest women in the country and placing them far ahead of their high-rolling brothers.

Caroline Hunt was a pleasant, self-effacing woman with the manner of an upper-middle-class matron, moderately involved in church and civic affairs but largely concerned about family. After graduating from the University of Texas at Austin, she married Dallas businessman Lloyd Sands. While rearing their five children, she pursued homey hobbies—needlepoint, embroidery, and baking. Distressed at the wasteful practice of discarding the flesh of jack-o'-lanterns, she collected pumpkin recipes, which she eventually published as a cookbook, *The Compleat Pumpkin-Eater*. But she blossomed as a businesswoman after she had divorced Sands in 1973 and married Old Dallas scion Buddy Schoellkopf, whom she divorced in turn in 1987. One of her ventures with Schoellkopf was a helicopter service called Pumpkin Air.

"I'm not the big businessperson everyone perceives,"

she said in 1984. "My children are very capable." Caroline Hunt had agreed to an interview for the slick Texas life-style magazine *Ultra*, which was doing a cover feature on Dallas. She sat in the living room of her comfortable contemporary house, where she had lived since 1957. Nestled at the end of a wooded cul-de-sac on one of the more modest streets in Highland Park, it was a house that called for a once-a-week cleaning woman, not live-in help. H. L. Hunt's billionaire daughter made and served coffee herself. There was a beige Dodge station wagon in the driveway.

The house was a sharp contrast with Caroline Hunt's hotels. Her first, the Mansion on Turtle Creek, was a twenty-one-million-dollar renovation of the extravagant Italianate residence built in 1925 for cotton magnate Sheppard King. Caroline Hunt had the stucco exterior painted her favorite color, pale pumpkin. Six-foot-tall bouquets of exotic flowers airfreighted from Hawaii dominated the black-and-white-tiled lobby. The hotel's restaurant was grandly formal and stunningly expensive. The rooms were large and decorated in restful beige with good traditional furniture; each had a sybaritic reading chair with a good light and a princess phone at the elbow. The soap in the bathrooms was from Hermès. And the service was unparalleled. If a guest was on the phone when another call came in, no tacky little red light flashed; instead, a uniformed runner slipped the message, tucked in a little envelope, under the door. It was as if Caroline Hunt were imbuing her hotel with all the luxe she could afford but denied herself.

"Our idea was to own the hotel and have somebody manage it, but we were so visible that we wanted to have a personal touch," she explained.

Rosewood, which was held by the Caroline Hunt Trust Estate, set up for her children, went on to build or buy six more upscale hostelries, which met with varying degrees of success. Caroline Hunt was uncomfortable with her image as queen of a hotel empire à la Leona Helmsley. She preferred to be thought of as a family person, interested in her children and grandchildren and in issues like education and job training.

"I think I'm the luckiest person in the world," she said

in a soft drawl. "First of all, I live in the most wonderful country in the world. I love my state, my city. I even love my street."

But not all of Caroline Hunt's luck revolved around such sweetly simple things. In 1987 she made thirty million dollars on a failed takeover bid for Phillips-Van Heusen.

Born in 1932, Lamar Hunt, the baby of the First Family, inherited his old man's reputation for penny-pinching. Although he lived on a twelve-acre estate in North Dallas, he always flew coach and drove elderly American sedans. In 1984 he spun around Dallas in a six-year-old Chrysler Cordoba. He told the *Dallas Times Herald* that the rumor that he owned only one suit was untrue; he simply enjoyed wearing navy blazers and gray slacks and owned several sets. However, he did admit to once pulling into a service station and asking for thirty-one cents' worth of gas. He seldom carried much cash, he explained.

Lamar, who graduated from SMU, was into sports in a big way. In 1959, at the age of twenty-six, he founded the American Football League. Three years later, he moved his pro team, the Dallas Texans, to Kansas City and named them the Chiefs. Initially his football ventures looked like a rich kid's plaything. When an acquaintance pointed out to H. L. Hunt that his son was losing a million dollars annually on his sports ventures, the crusty old wildcatter reportedly answered, "At that rate he can only afford to keep it up for fifty-one years." But Lamar soon turned the losses around. By 1966 the AFL's bold end run around the NFL had proved so effective that it precipitated a merger.

Under the gaze of the cigar-store wooden Indian chief that stood in his office, Lamar Hunt built an empire in what he candidly called sports entertainment. He owned part of the Chicago Bulls National Basketball Association team and an interest in the Tampa Bay Rowdies, a soccer franchise. During the mid-1970's he established World Championship Tennis; its televised tournaments transformed the country-club pastime into a big-bucks spectator sport. Lamar also had a limestone quarry and a chain of warehouses, as well as two theme parks in Kansas City—Worlds of Fun and Oceans of

Fun. One of his less successful real estate projects involved a scheme to develop Alcatraz into a shopping mall cum tourist attraction. After written protests from ten thousand appalled San Franciscans, he abandoned the plan.

With his pretty blond wife, ready sense of humor, and long-standing reputation for generous, though anonymous, philanthropy, Lamar Hunt was easily the classiest of the First Family sons. He prudently avoided getting involved in his brothers' catastrophic forays into soybeans and sugar. But he did keep his share of the family oil ventures, and he did have a minor part in the silver play. And he was still far less wealthy than he once was.

"That *Forbes* magazine story that said I was worth a billion dollars was hysterical," Lamar Hunt declared to the *Times Herald* in 1984. "I don't have any idea where they come up with those figures. . . . I think they've confused my debts with my assets."

His quip was uncannily prescient.

The Hunt brothers' fortune soared and fell under the stewardship of Nelson Bunker Hunt, born in 1926 and the oldest active son of the First Family. Bunker never got beyond his first year of college, but he played a more visible role in expanding his wealth than his brother Herbert, a geology graduate of Washington and Lee, who was three years younger and a partner in many of his high-flying ventures. Along with H. L. Hunt's millions, both brothers had inherited their father's love of gambling.

In 1986, as the Hunts' fortunes were falling, the *Wall Street Journal* ran an account of a poker game, years earlier, between Bunker Hunt and an Oklahoma oilman named Harry Schwarz. Holding nothing but a pair of threes, Bunker matched the fourteen-hundred-dollar pot between them. Schwarz called his bluff, explaining that if Bunker had bet less—say, two hundred or four hundred—Schwarz would have figured he held a strong hand, but when he bet fourteen hundred, Schwarz figured he was trying to buy the pot. "Bunker's been trying to buy the pot ever since he was a kid," an anonymous man who had observed the face-off told the *Journal*.

In person the man whose financial finaglings sent shud-

ders through the world economy seemed so ordinary he was
almost surreal. Although he didn't normally talk to the press,
Bunker Hunt consented to an interview in 1985—about his
racehorses. *Ultra* was doing a cover story on the state's top
horse breeders, and Bunker, independently of the rest of his
family, was one of the biggest Thoroughbred breeders in the
world.

Bunker Hunt was a large man with a short neck and a
round torso. His heft invited comparisons to the fat-cat industrialists caricatured with savage literalness by turn-of-the-
century cartoonists. Yet sitting there in an office plain to the
point of austerity—industrial-grade carpeting, black rubber
baseboards—and wearing an ill-fitting navy suit, with one
point of his shirt collar escaping across his lapel, he looked
like just another easygoing, good-natured country boy.

From the day in 1936 when his father first took him to
Arlington Downs, Bunker Hunt had liked horses. But watching them run wasn't enough for him. There was big money
to be made, not in betting on horses but in breeding them.
He pointed out that one of Seattle Slew's forty breeding
shares sold for over three million dollars. And there was
enough risk involved in horse breeding to keep it interesting.

Bunker Hunt reckoned that of the 150 foals his mares
produced a year, 15 were outstanding racing prospects. So
far he had never been lucky enough to produce a Kentucky
Derby winner, but since establishing his breeding operation
in 1964, he had come up with a number of international
champions. One of his horses, Dahlia, was the top money-
winning filly in the world; between 1973 and 1975 she ran
away with $1.5 million.

Thoroughbred breeding is the ultimate rich man's poker
game. "Monetary-wise, it's certainly not the best thing I'm
in on, but it's been an attractive thing," he said. "Horses
have been an excellent hedge. Their prices have gone up
really faster than inflation."

Asked how much his horses were worth, he declined to
name a figure. Instead, the man who had seen the value of
his silver, oil, and coal holdings soar and then plunge replied
with a knowing smile, "It's easy to say something's worth
something, but you still have to sell it."

During the 1960's Nelson Bunker Hunt was the world's

wealthiest man; for the time being he overshadowed even his father. A decade earlier he had begun exploring for oil in Pakistan and Libya. In 1961 he discovered Libya's massive Sarir oil field, and his stated net worth gushed to a staggering sixteen billion dollars. Then, on September 1, 1969, a dashing young army colonel named Muammar Qaddafi took over the Libyan government, promising to use the country's vast stores of petroleum to institute much needed social programs. Most of the major oil companies that had developed those fields greeted the new order with enthusiasm, at least publicly. Occidental Petroleum's Armand Hammer, deft at dealing with governments hostile to capitalism, went out of his way to cooperate. Not only did he agree to pay the higher royalties Qaddafi asked, but he also donated schools, hospitals, and highways into the desert. Bunker Hunt did no more than required under the lease he'd struck with the previous regime. And despite John Connally's negotiations on his behalf, in 1973 Bunker Hunt saw his wells shut down and the Sarir field nationalized. Armand Hammer kept on pumping.

Bunker's reluctance to make accommodations with Colonel Qaddafi may have been due in part to his political beliefs. Like his father, Bunker was an archconservative. He served on the national council of the John Birch Society and chipped in on Ollie North's private fund to support the contras. Bunker also was a backer of television evangelist Pat Robertson, head of the Christian Broadcasting Network, self-proclaimed prophet of God, and unsuccessful candidate for the 1988 Republican presidential nomination. Despite looming bankruptcy proceedings, in August 1986 Bunker threw a fund raiser for Robertson at his Circle T Ranch. Dominating the festivities was a hundred-foot-high gold-toned replica of the Statue of Liberty.

Hearing rumors of an impending world protein shortage, Bunker and Herbert Hunt began buying soybean futures "long" in 1976—picking them up cheap in exchange for an option to sell them at a higher price on a specific later date. By the spring of 1977 the brothers had tied up six million bushels of soybeans in their own names and eighteen million in those of their children. The price of a bushel had shot up from six dollars to more than ten dollars by April. Then the Commodities Futures Trading Commission called a halt in an attempt to force the Hunts to sell down to the three-million-bushel limit designed to guard against hoarding. Complaining that the CFTC was trying to push prices down, the Hunts sold off two million bushels. Bunker accused the regulatory agency of being an arm of the eastern establishment, bent on persecuting the Hunts for being conservative capitalists in a socialist world.

Bunker and Herbert Hunt and their offspring had staged an earlier foray into foodstuffs in 1974, when they bought majority interest in the Great Western Sugar Company and took it private under the Hunt International Resources Corporation, a subsidiary of Planet Investments. When the Hunts got their hands on it, Great Western was a profitable processor of sugar beets, mostly in eastern Colorado. It made $105 million in 1975. But on August 18, 1985, it filed for Chapter 11; four months earlier Hunt International had declared bankruptcy after defaulting on $295 million and being hit, along with Planet Investments and Offshore Investments, with a four-million-dollar tax lien from the state of Texas. At the time it cratered, Great Western owed $45 million, much of it to small family farmers whose beets it had already processed. The impact on the refinery towns was devastating.

Great Western might have stayed afloat if it hadn't had to support other Hunt interests. The company invested thirty million dollars in Godchaux-Henderson, its Louisiana cane processor, and wrote off seventy-nine million dollars to Godchaux-Henderson and to Hunt International, which also refined oil and was hit hard by tumbling petroleum prices. And it transferred money to Hunt International as dividends.

The stakes in the speculative poker games Bunker and Herbert dealt themselves into were unimaginably high. When they lost, they lost fortunes, but they remained fabulously wealthy men. On the other hand, their creditors were sometimes wiped out, despite having provided services and raw materials in good faith.

Of all the Hunt crapshoots, the one with the greatest potential for global repercussions was the silver play. Back in 1973, before U.S. citizens could buy gold, Bunker and Herbert began buying silver as a hedge against inflation. (They later got into ancient Greek and Roman coins for the same reason.) At the time silver sold for $1.94 an ounce. As the decade wore on, Lamar and their children joined them, as did several rich Saudis. The Hunts flew the ingots to private vaults in Switzerland, with gun-toting ranch hands guarding the cargo.

Double-digit inflation pushed precious metals through the roof. In January 1979 silver went to $16 an ounce. Using the silver they already owned as collateral, the Hunts borrowed billions to buy more, even after the Federal Reserve Board, in an attempt to cool inflation, clamped down on the money supply, forcing interest rates to skyrocket. By the end of the year the Hunts controlled fifty-nine million ounces— a third of the world's annual supply. Rumors began circulating that the Hunts and their Arab partners planned to mint their own money. The price hit $50.35 in January 1980, giving the Hunts a paper profit estimated at close to ten billion dollars. Around the world people sold heirloom flatware to be melted down into silver bars. Then the bubble burst. Seeking to regain control over the precious metals market, alarmed commodities exchanges slapped new restrictions on silver trading. Prices plummeted, but Bunker and Herbert, firm in their conservative conviction that precious metals were the only real money, didn't sell. By March 14, 1980, silver had dropped to $21 an ounce.

On March 25, Silver Thursday, prices collapsed, falling first to $15.80 an ounce, then to $10.80 by closing, sending tremors through the economy and threatening to precipitate a stock market crash. That same day Bache, the Hunts' silver dealer, hit them with a $135 million margin call. To the world's amazement, they announced that they couldn't pay. They owed $1.75 billion on silver that was now worth $1.2 billion.

Only a Brobingnagian bailout, in the form of a $1.1 billion loan engineered by the Federal Reserve, allowed the brothers to keep their bullion and refinance their debts. To cover their margin accounts, they had to persuade Margaret and Caroline, who hadn't been involved in the play, to allow them to pledge assets of family-owned Placid Oil. They also had to put up some of their personal possessions: antique furniture; Greek and Roman coins; five hundred Thoroughbred racehorses; a Mercedes; even a Rolex watch. In the wake of the debacle the Dallas-based Bonehead Club graced Bunker and Herbert with the 1980 "Bonehead of the Year" award.

Holding on to their silver tripled the Hunts' initial losses. Between 1980 and 1984 they paid $600 million to finance their loan, while the value of their holdings slid another $400 million. In all, Bunker, Herbert, and Lamar Hunt and their children lost $1.5 billion in the Silver Bubble. Asked how he felt about the disaster, Bunker reportedly shrugged and said, "A billion dollars isn't what it used to be."

The Hunts' silver problems were far from over. In 1987 the IRS claimed that Bunker, his wife, and their three adult children owed $358 million in back taxes. That bill stemmed from $147.6 million Bunker had given his children in 1980 to help them cover their own margin calls when silver crashed. On their 270-page 1980 tax return, the older Hunts claimed they'd lent the money to their children, believing that silver prices were sure to rebound; the continued decline made the loans uncollectible, turning them into short-term capital losses. The IRS insisted that the bailout was a gift. That meant Bunker and his wife couldn't deduct the money and their children had to pay taxes on all but thirty thousand dollars apiece.

Throughout the silver play and afterward the Hunts insisted that despite appearances to the contrary, they hadn't been trying to corner the silver market. In August 1988 a federal court jury in New York decided otherwise, ruling in favor of Minpeco S.A., Peru's government-owned state mining marketing agency, in a suit claiming the brothers and their Arab partners had tried to corral the world's silver. Lamar agreed to pay Minpeco $17 million in damages, but Bunker and Herbert fought their $132 million share of the judgment.

Meanwhile, the same oil slump that hit every other independent producer in Texas hit the Hunts. Only the blow was larger because they were bigger. When the First Family split its assets in February 1984, Bunker, Herbert, and Lamar got Placid Oil, which was a prosperous company, at least on paper. It held vast offshore leases in the Beaufort Sea north of Canada and Alaska, leases the Hunts had claimed were worth $2.27 billion in 1980. But drilling in that icy wilderness was incredibly difficult and expensive. With oil at $35 a barrel, it could be profitable; with oil at $15, it couldn't. By 1986 the Hunts' Beaufort Sea holdings were worth somewhere between 10 percent of their 1980 value and nothing. And with the energy industry in a shambles, the Hunts' lignite coal leases in the Dakotas, which they once valued at $400 million, also became worthless.

The collapse of oil prices delivered an even harder punch to Penrod Drilling, which the three brothers owned. Penrod floated the world's largest private offshore drilling fleet— thirty-five jack-up rigs, eleven other offshore rigs, nine submersibles, and two semisubmersibles, each worth millions of dollars. Because Penrod made its money drilling for other people and because oil under the ocean floor was a lot more expensive to bring up than oil under solid land, the company was particularly vulnerable. During the boom Penrod had 80 percent of its fleet working on an average day; after the fall that utilization dropped to 56 percent, even though Penrod had cut its lease rate.

For the Hunt brothers to stay afloat, Penrod had to make money. Bunker, Herbert, and Lamar had pledged its assets as collateral for loans on which they'd promised to pay $100 million a year. But Penrod was foundering. In May 1986, two months after Placid Oil defaulted on millions in obligations, Penrod was unable to pay $243 million in loans from four Texas banks—First City National and Texas Commerce Bank of Houston and InterFirst and Republic Bank of Dallas. Two years later Penrod, Placid, and the trust estates H. L. Hunt had set up for Bunker, Herbert, and Lamar all had declared bankruptcy. In July 1988 Herbert stepped down as managing partner of Penrod.

But the Texas loans were nothing compared with the Hunts' total debt. Altogether, creditors claimed that Bunker, Herbert, Lamar, and their family trusts owed $2.43 billion.

Liquidated, the brothers' interests in two hundred corporations and trusts were worth $1.48 billion, about a fifth of their value immediately after the Silver Bubble burst. If the creditors forced the Hunts into Chapter 7, the creditors would be stuck with a billion-dollar shortfall. Instead, they took another tack. Claiming that the brothers owned Penrod, which had secured the debt, as general partners, the banks argued they were liable as individuals. The banks went after the brothers' personal wealth, which was considerable, from rare coins to raw land to racehorses. And they didn't stop there. Although they were moving onto swampy ground, the creditors also included assets belonging to Margaret, Hassie, and Caroline, as well as those held by the Hunt children.

Threatening the Hunts with foreclosure was like wounding a charging rhinoceros: It only made Bunker, Herbert, and Lamar mad. On June 26, 1986, they filed a multibillion-dollar suit against twenty-three U.S. and foreign banks, from Paris to Tokyo—such big guns as Manufacturers Hanover Trust, Chemical Bank of New York, Citibank, and Bank of America. Essentially the suit accused the banks of trying to bankrupt the Hunts by lending them money they couldn't possibly repay. Then came a second suit, even more remarkable. It claimed that the banks had conspired to corner the world's offshore drilling business into a bank-owned cartel. The Hunts even said that they'd been invited to join in the scheme but had declined.

Together, the suits sought $3.6 billion in damages, plus cancellation or reduction of $1.5 billion of the debt.

After two years of expensive and acrimonious wrangling before federal bankruptcy judges, the banks settled out of court, agreeing to forgive $600 million of the Hunts' debt. The brothers would still have to pay back $803.5 million in addition to the millions they'd already disbursed to hundreds of smaller creditors.

Then the once unimaginable happened: Bunker and Herbert Hunt filed personal Chapter 11 bankruptcy. William Herbert Hunt listed property worth almost forty million dollars; Nelson Bunker Hunt's holdings totaled more than $249 million. But they were flooded with red ink. Bunker alone owed $1.25 billion, while Herbert's debts came to $887 million.

Yet with Penrod and Placid in Chapter 11 and the U.S. Bankruptcy Court looking over their shoulders, the Hunts were still busily drilling through the floor of the Gulf of Mexico, eighty miles south of Louisiana, hoping an undersea trench called Green Canyon would contain enough oil to rescue their empire. The discoveries they made in Green Canyon Blocks 254 and 301 looked promising, but the site was fraught with technical problems. The canyon floor was as much as thirty-eight hundred feet beneath the surface, so deep that the Hunts had to design a new drilling platform rising from a mammoth underwater template shaped to fit the curvature of the earth.

In early November 1988 the Hunts struck a deal with Exxon. The energy giant would take over fifty-eight Hunt leases in the Gulf of Mexico in exchange for 60 percent interest. The Hunt companies would hold on to the two blocks where they'd hit oil. But it was too late. By early 1990, the First Family brothers had irrevocably lost their spot among the ranks of the Big Rich.

After his assets were liquidated, Bunker emerged from bankruptcy still owing the IRS an additional $90 million from future earnings. He and his wife even had their Highland Park mansion on the market for $2.8 million.

"We're like everyone else whose children are grown," his wife told the *Dallas Times Herald*. "We don't need six bedrooms."

CHAPTER ELEVEN

★

The Wynnes

Dynasty III

Another eccentric and influential Northeast Texas clan, the Wynnes, may not have been as rich as the Hunts, but they seemed to have more fun making and spending their money. They were also more gracious losers.

Among other things, this quirky, creative family brought the world Six Flags Over Texas, the Styrofoam coffee cup, the Texas Pavilion at the 1964 New York World's Fair, the first successful private space launch, the Cattle Barons' Ball, four Democratic national conventions (1976, 1980, 1984, 1988), and Tango—a Dallas nightclub boasting a hundred-thousand-dollar cocktail computer and crowned by six giant motorized frogs, dancing and playing musical instruments.

The Wynne dynasty, in its fifth generation by the late 1980's, was comprised of the descendants of William B. Wynne, who in 1876 rode into Wills Point, forty-six miles east of Dallas, with nothing but a rifle and a pair of lawbooks in his saddlebags. With his wife, Margaret, Fat Dad, as his grandchildren came to call him, produced nine children. Eight of them—four sons and four daughters—survived to prolific adulthood.

Some Wynnes—like Jacque (pronounced "Jackie"), Shannon, both Toddie Lees, and all three Anguses—became household names in Texas; others operated behind the scenes. Some were liberal Democrats; others were conservative Republicans. Some were very rich; others, merely very comfortable. Because four members of the second generation were women, a number of prominent Wynnes didn't even bear that last name. One of them, Jimmy Harrison, held thirty patents; he literally cooked up the Styrofoam thermal cup in his kitchen in 1956. Three decades later, licensed by his patent, manufacturers worldwide extruded his invention at the rate of two billion a year.

If the rest of humankind had trouble figuring out which Wynne was descended from which, so did they themselves. To brief new in-laws, the family published its own *Cliff Notes* of recent genealogy, a volume called *Who's Whose Wynne*.

Like some secret society, the Wynnes wore distinctive rings and met every Memorial Day weekend for a three-day ritual that bound them together with the consistency of blackstrap molasses. "People keep accusing us of being a little clannish, which I think is fine," said Gordon Wynne, Jr., who practiced what he called "the three Ds of country law —deeds, death, divorce" in Wills Point (population 2,361) when he wasn't staging national Democratic political conventions. "I think it *is* a clan," he added. "The rings are our tartan."

For three generations every male member of the Wynne family (and more recently every female member as well) received the same ring on his or her twenty-first birthday. It consisted of three gold Serpents of the Nile intertwined into a band. Two had ruby eyes; one had emerald; each had a diamond in the middle of its head. The ring was a copy of the one a grateful client had bestowed on Fat Dad.

Despite his humble beginnings, Fat Dad was a natty gentleman who always wore a flower in his buttonhole and doffed his Panama hat to the ladies. Armed with style, drive, and a flair for showmanship that seemed to run in the Wynne genes, Fat Dad became a brilliant trial lawyer. Of the 179 men and 18 women he defended on capital offenses, none was executed, and only 18 received long sentences. The Wynne patriarch also enjoyed spectacular success with civil cases. One of his clients was Colonel William Fuller, a wealthy East Texan who raised Thoroughbreds. Leaving New York after winning the Brooklyn Handicap, Colonel Fuller's prize mare Tokalon was injured in a train wreck that killed another of the colonel's best horses. Summoned to New York, William Wynne, the boy from the provinces, won a handsome settlement against the railroad. (Family records didn't mention the amount.) Colonel Fuller was so pleased that he marched the spunky East Texas attorney into Tiffany's and bought him the ring that became the Wynne talisman.

According to the official Wynne family history, Fat Dad's wife, Margaret, a devout Presbyterian, considered the ring vulgar, like something a gambler would wear. But her husband never took it off his finger. His best friend was the local saloonkeeper who called on him to defend Wills Point's honor at the billiard table whenever a pool sharp drifted into town.

"Fat Dad liked a challenge," said the late Toddie Lee Wynne, Jr., in 1985, sitting in his den with a huge water buffalo, a Bengal tiger, a mammoth moose, a rhinoceros, a male lion, a warthog, a cheetah, and assorted deer and antelopes staring down from the walls. Fat Dad's idea of fishing, Toddie Lee explained, was landing trout on No. 10 sewing thread. For thirty years Fat Dad also reigned as pigeon-shooting champion of Texas. His secret was practice. Every day after work he'd tack a playing card on a stump and shoot all the color out of it.

Practical jokes were another of Fat Dad's favorite pastimes. To amaze his hunting companions, he taught his horse to point like a bird dog at a covey of quail—actually a response to subtle pressure from the rider's knee. Later, to amuse his grandchildren, he'd remove his false teeth and make them clatter.

When oil fever hit East Texas, William B. Wynne sent each of his sons—all University of Texas-educated lawyers—to a different boomtown, where they negotiated oil leases on behalf of local landowners. If a farmer was short of cash, as was often the case, the Wynne boys would take their fees in percentage points of the deal—a practice that yielded either nothing or a spectacular return.

Toddie Lee, Sr., didn't stop with representing clients in the oil business; he himself got into oil, in partnership with one of the state's most successful petroleum pioneers, Clint Murchison, Sr. While Toddie Lee was at it, he successfully attacked the existing law prorating oil production, taking the state of Texas to federal court several times until it finally revised the legislation to permit producers to pump more oil as demand increased.

True to his religious upbringing, Toddie Lee gave three million of his first thirty million dollars—a tithe—to the Presbyterian Church. He put part of the rest into a custom-outfitted DC-3. One afternoon, as he returned to Dallas from Matagorda—his forty-mile-long private island off the Texas coast—with a planeload of relatives, the pilot hit an alarming thunderstorm. Once the plane had ceased shuddering and the lightning had stopped bouncing off the wings, Angus Wynne Sr.'s wife, Nemo, remarked: "Can't you see the headlines in the papers tomorrow? 'Rich oilman's plane goes down with all his poor kin.' "

An oilman, a rancher, an international hotelier, and a space entrepreneur, Toddie Lee Wynne, Jr., inherited his grandfather's sturdy build and thick crown of white hair and his father's ability to make money. At the time of his death, in 1987, Toddie Lee, Jr., was chairman and president of American Liberty Oil and of American Home Realty and chairman of Plaza of the Americas, a plush hotel complex, complete with ice-skating rink, in downtown Dallas. He built the Hong Kong Hilton and owned the Malay Hilton and Tiger Tops, a Nepalese resort where guests rode elephants into the rugged countryside to view wildlife.

One of Toddie Lee Jr.'s last entrepreneurial ventures was Houston-based Space Services, Inc., which produced the world's first successful rocket launch on September 9, 1982.

The SSI chairman David Hannah persuaded both Toddie Lee, Jr., and his late father, who died three years before the landmark launch, to become major shareholders in the company. SSI didn't get its first paying payload—a communications satellite—until two years after Toddie Lee Jr.'s fatal heart attack. Still, the Dallas oilman was convinced the enterprise had a market niche with communications companies and other satellite users who might prefer to schedule a launch 120 days in advance, instead of waiting the years required by NASA. "There are certain things NASA doesn't want to do; they're old hat," Toddie Lee, Jr., said. "We'll do a launch for somewhere between thirteen million and fourteen million dollars and make a profit. That's not much compared to an offshore oil rig."

Fired by true Wynne entrepreneurial imagination, Toddie Lee, Jr., also pushed Space Services, Inc., into a less conventional direction: burial in space. One rocket could carry 10,330 two-by-five-eighths-inch packets of cremated remains at thirty-nine hundred dollars apiece. Enclosed together in a reflective canister, visible through binoculars from Earth, the packets would be shot into perpetual orbit, so that no matter what sort of life departed Uncle Harry had led, his survivors would be able to raise their eyes heavenward when they mentioned his name. At the time of Toddie Lee Jr.'s death, SSI had yet to launch its first Mylar mausoleum; his remains rested in Dallas.

If Angus, Sr., fitted into the "poor kin" category, it was only in comparison with his brother. He'd invested profitably in the East Texas oil fields and had done handsomely in law as well. A founder of the Texas State Bar Association, he had a flamboyant yet effective courtroom style. The press dubbed him King of the Boomtown Lawyers. His one significant failure was his defense of slantwell drilling rights, which would have allowed a producer to tap oil lying under any neighbors' land he could reach by drilling sideways.

"He was a big actor," said his grandson Shannon Wynne. A cool, lanky six feet four inches with storklike legs, Shannon had made his own mark by founding a series of trendy bars with names ending in O. "He could quote the Bible and cry big crocodile tears and pace the floor," Shannon continued. "He'd read two pocket westerns a day. While the other side was giving its arguments, he'd sit there reading a western."

Shannon's father, Gus—Angus Wynne, Jr.—interrupted his expected legal education to become a Navy commander in World War II. When he returned, he became a partner with his uncle Toddie Lee, Sr., in American Home Realty, which created the Dallas area's first combination commercial and residential development, 820-acre Wynnewood. To help capture the fancies of veterans flush with VA incentives, Gus named the streets after Pacific islands and battleships.

Then Gus formed the Great Southwest Corporation, which bought up the old Arlington Racetrack and the sprawling Waggoner 3-D Ranch midway between the two cities. And he started taking his kids to Disneyland. Much of the Arlington land became an industrial park, home to Pepsi-Cola, LTV, and the Greenhouse spa. The rest became Six Flags Over Texas, the most razzle-dazzle amusement park between Anaheim and Orlando.

"Dad was a history buff," said Shannon's older brother, rock and blues impresario Angus Wynne III, known to family and friends as Ango. He explained that Gus Wynne got the idea for the park's name from a little stand of six toy flags he saw on Ango's desk. "Originally they were going to call the park Texas Under Six Flags," Ango added. "Then I remember him saying, 'No, I can't do that because Texas isn't *under* nothing.' "

Six Flags opened in 1961 with an emphasis on cleanliness and wholesome entertainment loosely related to Texas history. It was an enormous success, and it brought Gus Wynne far more attention than his marriage to Camay Soap girl Joanne Ebeling, his development of Wynnewood, and his seemingly endless civic involvements, which ranged from the Boy Scouts to the Dallas Citizens Interracial Association to the American Leprosy Missions. Small wonder that his name came up in early 1964, when President Lyndon Johnson and Governor John Connally were looking for someone to stage an extravaganza worthy of Texas at the New York World's Fair.

No one had ever seen anything like the Texas Pavilion and Music Hall. Sprawling across three acres, the four-and-a-half million-dollar display of entrepreneurial optimism introduced the world to Dr Pepper, Tex-Mex cuisine, and mixed-media theater. The Lone Star's *pièce de résistance* was a lavish retrospective of the American musical, *To Broadway with Love*, the first show to blend film and live stage.

Gordon Wynne, Jr., produced it. He'd been Judy Garland's production manager and had several *Hallmark Hall of Fame* classics and a Broadway hit—*Write Me a Murder*—to his credit as a producer. But although it was a critical success, *To Broadway with Love*, like the Texas Pavilion and the entire 1964 World's Fair, was a financial fiasco. It languished in a remote corner of a fair with disastrously low attendance.

Angus Wynne, Jr., who'd financially guaranteed the extravagant enterprise, emerged with nine million dollars in personal debts. With true show biz pizzazz, he and Joanne responded with a party—an epic bankruptcy bash. "They had waiters with 'Soup Line' on their hats and 'Yes We Have No Bananas' on their shirts," Shannon said. "Everybody brought sacks of groceries and used clothes for us kids. It was all fun. They made big light of the fact that everybody went down the toidy."

But despite the brave face he put on it, the financial crash took its toll on Gus Wynne. Determined to pay off his creditors, he sold most of his stock in the Great Southwest Corporation to Penn Central. And he relinquished ownership of his beloved Six Flags, which went on to spawn, somewhat incongruously, Six Flags Over Georgia and Six Flags Over Mid-America. In 1969 Gus Wynne suffered a severe stroke. Then, after Penn Central went bankrupt in 1974, Great Southwest severed its relationship with him and sued him. It eventually dropped the suit, but he died of a heart attack in 1979.

In the wake of the World's Fair debacle, Gordon Wynne, Jr., fared better than his uncle. When most television production shifted from New York to the West Coast during the late sixties, he returned to Wills Point to practice law. Increasingly he used the technical skills he'd learned in show business to add drama to events for the Democratic party.

Between 1974 and 1988 Gordon produced four Democratic midterm conferences and four Democratic national
conventions. In between he served in the Carter administration—first in 1977 as special assistant to Ambassador Robert Strauss, later as executive director of the White House
Task Force on the Multilateral Trade Negotiations Agreement
and chairman of the Task Force on Energy Conservation.

When Mario Cuomo brought tears to the eyes of the
nation's Democrats watching the 1984 Democratic National
Convention, he did it with the help of Gordon Wynne's
backstage magic.

"There's not really a lot of difference between show business and politics," Gordon explained. "They both have their
plots and their subplots, their stars and their substars. The
entertainers aren't half as difficult to deal with as the politicians."

Like his uncle Gordon, Ango worked on the World's
Fair and emerged with a keen appetite for show business,
further whetted by an early taste for rock and roll and rhythm
and blues. He began booking funky bands for fraternity
bashes and deb parties. Then, together with fellow Dallasite
Jack Calmes, he formed Showco, which produced mammoth
concerts in Market Hall. They brought such messiahs of the
Sixties Sound as Bob Dylan, Janis Joplin, and Jimi Hendrix
to Texas. In 1968 they even opened Dallas's first interracial
club, Soul City.

Ango went on to found Central Casting, which began
as a music booking agency and later cast talent for Dallas's
growing film business, and a modeling agency, Industry/
Dallas, and he converted the Arcadia, a 1927-vintage vaude-
ville house, into a showcase for solo and small-group performances.

The Wynnes relished individuality, but they also relished tradition. The Serpents of the Nile rings were just the
beginning. Inspired by those rings, Fat Dad's descendants
called themselves Snakes; their spouses called themselves
Mongooses, since the mongoose was the one animal that
consistently bested the cobra. Mongoose brides had to learn
how to cook family specialties, like slang-jang—a vinegary
tomato, onion, and pepper relish. The most involved was

the spiced round—a giant round of beef packed with spice-dredged lard stuck into holes made with a sharpened broom-stick, then "put down" in brine for two weeks before being roasted and served at Christmas. Every bride got a huge spiced-round crock as a wedding present.

Most families have their own rituals for initiating new in-laws, indoctrinating children with shared lore and values, and inoculating all their members with a sense of group identification. But seldom are these as elaborate and for-malized as they were among the Wynnes.

At the 1987 Wynne family reunion the din was deaf-ening. A hundred and sixty people—many of them with the same high forehead, square jaw, and long, thin nose—crowded the nine-hundred-square-foot beige and brown par-lor of the Admiral's Villa, a $595-a-night three-bedroom suite at the Flagship Inn, across the freeway from Six Flags. Every-one seemed to be laughing, talking, yelling, and whooping at the same time. Dozens of children chased one another in and out among their elders' legs, hissing loudly like proper little Snakes.

"People who come from small families are sometimes overwhelmed by this," said clan historian Cookie Chilton Owen, a slender brunette with a gift for understatement.

Details of the reunion differed from year to year, but not the basic pattern. The consistency was part of what made the ritual work. The high point of the weekend was Saturday night, which began with a catered dinner of heavy East Texas food—fried catfish, hush puppies, and coleslaw steeped in mayonnaise. Although music and skits often accompanied the meal, they were only warm-ups for the Big Event—the initiation of new Mongooses. Thanks to his tenure in show business, Gordon Wynne, Jr., served as emcee.

The ceremony usually involved the bride or groom an-swering detailed questions on family lineage and lore. De-pending on the personality of the initiate, this good-natured pillorying could be hilarious or horrible. In 1985 the two new in-laws, both males, were swaddled in sheets and pillow-cases like hostages in front of some third world people's tribunal. In an overbearing voice Gordon fired off a series of arcane questions: Who was wrongly reported missing in action? Who had the first Mongoose pendant? What was the name of Uncle Bedford's ride at the New York World's Fair? Each wrong answer brought a hail of water balloons.

"If someone's inhibited, that's *their* problem," said Jacque Ryan Wynne, who married Toddie Lee Wynne, Jr., in 1972. Inhibition wasn't one of Jacque's problems. She invented the state's most flamboyant fund raiser, the Cattle Barons' Ball, and her private parties—most of which revolved around exotic themes—were legend. For her twenty-ninth birthday she hung her spacious contemporary brick Dallas house with white funeral wreaths. To celebrate her seventh anniversary, she threw a soiree based on the film *The Seven Year Itch* and came as Marilyn Monroe, complete with custom-designed blond wig. In 1982, to demonstrate her newly acquired proficiency in figure skating, Jacque donned a spectacular white tutu studded with emerald green glass. While hundreds of spectators watched, she skated to "O Holy Night" in the Plaza of the Americas Christmas pageant.

At ten forty-five Sunday morning, every Wynne at the reunion showed up for the traditional worship service, no matter when he'd cashed in his chips at the equally traditional all-night poker game. Family enforcers rousted the reluctant out of bed at ten-fifteen with ice cubes and cold towels. Fat Dad's only surviving son, Buck Wynne, opened the service with his mother's favorite hymns—"Church in the Wildwood," "In the Garden," and "Jesus Wants You for a Sunbeam." In a clear, warm tenor, Jimmy Spenser, a black family retainer in his sixties, poured forth "Have You Stopped to Pray Today?" Then Buck Wynne stepped to the podium and read the family credo, a letter Fat Dad wrote in 1916 to his four sons.

"I would not know how to live if I felt that some man that practiced law in the districts and counties that I lived in was held in higher esteem as a lawyer than myself . . . and this is the kind of lawyers that my boys must be and will be," Buck Wynne quoted in a wavering but emphatic voice as from the grave Fat Dad exhorted his descendants to succeed. "Inch by inch and step by step they must climb the ladder until they reach the top where they can sit quietly by and look down on those who are struggling far beneath them. . . . Nothing short of that place will satisfy."

The very site where the reunion took place reinforced this message. The Memorial Day after Angus Wynne, Jr., opened Six Flags Over Texas, the entire Wynne clan convened there to celebrate, their children armed with free passes. Even after bankruptcy forced Gus to sell Six Flags to Penn Central, ending the free passes, the family continued to hold their reunion there most years. To successive generations of Wynnes, that monument to real estate and show biz wasn't a symbol of defeat; it was hallowed ground. It embodied the family directive to go out and accomplish something in a public, even flashy way. This was a clan in which the sin was not overreaching but never trying.

Some families expect their children to become artists or musicians; others expect them to earn Ph.D.'s. The Wynnes were a large, cohesive, and prosperous clan partly because they gathered all eight branches together and told the kids that they could do anything they wanted to, that it was okay if they failed, and that they didn't have to be like everyone else.

"We might as well be sitting around the old tepee with the old chief saying, 'Here was our valley of laughter, and here was our trail of tears,' " Gordon Wynne, Jr., said after the 1987 reunion. "The bond perpetuates the party, and the party perpetuates the bond."

★

CHAPTER TWELVE

Mary Kay Ash

Eyeliner and Inspiration

Ten women dressed in silver lamé spaghetti-strapped dresses and pillbox hats and ten men decked out in silver lamé tuxedos danced across the stage of the Dallas Convention Center and up the risers outlined in blinking lights. "What is it that we're living for? What is it that we're giving for?" they sang with a brassy polish worthy of Broadway. "Applause! Applause!"

A year earlier this stage had been the focus of the 1984 Republican National Convention. On this sultry July night in 1985 it was converted to a slick show business fantasy for an event only relatively more modest—the annual Awards Night for Mary Kay Ash Cosmetics. On the surface, the four-million-dollar production looked like yet another example of ostentatious display, just what the world might expect of Dallas. But underneath, it was a crucial ingredient in the formula that had made multimillionaire cosmetics queen Mary Kay Ash the richest self-made female entrepreneur in

Texas and one of the most successful businesswomen in the country.

The slick song-and-dance numbers—with their original music, lyrics, and choreography, a new theme every year—swirled on through the evening. In between, women who were making seventy-five and one hundred thousand dollars a year gave ringing testimonials. With the fervor of true believers, they told how Mary Kay had saved them from a dust-choked North Carolina textile plant or a run-down tenement with a bare larder. It was the Academy Awards, *Queen for a Day*, and the Miss America Pageant bundled into one glittering package, then tied up with yards of sturdy, upbeat inspiration straight out of an East Texas tent revival meeting.

With her Mae West figure sheathed in sequins and chiffon, Mary Kay Ash was the fairy godmother of the event. Radiating that same charismatic optimism, that intense *belief* in every person in her audience that enabled her to raise, in a single Sunday, $2.3 million toward the fifteen-million-dollar Prestonwood Baptist Church building fund, she transported the crowd. She gushed encouragement and appreciation and handed out brown shadow mink jackets (with zip-out sleeves "for two elegant looks"), diamond bumblebee pins, five-thousand-dollar Neiman Marcus shopping sprees, and keys to pink Cadillacs, one of which revolved on a dais cloaked in fake fog. Sauntering self-consciously across the stage in pastel evening gowns, women of all ages, sizes, and ethnic backgrounds accepted with rapturous smiles and blissful tears the gifts, the royal sashes, the rhinestone crowns, and the long-stemmed roses. A few were young and pretty enough to have been contestants in local beauty contests, but most were ordinary-looking women transformed by the world's most potent cosmetic—ecstatic excitement.

"We make the Academy Awards look like an amateur production," Mary Kay later said bluntly as she sat in the soft beige corner office of her gold-skinned tower on Dallas's Stemmons Freeway.

The pageant was the key to the success of the $210 million company, with its national sales force of more than 150,000 women, who peddled moisturizer and lipstick to their friends and recruited them to do likewise.

"I don't think there's any woman in the world who

wouldn't want to be Miss America and walk down that runway with the roses in her arms and the crown on her head
and be presented with all the wonderful prizes that she gets,"
asserted Mary Kay, who apparently had never had a heart-
to-heart with a feminist. "But what chance does the average
woman have to be Miss America? There's no way you're ever
going to get to walk across that stage and get all those beautiful prizes. But we make it a reality."

The recognition was very public for the several hundred
women who sold the most and spread the Mary Kay gospel
to the biggest numbers of go-getting new "beauty consultants," as the company called its salespeople. Every woman
(only 0.5 percent of the sales force was male) who maintained
a given ambitious sales and recruitment level got two years'
use of one of the company's signature pink Cadillacs; Buicks
and Oldsmobiles went to those who sold somewhat less.
Otherwise almost all the performance prizes were frivolous
luxuries—no refrigerators or microwaves here. The psy-
chology behind this was shrewd. Sure, it would have been
simpler for Mary Kay Cosmetics to reward top performers
with bonus checks, as many other companies did. But that
five-thousand-dollar check would have been quickly ab-
sorbed into the household budget and forgotten. That mink,
that ring with its "rhapsody of rubies and diamonds," that
Wittnauer watch (for her husband) were constant reminders
to go out and hustle more business.

Mary Kay Awards Night was the climax of the company's annual three-day sales seminar. Hundreds of women
attended because they knew they'd be up there on that stage,
but tens of thousands came for the lectures on salesmanship
and time management, the hints on promoting the company's new products, the giggly camaraderie, and the inspiration of watching the members of the Queen's Court parade
across the proscenium and thinking, "Next year that could
be me." Despite the $95 registration fee (which didn't begin
to cover the cost) and the $160-a-night room rates at the
Loew's Anatole, where the Mary Kay legions bunked, the
event was so popular that the company put on four identical
seminars back to back, each named after a precious gem and
each with its own Awards Night. Altogether the company
spent five million dollars, served 130,000 lunches, and gave

employment to hundreds of Dallas dancers, lighting engineers, and stagehands during the normally somnolent last
two weeks in July.

On one level Mary Kay Cosmetics was the kind of enormous business success that proved women have the Right
Stuff to win in the male-dominated world of commerce. In
1984 the *Wall Street Journal* announced that Mary Kay had
more women earning fifty thousand dollars a year and above
than any other company in the United States, and the corporation itself claimed that it had more black, Asian-
American, and Hispanic women making fifty thousand dollars and up than any other company in the world. By the
end of 1987 eighteen women had raked in more than one
million dollars apiece in commissions.

Mary Kay Ash herself was one of only about thirty
women among the four hundred recipients of the Horatio
Alger Award, given to entrepreneurs and professionals who
had overcome early adversity to reach outstanding heights
in their careers. The meteoric rise of her company turned
heads on Wall Street. The stock was going for nine dollars
a share in 1982, when several analysts from Kidder, Peabody
and Merrill Lynch noticed it. By April 1983 it had jumped to
forty-four.

Yet there was something about Mary Kay Cosmetics that
made many feminists uncomfortable, even irate. Some objected to the whole idea of makeup, of exploiting society's
old message that women needed artifice to be attractive and
that for women, being attractive, especially to men, was terribly important. Others pointed out that while Mary Kay Ash
might be enormously successful, she was hardly blazing new
ground. Female cosmetics tycoons were nothing new; take
Helena Rubinstein and Estée Lauder. The cosmetics industry
was one of those few areas of endeavor, like clothing design,
long open to either sex. Even an insecure man would be less
threatened by his wife's making fifty thousand dollars selling
cosmetics than by her making the same money selling Xerox
machines or cars—lines where he might see himself competing. Then there were the official Mary Kay priorities, of
which even Phyllis Schlafly would have approved: "God
first, family second, job third."

But when they were prodded, what the feminist critics

invariably came down to was the cheerleaderlike vivacity the most successful Mary Kay minions exuded. When they got together for the annual seminar or for regional sales-training sessions, they even sang "I've got that Mary Kay enthusiasm" to the tune of the gospel hymn "I've got that joy, joy, joy down in my heart."

And wasn't there something about the sales *modus operandi* that smacked of preliberated adolescence? Unlike Avon ladies, who sold their products individually door to door, Mary Kay beauty consultants got friends to give "parties" for six to twelve women. Once she had them together, the Mary Kay saleswoman set a sample kit in front of each participant, took the group through the skin care ritual (four steps—cleanse, tone, and moisturize twice daily, retexturize once a week), and went on to show them how to apply the makeup appropriate to their coloring.

In her promotional photos the woman behind these legions of perky glamour peddlers looked like an aging movie star. The focus was soft; the lighting and expression were reminiscent of the "What becomes a legend most?" Blackglama mink ads. In person she was quite different—down-to-earth and natural, except for her huge, immobile blond coiffure. Mary Kay Ash was neither more nor less made up than a typical female bank vice-president or real estate agent, but her skin had an almost poreless perfection. She insisted that she used nothing but her company's products.

On a sunny afternoon in the middle of January 1987 Mary Kay Ash sat in her office under the glow of a crystal chandelier a good four feet across. Behind her Chippendale-style desk were four lighted curio cabinets filled with Boehm and Cybis porcelain—bisque birds; bleached-out youths and girls in melancholy poses; glazed flamenco dancers with skirts rimmed in yellow, fuchsia, and purple flowers. Some of these delicate pieces had cost seventy-five hundred dollars. All were Christmas or birthday gifts from her salespeople, who pooled their money in each of the company's fifty-eight geographical districts to buy them.

Instead of her signature pink, she wore a black suit trimmed in red. A diamond bumblebee the size of a deerfly adorned her blouson jacket. With twenty-one diamonds and a retail value of $3,660, it was identical to the pins she gave out at Awards Night to her Queens of Sales. The bumblebee was an inspirational symbol. Because of its weight and its limited wingspan, the bumblebee shouldn't have been able to fly, she explained in her soft, slightly nasal voice, but the bee didn't know that, so it flew despite its limitations. That was the message she pounded into her troops: Believe you can do the impossible, and maybe you can.

In her own early life Mary Kay overcame enough adversity to give this homily substance. Although she wouldn't discuss her age, she was born during the late 1910's in Hot Wells, Texas, a spa town twenty-five miles northwest of Houston. Hot Wells has since burned down and been replaced by suburban sprawl, but in those days Mary Kay's parents owned a hotel there. When Mary Kay was two, her father developed tuberculosis; the family moved to Houston, where he could get treatment. To support them, her mother went to work in a restaurant, and little Mary Kay looked after her father, standing on an orange crate to cook for him. When she had a question or felt overwhelmed, she called her mother at work. Their conversations always ended with an encouraging "Honey, Mother knows you can do it. You can do it, darling."

Mary Kay lifted the right side of her mouth in the asymmetrical smile that made her look world-weary and slightly ironic. "I grew up in a hurry," she said. "I lived for Saturday. That was my splurge day. I used to go downtown on a streetcar and buy the clothes I needed. I did it myself. I was seven, and the hardest job I had was convincing the clerks."

From an early age Mary Kay was fiercely competitive. If there was a prize to win, she went after it. She graduated from Reagan High School with honors, but there was no money for college, not even for Rice Institute (now University), where the tuition was free. Not to be outdone by her college-bound chums, she decided to marry her boyfriend, who was something of a local celebrity with a popular radio band called the Hawaiian Strummers. "He was the Elvis Presley of radio," she said wryly. "He was good-looking and he played the guitar and he sang. He was a real catch. There was just one little problem: That was all he ever wanted to be. He was not a responsible husband. All he wanted to do was play the guitar and sing and be the idol of all these girls.''

He joined the Army before World War II but blew his eighty-dollar monthly pay on guitar strings and tuxedos. With three children to feed, Mary Kay had to go to work.

One of the few things she could do and still spend most of her time with her kids was to to sell Stanley Home Products. In 1931, at the height of the Depression, Stanley Beveridge had come up with what the retail world now calls the party sales concept. The salesperson asked a friend to invite others to her house to drink coffee, gossip, and witness a product demonstration. The hostess provided the potential customers, the refreshments, and the illusion of a social event; in return she got a gift of the company's products and sometimes a percentage of the sales. The peer pressure was subtle but virtually irresistible. With their friends looking on, women felt they *had* to buy *some*thing. All the salesperson needed to do was interest some of her audience in an item, and they'd sell the others on it. In commissions per hour, the method had it all over door-to-door peddling.

Mary Kay flogged her wares to between twelve and twenty-four women at a time. (Nowadays, she noted, housewives willing to host such sales parties claim they don't know twelve available friends and don't have a dozen matching cups.) For the most part the Stanley products were better than those available in stores.

"We sold brooms and mops and toothbrushes and furniture cream and all that stuff to keep house—very glamorous," she said sardonically. "So I had to become more of an entertainer than a salesperson, because you can bore a group of twelve women stiff in five minutes with floor cleaner.''

After First Lady Eleanor Roosevelt told a reporter that she always tied a toothbrush into the bow of any Christmas gift (even if the recipient couldn't use another tie, he could use a toothbrush), Mary Kay added that celebrity hint to her repertoire of jokes and anecdotes. "I'd sell every woman there a dozen toothbrushes to put on her packages," she recalled.

She was phenomenally successful. During the late 1930's Mary Kay pulled in a thousand dollars a week in commissions. When she revealed her income to a female census taker, the woman announced in amazement that Mary Kay made more than the insurance company vice-president next door.

That fired Mary Kay's competitive spirit, but the prize she won for being Stanley's best producer in her region doused her enthusiasm. It was a flounder light, used to gig bottom fish. For years she kept the unsportsmanlike device on her bookshelf to remind her of how inappropriate performance incentives could be.

After thirteen years with Stanley Mary Kay moved on to another party-sales outfit, World Gift, because the products were prettier. This time she sold decorative items. She'd hit the house of the woman who'd agreed to be hostess, strip the living room of its pictures, flowers, and knickknacks, and substitute items from her stock of merchandise, color-coordinated to accent the upholstery. If the couch was brown, out would come orange candles in brass candlesticks, a print of a sunset for the wall, and an arrangement of artificial orange mums for the coffee table. "Most of the time, I sold the hostess everything I put up there," she said.

Mary Kay stayed with World Gift eleven years, rising to sales manager. One year she was responsible for 53 percent of its sales. After she remarried in the early sixties, she retired, but a few months of forced inactivity were all she could take.

More than a decade earlier, while giving her Stanley Home Products spiel in a neighborhood on Dallas's unfashionable south side, Mary Kay had noticed that every woman in the room had beautiful skin. She discovered that the secret was a skin cream the hostess's father, a hide tanner, had concocted. The woman was scooping it out into mayonnaise bottles and fruit jars, attaching directions written in longhand, and selling it to her friends. The goop looked and smelled like exactly what it was—slightly altered leather treatment—but Mary Kay took some home in a shoebox and began using it. And in 1963 she began to wonder if that hide tanner's cream might have commercial potential. Surely a good cosmetic chemist could do something about that revolting smell and appearance. Add some attractive packaging—a nice feminine pink, Mary Kay Ash figured—and the concoction could do as much for her as furniture cream had done for Stanley Beveridge.

Sitting down at the kitchen table with a yellow legal pad, Mary Kay began to list everything Stanley Home Products and World Gift had done wrong—not with their products but with their sales force. Sure, they'd made their founders millions of dollars, but she could make more. She could do it better.

"One of the things was the prizes," she explained twenty-four years later. "The prizes were never very interesting. For instance, I was Queen of Sales, and World Gift gave me an alligator bag. Period. We give things like a pink Cadillac. We do this in front of *everybody*," she added. "That's part of it."

Another thing Mary Kay didn't like was having all the prizes be competitive—even though personally she thrived on competition. "In Stanley and World Gift there was first prize, second prize, and third prize," she said. "Now, in every company there are three hotshots who are going to win those prizes year after year, so you think to yourself, 'What's the use trying?'"

Becoming a Mary Kay Queen of Personal Sales or Queen of Recruiting was purely a matter of selling the most cosmetics or signing up the most new salespeople. There were eight queens, two each for the Ruby, Emerald, Sapphire, and Diamond Seminars, plus a total of sixteen runners-up. But most of the prizes, including diamond bracelets and keys to cars, went to anyone who reached a preset performance level. In 1986, 425 women made it into the Queen's Court by selling at least twenty-four thousand dollars in products. Every one of them received at least a diamond or a diamond and ruby ring. And every one of them got bused out to Mary Kay's five-million-dollar pink mansion for pink spiced tea and cookies.

Sure, those rings may have cost the company a thousand dollars apiece. But if each of those women brought in six thousand dollars in profits without costing any overhead, the investment was worth it.

By 1987 Mary Kay Cosmetics had twenty-nine million dollars in leased cars running around the country. ("So you think pink Cadillacs are tacky?" a cover line on the June 1985 issue of *Savvy* asked slyly. "What color was the car your company gave *you*?") Every salesperson who sold six hundred dollars wholesale value in products for three consecutive months and recruited five new salespeople who together sold three thousand dollars for three months got the use of a lipstick red Oldsmobile Firenza for two years. For those who sold fifty thousand dollars for two consecutive quarters, there were pink Buick Centuries; for those who sold seventy-five thousand dollars, the coveted pink Cadillacs.

And there were other incentives as well. On her birthday each of the company's "beauty consultants" got a card from Mary Kay herself. The three thousand sales directors got gifts as well. That illusion of personal contact and reinforcement reflected the motivational philosophy the cosmetics queen expounded in her 1984 book *Mary Kay on People Management*, in which she exhorted executives to "praise people to success." The company's monthly newsletter, aptly titled *Applause*, listed the names of "Very Important Performers."

Perhaps the biggest flaw Mary Kay saw in companies outside the world of direct sales was their lack of appreciation for the plight of working women, especially working mothers. In the early 1960's there were no child care chains, no corporate flextime, no laws mandating comparable pay for comparable work. Yet the ranks of divorced women with children to support were growing, as was the number of households needing second incomes to move a notch up the socioeconomic ladder or just to get by. Direct sales had always offered women good potential earnings combined with flexible hours. Mary Kay decided to make that advantage explicit in her recruitment and sales training. Women had different priorities from men. Men might put their careers ahead of everything else, but for women it was "God first, family second, job third."

Mary Kay claimed that her company taught women to prioritize their lives and do what they felt was most important, instead of setting up conflicts between job and home. "A skin care class [her term for a Mary Kay sales presentation] never starts until ten o'clock," she said. "A woman can get her husband off to work, get her children off to school, and maybe plan the evening meal, then be back when the children get home. You make as much money in those hours as that gal who went to work at seven A.M. and comes home at six."

A lot of Mary Kay saleswomen came from very humble backgrounds, and the annual seminars featured elective workshops in diction and deportment to help them pass as middle class. Yet Mary Kay found even the two thirds of her sales force with some college lacking in self-confidence.

"We're selling a way of life," she declared with evangelical fervor. "So many times a woman comes into this company so inhibited, with such a bad self-image and no belief in herself. If you were to ask me what is the absolute common denominator among women, I would say it is the inability to have confidence in their own abilities. Men at least have sense enough to bluff their way through."

During the early 1980's the Mary Kay "way of life" enjoyed a sudden increase in appeal. The number of beauty consultants jumped from 50,000 in 1979 to almost 200,000 in 1982. But by the close of 1984 the sales force had slid back down to 151,615. Profits fell from $36.7 million in 1983 to $33.8 million in 1984, and stock skidded from a high near $45 in 1982 to $13.38 on July 7, 1985.

The company's official explanation of the drop was that layoffs accompanying the recession of 1980 and 1981 propelled many women into the work force and forced others to turn to moonlighting to supplement their paychecks. Once the economy improved, they didn't need the extra income. Also, by 1984 a growing number of large corporations had instituted flextime, on-site child care, and other progressive work schedule and benefit programs to fit the needs of working mothers.

Besides, for most Mary Kay saleswomen the money had never been all that great. While thousands made more than they could hope to bring in teaching school or working as secretaries, the average income each saleswoman earned from Mary Kay in 1984 was only $1,603. Presumably women with such lackluster sales sold mostly to their families and friends, making little effort to expand their circle of customers. That brought up another problem: Many people—male and female, feminist and male chauvinist alike—found something distasteful about a retail system that relied on selling to friends and relatives and then recruiting them to do likewise. It seemed to exploit human social relationships for commercial ends.

Yet it was a highly efficient sales mechanism. Mary Kay had no overhead for shops, no money laid out supplying drug and department stores. Apart from the eight-story Dallas office building and the sprawling, low-rise laboratory a few hundred yards down Regal Row, Mary Kay Cosmetics had three regional warehouses. That was it. President and chief executive officer Richard Rogers, Mary Kay's son, ran the company on just eleven hundred employees. The beauty consultants were all independent contractors. That gave them more freedom but less security.

Granted, consultants could buy into a group benefits program, which included health, life, and product replacement insurance. The products themselves were good quality and priced competitively. The cleanser, toner, and moisturizer compared favorably with higher-end drugstore lines like Revlon and Max Factor, although the makeup was more like the brands carried by supermarkets.

A new beauty consultant's initial investment was eighty-five dollars for a pink plastic case adorned with butterflies and filled with product samples and individual mirrored demonstration kits. She also bought however many bottles of cleanser, tubes of lipstick, and plastic compacts of blusher she estimated she'd sell during her first month or so. She paid for these in cash or with her Visa or MasterCard; the company didn't extend credit. She got to mark up the products 100 percent and keep the entire difference. Whatever she didn't sell, the company would buy back for ninety cents on the dollar.

But unless she sold directly to hundreds of women, each of whom consumed phenomenal quantities of cosmetics, a beauty consultant couldn't make a living peddling Mary Kay. She had to recruit others. Once a beauty consultant brought in thirty new saleswomen, she became a sales director. Sales directors were the ones who made the enviable incomes, but only 3 percent of the sales force reached that level.

In 1985 Mary Kay Ash and Richard Rogers anted up three

hundred million dollars and took Mary Kay Cosmetics private. It meant unloading the 176-acre tract of land northwest of Texas Stadium where Mary Kay had planned to put a hundred-million-dollar "cosmetics college," but the costly gambit erected an opaque curtain between the company and its critics.

"You don't have the stockholders on the line saying, 'Now that you are a *mature* company, don't you think that you should go to gray Cadillacs instead of pink Cadillacs and get rid of that frivolous pink image?' " Mary Kay Ash said, aping the rounded tones of a snooty matron.

All in all, pink had been very good to Mary Kay. She went home to her five-million-dollar red tile-roofed Mediterranean mansion in Prestonwood, the exclusive North Dallas neighborhood. Her nineteen thousand square feet of living space included twelve baths and a cavernous "great room" measuring sixty feet by thirty feet. After purchasing the house in 1984, she painted the stucco exterior blush pink.

CHAPTER THIRTEEN

★

Jarrell McCracken

Show Biz and Salvation

One characteristic that distinguished Texas from much of the rest of the country was the size, power, and wealth of the Baptist Church, the largest religious denomination in the state. Considering that more than a fifth of the population of Texas was Hispanic and overwhelmingly Catholic, this accomplishment was all the more remarkable.

Elsewhere families that rose from the working class to the ranks of wealth often shed their Baptist religion along with their polyester double knits, exchanging it for a WASP-ier creed. Not so in Texas, where the Baptist Church was the faith of some of the richest and most influential. The Baptists kept the sale of liquor by the drink at bay until 1970 and parimutuel betting until 1988. The Baptist Church also ran one of the state's largest educational institutions—Baylor University in Waco, a hundred miles south of Dallas.

In the late 1980's Baylor boasted an enrollment of eleven thousand, but it had only five thousand students when Jarrell McCracken, the son of a Baptist preacher in Dodge City, Kansas, matriculated in 1948. One reason McCracken came to Baylor was its athletic program. He had played football, basketball, and baseball in high school and entertained ambitions of becoming a professional baseball player. Baylor belonged to the Southwest Conference, and despite the school's modest size, its sports teams acquitted themselves well against the University of Texas, Texas A&M, and other larger rivals. Another feature that drew the boy from Kansas was the school's speech department, which offered training in radio announcing. He earned his B.A. in speech and religion in 1950, his master's in religion and history in 1953.

To support himself in school, Jarrell McCracken worked at KWTX, a local radio station. He spun records, reported news, and covered sports events. McCracken's favorite assignment was giving the play-by-play for the Waco Pirates, a Class B farm team for Pittsburgh. He broadcast live from all the home games, but when the team went on the road, he had to rely on wire service reports. Although these were pretty sparse, McCracken devised a method for giving them life. He recorded the sounds at one of the home games—the crack of the bat against the ball; the crowd cheering when a Pirate got a home run and booing when the umpire's call went against the team. Back at the studio he used these little reels of tape to re-create the action on the road.

"I'd get a report that said, 'So-and-so at bat. Two balls. One strike. Single to left,' " McCracken explained three decades later. "That's all it would say. So I'd have the pitcher giving the signal and winding up and throwing, and I'd say, 'It's low and outside.' I had all sorts of creative freedom." At the appropriate points he and the studio engineer brought in the sound effects from the home game they'd taped. "We got pretty good at it," he admitted. "In fact, most people around town thought we were really at the games."

This sleight of ear did more than mesmerize the listeners of KWTX; it transmogrified into a multimillion-dollar multimedia enterprise called Word Publishing, sort of a joint venture between God and Mammon.

At Baylor Jarrell McCracken seriously considered entering the ministry. He would have been good at it. McCracken was tall and handsome, with a straight nose and direct blue eyes. By 1985 his hair was gray, but it was thick enough to make him look ageless. His voice was firmly middle-register, with a residual midwestern twang and an underlay of optimism blended with compassion. Had he so chosen, Jarrell McCracken could have made it big as a television evangelist of the Pat Robertson school. Instead, he became to contemporary religious music what Ahmet Ertegun, cofounder of Atlantic Records, was to rock and roll.

One day while he was still at Baylor, a Baptist youth group in Hearne, a little town sixty-five miles to the southeast, asked the radio voice of the Waco Pirates to address it on the subject of Christianity and football. While casting about for something to say, McCracken came upon an article by Jimmy Allen, a preacher with a literary bent. Entitled "The Game of Life," it related an allegorical football game between Christianity and the forces of evil. Now there was an idea. Instead of lecturing the young Baptists on their chosen topic, why not use the opportunity to dramatize the eternal conflict? McCracken wrote up the play-by-play for just such a cosmic football match broadcast from the Stadium of Life over fictional radio station WORD. Dubbing in his old baseball sound effects, he recorded the imaginary contest, interjecting every ounce of descriptive drama he could muster. Instead of going to Hearne to preach, he sent the tape with the ministerial student who headed the youth group.

McCracken's friend returned the next Monday with raves about the football tape. The kids in Hearne loved it; in fact, eight or ten wanted to know where they could buy a record of the game. Other ministerial students borrowed the tape to use at the churches where they assisted on weekends.

"Pretty soon, I must have had fifty or sixty names of people who wanted copies, and I didn't know what to do," McCracken said. Finally he found a studio in California that could reproduce the tape on 78 rpm records. He had it do a hundred at first. To Jarrell McCracken the whole process was new. When the recording engineer asked what name he wanted on the label, he said the first thing that popped into his mind, the call letters of the imaginary radio station, WORD. The year was 1951. Jarrell McCracken was twenty-three.

Over the decades Word Publishing expanded to include religious books, sheet music, videocassettes, and a series of computer games based on C. S. Lewis's seven-volume Christian adventure fantasy *Chronicles of Narnia*. "The concept of Word is that we're a Christian communications company," McCracken explained in 1985. "And so whatever the media happens to present as an opportunity, that's what we're there for."

In 1986 Word even issued fifty thousand copies of a $9.95 paperback edition of the Meese Commission's report on pornography, available from the government for $35. In making its point that some forms of porn contributed to attacks on women, the document included unexpurgated excerpts from the likes of *Deep Throat* and *Debbie Does Dallas*.

But the greatest impact Word had was on the Christian music scene. Back in the fifties religious music was easy to identify by sound alone. There were masses and oratorios by classical masters, traditional hymns, and black spirituals. Pipe organs featured prominently. During the late sixties and early seventies, however, that changed. Successful rock and country musicians—many of them burned out on drugs, groupies, and the exhausting pace of road tours—began undergoing religious conversions and reawakenings. They wrote and performed songs similar in style to their previous work but reflecting their new experiences. Religious radio stations quickly recognized this trend as a godsend—the perfect way to reach rock-crazed youths and spiritually slack good ol' boys and girls. Pretty soon listeners tuning down to the left end of the FM dial could listen to heavy metal for fifteen minutes before realizing that the words were all about Jesus and redemption. They were "writing in the same idiom, just with Christian lyrics," McCracken said. "That's the way you end up reaching the young people, the people who are into rock music. You'd never reach me with it 'cause I can't stand to listen to it."

Really big-name recording stars like George Harrison, Seals and Crofts, Kris Kristofferson, and Willie Nelson simply included their new spiritual material on their general albums. But Word got those only slightly less established and with looser contracts.

Maybe Word wasn't producing the Mormon Tabernacle Choir, but as a business it was doing just fine. By 1985 the corporation had 460 employees and a whopping sixty million dollars in annual sales. Jarrell McCracken's secret was slick production, using the same Los Angeles and Nashville studios, the same recording engineers, the same backup musicians that gave that glossy sound to Top Forty hits. He also had a professional distribution network based in Winona Lake, Indiana, for North America and in London, England, for Europe, Africa, and Asia.

By that time Jarrell McCracken no longer owned Word. He'd sold it to media conglomerate ABC in 1974, although he stayed on as president until 1987. Neither McCracken nor ABC would reveal the price, but it was enough to bankroll the new venture he'd started on the side—Bentwood Farms, the largest breeder of Egyptian Arabian horses in the world.

McCracken, who didn't ride horses himself, got into his equine enterprise by dint of being a doting father. Lisa McCracken was horse-crazy, and she had a daddy who was able to indulge her passion. Lisa rode her first horse at two; by four she was riding alone. Her mother, Judith, taught her to read early and filled their white-columned house with figurines of animals.

Jarrell McCracken bought his daughter her first horse— an $85 mustang named Star—when she was eight. By the time she was in her early teens, Word was doing well enough that he could give her a $675 jumper. In 1969, when Lisa was sixteen, her horse's front legs began to wear out. Feeling pretty flush, McCracken decided to invest in a really good horse. He told Lisa to determine the best breed. She picked Arabians, the brave, beautiful equine heroes of her childhood novels.

Every other weekend Jarrell McCracken and his daughter traveled around Texas, looking at Arabian horses. In the beginning McCracken had figured that a "good" horse ought to cost about three times what he'd paid for the jumper, somewhere around two thousand dollars. After visiting a few breeding operations, he was just getting used to the fact that prices for registered Arabians were three thousand to eighty-five hundred dollars when he and Lisa spotted a pretty chestnut mare with a white blaze at Gleannloch Farms west of Houston. McCracken asked the owner what he wanted for the horse. The man replied that the mare wasn't for sale but that if she were, she'd bring forty to fifty thousand dollars. That was because she wasn't just an Arabian, she was an *Egyptian* Arabian.

"My first reaction to that price was that it was so ridiculous it made me sick at my stomach," McCracken said sixteen years later. "I couldn't understand why a nice guy like me was in a place like this. All the way home from Houston I kept thinking my mind was playing tricks on me. Did he say forty thousand dollars or four thousand dollars?"

But Jarrell McCracken was a rich man and an able scholar. If people were willing to pay those prices, horse breeding was a business worth looking into. After all, it didn't cost any more to feed a forty-thousand-dollar horse than it did to feed a four-hundred-dollar one. He began reading up on Egyptian Arabians, trying to find out why they were considered ten times more valuable than the domestic, Russian, Spanish, and Polish Arabians. "I began to see that it was a gold mine that nobody had found," he said.

Jarrell McCracken discovered that the story behind the breed was as romantic as *The Desert Song*. In 1805 an Ottoman Turkish soldier named Muhammad Ali became pasha of Egypt. A brilliant and ruthless tactician, he exterminated the leaders of the Mamelukes, who had ruled Egypt since 1250. He also set up schools and established a modern bureaucracy. Eventually his territory extended from the Sudan across the Arabian Peninsula to Syria. Muhammad Ali was a shrewd judge of horseflesh, and he demanded the best steeds in tribute from the nomadic tribes. Two out of three of these horses died crossing the desert, but eleven hundred made it to the imperial stables in Cairo.

Since the Arab tribesmen had bred their horses for strength, endurance, and courage in battle, Muhammad Ali crippled his vanquished foes' ability to wage war while he concentrated the best bloodlines in his own stables. When his grandson and successor, Abbas I, rose to the throne in 1848, he undid many of Muhammad Ali's progressive reforms, but he improved his horses. With a fierce dedication to perfection, he crossbred the top mares and stallions, developing a breed with rounded muscles, scimitar-shaped ears, and noble carriages. Confronted with new experiences, most horses shied away; descendants of Abbas's stables displayed courage and curiosity. Yet they were docile and affectionate. Compared with Thoroughbreds, they weren't particularly fast; compared with cutting horses, they weren't especially cunning; but in beauty and disposition Egyptian Arabians were without peer—the world's most beautiful and expensive pets.

Once Jarrell McCracken got the Egyptian Arabian bug, he got it bad. If he was going to invest in breeding these horses, only the best blood would do. Every day for eleven months McCracken spent three or four hours studying the top Egyptian bloodlines. He finally decided that a mare named Moniet el Nefous—which meant "the desire of all the souls in the world for beauty"—was the finest Egyptian Arabian horse ever. Even her birth in 1946 was special. With awe in his voice, McCracken described what he learned: "The people in Egypt who were there will tell you it was a moonlit night and the stars were out and they had straw down for her, which they don't normally do; their conditions aren't that great. The head of the Egyptian Arabian Organization and all those key people were there when that foal was born. It's like reading about Jesus Christ."

In March 1972 McCracken bought Ibn Moniet el Nefous, one of the mare's top sons. (It's traditional to give Egyptian Arabians Arabic names. *Ibn* and *ben* mean "son of"; *bent* means "daughter of.") He paid two hundred thousand dollars—a record price at the time.

Ibn died in 1986 but not before producing some stellar offspring. Some of his sons became geldings, but McCracken syndicated one, Moniet el Sharaf, for ten million dollars, and Ibn's daughter Fa Halima for a million. With something approaching the boldness of the Hunts in their silver play, the man who brought the world Christian rock virtually cornered the Egyptian Arabian breeding business. By 1985 there were still only twenty-five hundred Egyptian Arabians on earth; but a thousand were at Bentwood Farms, and half of those belonged to the McCrackens.

To develop beautiful, rounded muscles, the horses worked out in their own swimming pool behind the brick stallion barn, where the offices were furnished with Oriental rugs, polished oak, and flowered chintz. Ill or expectant Egyptian Arabians received the care of a full-time veterinarian at a special hospital barn with ten air-conditioned stalls. When the horses traveled, it was in a custom-designed hundred-thousand-dollar van.

At an average Bentwood sale the low-selling mare went for $125,000, the high seller for $400,000, sometimes as much as a million. Oilmen, medical specialists, real estate moguls, and professional athletes were shelling out this kind of money for horses that would never win the Triple Crown or the Silver and Gold cutting horse championship. There was some Arabian racing, but it was a small part of the Arabian scene and not very lucrative. They were paying for spirit and aesthetics, for those qualities that Jarrell McCracken could make sound as real and thrilling as he could make an imaginary football game between good and evil.

"A horse with great spirit, with its eyes flashing, its nostrils flaring, its tail up is a very exciting manifestation of something pretty magnificent," he said.

But people also bought Egyptian Arabians with the expectation that there would always be a fresh supply of newly rich buyers anteing up. And as oil collapsed and real estate and banking followed, prices for Egyptian Arabians plummeted 60 percent and more. In 1986 Bentwood had twelve hundred horses, half of which it owned. By 1988 it was down to nine hundred, and Jarrell McCracken, who had carried the notes on many of Bentwood's sales and whose charismatic personality and instinct for promotion had boosted the breed's popularity, found himself holding paper on horses worth less than two thirds of what he'd sold them for. Bentwood Farms filed for Chapter 11.

"If it doesn't work out, I still feel good about what I've accomplished," Jarrell McCracken said in early 1988. "I don't measure myself in dollars."

Even as he struggled to keep Bentwood Farms afloat, McCracken was launching a new venture, another Christian record company, this time devoted to traditional church music. "I am convinced that it's time to get back to the good, beautiful music, the great hymns and spirituals," he said.

★

CHAPTER FOURTEEN

Fort Worth

Where the West Still Begins

Oilman Bill Davis and his wife, Mitzi, raised miniature horses behind their rambling Tudor house across the street from Fort Worth's River Crest Country Club golf course, the premier residential area in this city of 450,000. But no one in their elegant neighborhood blinked an eye. Next door Edward and Elise Hay kept longhorn cattle in *their* yard. Nearby a camel once featured in the Neiman Marcus Christmas catalog grazed on Erma Lowe's lawn. Still another neighbor, Billy Gordon, raised African deer. "You couldn't do that in Dallas," Mitzi Davis observed.

Joined to Dallas by an umbilical cord of freeways and a sprawl of faceless suburbs, Fort Worth lay just thirty miles to the west. It may have been the longest thirty miles in the United States. West of the band of hardwood forest that divided this distance sprawled rolling ranchland broken by limestone outcroppings. East of it, flat farmland fell away.

Fort Worth was higher and drier than its sister city, with shorter trees and longer vistas. But the difference was more than geographic. Most of Fort Worth's family fortunes were grounded in cattle and oil; many of Dallas's were founded on real estate, banking, and merchandising. And with twice the population, Dallas radiated gloss and glitter, the excitement and confusion of new money.

"Dallas is so busy being sophisticated that they don't have any fun," said former Fort Worth City Councilwoman Shirley Johnson. "They have to bring visitors over here so they know they've been to Texas."

The late Amon Carter, Sr., put it another way: "Fort Worth is where the West begins. Dallas is where the East peters out." As publisher of the *Fort Worth Star-Telegram* from the 1920's until his death in 1955, Carter constituted a one-man establishment. He poured the money and influence his paper generated into promoting his city. The late Vice President John Nance Garner, a fellow Texan, once accused the powerful newspaperman of wanting the federal government run "to the exclusive benefit of Fort Worth and, if possible, to the detriment of Dallas." On those rare occasions when business forced him to visit his city's rival, Carter carried his lunch in a brown paper bag to avoid patronizing a Dallas restaurant.

When Dallas won the privilege of hosting the official Texas Centennial celebration in 1936, Carter countered with an alternative bash. Building a theater called Casa Mañana, he hired ace Broadway producer Billy Rose at a thousand dollars a day to stage a Texas-scale extravaganza and erected a 130-foot-long billboard at the entrance to the Dallas fairgrounds declaring "Forty-Five Minutes West to Whoopee."

The Fort Worth-Dallas rivalry began during the California gold rush. Fort Worth, established in 1849 as a military camp to protect prospectors headed west, was evolving into a full-fledged town. So was Dallas, launched eight years earlier as a remote trading post.

"When wagon trains rumbled through on the western track, Dallas men would stop them with lurid tales of danger to the west," said former House Speaker Jim Wright, a Fort Worth Democrat. "Picking up the challenge, the Fort Worth

settlement sent riders to intercept the wagons east of Dallas
and escort them to Fort Worth."

On a map Fort Worth appeared to be set in the middle
of the United States, but even in the late 1980's its western
flavor salted every aspect of local life. For example, the Reverend Gayland Pool, rector of St. Luke's in the Meadow
Episcopal Church, belonged to "a quiet little interdenomi-
national gathering" called the Cattle Country Clerics.

Generations of wealthy ranchers had described their
sprawling spreads by their distance north or west of Fort
Worth. This was the city where families whose acreage measured in the hundreds of thousands bought their lizard boots
and Resistol cowboy hats and sent their children for a little
Texas-style urban polish. Even if the ranch was up on the
Red River a hundred miles away, there was a house in town.

Along with its resident ranchers, Fort Worth also had a
western love of horses. The seven surrounding counties had
the highest per capita population of horses of any region in
the United States. Local equestrian passion leaned toward
cutting horses and rodeos. Since 1987 the annual Southwestern Exposition and Fat Stock Show had been the city's
top civic event. Fort Worth schools declared the first Stock
Show Friday a holiday so that children could watch community leaders ride down Main Street on silver-studded saddles during the opening parade. Rodeos had as much cachet
here as regattas did in Newport.

In the heart of Fort Worth's central business district,
Richard Haas's trompe l'oeil mural of cowboys herding long-
horns evoked the 1870's, when the Chisholm Trail ran down
Main Street. West of downtown, the Butterfield Overland
Mail Route—now brick-topped Camp Bowie Boulevard—cut
past the city's four museums a few blocks from the oak-
shaded mansions of River Crest. North of downtown lay the
Stockyards, once the capital of the Texas cattle industry.
Thanks to eight million dollars in federal grants and more
than twenty-five million in private funds, they'd become a
National Historic District and tourist mecca.

The Stockyards district grew up after 1876, when the
railroad replaced the long cattle drive north to Kansas. This
was where General Black Jack Pershing traded for mules and

horses and Buffalo Bill Cody took his ease at the White Elephant Saloon. Around the turn of the century both Swift and Armour established huge packing plants here, and Fort Worth—along with Chicago and Omaha—became one of the country's three major beef-distributing centers.

When the packing industry decentralized during the 1950's, Swift and Armour closed their local plants, but the area's quaint nineteenth-century buildings survived. Because Fort Worth remained the headquarters for the regional cattle business, the brick barns still housed cattle and horses, and real cowboys moseyed along the covered wooden sidewalks.

When those real cowboys got thirsty, they had to compete with crowds of European tourists and Dallasites in Neiman Marcus western chic. Trend-spotting *Esquire* magazine dubbed the once-humble White Elephant Saloon one of the nation's hundred best bars. And the Stockyards Hotel looked downright elegant done up in "cowboy baroque"—pressed tin ceilings and chairs upholstered in unshaved cowhide.

There were more elephants in Republican National Committeewoman Fran Chiles's office than there were in the Fort Worth Zoo. Maybe more than in all Texas zoos combined. Elephant pictures, elephant statuettes, elephant wall hangings. For an interview for a *Town & Country* story on Fort Worth, Mrs. Chiles wore a elephant ring and a wide belt adorned with a big gold and silver elephant. She was a tall, slender brunette, attractive in a no-nonsense way.

Before marrying Fort Worth oilman H. E. "Eddie" Chiles in 1973, "I spent twenty years in food service, and that prepared me for politics," she declared, referring to her stint as food and beverage manager for the Houston Club, the most democratic (with a small *d*) of Houston's private downtown watering holes. Her book *Parties, Parties* was a guide to entertaining, not a work of political analysis.

"I think it's great that she's in politics," said Eddie Chiles, a compact, weathered man a good twenty years her senior. "If we don't get into politics, we're going to have to suffer with the kind of government we get, and it'll probably be one we don't like."

In fact, most recent governments, particularly recent

Democratic Congresses, had been ones far-right Eddie Chiles didn't like.

By the time the Texas oil boom of the 1970's started, Chiles, a University of Oklahoma engineer, had already made several fortunes in oil field services. The Western Company, which he founded in 1939, began as a one-truck operation feeding hydrochloric acid down wells to milk the most possible oil from the rock. By 1948 Western had stimulated forty-five hundred oil wells, some of them as deep as twenty thousand feet, and had added pressurized water and live steam to its methods for coaxing petroleum from recalcitrant formations. Once Western worked its magic, a well bringing up ten barrels a day might bring up seventy or eighty. When there was a lot of drilling going on, it was an enormously profitable business. By 1967 Western was supplying custom-blended cement to secure drilling pipe in deep boreholes and had even bought itself some offshore drilling rigs.

One day in 1977 Fran Chiles and Bill Finn, Western's advertising man, were listening to Chiles work himself into a lather about Big Government—environmental controls, employment guidelines, rules for old oil, rules for new, and general meddling in the marketplace.

"He was very, very upset about the increasing control of government over free enterprise," Mrs. Chiles recounted later. "Eddie was ranting about the number of lawyers and CPAs he had to keep hiring to keep him in compliance with regulations."

Finn suggested that if Chiles was all that mad about it, he should go on the radio and say so.

"I really *was* mad because of the ultraliberal activities of the leading politicians of that day," Chiles admitted. "I saw our nation going toward socialism at an ever-increasing rate of speed. Our Founding Fathers intended our government to be capitalistic. The free-enterprise system will cease to exist when the government gets so large."

Eddie Chiles wasn't much of a cinema buff, but he'd heard about the scene in the 1976 movie *Network* where Howard Beale, the Mad Prophet of the Airwaves, played by Peter Finch, urged the American people, first from the television studio and then from a rooftop, to get up out of their chairs

and say, "I'm mad as hell, and I'm not going to take it anymore."

"I didn't find a rooftop," Chiles explained, "but I did
buy some airtime."

He began on West Texas radio, announcing that he was
mad about this and mad about that. "It's time to build a fence
between the hog and the trough," he liked to thunder against
Congress. His vituperative editorials prompted droves of his
fellow Cowboy Capitalists to switch their well service contracts to Western. His diatribes brought in so much business
that in 1982 he broadcast them on eight hundred stations in
fourteen states and Washington, D.C. And anyone who
called or wrote in received Western's companion pieces: one
bumper sticker declaring "I'M MAD, TOO, EDDIE" and another that said "I LOVE AMERICA." They were available in
English, Spanish, and French, for oil-rich Cajun South Louisiana. By 1984 seven hundred thousand "I'M MAD, TOO,
EDDIE" bumper stickers adorned the backs of pickup trucks
from Nome to Lake Charles.

To educate the public on the importance of the petroleum industry and to persuade American voters that oilmen
had been able to do just fine without government restrictions,
in 1978 Eddie Chiles hired historian Francis Munch to design
the Western Company Museum. Chiles gave Dr. Munch ten
thousand square feet of space in his corporate headquarters
and an unlimited budget. For an exhibit that had a definite
bias, the museum was surprisingly interesting and infor-
mative. The mixed-media graphic displays, which began
with the creation of the universe twenty billion years ago,
were varied and visually sophisticated. However, the full-
scale dioramas took the prize. Here, standing on old rigs,
talking mannequins recounted typical hardships and adventures of different periods in the history of the Oil Patch. Their
bodies were stiff, yet their faces were uncannily mobile, made
of flexible plastic shaped by molds taken from the heads of
the actors who recorded the lines. For six and a half years
droves of tourists marveled at the eerie effect. But in 1985,
as the oil bust deepened and the Western Company began
to crumble, Eddie Chiles mothballed his monument to free
enterprise.

At the peak of his prosperity Chiles funneled most of

his largess to conservative political and religious causes, but he did make a major civic contribution to Fort Worth in 1980. He bought the Texas Rangers and kept them from becoming a Dallas team. At the time Chiles made the purchase, Dallas was openly discussing building a downtown ballpark.

In early 1987 the Western Company pleaded guilty to seven counts of deceptive trade practices, all Class A misdemeanors, and acknowledged twelve similar incidents as part of a plea bargain for selling Mobil, Shell, Quintana Petroleum, and several smaller oil exploration companies drilling cement left over from other jobs, passing it off as custom-mixed for the task at hand. To be effective, the cement used to hold pipe in a borehole had to be blended with chemicals according to the specific rock and soil conditions found on that site. Because the cement also kept the oil and natural gas being pumped out from contaminating the reservoirs of groundwater it encountered along the way, the wrong cement could cause problems for the environment as well as for the drilling company.

The state district court in Victoria slapped Western with a thirty-thousand-dollar fine. This time Chiles's fellow oilmen weren't about to raise "I'M MAD, TOO, EDDIE" banners. But many seemed more saddened than outraged. Whatever they may have thought of Chiles's Texas Gothic style, they were quick to point out that the Western Company had operated for more than forty-five years with a reputation for honesty and sound management. To them, the sale of off-grade cement in 1985 and 1986 wasn't part of a long-term pattern; it was the regrettable corner cutting of a company desperate to stay afloat.

On April 25, 1986, Western defaulted on four hundred million dollars in loans, saying it couldn't pay either the principal or the interest. The company's net worth had dropped below three hundred million, and it was losing money at the rate of thirty-three million dollars a quarter. By the start of 1988 its unsecured debts had swelled to seven hundred million. On February 2, 1988, Western filed for Chapter 11 bankruptcy protection.

In terms of dollars involved, the Western Company bankruptcy was second only to the collapse of the Hunt family's Placid Oil.

* * *

Long before Eddie Chiles's day a Dallas newspaper columnist once sneered that so little happened in Fort Worth
that a panther could sleep unmolested in the street. By the
late 1980's, despite the distress of the Western Company and
other Oil Patch businesses, that panther would have been
busy dodging commuter traffic. Bell/Textron, the largest helicopter manufacturer in the free world, had its headquarters
here. So did Radio Shack's parent, the Tandy Corporation,
which was born in Fort Worth as a leather company.

Returning from World War II, Charles Tandy, the son
of the founder, had a brainstorm: producing leathercraft kits
for veterans' rehabilitation programs. Before long the company spawned and acquired other hobby businesses, including Radio Shack. In 1989 that one division boasted more
than nine thousand stores nationwide. It sold more telephones than anyone but AT&T. Tandy also manufactured
one of the country's most popular desktop computers, the
Tandy 1000.

Tandy's Fort Worth headquarters were a gadgeteer's
dream. It had the world's only privately owned subway,
which ran from the employee parking lot to the twin office
towers. Clear glass elevators and escalators revealed the
gears and pulleys. The corporate chairman, John Roach,
who'd convinced Charles Tandy to manufacture personal
computers, used a button under his desk to control the
drapes that shielded his corner office from the sun. Another
button allowed him to cut off the entrance to his high tech
lair by moving a wall.

Tandy's company was a model of corporate citizenship.
Lights arranged vertically on the sides of the twin Tandy
Towers trumpeted civic causes, from the United Way to the
Stock Show. And the Tandy Scholars program honored the
top 3 or 4 percent of the city's students in grades eight
through twelve with an annual steak dinner, at which John
Roach personally awarded two-thousand-dollar stipends to
the best math and science teachers at each of the city's high
schools.

Despite the historic rivalry, some of the biggest money
in Dallas invested in the Panther City. One major player was

computer services pioneer H. Ross Perot, who sold his Electronic Data Systems to General Motors in 1985 for $2.5 billion; he and his family owned ten thousand acres of real estate north of Fort Worth along one of the prime growth corridors. Nearby, Ray Hunt, the financially healthy scion of legendary wildcatter H. L. Hunt's Second Family, developed a 1,250-acre mixed-use project called Fossil Creek.

Just as Dallas money was coming to Fort Worth, Fort Worth business was reaching toward Dallas—literally. From 1975 on the major corridor of growth had been toward the Dallas/Fort Worth Regional Airport, the nation's largest in area. Every day 1,440 flights took off and landed there, and every year 32.3 million passengers passed through. "People in both cities refer to the regional airport as the equivalent of a deep-sea port," said Robert Crandall, chairman and chief executive of American Airlines. In 1979 American, the nation's third-largest carrier, further boosted the local economy by transferring its corporate headquarters from New York to Fort Worth. "It's easier to run a national and international airline like ours from the center of the country, rather than either coast," Crandall explained. "With any of our domestic cities, I can go there and get back the same day."

To the city's upper crust, the giant airport was a two-way pipeline to the world. "In twenty-five minutes we're at D/FW; then, in eight hours, we're in Paris," said Fort Worth artist James R. Blake. "You can get a cold, wet fish from just about anywhere now. And that's important."

One manifestation of Fort Worth's westernness was the extent to which its public amenities reflected individual vision. The city had 114 foundations with total assets exceeding a billion dollars—remarkable for an easygoing community of fewer than half a million people. In Fort Worth the rich traditionally had done what they thought needed doing without waiting for a mandate or support for their projects. And an astonishing number of Fort Worth's elite had the means to transform their civic visions into reality by signing a single check.

That signal sense of headstrong noblesse oblige gave Fort Worth two of its three art museums. Both had international reputations. The Kimbell, designed by Louis Kahn, and the Amon Carter, designed by Philip Johnson, faced each other across a terraced lawn west of downtown. The former stuck to non-U.S. art produced before 1900. The latter collected only American art related to westward expansion, but in quality and scope it went far beyond cowboy art. Except for its photography collection—one of the largest in the country—everything in the Carter was produced before 1940. Across the street the Fort Worth Art Museum restricted itself to the twentieth century. Combined, the three institutions constituted the finest visual arts complex in the state—much to the annoyance of Dallas.

The Carter and the Kimbell received all operating and acquisition costs from their foundations. The sole function of the two-hundred-million-dollar Kimbell Foundation, established by Fort Worth grain tycoon Kay Kimbell, was collecting and exhibiting art. Its annual acquisitions budget was more than seven million dollars—twice that of the National Gallery or the Metropolitan Museum of Art and second only to the Getty, which spent about a hundred million a year. When the museum paid six million dollars for Velázquez's "Don Pedro de Barberana" in 1981, it was hard to tell whether the acquisition itself or the resulting page one story in *The New York Times* was a greater source of civic pride.

The Carter grew out of a desire among the heirs of newspaperman Amon Carter to establish a fitting monument to Fort Worth's greatest booster. "When he died in 1955, we would not allow anybody to raise money to build a statue downtown or any of that foolishness," declared his daughter Ruth Carter Stevenson, chairman of the board of the $120 million Carter Foundation. A museum also solved the problem of what to do with the 350 Charles Russell and fifty Frederic Remington nineteenth- and early-twentieth-century oils and bronzes Carter had collected during the 1940's. Rather than build on the collection with the works of recent Carter and Russell imitators, the family added works by American painters as divergent as Winslow Homer, Grant Wood, and Georgia O'Keeffe, broadening its interpretation of "art dealing with westward expansion" to begin with the crossing of the Hudson River.

In 1985 the Carter unveiled Richard Avedon's dramatic "In the American West," which it had commissioned. The large-format black-and-white photo portraits shot outdoors against white paper took Avedon six years to complete. Far from romanticizing the West, some of the images of drifters and waitresses and oil field workers were grotesque, others poignant. Most were deeply disturbing yet very powerful. They reflected an unflinching, idiosyncratic vision on the part of both the artist and his patron. It would have been a daring exhibit for any art museum, even one in New York or Los Angeles.

The woman behind the Amon Carter Museum and the Amon Carter Foundation seemed jus as strong-willed as her father had been. Ruth Carter Stevenson had curly gray hair, bright Alice-blue eyes, and a direct yet patrician manner. She divided her time between Fort Worth and New York, where her husband, John R. Stevenson, president of the National Gallery in Washington, had his law practice.

Back during the early 1940's, when Ruth Carter was a student at Sarah Lawrence, she invited one of her roommates home for vacation. The Yankee girl's father forbade her to go. He thought Fort Worth was unsafe, full of gun-toting outlaws or maybe even renegade Comanches. " 'Texas' was an ugly word to easterners," Mrs. Stevenson said.

Amon Carter had sent his daughter East to school in hopes she would, as she explained, "go up there and see what the rest of the world is like but keep her Texas roots." She did, and she came back in 1949 with a well-developed taste for art, one quite different from her father's. Carter had strong opinions on the subject. Art ought to be representational, it shouldn't be too bloodthirsty, and it shouldn't promote bad social values. He once turned down an opportunity to buy a fine Frederic Remington bronze at a good price because the statue depicted polo ponies. He considered polo an effete sport.

Shortly after she graduated from college, Ruth Carter made her first major purchase. "In Chicago I went to the Art Institute and saw the Impressionist pictures, so I decided I wanted an Impressionist picture," she said matter-of-factly. She couldn't afford the Cézanne landscape she liked best (it's now in the National Gallery), so she bought a small Van Gogh, "Peasant Shouldering a Spade," on installment. When she showed her new acquisition to her father, his reaction was: "What in the name of God is *that*?" She replied: "The difference between your taste and mine."

As her taste and wealth grew, so did her confidence. "I had an eye, genetically perhaps," she said. "It took me a long time to trust it. Collecting is a *very serious* responsibility. I look back at Mr. Meadows and other people who've learned hard lessons," she added, referring to the Dallas oilman who unknowingly spent thirty-five million dollars on fakes by Elmyr de Hory, the late king of art forgers.

Thanks to Mrs. Stevenson's self-assured taste, Fort Worth had one of the most magnetic public spaces in the country, the Water Gardens. This square-block sculpture on the south edge of downtown lacked benches, grass, and many of the other amenities of city parks, yet it always drew visitors. In one corner a torrent tumbled down a steep cascade. In another a tranquil reflecting pool mirrored the sky. Along one side water slid serenely down a granite wall. Elsewhere a field of fountains blossomed into the air like giant Shasta daisies. During the long, hot, dry summers it was a true oasis.

The project began in the early 1970's when the heiress decided to do something personally about urban decay. "Downtown Fort Worth was a pretty crummy-looking place, especially that part of downtown," she later explained. So she called up New York architectural guru Philip Johnson, who'd designed the Carter Museum, and asked him what could be done in the way of a city park. After a couple of tries Johnson presented a plan she and her late brother, Amon Carter, Jr., liked. The two bought the property, bankrolled the work, and donated the finished project to the city in 1974.

No city council, no parks department committee could have come up with a space that better embodied two essential elements behind Fort Worth's western nature: individualism and the importance of water. At this point where the High Plains began their long, uneven amble toward the Rocky Mountains, water became scarce and precious and, therefore,

all the more beautiful and fascinating. Eastern, southern, and
midwestern cities had fountains. But they didn't have tem-
ples to water.

It took a singular vision to recognize that.

Retired oil and gas attorney Elton Hyder and his wife,
Martha, demonstrated further the paradoxical principle that
among the Fort Worth rich, eccentric individuality was the
best way to fit in. The Hyders' sprawling 1915-vintage Italianate villa easily, and often, accommodated 75 for a seated
lunch or 450 for a buffet. At some parties the guests congre-
gated on the huge columned stoa, two stories high and furnished like a living room but open on two sides to the
elements and to a sweeping view of the Trinity River valley;
at others, they moved indoors and were surrounded by a
wildly eclectic collection of art and oddments. The place had
the air of an English country house, filled with generations
of possessions bundled home by officers serving the empire
in exotic climes, but everything here was acquired in the last
forty years.

Martha Hyder's scores of Russian icons gazed beatifically
down from the antiqued chartreuse walls. Centuries-old tap-
estries draped the dining room, and medieval reliquaries
lurked on occasional tables. Pillows covered in mirrored fab-
ric glinted from sofas. Stuffed pheasants and quail, looking
freshly shot, hung upside down above a counter in the
kitchen; a heart-shaped white wooden plaque on the wall
declared: "Money isn't everything, but it sure keeps you in
touch with your children."

Elton Hyder's tastes were even more unusual: a ram's
head fashioned into a snuffbox for a British officers' mess,
numerous small cannons, and several polished human
skulls. One skull—that of an unfortunate British soldier—
had a spider web etched into the top by the Japanese in
Burma during World War II. Decorating Hyder's desk were
ten antique pistols, all pointed toward him as if to demonstrate perfect trust in his visitors. Antique guns and cannons
"keep people's tempers down," he explained, adding with
a chuckle, "I'd collect women if Martha would let me."

Before he retired in 1965 at forty-five, Elton Hyder had

a spectacular law career. At twenty-four he became the youngest attorney general in the history of Texas. A year and a half later the U.S. attorney general appointed him to prosecute defeated Japanese Admiral Hideki Tojo for war crimes. Hyder went on to become the oil and gas lawyer for Sid Richardson and other legendary wildcatters a generation his senior. Often he took a percentage of the action in lieu of an hourly fee. When his clients drilled dry holes, he went unpaid, but when they hit gushers, he raked in a fortune.

Using the profits from his lucrative practice, Hyder began collecting legal and patriotic memorabilia in 1949—everything from medieval and Renaissance courtroom furnishings to ancient deeds and writs to World War I posters. In 1984 Martha Hyder used the collection to redecorate the University of Texas Law School Library in Austin—a $1.5 million gift.

With his tall, military posture, elegant silver hair, and rakish grin, Elton Hyder was an accomplished flirt. After noticing Sotheby's executive Lee Thaw at a party, he told *The New York Times*'s Charlotte Curtis, "She's fabulous. She once smiled across a dinner table and three men left their wives."

If Elton Hyder seemed a tad awed by women, it might have been because of *his* wife. Blond and striking, with a square, determined jaw, Martha Hyder was a next-to-unstoppable organizer, fund raiser, and promoter of causes. Her most notable success was the Van Cliburn Piano Competition, which put Fort Worth on the worldwide cultural map. In international reputation it ranked second only to Moscow's Tchaikovsky Piano Competition.

No other event created more excitement among Fort Worth's social set, and the fact that it was held every four years only added to the interest. The Van Cliburn combined the thrill of great music with the exhilaration of spectator sports.

"There are all these kids from all over the world—from Russia and China and Texas—and you get caught up in what they're doing," said artist James R. Blake, whose wife sat on the Van Cliburn board. "There are always too many parties—parties for the judges, parties for the contestants.

But in the end there's this thing about talent that's the whole motivation. Everybody loves to be in on the ground floor of a talent."

The Van Cliburn began in the early 1960's, after the Texas pianist won the 1958 Tchaikovsky Competition. The late Dr. Irl Allison, a Fort Worth music teacher, offered ten thousand dollars to the winner of a contest set up in Cliburn's honor, and Martha Hyder gathered the money and organization needed to stage the event.

In 1986 Fort Worth got Van Cliburn himself. Born in Kilgore—a Deep East Texas town known largely for its girls' high school drill team, the Rangerettes—Cliburn made enough on his concert tours to buy the huge red-brick Kimbell mansion. He moved in with seven Steinway grand pianos and declared Fort Worth his residence.

Though it was three hundred miles from the nearest large body of water, Fort Worth had a yacht club. And sailing under a Texas-style burgee—an oversize pennant emblazoned with the head of a longhorn—the Fort Worth Boat Club managed to draw top sailors to man-made Eagle Mountain Lake. Sir James Hardy, who skippered the Australian entry in three America's Cups, was a member. So were Ted Turner, John Kolius, and Indianapolis 500 champion Johnny Rutherford, a Fort Worth native. Oilman Perry Bass, navigator for Ted Turner when he won the World Open Racing Championship, learned to sail here.

In fact, Fort Worth was sports-crazy—not just the spectator sports so dear to all Texans, but participatory sports. Home to golf greats Byron Nelson and Ben Hogan, the city boasted twenty public and private golf courses. Serious golfers joined the Shady Oaks or Colonial country clubs, site of the annual Colonial National Invitational Golf Tournament. Serious tennis players gravitated to Shady Oaks, where they saw fellow Fort Worther Martina Navratilova on the courts.

Socially River Crest was Fort Worth's top club. It also was the cause of one of the city's hottest disputes. In 1980 the stately sixty-six-year-old white-pillared clubhouse burned down. The building committee replaced it with a red-brick postmodern masterpiece by Taft Architects—John Casbarian, Danny Samuels, and Robert Timme, three Philip Johnson protégés from Houston.

"It was a federal case, World War Three. There wouldn't have been more outcry if you'd put public housing in the middle of the block," said River Crest member Byron Searcy.

"It was Fort Worth at its worst," added Searcy's wife, Lynn, former president of the Junior League. "People were saying, 'You will *not* touch that tree. I got my first kiss under that tree.' People were calling the board members all kinds of names."

One of those beleaguered board members was Dick Moncrief, who served on the River Crest building committee. He liked the new clubhouse but understood the dynamics fueling the flap. "The old clubhouse was the center of social life, literally," he said. "*All* the women in a certain social stratum had their wedding receptions there, so a lot of the people who grew up here remembered catching the bouquet thrown from the top of that old-fashioned stairway."

River Crest might have been the club to belong to, but Ridglea Country Club was the one favored for debuts. The unimaginative fifties-modern architecture of its clubhouse was unlikely to rouse anyone's protective sentiments, but along with the bland, institutional air went lots of open space just waiting to be transformed by Daddy's money. The first big Ridglea coming-out party was the all-night dance in the 1950's that the late Anne Burnett Tandy—heiress to the five-hundred-thousand acre Four 6's Ranch—gave for her daughter, now Anne Burnett Marion. Louis Armstrong provided the music, and a full-scale fireworks display marked the stroke of midnight. The William Youngs went Mrs. Tandy one better in 1983. To present their daughters, Marjorie and Kelly, they adopted a Route 66 theme. Each of six rooms in the Ridglea clubhouse represented the food and music of a different city between Chicago and Los Angeles: six cities; six lavish spreads; six live bands.

But some of Fort Worth's most inventive parties were given right at home. That's where Coca-Cola heiress Gloria Lupton Tennyson threw her huge dinner for local artist Scott Gentling, who with his brother Stuart painted Audubon-style pictures of Texas birds *in situ*. Mrs. Tennyson staged the banquet in honor of Scott's first set of bird paintings. The main course was wild dove. Because doves were out of season in Texas, she and her husband, Harry, flew down to Mexico and shot the birds themselves.

Though dispatching wild birds by the score may seem an odd way to toast art celebrating them, it apparently didn't to the Tennysons. This, after all, was Fort Worth, stronghold of individualism.

Midland oilman/rancher/long-distance tycoon Claytie Williams in his trophy-packed office at the ClayDesta National Bank. (*Barbara Laing/Black Star*)

Baron Enrique di Portanova's title was Italian, but his fortune was Texan as was his wife, Baroness Sandra di Portanova, the former Sandy "Buckets" Hovas. (*Janice Rubin*)

Houston's Carolyn Farb raised over a million dollars at one charity gala, but she was best known for her twenty-million-dollar divorce. (*Phyllis Hand*)

Harold Farb made his hundreds of millions building Houston apartments, then erected his own supper club, where he starred. (*Richard Carson*)

A cross between Scarlett and Zsa-Zsa, hostess and Honorary Consul Joanne Johnson King Herring Davis turned heads from Houston to Abu Dhabi. (*Phyllis Hand*)

Heiress Josephine Abercrombie, America's only female boxing impresario, gave her fighters (here, left to right, Olympic gold medalist Frank Tate, David Gauvin, and Hector Camacho) social polish. (*Ben DeSoto*/Houston Chronicle)

Faced with hard times, the King Ranch put the corporate reins in the hands of outsider Darwin Smith (left) instead of family scion Tio Kleberg (right). (*Will Van Overbeek*)

To keep the YO Ranch in the family, Charles Schreiner III not only bred his own strain of Texas Longhorns but raised exotic animals. (*Hal Swigett/YO Ranch*)

Foreman of his family's Kokernot 06 Ranch—the most scenic of Texas's big spreads—Chris Lacy, seen here with his wife, Diane, and their children, ranched much the way his great-grandparents had. (*Will Van Overbeek/ Ultra*)

After his dreams of becoming Big Rich vanished, John Connally and his wife, Nellie, took a last look at many of their possessions before his bankruptcy auction. (*Phyllis Hand*)

Stanley Marcus, shown here in front of a museum mockup of his family's original store, brought drop-dead chic to Texas. (*Janice Rubin*)

H. R. "Bum" Bright, onetime owner of the Dallas Cowboys, never lost his childhood fondness for the Arthurian legends, depicted in the custom-woven tapestry behind him. (*Phil Huber/Black Star*)

Caroline Hunt, daughter of legendary wildcatter H. L. Hunt, enjoyed high tea at one of her lavish hotels, Dallas's Mansion on Turtle Creek. (*Will Van Overbeek*)

As 1987 ended, the once-awesome fortunes of Hunt First Family brothers (left to right) William Herbert, Nelson Bunker, and Lamar were mired in bankruptcies. (*Phil Huber/Black Star*)

A wealth of Wynnes—(left to right) brothers Angus III and Shannon Wynne; Jimmy Harrison and his wife, Punkin; and Jacque Wynne and her husband, the late Toddie Lee Wynne, Jr.—assembled in Toddie Lee's trophy room. (*Shelly Katz Photo*)

With the inspirational talents of a TV evangelist, cosmetics queen Mary Kay Ash (shown here in one of the many baths of her all-pink Dallas mansion) launched legions of saleswomen. (© *1989 Danny Turner, for* Texas Monthly)

Ex-seminarian Jarrel McCracken's Word Publishing brought religious rock to the airwaves and Billy Graham to the bookstores with a record-breaking first printing of 800,000. (*Shelly Katz Photo*)

With her multimillion-dollar divorce pending, Priscilla Davis attended Fort Worth's Colonial Golf Tournament with her lover, Stan Farr. (*Gene Gordon/* Fort Worth Star-Telegram)

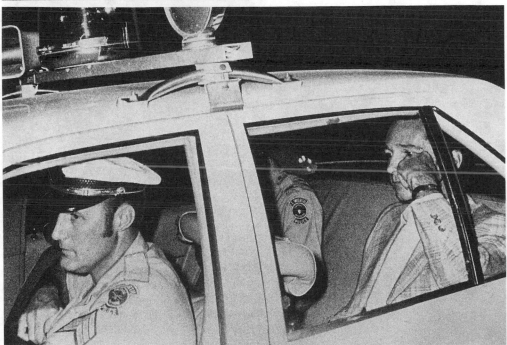

Fort Worth oilman T. Cullen Davis was the richest man ever tried for murder in America. (*Gene Gordon/*Fort Worth Star-Telegram)

In the midst of epic divorce negotia-tions, "Big Anne" Bass appeared alone but festive at the New York wedding of Laura Steinberg and Jonathan Tisch. (*Ron Galella*)

Above, the romance between Fort Worth billionaire Sid Bass and Iranian-born socialite Mercedes Kellogg (shown here leaving Bianca Jagger's birthday party) broke up one of Texas's biggest fortunes. (*Ron Galella*)

Left, Robert Bass and his wife, "Little Anne," his childhood sweetheart, leaving the wedding of older brother Sid to Mercedes Kellogg at New York's Plaza Hotel. (*Ron Galella*)

Rancher and sculptor Electra Waggoner Biggs was the toast of New York in the days when her portrait was painted. (*Will Van Overbeek*/Ultra)

Undaunted by three failed searches for the *Titanic*, Abilene oilman/adventurer Jack Grimm readied himself for finding Atlantis and engraving his mesa with a monument to the buffalo. (*Pam Francis*)

Amarillo broadcasting tycoon Stanley Marsh 3 did a rope trick in front of "Cadillac Ranch," his most famous work of ambush art. (*Wyatt McSpadden*)

No other individual gave more to New York's Metropolitan Opera than Amarillo oil heiress Sybil Harrington, shown here in her backyard with the Harrington String Quartet. (*John Bryson*/Town & Country)

Amarillo corporate raider T. Boone Pickens (left) and his lieutenant David Batchelder were frequently up at dawn plotting takeover strategies. (*Shelly Katz/Black Star*)

Late master cattle-breeder Henry Clay Koontz and his wife, Mary Sue, celebrated the hundredth anniversary of his family's HK ranch with their prize Bralers, a breed he originated. (*Lee Tilley*)

A descendant of the Canary Islanders who settled San Antonio, Walter Mathis, shown here at eighteenth-century Mission San Jose, became a major figure in the city's restoration movement. (*Will Van Overbeek*/Ultra)

Galveston-born oilman George Mitchell resurrected the island's Mardi Gras and the Knights of Momus, whose emblem he wore prominently at the krewe's annual ball where Cynthia Mitchell dropped her mask to join her husband *cognito*. (*Phyllis Hand*)

Austin techno-brat Michael Dell quit the University of Texas after his freshman year to found Dell Computer; by the time he was twenty-three his net worth was $125 million. (*Will Van Overbeek*)

Compaq Computer CEO Rod Canion sped his high-performance personal computer company to the ranks of the *Fortune* 500 faster than any other corporation in history. (*Janice Rubin*)

For billionaire Dallas computer services magnate H. Ross Perot, patriotic symbols—like the Gilbert Stuart behind his desk—were important, but so was personal involvement. (*Phil Huber/Black Star*)

★

CHAPTER FIFTEEN

T. Cullen Davis

Murder and Millions

With its high-pitched roof and leaded-glass windows, Nonesuch House, where Bill and Mitzi Davis lived and raised their miniature horses, exuded an atmosphere of antic whimsy. To gain entrance, one talked to the left of the pair of huge black lions flanking the gate, and the lion replied, thanks to the microphone and speaker hidden behind its fangs. Inside the fence a dozen or so bronze statues of slender youths or perhaps pixies, vaguely reminiscent of Maxfield Parrish, lounged about on the grass. On winter days Mitzi Davis decked them out in bright knit caps and mufflers. Inside, white marble busts on rosy brown marble pedestals gave a neoclassical fillip to the Regency decor.

Partly because of their taste and wit, the Davises were a very popular couple. But it hadn't hurt their social stock that even by Fort Worth standards, they'd been stunningly generous to local causes. Mitzi Davis's Mercedes sported a

license plate that read "STRAD 1" in honor of the Stradi-
varius she and her husband bought and put on permanent
loan to the Fort Worth Symphony. When Mark White, governor of Texas from 1983 to 1987, appointed fellow Democrat
Mrs. Davis to the Texas Arts Commission, she rolled up her
sleeves, went down to Austin, and set to work at her own
expense as a lobbyist for the arts. When the Fort Worth
Museum of Science and History decided that it needed something to attract paying patrons, Bill and Mitzi Davis anted
up $2.5 million toward an $8.5 million Omni Theater—a futuristic projection room where a 180-degree concave screen
drew viewers into three-dimensional documentaries on the
birth of the universe and the subtleties of plate tectonics.

Bill Davis was matter-of-fact about his philanthropies.
"The museum," he said, "was too dependent on an irregular
source of income. It needed something that was both educational and entertaining." Likewise, of the priceless violin
in the hands of the concertmaster: "The presence of a really
fine instrument was necessary to inspire the other players."

Davis obviously loved his city and appreciated its quirky
charms. He cited its old cemeteries, filled with pioneers,
cowboys, and notorious outlaws, as among its most under-
rated attractions. "We don't see fifty-story buildings as the
only road to progress," he declared. "We've had a lot of
people tell us we're not progressive because we're not plas-
tered over. I don't think progress is how much longer it takes
you to get to work this year than it did last year."

Despite their generosity and civic-mindedness, Bill and
Mitzi Davis might have found themselves out in the social
cold or at least shunted from the A list in a less relaxed, less
western city. For Bill was the younger brother of T. Cullen
Davis, the richest American ever tried for murder. And although Cullen had been acquitted, thanks to the highly paid
efforts of a team of lawyers led by Houston's courtroom
colossus Richard "Racehorse" Haynes, this was no simple,
single, straightforward homicide. It involved the deaths of
two people, the wounding of two others, and the alleged
planned murders of fifteen more. The scandal dragged on
for ten years, through four criminal trials followed by civil
suits. Month after month testimony from the witness stand

illuminated a dark, disturbing side to Fort Worth's tolerance for individual eccentricity, a strain of kookiness veering dangerously close to the pathological.

The family fortune began with Kenneth W. Davis, a contemporary of Amon Carter and wildcatter Sid Richardson. "They were not your average people," Bill Davis understated. "They were complete independents in thought and action." Ken Davis came to Fort Worth in the early 1920's to fly with the first Marine airborne unit, but he soon figured out that the greatest opportunities lay underground, in the newly discovered oil fields north and west of Fort Worth. At five feet six inches Davis was stocky, sturdy, and tough as a cheap steak. He picked up the soubriquet Stinky. Maybe it was a reference to the sour-smelling crude oil he was so good at getting out of the ground, but maybe it was a reference to his personality. Unlike Carter and Richardson, Stinky Davis had little interest in philanthropy or civic affairs, and he was a demanding and critical father.

Whatever his flaws, Stinky Davis was a gifted, hardworking businessman. He decided early that the way to make money in the oil industry was to play all the angles: do some exploration and production and provide other oilmen with equipment and services. Starting out with nothing in 1929, over four decades he built Kendavis Industries International, Inc. into a conglomerate with thousands of employees all over the globe. By the time Stinky Davis died in 1968, Kiii was worth $300 million.

Davis left an undivided third interest in his empire to each of his children: Ken, Jr., T. Cullen, and Bill. The boys grew up in the mock manor house where Bill and Mitzi later lived, but they weren't spoiled. The old man made them take turns mowing the vast lawn. He saw that all three got tough, inexpensive, no-frills engineering degrees at Texas A&M, and he kept his sharp, perfectionist eye riveted on them as managers of his companies. Apparently Stinky Davis thought the boys would do better running the family business together than they would splitting the assets. He was right. Within ten years of Stinky's death Kiii had quadrupled in value. The eighty-one companies that made up Kendavis Industries International, Inc. were worth $1.2 billion.

But that phenomenal increase in wealth wasn't what put the family name in the papers. It was Cullen.

When the middle son was born in 1933, Stinky Davis named him for a man he much admired, Houston wildcatter Hugh Roy Cullen. For the first three decades and a half of his life Cullen was reserved and unremarkable. Then, in 1968, he kicked over his traces.

The late sixties were a time of great social turmoil, and Cullen Davis wasn't the first uptight crew-cut businessman to shed his identity and begin behaving in hitherto unexpected ways. He ditched his wife, Sandra, a conventional member of Fort Worth's country club set, and on August 29, 1968—the day his father died—married Priscilla Lee Wilborn, a twice-divorced twenty-seven-year-old bleached blonde with a centerfold figure and a taste for miniskirts.

Priscilla hailed from Galena Park, a blue-collar refinery town on the Houston Ship Channel. Her first marriage at sixteen to twenty-one-year-old Jasper Baker lasted less than a year and produced one daughter. She had another daughter by Jack Wilborn, the used-car dealer she married when he was forty and she was eighteen.

Rather than persuade his new wife to adopt the low-key protective coloring of Fort Worth's upper crust, Cullen Davis seemed to delight in her flashy taste. She went along with his suggestion that she augment her already impressive breasts with silicone implants, then strutted into the Steeplechase Ball, the old guard's most venerable fete, in a spectacularly décolleté dress. On less formal occasions she wore a gold necklace with "RICH BITCH" spelled out in pavé diamonds. She appeared at a cocktail party for the *Apollo 13* astronauts in a fringed one-shoulder leather micro-minidress and at the Colonial Invitational Golf Tournament in a low-cut leather halter and breathtakingly brief leather shorts with open latticework sides. And she secured her place among Texas's legendary ladies when, as Gary Cartwright reported in his Davis saga *Blood Will Tell*, she had her pubic hair dyed pink and shaped into a heart.

As a monument to his new life-style, T. Cullen Davis built a six-million-dollar mansion on a 181-acre tract of family-held land bounded on one side by the Trinity River, on another by the Colonial Country Club golf course. His father had picked up the property in the 1940's. The house was striking but cold—an odd, nineteen-thousand-square-foot geometric jumble painted white and set very visibly atop a knoll.

The house was a showcase for Cullen's newfound interest in art. Paintings crowded the walls; sculptures loomed from tabletops and pedestals. A four-hundred-thousand-dollar Renoir greeted guests in the powder room. On one trip to New York Cullen bought out an entire gallery—115 paintings and bronzes. His collection of Oriental jade was particularly valuable. It included a white jade Ming dynasty vase, an $85,000 chess set, and a $350,000 pagoda. To protect these treasures, he installed a complicated electronic security system coordinated with the lighting.

The Mansion, as it came to be called locally, had twenty rooms and a large indoor pool, and Cullen supervised the design, construction, and decoration of each of those rooms save one—Priscilla's bath off the master bedroom. It was pink and pure Priscilla, with a sunken marble tub, a crystal chandelier, a cat box next to the bidet, and three walls of twenty-foot-tall mirrors to reflect the scene.

Not everyone found the new Cullen amusing. In 1972 Bill Davis purportedly became upset by his brother's extravagant expenditures on the Mansion and by the seven million dollars Cullen had lost in a variety of misguided business ventures with his friend Roy Rimmer, Jr. Cullen had used assets of the family conglomerate to borrow much of the money he'd lent Rimmer. Instead of remonstrating with Cullen, his older brother, Ken, sided with him. In August 1973 Ken and Cullen called a meeting of the board of directors and fired Bill from all his directorships of Kendavis Industries.

By that time Cullen wasn't getting along with his wife either. Claiming that she could no longer tolerate Cullen's temper, six years to the month after the wedding, Priscilla Davis filed for divorce. Even by Texas Big Rich standards, it promised to be a long, acrimonious battle. Cullen's lawyer produced a prenuptial agreement in which Priscilla apparently had waived her rights to a share of the Davis family fortune; she claimed that she'd thought she was signing a document regarding corporate taxes. Texas was a community property state. While husbands and wives were entitled to keep whatever assets they brought to a marriage, the courts, in the event of divorce, normally split the income those assets had earned from the wedding on. Before marrying a rich man, a woman might well consider a million-dollar settlement adequate security, but after she'd spent a few years as the wife of a multimillionaire, her perspective tended to shift. In practice, when a man's wealth increased as dramatically as Cullen Davis's had between 1968 and 1977—from a hundred million to four hundred million dollars—many divorce judges took a more sympathetic look at the wife's economic claims. The little lady couldn't have been fully aware of what she was doing when she signed her community property rights away.

Three months after Priscilla sued for divorce, Bill Davis filed his own suit against Ken and Cullen, saying his two older brothers were trying to squeeze him out of his inheritance.

During two years of depositions and delays in the Davis divorce, Judge Joe Eidson granted Priscilla thirty-five hundred dollars a month in temporary support (Texas had no alimony) and custody of the Mansion. As July 30, 1976, the date the first trial was set to begin, drew closer, he also issued a restraining order forbidding Cullen from visiting the Mansion or bothering his wife. Cullen had moved into the home of his girl friend Karen Master, a pretty blond divorcée, a born-again Christian with two young handicapped sons; they'd been dating since 1975, when she was twenty-six.

Priscilla had a parade of Cosmic Cowboy types crashing at the Mansion, including her two boyfriends: a scruffy motorcycle racer named W. T. Rufner and ex-Texas Christian University basketball player Stan Farr, a six-foot-nine-inch teddy bear of a man known around Fort Worth as the Gentle Giant. Priscilla's eighteen-year-old daughter, Dee, also lived with her; twelve-year-old Andrea lived with Jack Wilborn but visited overnight.

Priscilla's lawyers wanted to delay the divorce trial until later that summer, and Priscilla wanted her support payments raised to five thousand dollars a month; just air-conditioning those nineteen thousand square feet was enormously expensive. On August 2, 1976, Judge Eidson granted both requests.

That evening Priscilla and Stan Farr went out on the town. Returning home shortly after midnight, they found the security system turned off. A man dressed in black and wearing a woman's black wig stepped from the laundry room, said, "Hi," and shot Priscilla in the chest; her silicone implant slowed the bullet, mitigating what might otherwise have been a fatal wound. The gunman pursued Stan Farr upstairs to the master bedroom, where he shot the Gentle Giant four times, killing him. While the assailant was dispatching her lover, Priscilla escaped and ran across the huge field to her neighbors', where she pounded on the door, screaming, "Cullen is up there killing my children. He is killing everyone."

By the time Priscilla and Farr had arrived at the Mansion, Andrea, who'd come to spend the night, was already dead; police found her slumped against a basement wall, a bullet through her chest. Dee, still out on a date, had been spared. But as Priscilla stumbled across those acres of lawn, two visitors arrived: Dee's friend Bev Bass and Bev's boyfriend, Bubba Gavrel. The gunman shot Gavrel, crippling him from the waist down. Before the man in black could reload, Bev dashed down to the street and flagged a passing car. She told the driver that the man shooting people at the big house on the hill was Cullen Davis.

Initially the case seemed straightforward. T. Cullen Davis was charged with capital murder in the death of Andrea Wilborn and held without bond. Because of Judge Eidson's order forbidding Cullen from visiting the Mansion, the shootings constituted a capital offense—namely, murder committed during another felony, breaking and entering.

Cullen's $400 million didn't keep him out of jail; he spent a year behind bars awaiting his trial. However, he had a private cell where he could watch his own television, meet with Kendavis Industries functionaries, and enjoy meals catered by restaurants. And his money did allow him to hire the best lawyers and pay for services an ordinary defendant could never have afforded. Cullen's attorneys, for example, ordered daily court transcripts at $4.25 a page, often for two to three hundred pages. The transcripts were very useful in tripping up prosecution witnesses during cross-examination.

In the beginning Cullen hired Mike Gibson and Phil Burleson to plead his case. Burleson was the Dallas lawyer who with Melvin Belli had defended Jack Ruby in the shooting of Lee Harvey Oswald. Within a few months of his arrest Cullen added Houston defense legend Richard "Racehorse" Haynes as lead counsel. Haynes had earned his nickname as a running back at Houston's Reagan High School.

Cullen later stated that Haynes's fee in the murder trial was $250,000. The fees of the other defense lawyers and their expenses came to another $2.75 million. The state of Texas spent $300,000, not including the salaries of Tarrant County District Attorney Tim Curry and the seven other members of his staff involved. It was the most expensive criminal trial in Texas history.

The prosecution's expenses were so high because the trial ran five months and the jury was sequestered longer than any previous panel of twelve in the state. Even before the entire jury had been selected, Judge Tom Cave declared a mistrial because one of the jurors had discussed the case during an unauthorized phone call while she was visiting her terminally ill father in Illinois. The first juror on the second panel was picked on June 29, 1977, and spent the following 143 nights in hotel rooms. And the prosecution team slept and ate at taxpayers' expense as well, since the case was argued 350 miles northwest of Fort Worth in Amarillo. After the mistrial Judge Cave had ordered a change of venue, declaring that the case had generated too much local publicity to permit a fair trial in Fort Worth.

While Cullen was in jail awaiting trial, Priscilla's name, but not his, was dropped from the *Fort Worth Social Directory*. She, after all, was the outsider. And she wasn't much freer than her estranged husband. She stayed locked in the Mansion. When she did go out, it was with a silver-plated .32 strapped into a custom-made holster fitted to her right boot.

Just before the trial began, Bill Davis settled his suit against his brothers out of court for a sum rumored to involve forty million dollars in cash. Bill wound up with Nonesuch House and Davoil, a modest petroleum exploration and production company that at the time was far less valuable than the oil tool and oil field service arms of Kendavis Industries.

The defense team had its work set out for it. If Cullen had been accused of killing only Stan Farr, it wouldn't have been so hard. Traditionally Texas juries had taken a lenient look at the crime passionnel. But the cold-blooded murder of a sweet-natured, blameless twelve-year-old girl was another matter entirely. Cullen wasn't standing trial for the wounding of his estranged wife and the death of her live-in lover; he was standing trial for killing Andrea Wilborn.

The circumstantial case against Cullen was pretty damning. He'd had opportunity and ample motive; the afternoon before the shootings he'd taken another blow in the nasty knock-down, drag-out divorce. And two women who knew Cullen well, both fleeing in separate directions in fear for their lives, had identified him as the gunman. Still, there was no physical evidence linking Cullen to the crime, and Karen Master swore that he had been home in bed with her when the murders took place. (He said he'd spent the early evening alone at a movie theater seeing *The Bad News Bears*.) If Racehorse Haynes could scatter enough seeds of reasonable doubt for one to take root in the mind of a juror, he'd have at worst a hung jury.

Haynes was fond of describing his defense technique as follows: Suppose you say my dog bit you. First, my dog doesn't bite. Second, my dog was tied up that night. Third, I don't believe you really got bit. And fourth, I don't have a dog. That his defense scenarios often were mutually exclusive didn't seem to matter to Haynes's juries.

Besides being able to construct alternate explanations for the crime in question, Haynes was a master at dismantling the edifice erected by the state. He chipped away at the credibility of prosecution witnesses by attacking minute inconsistencies in their testimonies. The stultifying tedium this technique sometimes created was legendary in the Texas bar. Fellow Houston defense attorney Mike Ramsey, who once worked for Haynes, told of the time Haynes bored a juror to death. What really happened was that the unfortunate juror keeled over dead from a heart attack while Haynes was cross-examining a witness. "Can you imagine," Ramsey asked during an interview for a profile of his mentor, "the last thing you hear in this earthly world being Richard 'Race-horse' Haynes asking for the fourteenth time what time it was?"

In the Davis case Haynes's strategy was to persuade the jury that Stan Farr could have been the intended target of an unknown murderer and that Andrea, Priscilla, and Bubba Gavrel all had been accidental victims. The gunman, after all, had taken some pains to see that Farr was dead. If his primary purpose had been to kill Priscilla, surely he could have caught her as she ran across the field, hampered by high heels and a serious gunshot wound. The only reason anyone could have wanted Andrea dead was to hurt Priscilla or to prevent the young girl from testifying. Farr, on the other hand, might well have had other enemies than Cullen. Actually, although Farr had lived at the Mansion openly for fifteen months, he and Cullen had treated each other civilly when they'd met in public. But Farr had been involved in a number of hapless ventures, including the Rhinestone Cow-boy, a cosmic kicker bar, and plenty of witnesses testified that recreational drugs—particularly cocaine, marijuana, and Percodan—flowed freely at the Mansion. The shooting, Racehorse Haynes suggested, might have been the result of a soured business transaction, even a drug deal.

The flaw in Haynes's argument was that it seemed to require the jury to believe either that Priscilla Davis was so intent at getting back at her husband that she was willing to conceal the identity of her daughter's killer or that both she and Bev Bass had mistaken someone else for Cullen. And the former scenario involved the assumption that though fearing for their lives and running in separate directions, the two women had still managed to conspire to pin the crime on him.

Prosecutor Tim Curry might have been better off not calling Priscilla to testify. By the time Haynes finished cross-examining her and parading all the witnesses to the carry-ings-on under her roof, it was apparent that Priscilla was as much on trial as Cullen. And Racehorse didn't neglect to sprinkle the record with alternate explanations: Suppose Priscilla didn't recognize the gunman but saw an opportunity to implicate Cullen and thereby wreak her revenge and receive a better divorce settlement? After all, she didn't know for certain that Andrea was dead until after telling the neighbors it was Cullen. Or suppose she did recognize the gunman but was afraid to point the finger at him.

Haynes's technique won Cullen Davis an acquittal. Shortly thereafter, Karen Master left her two handicapped sons with her ex-husband, Walter Master, and she and Cullen went skiing in Aspen. While the couple was off celebrating, Master won a restraining order from a divorce court judge prohibiting Karen from taking the children near Cullen. Coincidentally, the judge involved was Joe Eidson, the same one hearing the Davis divorce. Karen eventually won out, defeating Master's play for permanent custody.

Under Karen's influence, Cullen became a born-again Christian in 1977, brought to tears by what he described as "an infilling of the Holy Spirit." He began contributing $250,000 a year to his church, Bethel Temple in Fort Worth.

Karen later claimed that her deaf ten-year-old son, Chesley, who'd lost his hearing in an automobile accident at eighteen months, had recovered miraculously when the Reverend Bob Tilton, pastor of the World of Faith Congregation and Bible College, put his hands on the little boy's ears at a meeting of twenty people at the Davis house on May 2, 1981. Chesley "went over and began playing the piano, and everyone there received the baptism of the Holy Spirit."

In 1983 Fort Worth evangelist James Robison persuaded Cullen Davis to join him in smashing one million dollars' worth of Cullen's collection of museum-quality jade and other Oriental carvings and dumping the smithereens into the Trinity River. Robison objected to the statues because they represented pagan dieties.

Whatever odd turns Cullen Davis's spiritual life was taking, the path his legal life took meanwhile was far more bizarre.

Despite Cullen's acquittal on the murder charge, he still faced civil suits from Priscilla, Jack Wilborn, Bubba Gavrel, and Stan Farr's children. Rather than have to demonstrate guilt beyond a reasonable doubt, the plaintiffs would be required to show only "a preponderance of evidence" in their favor. And the verdict didn't have to be unanimous; a ten to two jury vote would suffice.

After several delays Judge Joe Eidson set the divorce trial for August 14, 1978. Cullen had as his lawyer Haynes's partner Donn Fullenweider, as formidable in divorce cases as Haynes was in criminal litigation. To Fort Worth's surprise, Priscilla suddenly stopped fighting, perhaps figuring she'd be vindicated later in her suits for Andrea's wrongful death and her own injuries. She and Cullen agreed to limit the divorce proceedings to a simple no-fault property settlement.

Then, on August 30, 1978, exactly a year after he had been charged with the Mansion killings, Cullen Davis was arrested by the FBI. This time the charges were solicitation of capital murder and conspiracy to commit capital murder; both carried possible life sentences. Cullen allegedly had drawn up a list of fifteen people he wanted dead, beginning with his domestic court nemesis Judge Joe Eidson and including Judge Tom Cave, Priscilla, her daughter Dee, Bev Bass, Bubba Gavrel, and even his brother Bill.

The accusation stunned Fort Worth. Even the *Social Directory* now scratched his name. Had his acquittal on the Mansion murders so emboldened Cullen that he thought he could get away with bumping off whoever got in his way, including two judges? Or was this part of an elaborate plot to frame him?

The evidence seemed irrefutable. Hidden nearby in a van, FBI technicians had made audio- and videotapes of Cullen Davis arranging the hits through an intermediary and examining a faked photo of Judge Edison, his undershirt smeared with ketchup, playing dead in the trunk of a car.

Two months earlier Cullen had hired his old pool-shooting buddy David McCrory, a tenth-grade dropout, supposedly to be second-in-command for one of the Davis companies, Jet Air. McCrory's actual function had been to gather information that might help Cullen in his divorce:

investigating Bev Bass's and Bubba Gavrel's alleged drug use; discovering whether Priscilla's attorneys had been improperly friendly with Judge Eidson; digging up dirt on Priscilla's sex life. But when, McCrory claimed, Cullen had asked him to find a professional to do in his enemies, the tyro clandestine operative had called the FBI. Throughout the taped transactions, which took place on August 18 and 30 in the parking lot of Coco's Famous Hamburgers, McCrory wore a wire. Cullen sounded grimly taciturn as he clearly discussed such practical matters as who should be "done" next and how cash should be conveyed to the hit man, and he never once said, "What the hell are you talking about?" or anything else that might indicate that a more innocent exchange was being made to appear incriminating. Furthermore, the corresponding videotape showed Cullen handing McCrory something that looked like the white envelope stuffed with twenty-five-thousand dollars that McCrory handed over minutes later to the FBI.

Once again Racehorse Haynes led the defense team. Although Haynes wanted the case tried in Fort Worth, Judge Arthur Tipps ordered it moved to Houston. Judge Wallace "Pete" Moore, who heard the case, was tougher on Cullen and easier on the jury. He insisted that Cullen be treated like any other prisoner: no private TV; no catered meals; no business meetings in his cell. But Judge Moore let the jury go home at night.

Because of an equipment problem, the video- and audiotapes weren't synchronized; nonetheless, they were damning. The prosecution's problem was with its key witness. Under cross-examination, David McCrory admitted to stealing money from Cullen Davis and lying about problems with the IRS. He also testified that he'd lied to both Cullen and Priscilla on numerous occasions. Still worse, with his longish, slicked-back black hair and his hulking demeanor, McCrory looked no more credible than he sounded. Haynes deftly cast him as a cariacture of a con man and then raised the question of which side had been conned.

The jury might buy McCrory's pulling a double cross, but what about the FBI? For the defense, the challenge was persuading jurors that those supercops with their reputation for absolute integrity could have been unwilling dupes in an ingenious setup.

The defense case revolved around an extortion letter Cullen had received after his acquittal in Amarillo. He hadn't been satisfied with the FBI's investigation of the letter or with its attempts to identify the parties he said were making death threats against him, so, the defense explanation went, he'd decided to unmask the conspiracy against him on his own. Haynes also suggested that a week before the first meeting in Coco's parking lot, Cullen had received a call from someone purporting to be an FBI agent and asking him to go along with McCrory in order to trap the would-be death broker.

It seemed preposterous, yet the defense paraded forty-seven witnesses in its attempt to sell its conspiracy theory. Most of those testifying—admitted druggies, convicts currently serving time—ranked lower on the credibility scale than David McCrory. However, their sheer numbers were enough to shake the jury's confidence in the tapes.

Cullen hadn't taken the stand in the Mansion murder trial, but this time Racehorse Haynes called him to describe the arrival of the extortion letter, recount the call from the man claiming to work for the FBI, and explain that the twenty-five thousand dollars in the white envelope had been gambling winnings McCrory had asked him to hold in his office safe. The multimillionaire emitted an icy detachment that could have been either supreme arrogance or strength of character in the face of injustice. He struck many in the courtroom as a man used to getting his own way no matter what, a man who could hold himself in control under most stress but who, with enough of the right kind of provocation, might explode. He looked scary. But he managed to persuade four jurors that there was at least a reasonable doubt of his guilt. After forty-eight hours of deliberation, on January 22, 1979, the jury declared itself hopelessly deadlocked. Racehorse Haynes succeeded in getting the retrial set for Cullen's home turf. Later in 1979 a Fort Worth jury acquitted him.

For a few years it seemed as if the Davis drama were over. The divorce was finalized. Priscilla moved to Dallas and became a regular at trendy night spots and the Cattle

Barons' Ball. Cullen and Karen were married. Every so often tidbits about their religious experiences surfaced as human-interest items.

With both criminal cases behind him, Cullen Davis still faced civil suits levied by those injured in the Mansion shootings and by the families of those killed, suits that dragged on for seven years. The first to be resolved was Bubba Gavrel's. Still paralyzed from the waist down, he sued Cullen for fifteen million dollars. They settled out of court, reportedly for about $1 million, including $125,000 cash and 130 residential lots in a development southwest of Fort Worth.

In 1983 Davis sold the Mansion and the surrounding 179 acres for $33 million to the Dallas-based Cambridge Company, which planned to turn the property into a subdivision using Texas's most notorious residence as a clubhouse. He and Karen moved into a comparatively modest $750,000 house on the other side of town. Three years later Racehorse Haynes retired as Cullen's courtroom palladin. Plagued by twenty-three soured real estate deals in five years, Cullen could no longer afford him.

The drilling tools and oil field services that formed the backbone of Kendavis Industries were the hardest-hit sector of the Oil Patch. Because of its size, Kiii, like the Western Company, was able to hang on for a year after the price of a barrel of West Texas intermediate crude fell below ten dollars. But in April 1987, unable to pay the carrying charges on its half billion dollars in debts, the family conglomerate filed for Chapter 7 liquidation. Creditors took control and fired Ken and Cullen Davis. Stripped of his reported fifteen-thousand-dollar-a-month income, Cullen and Karen Davis were reduced to living on thirty-one thousand dollars a year and driving a 1979 Cadillac with 150,000 miles on it.

Despite Cullen's financial reverses, the following month Priscilla Davis and Jack Wilborn proceeded with the trial of their combined suit asking $16.5 million for Andrea's wrongful death and Priscilla's injuries. Although the jury was charged only with deciding where a preponderance of the evidence lay, on June 22, 1987, the foreman announced that it was deadlocked eight to four in favor of the plaintiffs.

"I want to give the Lord Jesus Christ all the credit for

what happened in this trial," Cullen announced in the best born-again tradition.

"That's good, because that's who he's going to have to answer to," Priscilla replied when the media asked for her reaction to the pious remark. She announced that she planned to refile separately, asking for ten million dollars.

It came as no surprise when the once richest American ever tried for murder filed for Chapter 7 on July 2, 1987. The only shock was the speed with which his debts had piled up and his fortune had declined. Cullen Davis owed $865 million, mostly in loans on failed real estate ventures. Apart from the $750,000 house he and Karen would be allowed to keep, his assets totaled less than $1 million.

Cullen Davis's bankruptcy effectively halted the raft of civil suits. At the end of August Cullen announced that he was selling his art collection to help pay his creditors. The public gawked at the inlaid Louis XVI tables, the eighteenth-century bronzes, the hundred-dollar crystal ashtray, and the bouquets of flowers fashioned from semiprecious stones.

That fall Priscilla agreed to a $5 million settlement of her $10 million claim, but she had to content herself with the satisfaction rather than the cash. Announcing that the court had distributed all but ten thousand dollars of Cullen Davis's estate, Judge Tillman released him on December 2, 1987, from $850 million in debt. Cullen would still be responsible for a five-hundred-thousand-dollar support payment to his first wife, Sandra, for Priscilla's five-million-dollar settlement, and for three million on behalf of Stan Farr's son and daughter.

As the 1980's drew to a close, Bill Davis—the nice-guy brother squeezed out of his inheritance—was doing just fine. Lean and well managed, his company, Davoil, made a modest profit even during the worst of the oil bust. With crude stabilized between fifteen and twenty dollars a barrel, Davoil looked downright prosperous as it continued to find and produce oil and gas all over the country, but mostly in West Texas and New Mexico.

The house at the center of the Davis drama stood empty. Plagued by the Texas real estate slump, the Cambridge Company had abandoned its project in 1987, leaving the Mansion to vandals. Thieves had pried the bronze tiles from the double front doors and stolen the gold-plated faucets from Priscilla's pink marble bathroom. Rain fell through broken skylights into the algae-encrusted swimming pool. And spray-painted obscenities decorated the walls that once displayed Impressionist masterpieces.

★

CHAPTER SIXTEEN

The Bass Brothers

Fort Worth's Baby Boom Billionaires

Despite the state's many vast fortunes, no one else in Texas had ever controlled so much wealth so early in life as the four Bass brothers of Fort Worth. Boyishly handsome and unnervingly fresh-faced, they looked even younger than they were: Sid, the eldest, was born in 1942; Lee, the youngest, in 1956. By 1989 their combined wealth approached five billion dollars. They owned hundreds of oil and gas wells, thousands of acres of real estate, and major stakes in *Fortune* 500 companies, which they traded for staggering profits.

Each Bass seemed to reflect a different segment of the baby boom generation. Sid was a brilliant businessman and major-league art collector. Born in 1946, Ed was a posthippie who organized and bankrolled such far-out New Age projects as a solar-powered hotel in Kathmandu, Nepal, and a self-contained environment in Oracle, Arizona, intended as a laboratory for the colonization of Mars. Bob, born in 1948, became a major player on the investment scene, but continued to devote much of his money and energy to buying and restoring historic buildings and to liberal and preservationist political causes. Lee was a sort of superyuppie, apparently being groomed as a successor to Sid, fourteen years his senior.

The Basses fitted the Cowboy Capitalist image of the Texas Rich in only one way: the amount of money they slung around. In personal style they seemed more like a New England dynasty; even Ed's New Age eccentricity was in the eastern tradition. All four went to Andover and Yale, where they received broad liberal arts educations. They wore exquisitely tailored but conservative suits. Their manners were polished; their tastes, sophisticated. They collected American contemporary art—not cowboy art—and they collected it seriously. Sid favored Morris Louis, Ellsworth Kelly, and Frank Stella, and was a trustee of New York's Museum of Modern Art. Ed was into the international avant-garde. Bob and his wife, Anne, were on the Collector's Committee of the National Gallery in Washington, and Lee and his wife, Ramona, who was from a well-established San Antonio family, the Seeligsons, were on the National Committee of the Whitney Museum of American Art in New York. The Basses contributed both money and effort to charitable causes. And they avoided publicity, Lee most of all.

Rather than submit the strict, detailed personal financial statements required by the New Jersey Casino Control Commission, the Basses ditched their 1983 bid for a piece of Atlantic City's Sands Hotel, even though that meant a seven-million-dollar loss. There was no hint that the Basses had anything to hide; they just valued their privacy and could afford to spend seven million to protect it.

In fact, the only Bass who would agree to talk to me was Bob, and that was for a *Town & Country* city profile of Fort Worth.

Tracking the Basses was like trying to spot meteors. They were there, and you could see them out of the corner of your eye; but if you stared at them directly, they disappeared. They weren't recluses. They were involved in Fort Worth's civic and social life. In low-key circles among the Texas social elite, their names came up casually. But if you asked about the Basses directly, those who knew them tended to clam up. Why were people so protective of the Basses' privacy? Perhaps because Fort Worth genuinely liked them and appreciated their civic contributions. The boys were objects of possessive community pride. They allowed Fort Worth to thumb its nose at Dallas and say, "Our billionaires are younger, more attractive, and more cultivated than your billionaires."

The Bass brothers became so rich so young for two reasons: First, the money they inherited skipped a generation, and secondly, they were remarkably smart and lucky at investing it.

The money came from Sid W. Richardson, a classic Texas wildcatter. Starting out with forty dollars he borrowed from his sister and pursuing his oil deals from a pay phone in a downtown Fort Worth sandwich shop, he made and lost three fortunes. Finally, in 1939, he discovered the Keystone field, one of the most lucrative plays in West Texas. Of the 385 wells he drilled there, only seventeen came up dry holes.

A handsome man six feet tall and about two hundred pounds, Sid Richardson was a lifelong bachelor; he once explained, "Women are always looking for a landing field, but mine's fogged in."

Among those seeking landing rights were some of the most glamorous women in the world. One summer during the late forties movie star Joan Crawford pursued Richardson relentlessly around La Jolla. The flustered oilman decamped from the Hotel del Charro in such a hurry that he left behind in a dresser drawer ten thousand dollars he'd won at Del Mar Racetrack.

Richardson was very close to his sister Annie Cecilia's family. In 1937 he took on her son, Perry Bass, fresh from Yale, as his partner. Since Perry's father, a Wichita Falls doctor, had died young, the relationship filled corresponding gaps for the wildcatter and his only nephew. Perry thought so much of his uncle that he named his first son Sid Richardson Bass.

Perry's third son, Bob, remembered his great-uncle as "a large man, very jovial, a lot of fun" and "quite a tease." Shortly after Dwight Eisenhower was elected, he invited Richardson to dine at the White House. The wildcatter replied: "Before I accept, Mr. President, what are you having for dinner?"

Richardson died in 1959, when Bob was only eleven and young Sid seventeen. The old wildcatter's fourth and last fortune totaled $105 million. He left $71 million to the Sid Richardson Foundation, which stood at about $133 million in 1989 and had given grants as high as four million dollars to educational, cultural, and medical charities solely within the state of Texas. Perry inherited only $450,000 worth of livestock, but at the time his partnership interest in the Richardson companies amounted to more than twelve million.

Sid Richardson also left each of his four grandnephews $2.8 million. Kids have blown legacies of that size on a few years of high living and bad business deals. But not Perry Bass's boys. They were trained to manage their money. Except for Ed, who took off for Santa Fe after graduating from Yale in 1968, they got M.B.A.'s—Sid and Bob from Stanford, Lee from Wharton. And while his sons were pursuing their educations, Perry wrapped their inheritances and his own share of the Richardson companies into Bass Brothers Enterprises. By 1969, a year after Sid returned from Stanford, Perry had nursed that collective stake to fifty million dollars. Then, saying he was going sailing, fiftyish Perry Bass, who had skippered his fifteen-and-one-half-foot Snipe to the national championship in the early 1930's, handed the company over to his twenty-seven-year-old son and took off as navigator on Ted Turner's yacht *American Eagle*.

Perry and Turner won the World's Open Racing Championship in 1972. Sid and his brothers won a place in American financial history.

In Bass lawyer Dee Kelly's office, next to autographed photos of Lyndon Johnson, Sam Rayburn, and John Connally, hung a sketch of the four Bass boys and Perry. At the top of the picture was a panther striding across a dollar bill. The panther was a reference to Fort Worth, the Panther City.

But more than that the panther was a quick, agile, clever predator, and it struck unexpectedly.

At one point in the mid-1980's the Bass brothers owned major chunks of more than thirty companies, including 24.8 percent of Walt Disney, 17.8 percent of Alexander's department stores, 30.8 percent of Munsingwear, 51 percent of Famous Amos Cookies, and 10 percent of Texaco. The Basses may have been publicity-shy, but no one could maneuver such enormous blocks of stock in private. By federal law, any entity acquiring 5 percent or more of a publicly traded corporation had to file a Schedule 13D with the Securities and Exchange Commission disclosing exactly who was involved in the deal and where the money was coming from.

Compared with those of other takeover artists, most of the Basses' gambits were passive; they bought undervalued securities and waited for them to appreciate over time. Although they didn't ride in roughshod, they made some of their money through what was known as greenmail: scooping up a big chunk of a company; threatening a takeover, then selling the stock back to the company at higher than market price. The Basses insisted that such an inflated repurchase was just one possible result of a stock play, and they defended their actions by saying they reinvested the money they made. But those profits could be staggering. In 1981, when white knight U.S. Steel rescued Marathon Oil from a joint takeover by the Basses and Dallas-based Sedco, the brothers sold their shares for $150 million more than they had paid for them. They turned another quick $50 million when Blue Bell, which made Wrangler jeans, bought back a block of Bass stock.

Then the Basses went after Texaco. The energy giant had made itself a prime takeover target through its own ill-fated 1984–85 attempt to snatch Getty Oil from Pennzoil. (That same move later prompted Pennzoil's successful $10.53 billion suit, settled for three billion in 1987.) Labeling Texaco's ten-billion-dollar offer for Getty "antishareholder," the Basses quickly raised their minor stake in the company to 9.8 percent. Rattled, CEO John K. McKinley bought the shares back for $1.2 billion, handing the boys from Fort Worth a fast $450 million profit.

Sometimes it was the Bass boys who were the white knights. In 1984 they rescued the foundering Walt Disney Company from the clutches of Saul Steinberg, Ivan Boesky, and Irwin Jacobs and supported CEO Michael Eisner as he turned the corporation around. The business world called it "saving the Mouse." The Basses' reward was $850 million in capital gains.

The Basses' *modus operandi* included setting up a separate company to handle each deal and bringing in their top advisers as partners. In fact, for sixteen years one of those advisers, Richard Rainwater, a Stanford Business School classmate of Sid's, was the major strategist for Bass Brothers Enterprises; while he was making the Basses billionaires, he earned his own spot on the *Forbes* 400 with an estimated 1989 net worth of three hundred million dollars.

Born in Fort Worth in 1943, Rainwater was a contemporary of the Bass boys but not part of the same set. His father was a mostly Lebanese wholesaler with some Cherokee Indian blood. While the Basses were hanging around the Fort Worth Boat Club, Rainwater was picking up trophies drag racing. While the Basses were getting their eastern polish at Yale, he was following thousands of other middle-class kids to the University of Texas.

Sid Bass and Richard Rainwater were the original business odd couple. Sid was blond with a medium build. Rainwater was tall, thin, and swarthy. Patrician to the core, Sid favored Savile Row suits. Rainwater went in for blue chambray work shirts and had a collection of funny hats. As an undergraduate Sid was a liberal arts major; his strengths were conceptualizing and communicating. Rainwater was a math whiz. Yet they had adjoining offices for sixteen years and shared a secretary for all but the last few.

Initially Sid hired his former classmate to assist him in diversifying the family oil fortune. With Rainwater's help, the fifty-million-dollar nest egg Perry Bass had left in his eldest son's hands mushroomed to four billion between 1970 and 1986. Granted, events worked in their favor: The 1973 Arab oil embargo pumped between ten million and fifteen million dollars a month into the Bass coffers. But rather than sink that windfall back into oil, they spread out. That was why the Basses continued to get richer throughout the Texas oil bust.

The first big move Sid Bass and Richard Rainwater made was putting eight million dollars in Idanta Partners, a California-based venture capital group that provided seed money for high tech start-ups. A decade later that investment was worth $200 million. Rainwater's sense of timing was uncanny. In late 1981 he wrapped up a 5.1 percent position for the Basses in Marathon Oil just a little over a week before Mobil and U.S. Steel duked it out for a Marathon takeover. The result: The Basses made a fast $160 million profit on a $165 million investment.

Back home they were reshaping Fort Worth. One of the first things Sid did when his father put him at the helm of the family fortune was begin buying up blocks of deteriorated real estate at the north end of downtown. The area had been abandoned virtually overnight in the late sixties, when developers had begun erecting suburban shopping malls and office buildings. By the early seventies the neatly kept emporiums that had lured the well-to-do from River Crest and Westover Hills had been replaced by a wig shop, a domino parlor, and musty stores where outmoded merchandise languished behind grimy display windows. The fanciful neoclassical iron fronts on the two-story turn-of-the-century buildings had begun to rust.

Bucking the trend toward flight, Charles Tandy erected his twin office towers. Fort Worth National Bank put up a shiny new building but couldn't rent the space. The problem was the surrounding area.

One day Charles Tandy invited Sid Bass, three decades his junior, to lunch. Over the meal Tandy made a proposition: I'll throw in a block, you throw in a block next to it, and we'll build a top-drawer downtown hotel.

Tandy didn't live to see the starkly contemporary wedge-shaped Worthington Hotel finished. But it did what he'd hoped it would: It provided a pleasant, convenient place for Tandy and other companies based downtown to house their visiting firemen. And with its austere interior softened by fresh flowers and framed posters from the Fort Worth Art Museum, it gave the area an instant aura of worldly style.

While the hotel was in the works, the Basses erected two dramatic office towers next door, smack on Main Street. Some people loved them, others hated them, but no one could miss them. At thirty-eight and thirty-four stories, they dominated the skyline of this low-rise city, and their silver skins flashed the Texas sun for miles. City Center, the Basses called the project. Designed by Yale architecture Dean Paul Rudolph, the skyscrapers were classic contemporary glass boxes, except that they sported indentations several stories high and tacked-on turrets, making them look like fortresses in a science-fiction film.

At the base of the futuristic towers the Basses renovated four square blocks of turn-of-the-century iron fronts and replaced the marginal tenants with merchants appealing to the young and upwardly mobile: a New Wave card shop; a bakery specializing in croissants and muffins; stylish restaurants serving quiche, homemade pasta, and gringofied Mexican fare. Trees laced with tiny white Tivoli lights sprouted from sidewalk planters. Clydesdales pulled hackney cabs down the brick-topped streets stripped of their asphalt thanks to a federal urban action grant. The Basses called their restoration Sundance Square after Harry Longbaugh, aka the Sundance Kid, who'd hung out nearby at Fannie Porter's bawdy house.

As sharp as the contrast was between them, in juxtaposition City Center and Sundance Square worked. The older buildings contributed a human scale and a streetscape that the new ones lacked. "There's so much about them that's vital, as opposed to having a glass canyon," Bob Bass said.

By 1987 City Center, Sundance Square, 6,886 acres of ranchland, and the family oil and gas holdings in Texas, Louisiana, and New Mexico were all that was left of Bass Brothers Enterprises. In 1985 the brothers started splitting their interests. Ed and Bob wanted to go their own ways. Because of the enormous amounts of money involved, the division wasn't easy. In fact, as a favor to the Basses, who had supported him, Texas Senator Lloyd Bentsen, Jr., tried to amend federal law to allow them to divvy up many of their assets tax-free. Initially the Treasury Department agreed; then it changed its mind. But a favorable IRS ruling had virtually the same effect.

Sid and Lee stuck together, with Lee becoming progressively more active in their business dealings, and *Forbes* estimated their 1989 combined net worth as at least $2.5 billion. They went in with their parents, Perry and Nancy, on several investments. *Forbes* called Bob Bass, who operated mainly through his Robert M. Bass Group, the richest and pegged his assets at $1.44 billion. Ed was the poorest, with a mere one billion. All four sailed smoothly not just through the Texas oil bust but through the 1987 Black Monday stock crash as well.

For a man who abhorred personal publicity, Sid Bass attracted the most prurient, persistent kind. In 1988 he found himself smack in the middle of a titillating divorce involving two beautiful women (one blond and cool, the other dark and exotic) and at least a billion dollars. No scriptwriter for a prime-time soap opera could have come up with anything juicier.

Sid first met Anne Hendricks at a birthday party; he was seven, and she was nine, the daughter of a prominent Indianapolis surgeon. Her mother was a former championship golfer whose father was a big Indianapolis builder named R. D. Brown. Through oil investments in Fort Worth during the 1940's, Brown had become friendly with Sid Richardson. Sid Bass and Anne Hendricks started dating when she was a senior at Vassar and he was a sophomore at Yale. On June 26, 1965, a week after Sid graduated, they were married.

Anne Bass was a slender, stylish woman with deep blue eyes and shoulder-length blond hair, which she parted in the middle and held back with barrettes. She went in for serious European couture—dresses with five-figure price tags—and drove a Rolls-Royce Silver Cloud.

The couple shared a genuine interest in art for its own sake, not just for its social cachet or investment potential. During the first year of their marriage, while Sid was working in Dallas before entering the Stanford Business School, he painted in their spare bedroom. In 1969 Sid and Anne joined the board of the Fort Worth Art Museum, which specialized in abstract contemporary works. Three years later the Sid Richardson Foundation, which had been giving the museum twenty-four thousand dollars a year, bankrolled its million-dollar expansion.

Museum-quality paintings decorated the walls of their cliff-climbing Paul Rudolph-designed house, which resembled a giant public sculpture. With five bedrooms and six baths, it cost five million dollars and sat on eight landscaped acres, including a formal rose garden, beds of annuals, lily ponds, and an orchid house.

The extravagant digs were the backdrop for the kind of serious entertaining that left even the most blasé easterners speechless. World-famous dancer Peter Martins, who succeeded George Balanchine as director of the New York City Ballet and the School of American Ballet, was no stranger to opulent parties. Yet he reported being floored when he, Mikhail Baryshnikov, and NYC Ballet principal dancer Heather Watts showed up for dinner at Sid and Anne's after a 1979 performance in Fort Worth and were greeted by a full orchestra.

Anne Bass, who had studied dance and continued to take daily ballet lessons, became one of the School of American Ballet's biggest angels and sat on its board of directors. She was named to the board of the American support group for the Paris Opera Ballet, and her picture began popping up in W. To accommodate her entrance onto the national and international social scene, the Basses bought a $5.25 million Manhattan *pied-à-terre*—complete with its own ballet studio—on Fifth Avenue overlooking Central Park. The fifteen-foot-high ceilings set off the exquisite European antiques, the Monets in the dining room, and the Mark Rothkos in the living room.

For a while it looked as if Anne Hendricks Bass would conquer that most formidable of America's social citadels, New York's *haut monde*. Then things started to sour. In 1984 Mary Porter—development director for the New York City Ballet and the School of American Ballet and secretary to Lincoln Kirstein, cofounder of the two related institutions—asked Anne to chair a fund-raising gala. Anne put together a party that raised $750,000 in one night, then went on to help Porter raise ten million to establish a permanent endowment for the school. Spurred on by their success, the

duo went after seven million dollars for offices and dormi-
tories. In the middle of this daring financial pas de deux,
Kirstein sacked Mary Porter after sixteen years of service.
Anne Bass retaliated by threatening to withdraw her support.

New York's cultural world was shocked. At seventy-
eight, Lincoln Kirstein, who had also helped found the Museum of Modern Art, was one of its elder statesmen. Did
this woman from Texas think that just because she had all
that money, she could challenge his power?

After several months the squall blew itself out. The millions Anne and Sid Bass had pledged found their way to the
coffers of the School of American Ballet and the New York
City Ballet; Anne kept her positions on both boards.

Then Sid bolted.

On September 16, 1986, society gossip columnist Suzy
announced in the New York *Post* that Sid Bass and Mercedes
Kellogg had fallen in love and had asked their respective
spouses for divorces. Apparently passion had been brewing
since the handsome Fort Worth billionaire and the vivacious
forty-two-year-old Iranian-born wife of career diplomat and
cereal heir Francis Kellogg, twenty-six years her senior, had
been seated together at the Black and White Ball at the duke
of Marlborough's Blenheim Palace in Oxfordshire, England,
two and a half months earlier.

On July 31, 1987, after twenty-two years of marriage,
Sid Bass filed for divorce in Tarrant County, Texas, citing
marital discord and a conflict of personalities. Since Texas
was a community property state, her lawyers argued, Anne
was entitled to virtually half of Sid's net worth, which had
swelled from ten million dollars or so to about one billion
during the course of the marriage. Rumors circulated that
she'd turned down a $500 million settlement. Separating
Sid's oil and real estate holdings from those of his brothers
and parents provided plenty of lucrative employment for
lawyers on both sides. The petitions, depositions, and settlement were sealed, but insiders reported that Anne had
received $275 million—about $200 million in cash, the rest
in cars, jewelry, artwork, and real estate.

The divorce was final in October 1988. At noon on Saturday, December 10, Sid and Mercedes were married in New

York. Suzy reported that guests cheered the occasion by shouting "yahoo" when the groom kissed the bride. But that famous gossip must have been mistaken. To express exuberance, true Texans don't holler "yahoo"; they holler "Yeehaw."

Bob Bass's personal life seemed as serene and wholesome as Sid's did turbulent and titillating. Bob was married to his childhood sweetheart, the former Anne Thraxton, daughter of a Fort Worth CPA. They'd met in dancing class during junior high. For national Rich watchers, the fact that both brothers had wives named Anne was confusing, but not for locals. Fort Worth called Mrs. Sid Bass Big Anne and Mrs. Robert Bass Little Anne. And they looked different. Little Anne was petite, about five feet tall, with a brunette pageboy and understated taste in clothes and jewelry.

By 1987 Bob, not Sid, was the Bass with the buckets of business-page ink and the highest estimated net worth. At the close of 1986 he owned stock in twenty-four corporations and forty-three partnerships. He seemed to have an uncanny knack for buying up undervalued companies at just the right time and doubling his money, usually without ditching top management. His net worth was well over a billion dollars. If he was playing that big that well at thirty-eight, *Forbes* marveled, what would he be doing at fifty?

The second-youngest brother began staking his own claim on Wall Street in 1985, when he bought 24.9 percent of Taft Broadcasting for $205 million. The company included twelve television stations and Hanna-Barbera, the creator of Yogi Bear and Huckleberry Hound. In September 1987 Bob Bass split Taft up, selling all but one of the television stations. His investment partnership, the Robert M. Bass Group, emerged with $157.5 million in cash, large chunks of two cable companies, and the Columbus, Ohio, ABC affiliate— a total of about half a billion dollars.

The quake that set Wall Street reeling on October 19, 1987, barely broke Bob Bass's stride. That same month he and Aoki—the Japanese construction company that owned the Algonquin, New York's literary landmark—purchased Westin Hotels from Allegis for $1.35 billion in cash and the assumption of $180 million in debt. In March 1988 he spun off the Plaza Hotel to Donald Trump for $410 million. Two months later shareholders approved his $702 million leveraged buyout of Bell & Howell, the erstwhile movie camera company that had diversified into everything from cable TV to Katharine Gibbs secretarial schools to Gump's specialty stores.

For one of the most powerful financiers in America, Bob Bass was remarkably unassuming. His face was so boyish that his thick, prematurely gray hair and rimless glasses only made him look younger than he was. Except for the little booth manned twenty-four hours a day by a security guard, the house where he and Anne lived could have belonged to two successful young doctors or attorneys. Shielded by trees at the top of a steep hill, the structure was blond brick, contemporary but unobtrusive, designed not by an international name but by Dallas architect Dan Oglesby. A basketball hoop hung over the driveway. The day I visited, there were two Volvos parked behind the house—a green station wagon and a burgundy sedan. Not a Rolls-Royce in sight. (Granted, Bob owned a Volvo dealership.) A window to the right of the front door showcased a Morris Louis the Fort Worth Art Museum would have been proud to call its own, and inside, canvases by Richard Diebenkorn and Jasper Johns decorated the ivory-colored walls. But nothing about the house seemed to have been designed to impress or intimidate.

If anything, Bob and Little Anne seemed to be trying to overcome the barriers created by their great wealth. As a benefit for Trinity Valley, a private Fort Worth day school, they threw a fifties sock hop, to which they wore matching letter sweaters. And Bob's office on the thirty-first floor of First City Tower was virtually identical with those of his associates: gray industrial-grade carpeting; a computer atop a white laminate desk; a glass wall looking out on the reception area.

In person Bob and Anne Bass were refreshingly unpretentious. They both laughed easily. While they seemed more relaxed talking about Fort Worth's virtues and problems than about Bob's business ventures or anything personal, they came across as witty and genuine.

Bob, who was chairman of the board of the National Trust for Historic Preservation, had a long-standing interest in bringing old buildings back to life. When the Robert M. Bass Group wasn't busy taking over *Fortune* 500 companies, it occupied itself with new commercial construction and restoration of historic structures from Denver to the nation's capital. It renovated Washington's century-old Bond Building, famous for its terra-cotta facade. As a personal project, Bob and Anne bought Ulysses S. Grant's Georgetown mansion for two million dollars and redid it into a showplace second residence.

To Bob Bass, saving old buildings was less a matter of sentimental nostalgia than of efficient and appropriate land use. "There is a need to use resources to preserve attributes and correct deficiencies, rather than ignoring what is there and sprawling outwards," he said. Anne even laid many of urban America's social problems at the feet of developers who deserted central business districts and older neighborhoods to chase cheaper suburban real estate. "Having an inner city that is decaying, that is not providing the proper job opportunities or home environment is just unhealthy," she said. Although the Basses' spokespeople presented the eclectic downtown redevelopment as an expression of one entity, Bass Brothers Enterprises, Sundance Square was clearly Bob's.

Bob and Anne were the most civically involved of the Basses. He was chairman of the board of the Cook-Fort Worth Children's Medical Center, and both were on the Van Cliburn's cabinet, or board of directors. Like a turbocharged Junior Leaguer, Anne radiated an intense commitment to social services, not necessarily the most fashionable causes. She'd startled other members of worthy committees by showing up when it was time to do mailings and sitting on the floor, with everyone else, stuffing envelopes.

In spite of her size, Little Anne Bass could be formidably assertive and articulate.

"There's very little public support for social services in Fort Worth," she said bluntly. Here, as in most of Texas, shelters for the homeless, free testing for children with developmental problems, and similar responsibilities that a compassionate, farsighted government would have assumed were left to volunteers like her. But Anne seemed free of the condescension that afflicted so many rich Texans involved in good works. She spoke not of "the poor," but of "people who may be down on their luck or who for whatever reason may be unable to provide for themselves," as if she could actually imagine herself in that position.

Both Bob and Anne were intensely involved in I-CARE (Citizen Advocates for Responsible Expansion). I-CARE's broad agenda was to steer Fort Worth's development in the direction of greater livability. "The city is going to grow," Bob said. "The challenge is to bias the growth to be better growth than it would be if it were left alone."

I-CARE successfully blocked two proposed elevated freeways. One would have cut through the heart of the museum district; the other would have slashed across the south end of downtown, casting its shadow over the Water Gardens and destroying several of the city's most pleasing historic buildings.

Rather than attempt to block freeways altogether, the group proposed practical alternative routes that didn't require raising the road surface above street level. "Elevated freeways become impenetrable barriers to development," Bob explained. "You end up with no form of human life within a block of the freeway."

I-CARE couldn't have taken on the Texas Department of Highways and Public Transportation, the Federal Highway Administration, and the U.S. Department of Transportation without Bob Bass's money—money to develop workable alternatives, money for lawyers to fight the agencies in court. But Bob and Anne Bass didn't just go ahead on their own Fort Worth rich style. They got thirty organizations involved.

"The freeway thing is a very interesting situation just by itself," Anne said. "But what's really significant is that for the first time in the city of Fort Worth a coalition of very diverse groups came together to work on a project."

"Everything from the Sierra Club to the teamsters' union," Bob interjected.

For Fort Worth, the freeway fight marked a movement away from the Carter and Kimbell style of philanthropy, which gave people things at the expense of their feeling of ownership. "The city is being opened up in terms of the process of participation," Anne said. "I think that's very healthy. It adds a new dimension."

For Bob Bass, I-CARE marked an entrance into politics. In 1986, with the freeway fight in full froth, Governor Mark White, a Democrat, appointed Bob to the three-member Texas Highway Commission. He accepted, even though it meant filing a twenty-seven-page public declaration of his financial holdings. But he kept the position less than a year. After Republican Bill Clements defeated White, the new governor replaced Bob with Dallasite Robert Dedman, founder of the Club Corporation of America.

Perry Bass had served a stint as chairman of the Texas Parks and Wildlife Commission, but for the most part the Basses had left the governing to others. They had two political war chests—the Good Government Fund and the Bass Brothers Political Action Committee, which gave to both Republicans and Democrats, sometimes in the same race. But on his own Bob Bass emerged as an active backer of liberal Democrats. In 1984 Perry and Sid supported conservative Phil Gramm for the U.S. Senate; Bob backed Austin attorney Lloyd Doggett, a fellow baby boomer who'd fought for progressive social and environmental legislation during his eleven years in the Texas legislature.

Fort Worth's state senator, Hugh Parmer, who also went to Yale, observed that the boyish billionaire had "put together an interesting political coalition, focused mainly on environmental issues, that may give him power beyond his economic clout." Parmer added: "Sid hires people to worry about politics. Bob worries about it some himself."

After Bob Bass's purchase of the Grant mansion, rumors persisted that he might even have national political ambitions of his own.

The Bass who might eventually have the greatest impact and even the greatest wealth was the least conventional— Ed. He bankrolled Decisions Team Limited, an international group of free-form intellectuals. Their detractors called them a cult, but they called themselves synergists, after Buckminster Fuller's concept of synergy, the hypothesis that the behavior of the whole couldn't be predicted by the behavior of its parts.

During the late 1960's thousands of hirsute idealists discussed the far-out things they'd do to change the world if only they had the money.

Ed Bass was different. He had it.

After graduating from college in 1968, Ed, who'd been interested in architecture since his prep school days at Phillips Academy, stayed on in New Haven and enrolled in the Yale School of Architecture. But he dropped out after a trip to New Mexico during spring break in 1970. That part of the country had long been a mecca for artists and writers, and it had evolved into a major nexus for hippies. Ed stayed and began building adobe houses and condos in and around Santa Fe.

Some of Ed Bass's real estate projects involved a commune led by John Allen, a charismatic Oklahoma native of about forty. For a subculture guru, Allen had exceptionally solid academic credentials. He'd attended Oklahoma University, Northwestern University, Stanford, and the Colorado School of Mines, and he'd received an M.B.A. from Harvard in 1962. He also had a philosophy based partly on the teachings of the early-twentieth-century Armenian mystic G. I. Gurdjieff, who likened ordinary life to a state of sleep and promoted the use of dance and other art forms as means of awakening the spirit. Dubbing itself the Theater of All Possibilities, one arm of Allen's tribe toured the country in a yellow school bus, performing avant-garde dramatic productions.

Ed didn't join Allen's commune, but he did become a director of Decisions Team Limited, the international corporation that grew out of it in 1980. At the core of DTL was a closely knit group of about forty people, mostly from North America and Great Britain. They went by fanciful nicknames—among them, Moondancer, Chutney, Firefly, Honey, Houlihan, and Horseshit. Ed was Sharkey; John Allen was Johnny Dolphin; Allen's wife, Marie, was Flash. They dedicated themselves to forging a new civilization capable of surviving the collapse of Western culture.

To that apocalyptically ambitious end, DTL undertook a mixed bag of expensive projects, from the aesthetic to the technological, in eight countries. The eighty-room solar-powered Hotel Vajra in Kathmandu, Nepal, offered moderately priced accommodations for high-altitude tourists. October Gallery and Lundonia House in London's bohemian Bloomsbury district exhibited and published avant-garde works of art and literature. In eight hundred acres of rain forest outside San Juan, Puerto Rico, Las Casas de la Selva developed new plant species. Synergia Ranch near Santa Fe, New Mexico, explored innovative irrigation methods. At Aix-en-Provence, France, Les Marronniers Conference Center provided a forum for free-form interdisciplinary debate. Overseeing all this was the Decisions Team Limited Management Company in Hong Kong.

Ed spent six months out of every year in the outback of western Australia, where DTL's Savannah Systems Corporation experimented with dry-land sheep ranching and drought-resistant grasses at two facilities—Birdwood Downs (five thousand acres) and Quanbun Downs (three hundred thousand acres)—grappling with the problems of ecological degradation facing much of the world. The closest city, Perth, was twelve hundred miles away.

DTL's quasi-academic arm, the Institute of Ecotechnics, dispensed degrees from its centers in London, India, France, and New Mexico and aboard the RV *Heraclitus*, a 140-ton research-equipped ferroconcrete Chinese junk, which studied the world's oceans. But the value of these degrees was open to question since they demanded little or no grounding in conventional disciplines. Some traditionally trained academics described the DTL-sponsored conferences they attended as exciting; others derided them as loosely organized and fraught with fuzzy thinking.

Two things were certain: First, Synergetic Civilization, the decision-making core of Decisions Team Limited, took itself seriously. Secondly, its endeavors cost a whole lot of money. How much of that money came from Ed Bass? A bunch. Perhaps almost all. But Ed never put more than 10 percent of his capital into these projects. The rest he kept in conservative investments.

DTL's most accessible venture, Caravan of Dreams, was all Ed's. In fact, it came into being after he'd moved back to Fort Worth in 1979 and discovered that there were no apartments in the middle of the central business district, where he wanted to live.

Named for the last tale in the *One Thousand and One Nights*, the story that wins Scheherazade her life and freedom, Caravan was a $5.5 million island rising between the twin Tandy towers and Sundance Square in downtown Fort Worth. The face it presented at street level was relatively bland: the neatly restored storefronts of four late-nineteenth-century commercial buildings. From lighted glass cases, posters and photos announced coming performances by such jazz greats as Wynton Marsalis, Stan Getz, Carmen McRae, Sun Ra, and Dizzy Gillespie. Ed had loved jazz since prep school, when he'd discovered saxophonist Ornette Coleman, a Fort Worth native who blended American jazz, rock, and rhythm and blues with ethnic musical forms from the third world. (In 1987 Caravan of Dreams launched its own record label, featuring Coleman and his disciples.)

Inside, Caravan's first floor was a nightclub. Sprinkled with aging hipsters and mixed-race couples, the lounge could have been a cellar dive off Bleecker Street in New York's Greenwich Village. A neon rendition of a yogi playing a saxophone hung above the bar. A mural depicting the history of jazz surged in strong primary hues across the long wall flanking the stage. On the shorter wall opposite was a mural dedicated to the world of dance, from Martha Graham to Australian aborigines. Poking out from behind the Chrysler Building in the jazz mural were two rockets, one a red and black war missile threatening to destroy the world, the other a radiant white starship promising a new, more harmonious home for humankind on other planets.

On the second level, a 212-seat theater presented dance, fringe drama, classics by Aeschylus and Shakespeare, mixed-media performance art, and stand-up acts by William Burroughs and Timothy Leary. Sharing this floor were an art gallery, a studio for dance and the martial arts, and several apartments, one of them Ed Bass's. But the most popular part of the whole artsy amalgam was the roof. For those who could get seats, its Grotto Bar, complete with a waterfall flanked by full-size palm trees, was the best spot in Texas for a quiet drink. Crowning one side of the roof, a fifty-foot glass and steel geodesic dome housed cacti and succulents from Tehuacán, Namibia, Malagasy, and the shores of the Sea of Cortés. Neon galactic spirals and a crescent man in the moon decorated the dome's surface.

Ed Bass's New Age interests may have been eccentric and extravagant, but until March 10, 1985, they seemed harmless. That was the day Texans woke up to find EDWARD BASS FUNDS "INTELLECTUAL CULT," leaping at them from the front page of the *Dallas Morning News*. Lennox Samuels, staff writer for the largest-circulation paper in the Dallas-Fort Worth Metroplex, focused the day's lead story on allegations by former Caravan of Dreams associate artistic director Carol Line that the group John Allen had established was an intellectually elitist cult. She recounted meetings of Synergetic Civilization at which Allen dressed down recalcitrant members, accusing them of being too attached to material comforts; Samuels quoted another participant's anonymous description of the browbeatings as "mental torture." Had one of the richest men in Texas fallen under the spell of some Jim Jones of the avant-garde?

There were several problems with the exposé. Ms. Line, a Fort Worth native, had left her position under a cloud: Artistic director Honey Hoffman had accused her of stealing between $750 and $20,000. Beyond that, the term "cult" was thrown around pretty loosely. Sure, Ed Bass was involved in some radically unconventional ventures, all with the same bunch of people. But the picture of him as a victim of financial exploitation simply didn't come into focus. His relationship with John Allen might not have been that different from Sid Bass's symbiosis with Richard Rainwater. Rather than being stripped to poverty by a charismatic leader, Ed had increased his personal wealth enormously, albeit passively, through his ventures with his brothers. Like his great-uncle Sid Richardson, he was a childless lifelong bachelor; all his nieces and nephews were so well fixed that he didn't need to worry about anyone's financial security but his own.

Besides, some of his far-out ventures, especially the development of new plant species for dry-land farming, had considerable commercial potential.

And Ed Bass held the patents.

In 1984, at Sun Space Ranch and Conference Center in aptly named Oracle, Arizona, DTL began its most ambitious project to date. It was a two-and-one-half-acre miniature earth, a self-contained ecosystem intended as a working laboratory for the colonization of Mars. Buckminster Fuller had called the earth the biosphere, so DTL dubbed its bonzai world Biosphere II. Inside a white-girder and glass structure that some observers likened to a new Hyatt Regency were a marsh, a desert, a rain forest, a savanna, a shallow sea with a coral reef, and a lagoon—all in miniature. Off to one side were a farm, with yard-square plots of wheat and rye, and a microcity, with room for eight biospherians. Fish swam in the biosphere's ponds; Vietnamese pigs wandered its forest; this cross between Eden and Noah's Ark even had 250 species of insects, including mosquitoes, but they were a variety that bit frogs rather than humans. Biosphere II was a closed, self-sufficient system.

Starting in fall 1990, eight volunteers were to be sealed into this giant vivarium, linked to the outside world only by telephone, computer, and video camera. When they weren't tending the crops or conducting experiments on their Lilliputian environment, they could snorkel in their tiny sea. Ed Bass decided not to become one of the biospherians but told *Texas Monthly*'s Joe Nick Patoski, "They will be able to lead a much richer life than most people."

And Ed paid the entire thirty-million-dollar tab.

Guided through Biosphere II by Space Biospherics staff dressed in stylish red jumpsuits with Buck Rogers shoulder flanges, the media blinked, but they didn't scoff. Maybe expensive long-term projects like the colonization of space were best left to private visionaries like this child of the sixties with his billion-dollar bankroll.

CHAPTER SEVENTEEN

★

The Unsinkable Jack Grimm

From the time they were first homesteaded in the 1870's, the rolling plains north and west of Fort Worth spawned a breed of individualists whose idiosyncrasies flourished unabated by the restraining forces of urban society. Take Abilene's "Cadillac Jack" Grimm—independent oilman and adventurer, formidable poker player, and Cowboy Capitalist. He had a penchant for such fanciful projects as the search for the Loch Ness Monster and the quest for the wreckage of Noah's Ark.

Grimm didn't much like the nickname Cadillac Jack, bestowed by his friend Nelson Bunker Hunt. In the Mercedes and Rolls days of the Texas oil boom, it had lost the connotations of flashy wealth it had had during the Depression, when Cadillac Jack was the *nom de guerre* of a notorious local bootlegger in southeastern Oklahoma, where Grimm grew up. But despite Grimm's objections, the handle stuck.

With his five feet nine inches of condensed energy wedged into his cramped office 150 miles west of Fort Worth, Grimm explained that he'd been chasing buried treasure since he was twelve. Hearing from his grandfather, a pioneer wildcatter, that the sixteenth-century Spanish explorer Francisco Vásquez de Coronado had stashed gold on the family ranch, young Grimm and a friend bought a case of dynamite from the hardware store and blew up part of a creek bed. They didn't find any doubloons, but they did blast loose two handfuls of lead shot, some arrowheads, and an old iron skillet. A decade later, seeking to learn more effective methods of extracting the earth's bounty, Grimm earned a degree in petroleum geology from Oklahoma University. Then he set off with his bride, Jackie, on a three-month honeymoon panning for gold in California.

As Grimm described his early exploits, his brown eyes, set well back from his imposing nose, glinted out from under his bushy salt-and-pepper brows. With his longish ruff of white hair grazing the collar of his shirt, Jack Grimm looked like an American bald eagle, an endangered raptor still intent on his prey. His gaze darted back and forth across his desk from the bottle of Maalox to the clear plastic container of Chupa Chups lollipops. After several seconds of intent study he snatched a lollipop.

Right out of college Grimm did something virtually unheard of: He struck oil on the first well he drilled. "I thought I was so smart," he said. "It wasn't until I drilled twenty-five dry holes in a row in 1955 that I knew how dumb I was. They took out my phone and everything." Eventually Grimm's luck changed. He went on to find forty oil and gas fields, as well as a couple of veins of gold and silver in Nevada and Utah.

Jack Grimm liked finding things. When he wasn't digging for oil or prospecting for precious metals, he was mounting a number of quixotic expeditions: one to capture Bigfoot, the elusive man-ape of British Columbia; another to photograph the legendary Loch Ness Monster; another to locate evidence, such as ancient ship's timbers, that Noah's Ark had landed on the rocky summit of Turkey's Mount Ararat; yet another to mine for emeralds (his favorite stone) in Colombia, where he had to defend his treasure from bandits.

In 1980 he made the first of his three attempts to find the *Titanic*. In 1981 he underwrote the efforts of five Christian fundamentalists who smuggled four thousand miniature Tibetan-language versions of the New Testament into Tibet, and in 1983 he came up with the cash to allow three wheelchair-bound paraplegic Vietnam vets to climb the highest mountain in Texas—8,751-foot Guadalupe Peak. In 1984 Grimm set out on yet another quest, one to locate and salvage a paddle-wheeler that sank off Charleston in 1850 with at least five million dollars in gold coins and all the nuggets carried by four hundred New York-bound forty-niners. Grimm found what looked like an outline of the doomed *South America*, but a Carolina treasure hunter claimed he'd found it first and chased the Texan away from the site with a court injunction.

By 1989 Grimm was putting together a search for the submerged ruins of the fabled city of Atlantis. He thought he'd located the spot—the Amphire Banks 450 miles west of Gibraltar and 135 feet deep. He planned to use a small, highly maneuverable underwater vessel owned by French deep-sea exploration company IFREMER and equipped with arms capable of recovering relics of the lost civilization. He also intended to film the search and salvage operation.

Even Grimm's more modest expeditions, like the three-hundred-thousand-dollar thwarted search for the *South America*, were staggeringly expensive. To recoup some of the costs, Grimm turned them into real-life cinematic adventures narrated by the likes of Orson Welles and Joseph Cotten. Then Jack F. Grimm Productions—whose logo was an oil derrick spouting strips of movie film—sold the rights to cable television.

Grimm didn't foot the bill for his enterprises alone. He had a knack for getting others to invest in his adventures even though all the most glamorous ones lost money, except for the search for Noah's Ark, which resulted in a profitable documentary, *Expedition to Ararat*. As with oil wildcatting, only part of the appeal was in the enormous potential for profit. Grimm's investors were mostly fellow Cowboy Capitalists who preferred to make or lose money in things they could brag about at the Petroleum Club.

"Part of the fun of doing these projects is trying to structure them as successful business ventures," Grimm said. "If there's a profit, we take it. If not, it's a write-off." He paused and frowned pensively, as if trying to deflect the troublesome truth that much of the money that supported these exploits might otherwise end up in the federal treasury shaving a millimeter off the deficit. "I don't like the word 'write-off.' " He edited himself. "It's a business loss."

Whenever articles appeared about his exploits, Grimm was flooded with requests for backing. He responded positively when evangelist Edward Ainsley asked him to finance the Bible-smuggling mission to Tibet, demanding only that the four thousand miniature New Testaments contained in the luggage be piled on top of some heavier contraband: two 16 mm cameras, prohibited to outsiders not accompanied by Chinese government escorts. The five missionary smugglers accomplished their objectives while Grimm's two cameramen roamed freely through villages barred to Westerners since the forties and came back with the uncensored footage for two movies, *The Tibet File* and *The China Experience*.

Grimm claimed he agreed to help Ainsley with his Bible smuggling after being miraculously cured of some old shrapnel wounds in his hips while watching the evangelist on TV. But his generosity toward religious causes had its limits. When another fundamentalist preacher called and said, "God came to me in a dream last night and said you were going to give me a Learjet," Grimm replied curtly, "God didn't come to *me* in that dream."

Jack Grimm's fascination with the *Titanic* began in his childhood. His devoutly Baptist mother had told him about the disaster, explaining that the ship had been a boatload of sinners and that the iceberg had been God's vengeance on them all. But it wasn't until 1980 that he seriously considered looking for the doomed luxury liner. While searching for silver in Utah, Grimm rummaged through the debris left in an abandoned prospector's cabin. He found hidden among the papers a perfectly preserved copy of the Salt Lake *Herald-Republican* dated April 15, 1912—the day after the night the *Titanic* sank.

Along with news of the disaster, the paper mentioned all the wealthy and prominent people on board, among them John Jacob Astor, the American journalist and painter F. D.

Millet, Grand Trunk Railroad President C. M. Hayes, rough-hewn Denver widow turned international socialite "The Unsinkable" Molly Brown, and Macy's owner Isidor Straus. Delighted to be on the maiden voyage of the world's premier passenger ship, many were returning to New York from the lavish European social season. Their luggage was stuffed with expensive mementos. Their most valuable jewels were locked in the purser's waterproof safe, along with a ruby- and pearl-encrusted volume of the *Rubáiyát of Omar Khayyám.* (The much ballyhooed opening of that safe on live television in October 1987 showed that someone had had the presence of mind to clean it out before the ship sank.)

Resolved to find the *Titanic,* Grimm spent more than two million dollars on three serious attempts—1980, 1981, and 1983—and went along on every one of them. The 1980 and 1983 expeditions were washouts, but the 1981 trip had some interesting results.

Getting even a shot at finding the legendary ship buried under two and a half miles of water involved developing special deep-sea research equipment: a seven-foot-long platform mounted with sonar devices, a million-dollar magnetometer, and cameras that could be towed at depths that would crush any but the most experimental submarines. Called the Deep-Tow, this package was the result of twenty years of work by the Marine Physical Lab at the Scripps Institution of Oceanography in La Jolla, California. Although they would have liked more than the scheduled two weeks at sea, the Scripps scientists were happy, for a price, to lump the *Titanic* search with an ongoing project to map the magnetic and sonar properties of that part of the North Atlantic, a featureless expanse littered with debris dropped by icebergs.

The second *Titanic* expedition cost more than $450,000. Investors included Bunker Hunt and James Drury, television's erstwhile "Virginian." Drury also went along on the search to provide shipboard narration for *Return to the Titanic.*

Grimm's conviction that films that allowed people to participate vicariously in real-life adventures could make a lot of money led him to try embellishing the *Titanic* saga by taking a trained monkey aboard the research vessel *Gyre.* The monkey, he reasoned, would add visual interest to the film by pointing to navigation charts, indicating spots where the luxury liner might lie. One of the heads of the science team, Dr. Fred Spiess of Scripps, gave Grimm a flat ultimatum. "Either the monkey goes or I go," he insisted. The monkey stayed ashore.

To promote the expedition further, Grimm hired ghost-writer Bill Hoffman to write a book about it. He also dreamed up a contest timed to coincide with the book's release. The object was to find a photo of an eighteen-inch gold model of the *Titanic* that Grimm had commissioned as the prize. Cast of fourteen-carat gold with rigging of platinum wire, the model was a marvel of realism. The little gold propellers even turned. The photo was inserted in a volume of *America Yesterday* on a shelf of the New York Public Library. Grimm published the clues—cryptograms drawn from the *Titanic* book—in newspapers across the country. Although he had hoped the contest would drag on for a well-publicized year with mounting book sales, two Pentagon cryptographers and a New York banker teamed up and found the snapshot in five days. Because the three would have had trouble sharing the prize, Grimm bought it back from them for twenty-five thousand dollars, then stored it in a vault at an Abilene jewelry store.

Throughout our interview Jack Grimm reiterated his claim that his team did find the *Titanic* on that second trip and just didn't have time to record its features fully. Confidently pulling a set of computer-enhanced strobe-lit photos from his desk drawer, Grimm explained that they showed the *Titanic*'s propeller, standing upright as it would if it were still attached. The image was of a flat object with curving edges. It did, indeed, look man-made, and it resembled another picture Grimm pulled from the drawer, this one of the propeller of the *Titanic*'s sister ship, the *Olympic*.

The 1981 expedition's scientists were more skeptical than Grimm. "Jack wanted to make it a propeller so bad that if there was any way he could have made it a propeller, he would have," said Scripps engineer Tony Boegeman, who helped design the Deep-Tow and used it on the 1981 *Titanic* expedition. "Very interesting picture, though," he added.

Grimm's picture was snapped on the ocean bottom 12,800 feet down and only half a mile from the spot where the forward portion of the ship—which by some reports may have broken in two on the surface—was found in 1985 by a consortium from the Woods Hole Oceanographic Institution and IFREMER. (Grimm wasn't involved in that find.)

For all their objectivity, even the most hard-nosed scientists were caught up in the romance of Grimm's search. Everybody brought and read *Titanic* books. Grimm traded *Titanic* jokes with the scientists and crew. But he also took his share of the boring winch watches, keeping an eye on the line that held the Deep-Tow, maintaining his humor during weather so rough it turned even the ship's sea-seasoned crew green. And he engaged in that venerable Cowboy Capitalist pastime, poker.

When it came to poker, Cadillac Jack was used to winning. In 1976 he placed second against some of the country's top professional players in the World Series of Poker at Benny Binion's Horseshoe Club in Las Vegas, where he was also named "Most Congenial Participant." ("That means," he quipped, "that I could lose ten thousand dollars and still smile.") Although poker playing was endemic on research ships, Grimm ate the *Gyre*'s crew and the scientists alive. He later said that his biggest problem was letting them recoup their losses, including the pickup truck and the three rifles for which he held IOUs, without telegraphing that he was throwing the hands.

"I play cards at sea quite a bit, and I usually come home with two or three hundred dollars," said Tony Boegeman. "I don't play when I'm tired, and I don't play when I'm busy, and I don't play when I don't think I can win." He added, "I didn't think I could win against Jack Grimm. I watched, and I watched very carefully. He's very careful about increasing the odds in his favor. He's one hell of a poker player."

Politically Jack Grimm was a self-styled progressive conservative. "I believe in forward progress with caution," he explained. "I'm fiercely patriotic, and all I hope for is to see this great nation survive the threat of communism." One way to discourage a potential Communist takeover, he contended, was to arm the citizenry. "If everybody has guns, there's no way anybody could take us over," he said.

Grimm thought that what the country needed was more

great men. "Where are all the American heroes?" he asked, adding, "Do you know who I think would have made a great President? John Connally." Harry Truman and Teddy Roosevelt also ranked high on Grimm's roster of greatness.

One topic Jack Grimm and Teddy Roosevelt would have agreed on was the buffalo. Until the 1970's millions of bison migrated through the gap between the hills on Grimm's twenty-four-hundred-acre ranch eighteen miles south of Abilene at Buffalo Gap. On one day, Grimm said, buffalo hunters—lusting for the dollar per skin traders offered for the hides—shot five hundred thousand buffalo, leaving their carcasses to rot in the draw at the foot of Grimm's Mountain, a mesa that was called Nelson's Mountain up until Jack Grimm bought the land.

To honor "the only living creature on earth that could furnish a complete life-support system to an entire civilization," Grimm planned a bas-relief tribute two-thousand feet long, three times the size of the Mount Rushmore carvings. Chiseled into the limestone cap rock at the top of Grimm's Mountain, it would depict the chronology of the shaggy beasts that once made the Great Plains tremble beneath their hooves. At one end would be the huge herds that thundered across the prairie before the coming of humans; at the other would be the advent of the buffalo hunters and the locomotive. As Grimm described it, when the light was right, the shadows would shift, and the buffalo would seem to move.

He was also thinking of adding something else to the giant frieze: the heads of the seven *Challenger* astronauts.

In a pen at the foot of his mesa Jack Grimm kept about twenty buffalo. When he drove up, they trotted toward the fence, looking hopefully for the oat cakes he fed them during snowy winters. Grimm and the buffalo seemed to feel a kinship for each other. It hadn't been so long since it looked as if the American independent oilman might be in as much danger of extinction as the American bison.

But like the buffalo, Grimm and his species were hanging in there, although in smaller numbers. "Nowadays we independents drill among ourselves," he explained. "It's 'I'll take a quarter of your deal if you'll take a quarter of mine.' "

Jack Grimm might have found it easier to round up capital if he'd lived in Houston, Dallas, or Fort Worth, but he seemed firmly planted in Abilene, where people recognized him in restaurants and shouted to him from across the street about getting together to hash out deals. He got to be utterly himself and still the most famous man in town. If he had lived in one of the state's capitals of commerce, he might have had to spend money on things he didn't consider potentially profitable, inspiring, or fun. He might even have been overshadowed by other eccentrics, although he didn't like that term.

"Do I seem like an eccentric to you?" he asked. "I'm not an eccentric. I'm just an ordinary person who does these things."

CHAPTER EIGHTEEN

★

Electra Waggoner Biggs

Haut *on the Range*

The country along the Red River, which separated Texas from Oklahoma, was a flat expanse of rust-colored clay topped by buffalo grass, mesquite, rattlesnakes, and equally rust-colored dust. Until the late 1800's most white people were content to leave this stretch of unpromising-looking real estate to the Wichitas and Comanches. Not Dan Waggoner.

Waggoner had inherited a modest legacy: one filly, twelve sheep, fourteen head of cattle, 21½ acres of land, and $3.45 cash. In 1854 he used the profit from his little farm to buy fifteen thousand acres near Decatur, forty miles northwest of Fort Worth. It was a hardscrabble existence, what with Indian raids and droughts, but he made it through the Civil War by selling cattle to the Confederate army for ten dollars a head. In 1870 Waggoner and his son W.T., known as Tom, drove a herd of longhorns to Kansas and returned with $55,000, a fortune in those days. They moved northwest

125 miles to Vernon (the town's original name was *Mount Vernon*, but its realistic solons soon dropped the reference to topography), where they put forty thousand into dollar-an-acre land. The Waggoners kept expanding, increasing their herd, making more money, buying more land. At one point after Dan Waggoner's death a fellow rancher reportedly asked Tom whether he planned to purchase all the land in Texas. "I only want mine and what joins it," he replied.

Tom Waggoner put together 535,000 acres, all inside one fence; it was still that way in 1989. Stretching into six counties, the Waggoner Ranch was the largest contiguous spread in the country. (The King Ranch was more than half again as big, but its five separate divisions hopscotched across South Texas.) It was also the biggest ranch in private hands. It all belonged to a trust controlled by Tom Waggoner's granddaughter Electra Waggoner Biggs and his great-grandson A. B. "Bucky" Wharton III.

The Waggoner brand—three backward *D*'s—was hard to doctor, so Tom Waggoner seldom lost cattle to rustlers. But scarcity of water limited the number of animals he could run on the ranch. One day in 1902, decades after rail shipment to Fort Worth had replaced the long cattle drives, he was drilling a deepwater well when he struck oil. "Damn the oil," he said, cursing the sticky black stuff spraying out over his field. "I want water."

Once Waggoner had overcome his resistance to poking unsightly holes in his pasture, his ranch was soon producing enough petroleum to pay for all the water tanks he could ever want. By the end of the 1920's rigs operated by nineteen companies clustered around the northeast section of the ranch, near the former town of Beaver, since named Electra for the cattle and oil baron's only daughter.

The family came to refer to the original Electra Waggoner as Electra I. In Greek mythology there were three Electras: the daughter of Agamemnon and the treacherous Clytemnestra; one of the Pleiades and the mother by Zeus of Dardanus, the founder of Troy; and a sea nymph, mother of the Harpies and of Iris, the rainbow. Tom Waggoner didn't name his daughter for any of these; he named her for her maternal grandfather, Electius Halsell.

Electra I was her father's darling. Even before he struck

oil, Tom Waggoner couldn't do enough for her. Her shopping sprees were epic. Shortly after Neiman Marcus opened,
she spent twenty thousand dollars there in one day, then
came back the next for twenty thousand more. She stocked
her closet with 350 pairs of shoes at a time.

Waggoner also tried his best to give his little girl the
subtle advantages enjoyed by daughters of the rich in the
East. On one of those around-the-world cruises considered
the capstone of a young Edwardian lady's education, she
met her future husband, A. B. Wharton. He was a scion of
a Main Line Philadelphia family that had come to the New
World with William Penn, made a fortune in steel, and gone
on to found the University of Pennsylvania's Wharton School
of Finance and Commerce.

Tom Waggoner also had two sons, Guy and E. Paul.
Guy married and divorced eight times; his heirs eventually
settled for a passel of land the family had picked up in New
Mexico. Paul loved horses and made the Waggoner Ranch
world-famous for its quarter horses. He once turned down
five hundred thousand dollars for his favorite, a stallion
named Poco Bueno, who was still siring foals at twenty-six.
When Poco died, Paul buried him standing up just inside
the main gates to the ranch and topped the grave with an
elaborately carved granite marker.

E. Paul Waggoner named his only child after his sister.
Electra II was a brown-eyed blonde with a strong profile and
elegant carriage. Like the children of many Northwest Texas
ranchers, she was born in Fort Worth, spent her early childhood on the ranch, then moved back to Fort Worth when
she was six, ready to start school and learn to be a proper
lady. Her parents sent her off at twelve to Miss Wright's in
Bryn Mawr, the heart of Philadelphia's Main Line. The girls
there called her Tex and teased her about being a ranch girl,
"especially about my accent," she said during an interview
at Santa Rosa, her fifteen-room red tile-roofed Spanish colonial villa on the Waggoner Ranch.

With its acres of lawn and formal gardens, its marble
floors and pickled-pine woodwork, its regal portrait of a
young Electra II in the living room and its Remington of a
mustachioed cavalryman at the foot of the stairs, Santa Rosa

was an oasis of gentility on a rough red-dirt prairie unbroken except by oil pumpjacks and windmills. On this January afternoon a heavy snowfall cushioned the countryside. The runoff made the water in the fourteen-hundred-acre artificial lake next to the house as red as the coats on the white-faced Herefords the Waggoner ran.

Despite her schoolmates' teasing, Electra II loved the East. She finished at Miss Hourigan's School for Girls in New York and made her debut at the Bachelors' Cotillion in Baltimore. Urged by her mother to acquire a strong business background in preparation for sharing the management of the ranch with her cousin A. B. "Bucky" Wharton, she enrolled in accounting courses at Columbia. She hated accounting, although a Columbia business student she'd met the previous summer aboard a ship to France helped her with her homework. When she married the helpful young man, Arthur Gordon Bowman, in 1933, she was eighteen.

The marriage lasted only a year, and she kept the name of the groom as close a secret as her date of birth; but Edward Steichen's bridal portrait, which appeared in that July 15's *Vogue*, became one of his most famous photographs. Electra II was ethereal in a gown with great wings of white tulle floating from the shoulders. She carried a bouquet of huge white orchids. Crowning her short coiffure was Electra I's wedding veil, which had cost Tom Waggoner ten thousand dollars a generation earlier.

Electra II may have become disenchanted with her groom, but she was still enamored of New York. To persuade her parents that there was a valid reason for her to stay in Manhattan, she took up sculpting, thinking she might enjoy the feel of the clay. Somewhat to her surprise, she was very good at it.

While other aspiring artists shivered in lofts, Electra Waggoner entertained in her eleven-room apartment with a balcony overlooking the East River. Aided by her beauty and vivacious personality, and her family's money, she was an enormous social success.

Electra II's social contacts helped her get her early commissions; the quality of her work did the rest. Her first major piece was a bust of Notre Dame football great Knute Rockne

for inventor-industrialist Vincent Bendix, whose aviation corporation made some of the fastest planes in the world. In
Paris she apprenticed in a bronze foundry and learned to cut
marble. While in France, Electra Waggoner won third place
in the prestigious Salon d'Automne for "Enigma," a head of
her half-black, half-Indian maid done in black Belgian marble.
The piece became part of the permanent collection of the
Huntington Museum in Pasadena, California. She had ex-
hibitions in New York galleries. She did a large bust of Bob
Hope. But her most famous sculpture was the thirteen-and-
a-half-foot bronze of Will Rogers on his horse, Soapsuds.
One casting stood at the entrance to the Will Rogers Coliseum
in Fort Worth, another on the campus of Texas Tech University in Lubbock, and the third in front of the Cowboy Hall
of Fame in Claremore, Oklahoma. The piece took her five
years to complete, but she didn't need to come back to Texas
to do it. She used a New York City police horse as a model
for Soapsuds.

At a friend's suggestion, shortly after her divorce, Electra
Waggoner called fellow Texan John Biggs, a young executive
in International Paper's New York office. She'd met him on
a blind date when she was seventeen and he was a football
and baseball star at the Virginia Military Institute. This time
he took her to Coney Island and won her heart.

After her marriage to John Biggs, men found the Texas
heiress, if anything, more fascinating than before. One evening at dinner she was seated next to the chairman of Lockheed. "He kept looking at me," she recounted. "Finally, he
said, 'That's a hell of a name for an airplane.' " Which is
how the Lockheed Electra came to be. And it wasn't the only
glamorous machine christened in her honor. John Biggs's
brother-in-law, General Motors president H. H. "Red" Curtis, named the Buick Electra for her.

At the end of World War II the socialite sculptress and
her husband moved back to the ranch. A native of Sherman,
a small city north of Dallas, John Biggs adjusted more easily
than the rancher's daughter did. He managed the Waggoner
Ranch from 1953 until his death in 1975, moving it to the
threshold of the era when it would keep its breeding records
on computers and use helicopters to check the cattle.

Although she had learned to ride at six, Mrs. Biggs never cared much for horses. She preferred dancing, and frankly feminine ball gowns suited her better than boots and jeans. But her younger daughter, Helen Biggs Willingham, had Paul Waggoner's love of quarter horses and grew up to take care of that part of the ranching operation. The Waggoner Ranch continued to produce some of the country's finest cutting horses, many of them descended from Poco Bueno.

Mrs. Biggs loved to travel—to New York twice a year, to Europe, and especially to Hong Kong, where she made regular pilgrimages. During hunting season she entertained houseguests from all over the world at Santa Rosa. She also owned part of Château Bouchaine, a Napa Valley winery.

In between international jaunts, Electra Waggoner Biggs sculpted. "I *like* to do it," she said. "I like to be told I'm good." It was more than a hobby. Some of her bronzes sold for as much as sixty thousand dollars. Perched above the sitting room, her studio was a liberating space about forty feet long, with windows on three walls. It smelled earthily of clay. Along the blank wall, a three-sided glass case displayed sculpted portraits of her friend Mary Martin and of Harry Truman, Dwight Eisenhower, Sam Rayburn, Van Cliburn, and other notables.

Mrs. Biggs didn't ride the range, but she had a keen interest in ranching as a business. She was an honorary vice-president of the Southwest Cattlemen's Association and worried as much as any other rancher about the decline in the consumption of red meat.

"I think the cattle industry is coming back," she said, "but we have to combat these doctors who say you're going to die if you eat a piece of beef."

While she would no more discuss the number of cattle on the ranch or the extent of its depleting petroleum reserves than she would reveal her age, Electra Waggoner Biggs clearly identified more with ranching than with oil. "I think there'll always be a ranching mystique," she explained. "There's a romance to it. You can have millions and millions of dollars in oil, and it doesn't have the appeal of ranching."

★

CHAPTER NINETEEN

Stanley Marsh 3

Cristo of the Cap Rock

Slicing diagonally across the Texas Panhandle—the northern extension of the state that juts up through Oklahoma almost to Kansas and Colorado —is a dramatic escarpment more than a thousand feet high. It goes straight up, a wall of rock in varicolored stripes, slashed here and there by water and wind. From the air it looks like a deep one-sided canyon or the start of a mountain range that rises but never comes down.

At its top, above the layers of orange and rust and ocher, is a stratum of buff-colored limestone. Texans call it the cap rock. It marks the High Plains, starting at about thirty-five hundred feet and sloping gradually to a mile in elevation at the base of the Rocky Mountains. Except at the edge of the escarpment, the land is so flat it gives the illusion of being convex, as if the bowl of the sky extended more than 180 degrees. When the Spanish explorer Coronado came through in 1541 on his search for the Seven Cities of Cibola, he found grass so high that it brushed the bellies of his horses and disoriented his men. He christened the region the Llano Estacado (the staked plain).

The Panhandle got about twenty inches of precipitation a year. Ephemeral playa lakes provided the only surface water. These former buffalo wallows filled up like giant round puddles during a good rain, then vanished after a few weeks of dry weather. With irrigation from the underlying Ogallala Aquifer, wheat and long-staple cotton thrived here. So did cattle, provided a rancher allowed twenty acres for each mother cow. Like South Texas and the Trans-Pecos, this was a region of sprawling spreads. Even with modern agricultural methods, a ranch needed to be at least ten thousand acres to make money.

Up on the cap rock, the sun was piercingly bright, the almost ceaseless wind often laden with dust. In January and February blue northers roared through, dropping the temperature to below zero while eight hundred miles south in Brownsville, tourists tanned themselves in seventy-five-degree sunshine. It hardly seemed like the same state.

Most Texans considered the Panhandle the provinces. The Texas expression "He just came down off the cap rock" was roughly equivalent to "He just came in on a load of posts." But this wasn't truly the sticks. Although it had a population just under 150,000, Amarillo, the Panhandle's major city, was the commercial and cultural nexus for half a million people in five states.

Amarillo meant "yellow" in Spanish, and there was a pervasive wheat straw yellow to the landscape and the light. Around the city's perimeter, green and black hazardous cargo route signs served as disquieting reminders that the Pantex plant nine miles east of the airport manufactured the warheads for the country's nuclear missiles. All of America's helium came from here as well, siphoned out of underground rock formations.

This was not a town for people worried about their cholesterol. Forty percent of the beef consumed in the United States was slaughtered within three hundred miles of here; feedlots and slaughterhouses were big business. Amarillo

was full of barbecue joints and steakhouses. The Big Texan
Steak Ranch boasted a gaudy movie-set Old West decor and
a possibly heart-stopping deal: Anyone who could eat a sev-
enty-two-ounce T-bone in an hour got it free.

The Big Texan sat alongside Interstate 40, formerly Route
66, that mythical continent-spanning highway that stretched
across the Panhandle. From this perspective at sixty-five
miles an hour, Amarillo seemed all fast-food restaurants and
giant gas stations doing a bang-up business in diesel fuel
and coin-operated showers.

That was why it was so mystifying yet so appropriate,
when you topped the almost imperceptible rise on I-40 eight
miles west of town, to look south and see a row of ten
Cadillacs—one of every model from 1949 through 1964—
planted nose down in a cow pasture. They appeared to have
crashed from heaven. Tilted toward Tucumcari at precisely
the angle of the sides of the Great Pyramid of Cheops, their
chassis were arranged to show the evolution of the tail fin.

"Cadillac Ranch," as this installation was called, was the
Stonehenge of the American West. Long-haul truckers and
California-bound tourists alike stared at it in wonder as
mixed-breed cattle grazed nonchalantly between the cars. No
signs explained the phenomenon; no security guards protected it. In the decade and a half they'd inclined at the
intersection of Route 66 and Helium Road, the Cadillacs had
been sprayed with red and gray primer, battered by tire irons,
and encrusted with graffiti, giving them an incongruous
punk, urban quality.

"Americans know how to treat their monuments," said
Amarillo oil and gas heir and broadcasting mogul Stanley
Marsh 3 (never III or 3rd), who owned "Cadillac Ranch,"
along with "Floating Mesa," the "Phantom Soft Pool Table,"
and other large-scale works of ambush art. "I think it's just
fine. Since I go out there with people all the time, it makes
it a little different. It's kind of like a new adventure."

Three California architect-artists—Chip Lord, Hudson
Marquez, and Doug Michels—dreamed up the "Cadillac
Ranch" in 1974; Marsh supplied the land and the cars. In the
whimsically countercultural mood of the late sixties and early
seventies, the trio named their firm the Ant Farm for nature's

great underground architects. Their other projects included a house modeled on tumescent male genitalia and a floating salon designed to permit humans to communicate comfortably with porpoises.

To Marsh, the existence of an underlying ideology was what made the cathedral at Chartres, "built by people who'd work a hundred years for something they believed," better than the Empire State Building or the World Trade Center, erected for commercial purposes.

Scrunching down in a green suede armchair in his office on the tenth floor of the tallest structure between Oklahoma City and Denver—the thirty-one-story Texas American Bank Building—Stanley Marsh explained the Ant Farm's credo. His appearance was as eclectic as his interests: the neatly styled white-gray hair and mustache of a middle-aged media executive; the owlish round-rimmed glasses of a curious child; the blue blazer and broad-striped blue and white shirt of an Ivy Leaguer; the faded jeans and soft-soled brown moccasins of an erstwhile hippie. Blown-up black-and-white photos of Marsh's family and friends covered one wall; stacked two deep, seven television sets—one for each network affiliate plus four cable companies—stared out from another. As Marsh talked, he took swigs of Perrier, pausing occasionally to toss an empty little green bottle over his shoulder into a city park-size wire trash basket.

"The Ant Farm believes in the history of consciousness," Marsh explained. "What defines human beings is that we can think of now and then and make plans." The automobile changed consciousness because it allowed restless adolescents to imagine themselves not just in another house or another village but roaring down the highway of endless possibilities.

"The car represented sexual freedom," Marsh said. "It represented value. It changed our whole idea of what we could do with our lives."

And the ultimate car was the Cadillac. It was a mass-produced status symbol, expensive but attainable. Hitting Highway 66 in a tail-finned Cadillac was the American Dream, Marsh said, adding: "So these are buried as a monument to the American Dream—before we felt guilty about the undeveloped world and fossil fuels and using up more than our share of this and that, when we were young and innocent. And they're a monument to our changed consciousness."

Intellectuals debated whether "Cadillac Ranch" was art or kitsch. To the unimaginative, it was an outrageous example of stereotypically Texan conspicuous consumption. (How could they know that the Ant Farm bought most of the cars for one or two hundred dollars through want ads in the Amarillo paper?) But to most people who saw it, that automotive chorus line was simply one of America's more arresting roadside attractions.

That was fine with Stanley Marsh 3. "Driving from Tucumcari, you may see the 'Cadillac Ranch' and you may hate it, but at least it's your decision," he declared. "I don't believe in anything in a museum. Once you walk in and you see the guard and they take your picture with the video camera and you go past the curio shop and the docents and then you go see the painting, you're so intimidated you're either going to like that painting or you're going to hate it depending on how thick the front door is and how fancy the design of the frame is. It says, 'Worship me, worship me, worship me.' So my hobby is to make art things and hide them. I want to create a series of rewards and a surprise for cowboys and hippies."

Stanley Marsh's hobby began with a visit to a Claes Oldenburg exhibit at New York's Museum of Modern Art in 1969. Marsh was so impressed with Oldenburg's fanciful oversize soft sculptures that he went home and constructed two Brobdingnagian neckties: a forty-foot-long, eight-foot-wide four-in-hand for his mother's chimney and a fourteen-foot-wide bow tie for his grandmother's. Then he set about turning his ten-thousand-acre spread into a hidden art ranch.

For months at a time young artists stayed with Marsh, his wife, Wendy, and their five children, creating sculptures. Some, like Roger Dainton's "Night Tree"—a twenty-foot-tall neon spire changing colors with shifting wind speeds—and John Chamberlain's dozen assemblages from wrecked and compacted cars, might have found places in museums. But most were too large and outlandish for any urban venue.

Jack Goddard, one of Marsh's cowboys, squired me around the hidden art. He wore scuffed boots, jeans, and a black Genesis 1987 Tour T-shirt. We bounced down a dirt path to the "Amarillo Ramp," an earthwork fifty feet wide curving four hundred feet in a gradually sloping spiral. The only people likely to stumble across it were cropdusters. Surrounded by mesquite, sotol, and thorny, yellow-tipped cholla, the "Ramp" looked like an Indian burial mound, an eerily appropriate resemblance since the artist, Robert Smithson, died in a plane crash while inspecting his oeuvre.

The "Phantom Soft Pool Table" lurked off another rutted trail. The "Pool Table" was Marsh's own sculpture, executed in canvas, wood, and foam rubber. Everything was twenty times scale. The playing surface was eighty feet by a hundred feet of mowed grass sprayed with bright green watercolor. The soft pool cue was sixty feet long, each of the full set of squooshy balls forty-two inches in diameter. There were even a triangular wooden rack and a giant cue chalk. Unlike the "Amarillo Ramp," the "Phantom Soft Pool Table" could be moved from one location to another.

"The next time you're here, it could be someplace else," Marsh said, adding that part of its point was its inaccessibility. "It's like the Taj Mahal. I always thought the Taj Mahal was a wonderful work of art because no one I know has ever seen it. The best art creates its own myth."

Marsh planned future surprises for those who got lost in their pickups or blown off course by a tornado. He talked about planting wheat, then cutting it into the shape of a hand and calling it the "Great American Farmhand." And about building a hand-shaped corral and filling it with cattle—the "Great American Cowhand." And a soft full-size Statue of Liberty might be fun. She could be moved from place to place and maybe get to hold something besides a torch and a book.

In his monumental eccentricity, Marsh stood somewhere between Jack Grimm and Ed Bass, yet off to the side. Although he shared Grimm's delight in diversion, Marsh didn't try to make money from his projects; that was what his television stations, ranches, and oil and gas interests were for. And unlike Grimm, he was a self-avowed intellectual. He seemed aware of the place he and the works he sponsored

and created had in the broad plain of contemporary culture.
He read voraciously. He formed opinions about contemporary artists. He went to a lot of movies. He was hip. But it
was a whimsical hipness, not the didactic hipness of Ed
Bass's Decisions Team Limited. Marsh's vision was playful
rather than apocalyptic.

Despite a fondness for preposterous overstatements (he
once told a writer for *Accent West*, an Amarillo city magazine,
that the "Phantom Soft Pool Table" was "the greatest un-
dertaking of man since the Tower of Babel"), Marsh didn't
take himself too seriously. He admitted that his oft-quoted
suggestion that all museums should be sealed up, preferably
with their directors and curators inside, was "just idealistic
talk." But his contempt for collectors who valued art for its
investment potential was genuine. He told *Dallas Times Herald*
columnist Molly Ivins: "You know the kind of people who
show you their paintings and say, 'The little lady and I paid
eight thousand dollars for that just a few years ago and another one by the same guy sold at auction the other day for
fifteen thousand, and it's not near as good as ours. Ours is
six inches bigger.' They might as well frame a share of Xerox
and look at that."

Stanley Marsh 3 came from Panhandle pioneer stock.
Since this was one of the last areas of the country to be settled,
that meant he was third-generation. When his grandfather,
a bookkeeper, announced that they were moving to Amarillo,
his grandmother, the first woman in Ohio to earn a Phi Beta
Kappa key, opened her geography book and saw that the
town sat in the middle of a region labeled the "Great American Desert." But she came anyhow and stuck it out through
all sorts of hardships.

"What we got in the Panhandle were the keepers,"
Marsh said. "They made it through the Dust Bowl and the
Depression. They kept the farm and are proud of it."

Even if that farm was 150 miles away, they came to
Amarillo to see the orthodontist or to buy a new sofa. "Amarillo is like the capital of a small, unrecognized state," Marsh
explained. "You can get anything here. You can buy a mink
coat; you can get a face-lift. Since we're small and haven't
grown much, we all know each other. We're somewhat of a
law unto ourselves."

Billy the Kid lived here. So did Georgia O'Keeffe.

"What makes Amarillo a terrifically interesting town," Marsh continued, "is that it has enough people that are so isolated that we create our own culture. It could be an island. We have to make our own fun. People in Austin make a lot of fun, but there's a lot of canned fun you can buy. In Wichita Falls or Waxahachie you're only an hour from Dallas. Those towns lack a certain luster because people go elsewhere to have their fun."

Stanley Marsh's grandfather moved to Amarillo in the 1920's, when the first wildcatters hit oil and gas in the Panhandle. The nearest gas well was fifty miles from town, but Amarillo was where the railroads and the telegraph lines came, so Amarillo was where the oil companies had their offices. One field stretched north toward Liberal, Kansas; another spread out around Borger, Texas. The largest sprawled east almost to Oklahoma City. That's the one Stanley Marsh 1 had a piece of.

Stanley 3's mother encouraged his creativity, but when it came time for college, he went to the University of Pennsylvania's Wharton School of Finance and Commerce for some practical training in managing money. Deciding that he "needed to be cultured," he stayed to earn a master's degree in American civilization. Then he returned to Amarillo and opened a bookstore. In 1967 his father died, and he and his younger brothers, Tom and Mike, had to decide what to do with the money they inherited.

"I wanted to do something of interest in the community," Marsh said. "I did not want to just invest in stocks and bonds. I did not want to buy a ranch because that would've meant I would've hung out at the bar in the country club."

Amarillo's financially troubled ABC affiliate, KVII (Channel 7), was for sale. The Marsh brothers bought it, and Stanley set about turning it around. He built a new broadcast tower. He beefed up the staff. Twenty years after the purchase KVII had a larger share of its market than any other ABC station.

Stanley Marsh credited his success in part to his feeling for the community. "It's a luxury to live in your hometown and to be in the media, because that's reporting on where you're from," he said. "I have an advantage over my competitors. I remember when they built the high school. I remember when they integrated the high school. I'm not one of those people who've come home again; I've never left."

Despite its reliance on two troubled industries—oil and gas and agriculture—in the late 1980's the Panhandle was still doing well enough for KVII to prosper. "There are people hurting here, and there are millionaires mowing their own lawns so they can pay their country club dues," Marsh said. "But there's a kind of feeling that we beat 'em before; we can beat 'em again."

Still, Marsh hadn't restricted his ventures to the Panhandle. When they became available, Marsh Media scooped up KVIA in El Paso and several out-of-town cable franchises.

"Buying and selling broadcast properties has been the perfect business for me," Marsh declared exuberantly. "It's just made me happy. I like to go to plays. I like news. I like the entertainment. I like to talk about 'Is Sam Waterston a good Lincoln?' "

Furthermore, Marsh noted, the world tolerated eccentric bookstore owners and television tycoons, but not eccentric bankers. "I knew a banker once I really liked," he explained, "and he said to me, 'Stanley, I saw something I'm just sure was a flying saucer. I put my hand up and it flew this way.' And he said to me, 'Good bankers have not seen flying saucers.' "

Marsh put in full days at his office, but he delegated routine management to a handful of top associates and kept his schedule flexible. "My particular job is I'm like the top of the pressure cooker," Marsh explained. "If I started to do a lot of managerial tasks that someone else could do, then I wouldn't be free for the crises."

While he waited to go into entrepreneurial action, Marsh read, planned art projects, and carried on a literally large correspondence on oversize stationery.

"Here's what I did today." He crowed with an infectious hee-hee-hee laugh. "There are twenty-eight kids in Amarillo who go away to prep school or college and are my godchildren or my nieces and nephews. I call them the preppies. And today I subscribed them all to the *Daily Worker*." He chortled as he referred to the house organ of the American Communist party. "It's not called the *Daily Worker* anymore. It's called *People's Daily* or something. [It's the *Daily World*.] But can you imagine at Choate or Andover or Vanderbilt having the *Daily Worker* come in your mailbox?"

Media wasn't Marsh's only business. He and his brothers had some oil and gas properties. He helped found a local bank. And he did some ranching. On his office wall next to the seven televisions was a map of the Panhandle, much of it covered with a checkerboard of pink, orange, and turquoise. Each little colored square indicated a section, or square mile, of the Frying Pan Ranch, which belonged to his wife, Wendy Bush O'Brien Marsh, and her family. Her grandmother's second husband had made his fortune pioneering machine-made barbed wire. By the 1980's the cattle that grazed on both Wendy's part of the Frying Pan and on the smaller Marsh Ranch wore the frying pan brand—a circle with a slightly curved handle sticking off to the upper right, the logo of the Marshes' Dripping Springs Cattle Company. The Frying Pan also raised wheat and grew barley and milo for feedlots.

Wendy Marsh was far from the rough-hewn Hollywood stereotype of a lady rancher. She majored in art history at Smith, received a master's in French from Cornell, then went on to earn a law degree from the University of Texas. She was a midwestern-style Republican who devoted a lot of time to civic causes and served as chairman of the board of Amarillo Community College.

But Stanley didn't fit the rancher mold either. "I'm not a cowboy," he declared. "I don't look like one. I can't do the ropes. The worst thing I could've done as far as getting along with the people who work the ranch would have been to go on roundups and try to show off. I can't even walk very well in boots."

Stanley Marsh 3 had yet to make it into the *Forbes* 400, but he probably enjoyed his money a lot more than most of those on that gilt-edged list. Most Big Rich used their fortunes primarily to increase their fortunes. Marsh used his to have fun.

Once a year that fun took the form of a far-flung foray

with a handful of long-standing buddies: Dean Cobb, a law-yer-lobbyist from Austin; Scott Elliott, a dealer in Frank Lloyd Wright memorabilia from Chicago; Phillip Periman, head of the Harrington Cancer Center in Amarillo; and Joe Howell, David Weir, and John Rheinhart, all of whom worked with Marsh Media. The annual tradition of exotic quests began in 1972. Since then they'd gone trekking in Nepal, taken a fishing boat up the Amazon to visit a tribe of headhunters, journeyed to Lapland to check out reindeer husbandry, climbed Mount McKinley in old-fashioned Boy Scout uniforms with broad-brimmed hats and knee socks, and gone to Indonesia to see the giant Komodo dragons—three-hundred-pound lizards.

Their most bizarre trip, at least in Marsh's retelling, was one to Rwanda, where they sought out mountain gorillas. Hoping to get close to the wary primates, they donned gorilla suits and had their guides do likewise. The stifling costumes failed to fool the gorillas, but they created a stir in the African village. As Marsh and his buddies strolled into town, the local men rushed home to don their best attire—used American and European coats and ties—then took turns posing with their neighbors.

"It looked like a black Rotary Club from the movie *Ironweed*," Marsh said. "I thought they wanted to take our pictures, but they wanted to have their pictures taken with the guides in the gorilla suits."

Stanley Marsh 3 lived on the northwestern edge of Amarillo in a rambling contemporary fieldstone house named Toad Hall, after the residence of another rich eccentric, Mr. Toad, protagonist of Kenneth Grahame's children's classic *The Wind in the Willows*. "You need heroes," Marsh explained. "And after Lincoln and Kennedy, Mr. Toad is my hero—better than George Washington with his wooden teeth."

Once Toad Hall had been out in the country, but lately anonymous subdivisions had encroached on two sides. In an effort to discourage one, which included a fundamentalist church, Marsh erected a billboard on his property: FUTURE HOME OF THE WORLD'S LARGEST POISONOUS SNAKE FARM. It didn't work. After all, some fundamentalists handled venomous vipers to demonstrate the strength of the Lord's protection.

In front of Toad Hall, a giant American flag waved above a tomato red Volkswagen Bug buried in the lawn nose first—a surprise gift from Marsh's brothers, who dubbed it "Cadillac Ranchette." Climbing the cottonwoods that ringed the house, peacocks shrieked shrilly; Marsh replied with raucous screeches, which appeared to impress the birds about as much as the gorilla suits had impressed the Rwandan mountain gorillas. Three eight-foot-high plastic-covered foam letters—a red *A*, a yellow *R*, and a blue *T*—leaned tipsily against the back fence, clearly visible from the dining-room table, enabling Marsh to answer with a sweeping gesture when dinner guests asked, "What is art?"

The evening following my tour of the hidden art capped a big news day, and Stanley Marsh 3 was ready for it with his daily ritual: the simultaneous viewing of all three local versions of the six o'clock news. He settled down in Toad Hall's library, remote control in hand, and turned up the sound on first one, then another, appraising Channel 7's news judgment and presentation.

Hanging in Toad Hall's dining room was what appeared at first glance to be a Matisse. It was actually a clever fake by the late pharaoh of forgers Elmyr de Hory. Marsh bought the painting over the phone from John Connally's bankruptcy auction, partly because Wendy had always wanted a Matisse and the price was right, partly to remind him of his long-standing antipathy toward the former governor. For the erstwhile secretary of the treasury's 1975 milk fund bribery trial, Marsh and several of his friends showed up at dawn at Washington's U.S. District Court in a milk truck, dressed as cowboys, right down to the fresh manure on their feet.

Marsh voted for Paul Simon in the 1988 Democratic primary and described himself as an Eleanor Roosevelt liberal and an e. e. cummings (as opposed to a Jack Kerouac) beatnik. "I'm too old to be a hippie," he explained. "I'm predrug culture."

During the sixties and early seventies he fought for civil rights and against the Vietnam War, but always from a privileged base. After Stanley 3 took the first black man to lunch at Amarillo's Kresse's, his father had him paged at the country club swimming pool and summoned to his office. Rather than order his son to curtail his activism, Stanley Marsh 2 merely asked him to sign a will specifying that Stanley 3's brothers would inherit his estate if he were killed.

Marsh's antiestablishment antics earned him a place on Richard Nixon's notorious enemies list, putting him in the company of only two other Texans: state legislator and gubernatorial candidate Frances "Sissy" Farenthold, head of the National Women's Political Caucus and a vocal opponent of the Vietnam War, and Bernard Rapoport, a Waco financier noted for his generous contributions to liberal causes. Marsh made the list for a blatantly irreverent letter he wrote late in 1973 to the First Lady. Hearing from Halston, who was then designing millinery, that Mrs. Nixon had cried as she told him her husband had forbidden her to wear ermine hats until they were out of the White House, Stanley Marsh 3 was moved to satire. The letter, he said, had disappeared from his files, but it went something like this:

Dear Pat:

I am a practicing capitalist, and I am worried that the policies of your husband will cause a revolution and we'll be taken over by the communists. I feel confident of my ability to succeed in any meritocracy; but I think that the new regime will be prejudiced against people like myself, and I will be forbidden to compete for position in the communist world. I've thought and thought about what I can do to feed my wife and family after the revolution, and I've decided that they probably would not bar me from starting and directing a Museum of Decadent Art. To that end, I've designed one, and I've decided to dedicate the entire bottom floor to your hats.

Not only did Marsh mail the mischievous missive to Pat Nixon, but he fired off copies to every designer in that week's *Women's Wear Daily*.

The letter wasn't serious, but the response was. "I was

audited," Marsh declared. "The licenses for my TV stations were held up." Three months later Richard Nixon penned an apology. Stanley Marsh 3 had it framed on his office wall.

Middle age only made him more subtle. At one point during Cullen Davis's first murder trial in Amarillo, Marsh called every airline serving the city and booked reservations to Rio de Janeiro in the name of the accused. One night during the proceedings the "Phantom Pool Table" vanished from its pasture and reappeared on the roof of a building across from the county jail, where Davis was housed. To mark the city's longest-running judicial production, Marsh opened Toad Hall for a "cast party" for all the lawyers, then threw a "wrap party" for the attorneys, jurors, witnesses, and Davis himself at the end.

Even Mother Nature wasn't safe from Marsh's shenanigans. He had his pet pig, Minnesota Fats, tattooed with wings like an Assyrian idol, then rechristened the animal Pigasus. When Pigasus rooted out a stash of chocolate Easter eggs and ate himself to death, Marsh had the porker preserved by taxidermy, then repeated the artwork on two hairless dogs.

At times Toad Hall resembled a menagerie. Marsh rented lions, tigers, and elephants; he raised llamas and what he proudly described as "the largest herd of two-hump camels in south Potter County." He named the male Columbus and the females Nina, Pinta, and Santa Maria. He wanted the first baby to represent the New World, so he called her Sally Tomato after an American mafiosa. "I had a yak that I crossed with a cow to produce a cattle-yak," Marsh declared absolutely straight-faced.

During the late 1980's Marsh's five teenage children were absorbing much of his antic energy, but he was having a good time mulling over what he might do next. "I have a lot of hobbies," Marsh explained. "One is making roadside attractions—my artworks. Another is raising animals. I don't see the difference between raising rheas and building the 'Cadillac Ranch.' I want to do the most exciting things."

Maybe he'd breed those rheas, for the fun of observing the ostrichlike birds' nesting habits and talking to zoologists. "You have total access to people you'd never have access to otherwise," he said. "You can call up the head of zoology at Harvard if it has to do with what you should do with the rheas. I'm sure that he doesn't want me to ask him what he thought of *Biloxi Blues*."

Or maybe he'd cross horses and zebras to produce a black-and-white striped horse called a zebrule. "I could have Twenty-Zebrule Team Borax," he exclaimed. "And if I did that, I could hang out with the head of the San Diego Zoo and the St. Louis Zoo and the Bronx Zoo. For all I know, the head of the San Diego Zoo is a Pygmy or a dwarf or an eight-foot-tall woman who sings opera. I probably have nothing in common with her whatever except for the fact that we'd both be intrigued by whether you can get a domestic temperament into an animal that has a zebra color."

★

CHAPTER TWENTY

T. Boone Pickens

The "Attila of Amarilla"

"I'm just going to talk to you-all for a minute," T. Boone Pickens announced, settling behind the desk in his oak-paneled office in downtown Amarillo. "I have a pigeon lined up for a racquetball game."

Pickens looked eager for his daily taste of combat at the T. Boone Pickens, Jr., Fitness Center, across the street from the headquarters of Mesa Limited Partnership, his oil and gas company. With a weight room, a gym, a jogging track, and four glass-walled racquetball courts, that plush perquisite for Mesa's four hundred Amarillo employees was a monument to the corporate corsair's hardball competitive drive. At the entrance was a life-size bronze of Pickens himself crouched to deliver a devastating backhand shot.

On the rare occasions that he lost a game, Pickens had been known to walk off without the customary handshake. As he explained, "Why do I want to be friendly with someone who's beaten me?"

If there was a modern embodiment of Thorstein Veblen's predatory capitalist, Boone Pickens was it. *Time* likened him to Jay Gould and Jim Fisk, the nineteenth-century financiers who forced the consolidation of the railroads. By his own reckoning, Pickens had made over $107 million, most of it through failed hostile takeover attempts against such industry giants as Gulf and Phillips Petroleum. Fond of citing the separation of ownership and control as a major cause of the decline of corporate America, he'd gone on the attack, excoriating corporate chief executives, as a class and individually, for being more interested in what he called the Four Ps—pay, perks, power, and prestige—than in the welfare of their shareholders. "Chief executives, who themselves own few shares of their companies, have no more feeling for the average stockholder than they do for the baboons in Africa," he told *Time* in 1985. (At that point he owned 2.2 percent of the company he headed; three years later he held 5.5 percent, which by his own estimation represented 90 percent of his net worth. In fact, 95 percent of Mesa's employees held stock in the company. Big Oil chiefs held, on average, three tenths of 1 percent of their companies' stocks.)

Even Pickens's hobby—hunting quail, duck, geese, and pheasant—was predatory. He also loved gambling, especially high-stakes poker, and made no apologies for it. He once dropped fifteen thousand dollars on the Super Bowl, and in 1973 he parlayed thirty-four thousand into $6.6 million in six months on cattle futures. In his ghostwritten autobiography, *Boone*, he declared, "A commodity futures play is one of the purest forms of entrepreneurship."

Never mind the part of entrepreneurship that involved organizing and managing a business to provide goods and services and jobs. To Boone Pickens, entrepreneurship was risking money for a chance at quick and often staggering gain.

"The fact is, Pickens loves making deals," said Joe Nocera, who spent weeks during the 1984 Gulf takeover attempt following Pickens for *Texas Monthly* and was ultimately one of several ghosts on Pickens's book. "They fuel him and excite him and challenge him in a way that the everyday business of his company does not."

Pickens seemed to believe in a corporate version of Social Darwinism: If he could snatch a company or weaken it so that another Wall Street nimrod could grab it, then the company deserved to be snatched. "A company that's ripe for takeover is a company that has sorry management," he told me during our March 1988 interview in Amarillo.

"I'm always amused when somebody calls me a raider," Pickens proclaimed in his broad High Plains twang, "because a raider is somebody who doesn't invest anything except maybe a few bucks in a gun to stick in your ribs. What we have done is become very large stockholders. You take the eight companies we've become involved with; there were nine hundred fifty thousand stockholders who made fifteen billion dollars, and our part of it was five percent. So we've helped 95 percent of the stockholders make that money, and it was money that would not have been made had we or some other large stockholder not forced the issue."

Never mind that it was money that the company management anted up to protect its positions, or that it was borrowed money, or that it was money that might otherwise have been used to build new refineries, find new oil and gas, or expand into new markets. When reporters lobbed the last criticism at him, Pickens retorted that considering current oil and gas prices, it wouldn't make sense for those companies to put that money into exploration and production, so the cash might as well be doled out to shareholders to pump back into healthier parts of the economy. Presumably the interest for servicing that debt and the fees charged by the lawyers for both sides were another way of redistributing wealth—to financial institutions and to the world's least needy profession.

Boone Pickens resembled the land he came from. Except for his intensely blue eyes, he was monochromatic. His weathered skin, graying reddish blond hair, and light but bushy brows blended into a single tone of sun-bleached auburn. He talked like a Texas oilman, calling business "bidness" and peppering his speech with such regionalisms as "It's better than a poke in the eye with a sharp stick." A Charles Russell painting of cowboys roping a steer decorated the wall behind his desk, and other western genre art by

Russell, G. Harvey, and Melvin Warren hung above the oak wainscoting in the hall. Otherwise the decor was as traditional as a venerable Manhattan men's club—comfortable leather armchairs and rich-hued Oriental rugs on pegged wood floors. And Pickens dressed like a Wall Street arbitrageur in conservative suits and wing tip shoes.

When Diane Jennings of the *Dallas Morning News* asked Pickens in 1987 what one thing he'd change about himself, he replied, "I'd be six feet tall." Standing a compact, muscular five feet nine inches, Pickens was a fanatic about fitness. In 1972 he took up racquetball with the same bulldog competitiveness he brought to leveraged buyouts. He bragged that he might be the best racquetball player of his age in the country but added that there weren't many contenders. He jogged several miles every day before breakfast, then sat down to a bowl of cereal, fruit, and low-fat milk. He didn't smoke, and a sign in his ten-passenger Falcon 50 business jet (one of two; he also had a personal Cessna) remonstrated: IF YOU MUST SMOKE, PLEASE STEP OUTSIDE.

In 1980, when Mesa Petroleum gave him $7.86 million in salary and stock options, Boone Pickens was the best-paid corporate executive in the country. "Money is a report card," he wrote in his autobiography. "I get a big thrill out of making money, but I don't get much of a thrill out of spending it."

As rich Texas oilmen went, Pickens wasn't flashy. He and his wife, Bea, had a condominium in Houston, a house in Palm Springs, and their fourteen-thousand-acre Two B Ranch in the Panhandle; but their primary residence was the Woodstone, a walled compound he built on the western edge of the Amarillo Country Club golf course. The exteriors of the enclave's five town houses were understated sand-colored stucco. All the units were big, but there was no hint from the outside that the Pickenses' home concealed two courtyards and an indoor tennis court. In 1986 Bea reportedly spent three million dollars redecorating the courtyards and den, installing a fireplace from a European castle. After the redo, the Pickenses threw a party for artists and sculptors featured in a Houston Museum of Fine Arts group show. The fete was a mock African safari, complete with palm trees, live African animals, and jungle sound effects. Bea even flew in chefs from Africa to provide a Dark Continent spin to the catered barbecue.

That night at the Woodstone was a long way from Holdenville, the little railroad town in eastern Oklahoma where Pickens was born in 1928. His father, Thomas Boone Pickens, who shared a distant ancestor with Daniel Boone, was a petroleum landman. He'd acquire mineral leases from farmers and sell them to oil companies. Although Thomas Pickens was the son of a Methodist missionary, he was an inveterate gambler. He played poker, bet on football games, and invested in mostly unsuccessful wildcat wells. He lost so much money on the wildcats that he had to go to work as a hired hand—for Phillips Petroleum.

Boone Pickens's mother was strict to the point of rigidity, starched with the kind of toughness useful for survival on the frontier. She put principles above compassion. During World War II Mrs. Pickens ran the Office of Price Administration for the three counties surrounding Holdenville. When a gas station owner explained that he'd accidentally left the pump on all night and lost his month's ration of gas, she refused to give him more, even though he'd given Boone a summer job and been very kind to the boy.

In 1944 Phillips transferred Thomas Pickens west to Amarillo.

Boone studied geology at Texas A&M, then switched to Oklahoma A&M at Stillwater in order to be closer to his girl friend, Lynn O'Brien, a high school student from the same prosperous and well-regarded Amarillo pioneer family that produced Wendy O'Brien Marsh. Lynn and Boone married in February 1949, while he was still in college. By the end of the year they had a baby daughter.

Boone Pickens graduated in 1951. It was the middle of an oil slump, but he landed a job with Phillips Petroleum in Bartlesville, Oklahoma. He made $290 a month, rode a bicycle to work, and hunted squirrels, which he brought home for Lynn to cook. Phillips bounced him around to Corpus Christi and then to Amarillo. By November 1954 he'd had enough of Big Oil bureaucracy and quit. The man who launched a frontal assault on Phillips three decades later was twenty-six and had a wife and two daughters to support, but he was unencumbered by self-doubt or, for that matter, by patience.

After a year of putting together mineral leases for established independent oilmen, Pickens got himself some backers. His uncle-in-law, cattleman John O'Brien, and Eugene McCartt, whose family owned several Amarillo supermarkets, each put up $1,250 for 25 percent of the stock; they let Pickens buy his half with a $2,500 promissory note and gave him a hundred-thousand-dollar line of credit. Pickens hired a landman, a geologist, and a secretary and began buying leases himself. He called his company Petroleum Exploration Incorporated.

To finance the drilling, Pickens put together limited partnerships, each encompassing a number of wells; if one came up dry, the investors would get a chance on the others. He raised the money locally and, on McCartt's advice, named each partnership after one of Amarillo's leading citizens. The ploy was shameless, but it helped lend the "boy geologist," as he was called, much needed credibility; he was twenty-five years younger than any other independent oilman in the Panhandle. The first time around, the wells all came up dry; but the second batch of fifteen brought in one good oil well and seven gas wells.

In 1963 Pickens took PEI public, renaming it the Mesa Petroleum Company after the tabletop geological formations that broke the flatness of the Panhandle landscape. The public offering allowed Mesa to use its proven reserves as collateral to borrow money for more exploration and development. Erstwhile partners became shareholders; Pickens, the CEO, was the largest, with 15.8 percent of the new company.

Mesa took off, but Boone Pickens's family life suffered. He and Lynn divorced in 1971. Some old-line Amarillans proclaimed their disapproval, pointing out that Lynn's uncle had set Boone up in business, as if that obligated Boone to stick with the marriage for longer than twenty-two years. But John O'Brien hadn't done badly on the deal. By 1986 his $1,250 investment was worth seven million.

The year following his divorce, Pickens married Oklahoma City socialite Beatrice Carr Stuart. They were well matched. She was a crack shot, although she preferred big-game hunting to bagging quail. And right after the honeymoon she enrolled in a geology course at Amarillo College.

Branching out into Canada and the North Sea, Pickens made the most of the seventies, when the Arab oil embargo sent prices through the roof. During the oil boom Mesa had fifty-one rigs working, including five jack-ups in the Gulf of Mexico, more than any other company except Arco. But it was costing half a million dollars a day to keep those rigs pumping, a lot of money for an outfit worth six hundred million. The price of everything, from offshore platforms to caterers for the crew, was exorbitant. In March 1979, with Mesa's annual budget at four hundred million dollars, Pickens announced that since the company couldn't afford to replace its reserves, it ought to get out of the oil business. He sold his Canadian operations to Dome Petroleum for six hundred million dollars and backed out of the North Sea.

"Boone dug his share of wildcats," Dr. Jared Hazleton, Mesa's vice-president for economics, explained in 1988. "But he figured out early that oil prices wouldn't keep rising and the cost of finding oil was more than you could get for it."

Taking advantage of a short-lived tax wrinkle, Pickens put half of Mesa's gas reserves into a royalty trust. Instead of the income going to the corporation, which would have had to pay taxes on it before sending out dividends, it went directly to the stockholders. When the Tax Reform Act of 1984 nixed royalty trusts, Pickens established Mesa Limited Partnership. By February 1987 he'd converted all of Mesa's shareholders into limited partners and transferred all of Mesa Petroleum's assets to the new entity. Boone Pickens's title changed from chairman of the board to general partner.

Although Mesa was trading only between nine and fifteen dollars a share in 1988, it was paying a whopping two-dollar annual dividend—an 18 percent return, virtually unheard of in the oil industry. In the first two years of the limited partnership Mesa paid out five hundred million dollars to its erstwhile shareholders, now partners. But those yearly payments were really like annuity checks since the company's assets were being depleted. Pickens contended that the entire Texas economy was in the same fix.

As for where Texas was headed, he said, "Being a geologist, I look for look-alikes. And what do you look at? You
look at a producing state that's no longer a producing state
—Pennsylvania."

Pickens figured that while it didn't pay to search for oil
and gas in the ground, it might pay to search for it on Wall
Street. He made his first hostile takeover in 1969, when he
picked up Hugoton Production, a gas company based in
Kansas City. But it wasn't until the mid-seventies that he
started seriously stalking vulnerable corporations. His formula for spotting acquisition targets was simple: If a company's stock was trading below the value of its assets, it was
poorly managed and ripe for takeover. The tricky part was
determining the true value of its assets.

In 1976 Pickens flew to four companies in one day and
made each CEO an offer at least 50 percent higher than the
stock was selling for. No takers. Six years later he startled
the business world by making a run at Cities Service, a six-
billion-dollar company with stock going for half its value.
Mesa's assets were two billion dollars—great for an independent oil company but not for challenging the thirty-ninth-
largest corporation in the United States. Up until then it was
unheard of for a smaller company to attempt an unfriendly
takeover play against a larger one. Pickens didn't get Cities,
but he forced it into the arms of Gulf, making thirty million
dollars for Mesa after taxes.

Because Mesa didn't have the financial heft to tackle
industry giants on its own, Pickens brought in outside partners, but they were silent backers. He played his own hands
and played them close to the chest. By moving money around
from bank to bank in fifty-million-dollar chunks and giving
each takeover target a code name, he avoided tipping off
Wall Street watchers before he was ready to scoop up controlling blocks of stock. Once he had acquired a major position in a company, he announced publicly that he could
run it better than its present management. Fearing for their
jobs, the jittery executives would buy back the stock at much
higher prices or find a white knight—a third company that
would take over the corporation but keep its top management. Either way Pickens, Mesa, and its partners won.

This may sound a lot like greenmail, but Pickens insisted that there were two crucial differences. First, in true greenmail the defending company offered to buy back the raider's stock for more than it would pay to the average shareholder; Pickens always insisted that his prey give the same price to everyone who tendered shares. Secondly, he claimed that all his takeover attempts had been serious; he wanted the companies' reserves. "The shareholders really don't care where you get the oil—whether you find it or buy it," he told me. "They just want to be sure you did a good job with whatever you did with their money."

Pickens employed his Cities *modus operandi* in 1983 and 1984 against Gulf itself, the world's sixth-largest oil company, with twenty billion dollars in assets and forty thousand employees. After a bitter proxy fight he forced Gulf to sell out to Chevron for $13.2 billion. Mesa and its six partners made $760 million on the deal before taxes.

In celebration, fifty Wall Street speculators who'd ridden along on the wave threw a dinner for Pickens at the Regency Hotel. To thank him for bringing fifty million dollars in legal and related fees to New York, Mayor Ed Koch presented him with a Steuben crystal apple, the city's symbol. At the end of the meal a trained chimpanzee wearing a Gulf service station attendant's uniform zoomed in on roller skates, sat down next to Pickens, and began licking his face. Someone introduced the chimp as Jimmy Lee, Gulf's chief executive officer. Pickens later denied that he had anything to do with the monkey business.

During 1984 and 1985 he took to the road. Like a circuit-riding preacher, he delivered the same gospel day after day to lunch and breakfast clubs: The problem with corporate America was the separation of ownership and control. No one was looking out for the shareholders. He was a good speaker, concise and entertaining, relaxed and affable with the press. T. Boone Pickens emerged as part of a new breed: the businessman as celebrity.

When Pickens went after Phillips Petroleum in December 1984, the residents of Bartlesville, Oklahoma, where Phillips employed sixty-eight hundred, wore Boonebuster T-shirts and held twenty-four-hour prayer vigils. Pickens later insisted that he'd had no intention of shutting down the Bartlesville headquarters operation, but people there suspected that the takeover fight was something of a grudge match.

When Bartlesville learned that Phillips had escaped Pickens's clutches, churches set aside sixty-six seconds (as in Phillips 66) of their Christmas Eve services for a prayer of thanks. But the one-two punch—first from Pickens, then from Carl Icahn—left the company reeling. It sold off two billion dollars in assets and borrowed $4.5 billion to buy back 72.5 million shares. Union employees agreed to forgo raises to help the company bail itself out. Phillips Petroleum's debt rose from 35 percent of total capital to 81 percent, and its bond rating dropped two notches to just above the speculative level.

But Mesa made eighty-eight million dollars off the deal.

"Those managements are big boys," Pickens said when questioned about the damage done by such a debt load. "If they want to go out and borrow four billion or five billion dollars to keep their jobs, that's their business. And if the stockholders want to go along with that kind of gag, that's their business, too."

When Houston independent oilman Michel Halbouty said that Pickens's practice of hunting for oil on Wall Street rather than in the ground was bad for national security because it ultimately tied up money that could be used to free the country from dependence on foreign oil, Pickens countered that national security was the Army and Navy's responsibility, not his.

Spurred on by the success of *Iacocca*, which spent a year on *The New York Times* best seller list, most of it at the top, Houghton Mifflin shelled out a $1.5 million advance in the fall of 1985 for the rights to Boone Pickens's autobiography. Pickens had started working with San Francisco writer Moira Johnston, the third journalist he'd invited to Amarillo for consideration. After she'd stayed with the Pickenses for several months, Boone let her go, reportedly because he doubted her ability to understand and convey the business details. (She went on to write *Takeovers: The New Wall Street Warriors*, which Pickens recommended to me without mentioning that she'd ever worked on his book.) The next writer, former *Texas*

Monthly senior editor Joe Nocera, drafted the proposal that excited thirteen publishers into a bidding war, but Pickens unloaded him twenty pages short of a completed first draft, bringing in the *Washington Post*'s Jim Conway to finish the job. Pickens failed to mention either Moira Johnston or Joe Nocera in his acknowledgments, and Nocera sued for his share of the advance.

Boone hit the stores in March 1987, but the book never quite lived up to expectations. Houghton Mifflin refused to give sales figures but claimed the book was a success, presumably because it handled the paperback itself. After fifteen weeks on the best seller list, sales dropped off fast. *Boone* just didn't have the appeal of *Iacocca*. Chrysler's chairman, after all, had rescued a company and saved jobs; Pickens was involved in a game that killed and disabled companies and cost jobs. Even as a champion of stockholders, it was hard to see him as a hero. Besides, the book attacked its natural audience—the fast-track corporate types who buy most business bios.

In 1986 Pickens anted up $1.43 million to form the United Shareholders Association with the stated purpose of pushing for corporate accountability to the forty-two million Americans who owned stock. The nonprofit group would try to get regulations established that would call for secret ballots in proxy votes (they were signed by shareholders and counted by management) and make boards of directors independent of corporate executives. And of course, it would fight to repeal restrictions on takeovers.

After Phillips, Pickens stayed out of the takeover arena until 1987, when he made a two-billion-dollar play for Diamond Shamrock, emerging with a paltry few million in profit. That summer he switched strategies and started going after defense industry targets Boeing and Singer and after Newmont Mining, with the largest gold reserves in North America. All three bids failed. Mesa's earnings, which were $70.6 million in 1986, slipped to $31.9 million in 1987.

With the Federal Reserve's new regulations hampering his takeover plays, in 1986 Boone Pickens began turning his formidable aggressive energy loose on Amarillo. It was like watching a grizzly bear run amok in a cottage.

Both Mesa and the Pickenses contributed hundreds of

thousands of dollars a year to local charities, although Pick-ens had been known to withdraw his support if the director of a beneficiary institution refused to do something he asked. One of the Pickenses' favorite causes was West Texas State University, a former teachers' college seventeen miles south of Amarillo in Canyon; they gave the school $2.5 million. Soon WTSU had the T. Boone Pickens College of Business, the Beatrice Carr Pickens chair in music, and the Bea and Boone Pickens Distinguished Lecture Series. Governor Bill Clements made Pickens chairman of the board of regents.

WTSU itself had never pretended to be distinguished. (Georgia O'Keeffe taught art there in 1916 but left after a year.) It drew its fifty-seven hundred students from Amarillo and from little Panhandle ranching towns; a lot of them were the first in their families to attend college.

Since many of Mesa's employees came from WTSU, Pick-ens had a natural interest in transforming the university into a corporate training ground. When a new president, Ed Roach, came aboard in 1984, the two men hit it off imme-diately. Roach was former dean of the business school at Lyndon Johnson's alma mater, Southwest Texas State Uni-versity, in San Marcos. He and Pickens shared a vision: They wanted to turn mediocre WTSU into a respected, efficiently managed university.

Roach froze faculty salaries and consolidated depart-ments, but he spent a million dollars—twice the original estimate—building himself a seventy-three-hundred-square-foot official residence. By 1986 the faculty was disenchanted and handed Roach a 78 percent vote of no confidence. But Pickens stood solidly behind him. When the *Amarillo Globe* and *News*, both owned by Georgia-based Morris Commu-nications, began running critical stories about West Texas State, Pickens launched a campaign to get readers to cancel subscriptions and merchants to pull ads. Pickens's Panhan-dle Citizens for a Better Amarillo Newspaper distributed but-tons with the names of the newspapers cut by a red slash— not unlike the emblem on Bartlesville's Boonebuster T-shirts. Reporters countered with a button of their own: the same red slash across "Attilla of Amarilla."

Pickens won—sort of. After flying up to meet with him,

William S. Morris III transferred the papers' general manager to Georgia. Pickens marked the occasion by draping Mesa's headquarters with a banner saying "Good-bye, Jerry."

Not that Pickens didn't have his local supporters. At the beginning of March 1988 fifty billboards popped up all over town. They read: "Boone & Bea—You love Amarillo, and we love you." They stayed up for a month at a total cost of ten thousand dollars.

Asked where they came from, Pickens quipped, "Bea and I put those up at night. We can't stand empty billboards." In truth, the people behind the fawning display were Gene Hill, owner of Hill's Sport Shop, and fourteen other merchants, alarmed by the rumor that Pickens was considering pulling up stakes and moving Mesa's headquarters to the Bass brothers' towers in Fort Worth.

On April 5, 1988, the lead story of the *Wall Street Journal* called Pickens a "cranky cowboy." He had reason to be cranky. The city of Amarillo was suing Mesa, claiming it was charging too much for natural gas. And three of his top men had quit within a month of each other. All in their thirties, all key lieutenants in his lucrative takeover attempts, they had jumped on their own. They claimed personal reasons and insisted that they weren't unhappy with either Pickens or Mesa. One, David Batchelder, told the *Wall Street Journal* that the problem was Amarillo; the town was "nothing but one big truckstop." One of the truck stops on I-40 sent Batchelder a gimme cap in appreciation.

By June 1988, with four hundred employees, down from six hundred, Mesa looked less like a lean, mean corporate raptor than a company gradually going out of business.

★

CHAPTER TWENTY-ONE

Sybil Harrington

Philanthropy con Brio

On December 8, 1988, Lincoln Center's gold curtain rose on the Metropolitan Opera's opulent new production of Puccini's *Aida* designed by Gianni Quaranta, the young Italian who won the 1986 Academy Award for Best Art Direction for *A Room with a View*. Inspired by nineteenth-century watercolor fantasies of ancient Egypt, the sets formed a dreamlike backdrop for a chorus clad in elegant white robes adorned in glistening brass. Leona Mitchell was thrillingly tragic in the title role of the exiled and enslaved Ethiopian princess; Placido Domingo sang the young general Radames with touching nobility; the pageantry of the triumphal march, complete with live exotic animals, elicited peal after peal of bravos. And sitting in her parterre box, the petite white-haired lady from Amarillo who had made the production possible applauded with as much spontaneous enthusiasm as anyone else in the house, even though she had sat through weeks of rehearsals.

Grand opera was Sybil B. Harrington's grand passion.
"All of it's there—beautiful sets, great costumes, great music.
What more could you want?" she declared the summer be-
fore the *Aida* premiere as she sat in the living room of her
Amarillo house overlooking a rare acre of verdant garden.
She migrated seasonally from this High Plains oasis to her
neoclassical villa in Phoenix and her apartment in Manhattan.

The biggest individual contributor in the history of the
Metropolitan Opera, this vivacious widow of a pioneer Texas
oilman had since 1978 bankrolled eleven new productions.
She had also been enormously openhanded toward the Met's
unrestricted fund. In fact, though neither she nor the Met
would specify exactly how much she'd contributed, the total
was well over ten million dollars. Assistant general manager
and former development director Marilyn Shapiro acknowledged that Mrs. Harrington had given more to the company
than any corporate donor save Texaco, which underwrote
the *Live from the Met* broadcasts on PBS.

Before Mrs. Harrington arrived as its major angel, the
Met lacked the funds to mount badly needed new productions. "The Met was in serious financial trouble. What she
did was give the theater its life," Ms. Shapiro said.

The Big Rich could do whatever they liked with their
money, and what Sybil Harrington liked was to give it away
where it was appreciated. Through the Don and Sybil Harrington Foundation, she had contributed close to sixty million
dollars to eighty-nine little-known charities in and around
her hometown. Virtually every corner of the 23,200-square-
mile Texas Panhandle had benefited from her generosity,
from lights for the softball field at Gruver to books for the
Friona Public Library, from the Opportunity School—a pre-
school for poor children in Amarillo—to costumes and sets
for the summer outdoor pageant *Texas* at Palo Duro Canyon
State Park. Thanks to the Harrington Foundation's sixty-
eight-million-dollar endowment, this remote and often desolate region, where the total population was three hundred
thousand and where seven counties lacked even a single
doctor, had a state-of-the-art cancer center, an award-
winning string quartet, and many of the other amenities
associated with large cities.

Sybil Harrington's name didn't appear on many lists of

contributors to high-profile national charities. "I'm a loner. I was an only child," she explained, lifting her graceful but slightly skeptical semicircular brows.

In the causes she chose to support, as in everything else, Sybil Harrington thought for herself.

"Independence of mind is a Panhandle trait," said Dr. Phillip Periman, president and medical director of the Harrington Cancer Center and, coincidentally, a lifelong friend of Stanley Marsh 3. "You see it in Boone Pickens. You see it in Stanley Marsh. The people who came out here were risk takers. I think Sybil is that way. She doesn't do anything the way anybody else does."

He added: "She's not all bubbles and champagne. One of the reasons she's been so smart about giving her money is that she doesn't have a fairy-tale view of the world."

Dr. Periman first met Mrs. Harrington at an Amarillo dinner party shortly after she had contributed the money for the cancer center's airy human-scale thirteen-million-dollar building designed by Yale architecture dean Paul Rudolph; it cost 15 percent more than a traditionally institutional structure of the same size. "The first thing she did was chew me out," Dr. Periman recalled. "I'd said something like 'If we only had a few million more, we could do this and that.' She felt I was being ungrateful and inappropriate, and she let me know it in no uncertain terms. And I was just being brash and aggressive and visionary. She said, 'Young man, you have to learn timing.' "

Consistent with her conservative political philosophy, Mrs. Harrington was a fierce champion of private philanthropy, as opposed to government funding for social programs and the arts. "We've got to have that free enterprise," she asserted. "It's important in charitable institutions as well as in business. Art has to have freedom."

Sybil Buckingham Harrington was born and reared in Amarillo, the granddaughter of some of the town's first settlers. As a child she learned how to fish and shoot, but she also loved music and dance and pursued them with a self-reliance born of necessity. She studied piano and church organ, and when the Paramount Theater opened in town, she persuaded the organist to teach her how to play popular tunes on his Wurlitzer. Her mother timed their shopping trips to Neiman Marcus in Dallas 363 miles to the southeast to coincide with concerts.

Although she'd never seen classical ballet, which Amarillans then called toe dancing, Sybil Buckingham decided that she wanted to be a ballerina. After sending off for a pair of toe shoes from a mail-order catalog, she took lessons from a Fort Worth dance teacher who spent her summers in cooler Amarillo. Seven decades later Mrs. Harrington still carried her five-foot-two-inch frame like a dancer.

"I've *always* loved music," she said. "My whole family did. My father had a terrific collection of Red Seal records—the Victor classical label. I'd listen to Caruso on his Edison record player. Schumann-Heink played here; so did Paderewski. I remember every one of them, even though I was really small."

With her pert nose, heart-shaped face, and penetrating brown eyes, Sybil Buckingham was one of the prettiest girls in the Panhandle. In 1935 she married Donald D. Harrington, a phenomenally successful independent oilman with a rakish resemblance to Fred Astaire.

Don Harrington had come to Amarillo in 1926 with the Marlin Oil Company. He served as a landman, identifying ranch acreage that looked as if it might contain oil and gas beneath the surface, then securing the rights to drill. A year later he and Amarillans Stanley Marsh, Sr., and Lawrence Hagy went into business. Sometimes the partners arranged leases for major oil corporations; sometimes they drilled for the oil and natural gas themselves. They even went on to build their own gasoline refineries. By the end of World War II Don Harrington had a major interest in hundreds of oil and gas wells spread across hundreds of thousands of acres in the Panhandle and Hugoton fields.

Wealthy Amarillans had always traveled, but few so frequently or to such fashionable places as the Harringtons. They summered in La Jolla and wintered in Phoenix. As a child Mrs. Harrington had heard her first opera on the Met's early radio broadcasts; now she indulged her passion in person in New York. She traveled to Paris for fittings by Dior and Balmain. The former Sybil Buckingham, who had once dreamed of becoming a ballerina, counted among her close friends Adele Astaire, Spencer Tracy, and Greer Garson.

Her good looks, gregarious charm, and lively wit—not to mention her money—made her a café society hit, but she never had much patience for the pompous. With a musician's deft ear for mimicry, she punctuated our interview with arch imitations of pretentious New York matrons and self-important celebrities like Joan Crawford, who, when Mrs. Harrington asked why she came to the beach in La Jolla wearing pearls with her slinky black maillot, replied, "Dahling, the seawater is good for them. They *come* from the sea."

In Amarillo the Harringtons bought a fifteen-thousand-square-foot house built in 1914 by a cattle baron who had had the grand Ionic columns that supported the portico hauled from Kansas City by mule team. Mrs. Harrington bleached the oppressive mahogany woodwork, decorated the walls with French Impressionists, and entertained everyone from local ranchers to Clark Gable.

Don and Sybil Harrington maintained their attachment to the land where she had grown up and he had made his fortune. In 1951 they established the Harrington Foundation, initially capitalized by three thousand shares of Southwestern Public Service Company stock. From the beginning most of the money went to local causes.

In a contemplative moment Sybil Harrington told her husband: "My worry is that you'll die and leave me with all that money."

Then, in 1974, both Mrs. Harrington's husband and her only child, Sally Harrington Goldwater, wife of the former Arizona senator's younger brother Robert, died unexpectedly only months apart. Stunned by her grief, she sought solace in découpage and her piano.

"It takes people a different amount of time to heal," she reflected fourteen years later. "It probably took me longer than others. Then I woke up and said, 'He left you with the ability to do so much. Get out there and do it!' "

She took on the responsibility of chairing the Harrington Foundation herself. "Giving away money is hard work," she said. "But I got a kick out of it. I felt important for once in my life."

Prompted by her love of music, Sybil Harrington also

began attending the Metropolitan Opera—alone. One day in 1978 she mentioned to Met board member Mrs. Louis Douglas that she wished there were something she could do for the company, apart from the regular contributions she and her husband had long given. To Mrs. Harrington's surprise, Mrs. Douglas leaped at her offer.

"Like everyone else, I thought the Met was this rich house that all these New Yorkers gave all this money to," Mrs. Harrington recounted. "But the Met doesn't have that much money. Opera is the most expensive of all the arts to produce."

The next thing she knew, Sybil Harrington was committed to underwriting a new production of Verdi's *Don Carlo*. This wasn't a foundation project; she bankrolled it from her personal wealth. "I was *so* excited," she said. "I didn't even know it was possible. I didn't know there was such a thing as a donor putting on a production."

Week after week she sat in on rehearsals, fascinated by the whole process of bringing an opera to life. When someone suggested scratching the white horse and Irish wolfhounds from the spectacle, she declared, "If it's grand opera, it's got to be *grand*." The live animals stayed.

On opening night, February 5, 1979, she was thrilled. She recalled: "At the premiere of *Don Carlo*, I'd sit there and think, 'Am I responsible for all this? Yes, I am. Isn't it wonderful?' "

She went on to underwrite new productions of *Un Ballo in Maschera*, *Manon Lescaut*, *La Bohème*, *Francesca da Rimini*, *Tosca*, *Die Fledermaus*, *Turandot*, *Das Rheingold*, *Aida*, and *La Traviata*—perennially popular operas performed so frequently that the sets and costumes wore out. With more than a thousand full-time employees, the Metropolitan Opera had an annual budget of eighty-five million dollars, only two thirds of which was covered by ticket sales. The cost of a new production ranged from six hundred thousand dollars to $1.5 million or more, with the operas set in palaces coming in on the high end. These were the very ones Sybil Harrington loved.

"I have to have beauty," she said. "And I think the Met needs a few spectacles that make money."

As generous as she was to the Met, she didn't play

director. "She's very careful about that, like the separation of church and state," said Marilyn Shapiro.

After a season's list of productions had been drawn up, Mrs. Harrington went over it and decided which she'd like to bankroll. Invariably it was one or two grand, traditional operas calling for lush sets and lavish costumes. Others could back Benjamin Britten's *Billy Budd* or the world premiere of Philip Glass's *The Voyage*; Sybil Harrington preferred Verdi, Puccini, Mozart, and Wagner.

Let anyone attack these productions as *too* lavish, and Mrs. Harrington sprang to the company's defense. *Turandot*, with Placido Domingo and Eva Marton, was a case in point. For Act II, Scene 2, the curtain rose on blinding opulence. Three gold pagodas towered above a lagoon of shimmering glass tubes lit from beneath. Clad in exquisitely embroidered silk kimonos, dancers swirled fans and sleeves in mesmerizing motions. The audience rose and cheered, but *New York Times* critic Donal Henahan likened the spectacle to the Ice Capades.

"It's a Chinese fairy tale," Mrs. Harrington remonstrated. "How can you do a Chinese fairy tale and not have it all iridescent and glamorous?"

The company loved her, not only for her financial backing but also for her unfailing emotional support and interest. She fluttered backstage with the unfeigned enthusiasm of a fond aunt, telling all of them, from chorus members to carpenters, they were doing a wonderful job, and accepted graciously when burly lighting technicians invited her to the employee cafeteria for coffee. At the Metropolitan Opera Guild's annual luncheon on March 26, 1987, the Met renamed its main hall the Sybil B. Harrington Auditorium. To commemorate the occasion, the company presented her with a Steuben crystal cube etched with the Met's signature arches on three sides and five costumed singers on the fourth. The lighting crew added its own memento: a heather green T-shirt, just like they wore backstage, with the Met logo on the front and the productions she'd underwritten listed on the back.

"Her support is a considered and well-thought-out effort," explained the Met's general manager, Bruce Crawford, who resigned at the end of 1988. "It's really based on very intelligent and hardheaded assessments of what's going on."

Sybil Harrington brought that same creative pragmatism to her foundation. "Most people who give a lot of money to an institution want control. Not Mrs. Harrington," said Carol Cline, director of exhibits for the Panhandle-Plains Historical Museum, in Canyon, Texas, which received a $5.25 million Harrington Foundation grant to build the seventy-five-thousand-square-foot Don Harrington Petroleum Wing—the most thorough, sensible, and attractive of the state's numerous oil and gas exhibits.

Mrs. Harrington explained her approach as follows: "We just give the money and pray. *They* know how to do what they do best."

Sometimes she structured her giving so cleverly that her money did triple duty. Thanks to her generosity, Amarillo may have been the only city of 150,000 with its own resident ballet company; she gave more than $250,000 for sets, costumes, and special effects for its annual *Nutcracker* production alone. But the way her underwriting worked, the Lone Star Ballet's principals were required to teach dance at West Texas State University, and the company's director also headed the WTSU dance department and directed the musical *Texas* in the summer. A similar strategy gave the Amarillo Symphony four principal musicians, WTSU four talented young professionals—none of them from Texas—on its music faculty, and the Panhandle the Harrington String Quartet.

When the quartet won the grand prize in the 1987 Frischoff National Chamber Music Competition, critics were stunned. "People said, 'Where are you from? Isn't it all cactus?' " violinist Dawn Harms said later.

The quartet toured the United States and Europe, but they also enjoyed giving performances in White Deer, Dalhart, and the other little towns in the Panhandle. "They need us," Ms. Harms said. "We're the culture in this area. Frankly I wouldn't want us to be another chamber group running around New York City, having to work part-time serving hamburgers at Wendy's."

Sybil Harrington took great delight in the tributes showered upon her for her philanthropy, from the local Boy Scout council's Silver Beaver Award and the Amarillo Junior League's Outstanding Community Philanthropist citation to *Town & Country's* Generous American Award and the highest honor granted by the American Medical Association to a nonphysician. The only time she scoffed at recognition was when she was named to the International Best-Dressed List in 1986. "I never laughed so hard in my life," she said. "It was ridiculous, but I appreciated it. When I was young and had all my clothes made in Paris, nobody had heard of me."

She especially treasured the book Amarillo writer Sally Bivins assembled for her birthday on October 13, 1983. In it each of the Panhandle charities benefiting from Harrington Foundation grants pledged to take on a specific project as a birthday gift. The Amarillo Council of Garden Clubs lighted the fragrance garden she'd contributed for the blind. The local council of Camp Fire (now coed) promised to undertake an annual ecological project. The Amarillo-Panhandle Humane Society established the Tutu Harrington Fund, named for Mrs. Harrington's poodle, to spay and neuter animals adopted by low-income families.

The same year Sybil Harrington donated her grand white-columned residence to the Panhandle-Plains Historical Society, along with a million-dollar endowment to provide for it to be maintained and open on a limited schedule for tours. She wasn't feeling morbid; she simply wanted to be sure she herself would be there to see that everything was properly arranged, a process that took five years.

On January 1, 1988, she also relinquished control of the Don and Sybil Harrington Foundation, transforming it into the income-generating arm of the public Amarillo Area Foundation, which her husband had helped establish in 1957. Its directors were elected by everyone in the community who contributed at least $250 a year.

In structuring the transfer, Sybil Harrington may have found what so many philanthropists had sought in vain: a method for assuring that her money would do what she would have it do long after she was gone. She wasn't relying solely on the wisdom of future civic solons. Of the more than six million dollars that the sixty-eight-million-dollar Harrington Foundation's assets generated annually, she designated

65 percent to go in fixed percentages to twenty charities, eighteen local causes plus the Retina Foundation in Dallas and the Harrington Arthritis Foundation in Phoenix. The Amarillo Area Foundation distributed the remaining 35 percent at its discretion within the twenty-six counties of the Texas Panhandle.

The confidence demonstrated by that local commitment was almost as important as the money itself.

"When you live in an isolated place, you get the feeling that it can't be any good if it's in the High Plains—which is nonsense," said Dr. Phillip Periman, whose Harrington Cancer Center was to use the two million dollars it would receive annually from the foundation to conduct research in biological response modifiers, the most promising new direction for cancer treatment. "It's important to have a patron with this spirit that says, 'You *can* do it, and you can do it as well as they can do it in New York.'"

CHAPTER TWENTY-TWO

★

San Antonio and South Texas

Prickly Pears and Patrónes

The brush country of South Texas lay seven hundred miles from the Panhandle, at the opposite end of the state, yet the two regions shared a similar desolate, flat landscape, a similar insular outlook, and a similar reliance on cattle and oil. The ranches surrounding both sprawled into the tens and even hundreds of thousands of acres, and the people who owned them were used to doing things their own way.

But two important differences—climate and culture—distinguished the regions. South Texas formed a rough triangle bounded on the southeast by the Gulf of Mexico, on the southwest by the Rio Grande, and on the north by the southern edge of the Edwards Plateau and the Guadalupe River. The weather was semiarid and subtropical, with long, steamy summers and mild winters. In fact, the climate in the southernmost countries resembled South Florida's; freezes were so rare they were considered natural disasters. The Lower Rio Grande Valley was famous for its sweet ruby red grapefruit, and given irrigation, vegetables grew year-round. But left to its natural inclinations, this coastal plain sprouted prickly pear, jimson weed, hedgehog cactus, tasajillo, peyote, and catclaw. In fact, there was a saying that in South Texas everything either had thorns on it or was poisonous or both—including the people.

This was the land of notorious Box 13, the Duval County voting district where the dead rose in alphabetical order to give Congressman Lyndon Johnson an eighty-seven-vote victory over former Governor Coke Stevenson in the crucial 1948 Democratic senatorial primary. South Texas was also the native turf of Clinton Manges, the Freer rancher and Democratic power broker who won four hundred million dollars by suing Mobil, forcing it to surrender its oil and gas lease covering sixty-four thousand acres of his hundred-thousand-acre ranch.

Back in the 1930's, Lon Hill II, then head of Corpus Christi's power company, knocked on doors up and down Wall Street in search of financing for roads, bridges, and other public works projects. South Texas was a land with great potential; all it needed was "water—and a better class of people," he declared. "That's all that hell needs," one banker retorted.

The true mark of South Texas wasn't the landscape or the vegetation, however; it was a subtle sensation of being in another country, as if one had dozed through a border crossing, then snapped awake not in the United States, not in Mexico, but in a broad frontier zone that was both and neither. Everyone who grew up here spoke Spanish—not necessarily as a first language and, in the case of Anglos, often badly and with a pronounced twang, but with fearless fluency. Except for their national hamburger and frozen custard franchises, the small, dusty towns could easily have been in the northern Mexican states of Tamaulipas or Nuevo León. The land, the cattle, the oil and gas—in short, the wealth—lay mostly in the hands of a few Anglo dynasties that had owned it since the mid-1800's—the Klebergs of the King Ranch, the O'Connors, the Kenedys (who spelled their name with one *n*), the Welders, and the Armstrongs—and the Yturrias and the Garcias, who had held on to their early-nineteenth-century Spanish land grants. The middle class was small, and self-made success stories were few.

One notable exception was Lloyd M. Bentsen, Sr., father of the 1988 vice presidential candidate and senior senator from Texas. Born in 1894 in a sod hut dug into the South Dakota prairie, ninety-five years later Bentsen was still rising at 5:00 every morning, leaving his estate Acres de la Primavera (Acres of Springtime) near Mission before dawn, and driving a hundred miles up and down the fertile Lower Rio Grande Valley to check operations on his forty-two thousand acres of farmland. In fact, he died on one of those early-morning surveys. Shortly after 7:30 A.M. on January 17, 1989, at a stop sign outside Edinburgh, the elder Bentsen failed to yield to oncoming traffic on a heavily traveled highway and was killed instantly when his Buick Park Avenue was broadsided by a Thunderbird.

In 1988 *Forbes* researchers estimated Lloyd Bentsen Sr.'s wealth at $180 million—shy of the Rich List's $225 million cutoff, but enough to make him the richest man in the Lower Rio Grande Valley. His Bentsen Palm Nursery coddled half a million juvenile palm trees—both the towering sixty-foot Washingtonians that formed the valley's only skyline and the lovely *Cocos pumosa*, a shorter tree with fernlike fronds. His LMB Corporation grew truckloads of grapefruit and oranges. In 1987 he raised enough maize to fill 1,358 railroad cars.

It helped to have other business interests, like the six banks he founded. They acted as clearinghouses for money moving back and forth across the border. And it helped to have a son highly placed in Washington. In March 1988, four months before Michael Dukakis tapped him for his running mate, Senator Bentsen proposed to use accelerated corporate tax payments to give farmers relief from the diesel fuel tax.

Like his son, the Bentsen patriarch was a South Texas-style conservative Democrat. "In the old days the bankers ran the banks," he told me during a March 1988 interview. "Now regulations run the banks. I think we've got far too much regulation."

A dapper man with a neatly trimmed white mustache that didn't quite make it to the corners of his mouth, Mr. Lloyd, as his secretaries called him, stood well over six feet tall. His back was straight; his voice was firm and steady as he handled three business deals over the phone, turning down one and saying, "*Bueno*," to the others.

Bentsen's parents had been Danish immigrants who came directly from Europe to the wind-blasted plains of South Dakota, where they settled next to the Sioux Indian reservation. The lure was land, free for the homesteading.

But in human terms the price that free land exacted was exorbitant. From the time they could walk, all six children worked planting wheat, millet, and flax. The Bentsens trained their milk cow to work in harness alongside their single horse to pull the reaper at harvest. Lloyd quit school at thirteen to handle more chores.

The hardships overwhelmed a lot of homesteaders. More prairie schooners rumbled down the road near the Bentsen farm headed east than headed west. Emblazoned on the side of one was "Thirty miles from water, three hundred miles from wood. To hell with North Dakota. We're leaving here for good."

When World War I broke out, Lloyd enlisted in the Army. A motorcycle accident in 1915 almost killed him, but when he recovered, he decided to try something even more daring: becoming a pilot. During flight school in San Antonio, Bentsen met a young South Texas soldier, Ray Landry, who invited him home to Mission for the weekend. Walking down the main street, they spotted an angelic-looking young blonde in a Red Cross uniform with silver shoulder bars. Bentsen gave her the snappiest salute he could muster, but she ducked her head in annoyance.

"Who the devil is that girl?" he asked his buddy.

Landry explained that she was Edna Ruth Colbath, an orphan being reared by her grandparents and that the only way to meet her was to go to church. So Bentsen asked another girl to take him to the Baptist service the next day and introduce him to the blonde in the choir.

For three years Bentsen corresponded with Edna Ruth, whom he called Dolly. When he was discharged in 1920, he

came back to Mission and talked her into marrying him. He
had $1.50 in his pocket. They rented a little shack beside the
Edinburgh irrigation canal.

Dolly had been to college, but she had never learned to
cook, sweep a floor, or even make a bed. She was also penniless. Her wealthy grandmother, who had reared her to be
a lady of leisure, had died in a flu epidemic, and Dolly's
guardian had embezzled her inheritance to cover his losses
on cotton futures. But she bore her situation with good grace.
"Through all the hardships we endured trying to eke out an
existence on nothing, I never heard a complaint," Bentsen
said.

With a five-hundred-dollar bank loan, Bentsen hired a
crew of a thousand men and started clearing the dense,
thorny brush from acreage owned by the old land-grant dynasties. For a share of the profits the *patrónes* allowed him
to cultivate the land until they found buyers for it. In turn,
Bentsen made a deal with twenty-five or thirty *campesinos*
living across the river: He'd give them the seed, equipment,
and mules they needed to farm the cleared land and split
the income from the crops with them fifty-fifty. Before long
he was growing thousands of acres of cotton, corn, cabbage,
carrots, and onions. If the terms were right—like nothing
down and twenty years to pay—he used his profits to buy
the land.

Bentsen later insisted he got rich because he had to. It
was the only way he could support Dolly.

For the first few years of her marriage Dolly made do
with the dresses she'd bought during her days as a coddled
heiress. Eventually she started appearing at breakfast in evening gowns, but Bentsen didn't take the hint. "Because this
was the first wife I ever had, I didn't know you had to buy
clothes for them," he said. One day she announced plain-
tively that she didn't have anything to wear.

Using $387 he'd made clearing brush, Bentsen had
bought a new Ford with all the accessories. As a belated
honeymoon, he offered to drive his bride to San Antonio
and buy her a new dress. The trip took seventeen hours over
rutted wagon roads. The next morning, with the dust washed
off, Lloyd and Dolly Bentsen walked into Frost Brothers, the

best store in town. A saleslady who recognized Dolly from her wealthier days took her in tow. She emerged in a stunning form-fitting baby blue frock.

"In those days, you could buy a lovely dress for five dollars," Bentsen recalled. "I thought because it was for her, we'd really splurge and spend ten or twelve dollars. I said, 'Dolly, with what that dress does for you and what you do for that dress, you've got to have it.' " Then he asked how much it cost. It was sixty-seven dollars—more than twice what the average American worker at that time made in a week.

"I caught my breath and said, 'I don't care,' " Bentsen continued. "Moments later she came back, and she had a little hat on the side of her head and a pair of blue slippers. And she said, 'Lloyd, I've got to have the hat and pumps to go with the dress.' "

Figuring that each of the accessories couldn't cost more than a few dollars, he agreed. Because he'd brought only enough cash to cover travel expenses, he told Dolly to write a check for her purchases. He didn't have the money in his account to pay for the dress, but he figured he could take out another loan.

Rushing home to make the check good, Bentsen drove all night with Dolly dozing on his shoulder. At dawn, as she began to wake, he asked her how much the hat and shoes had cost. "I believe they were a hundred and twenty-five dollars," she replied.

"I told you I didn't have any money in the bank," he groaned.

She smiled sweetly and said, "That's why I did it, Lloyd. It shows the confidence I have in you."

On the subject of Dolly, Lloyd Bentsen, Sr., was unabashedly sentimental. When a blizzard left him stranded in Iowa on March 18, 1947, his wedding anniversary, he stayed up all night writing an eight-stanza poem, comparing her favorably with lilies and cherubs, which he sent by Western Union. Over the years he continued writing love verses, which he compiled into a memorial book when Dolly died in 1977.

Lloyd Bentsen, Sr., was decidedly *unsentimental* about

his business dealings. He always bought and sold land with a cold eye toward maximizing his profits.

Soon Bentsen began buying big parcels of land, then selling off part of the acreage in twenty- and thirty-acre tracts to help pay for it and give himself accounts receivable to use as collateral at the bank. Some of the land was good for citrus; some was only good for grazing cattle. But a lot of it was good for peddling to Yankees.

Bentsen's first big purchase was thirty thousand acres —the Los Guages and Los Magueyes ranches. The owner was selling them for seven dollars an acre at no money down and 5 percent interest for twenty-five years. The hitch was that the owner got to keep the mineral rights. There was a little oil and gas on the property, but that didn't concern Bentsen; he figured he could make the payments easily growing cotton and maize. Other Valley businessmen were shorter on vision. As Bentsen drove his Ford into Mission after signing the deal, the good old boys lounging around on the board sidewalk razzed him. "Is there gold under that land?" they jeered. "That's three-dollar-an-acre land, and it'll never be worth a penny more."

By 1955, when Bentsen paid off the note, the Los Guages and Los Magueyes were worth $150 an acre. By the time of his death even the most remote, unirrigated sections would have gone for at least five hundred an acre.

Bentsen sold Valley real estate as though he were a preacher on a fifty-thousand-megawatt border radio station selling salvation.

"I'm a firm believer that every section of the United States is destined to increase in value until it duplicates the value of the already settled sections with the same natural advantages," he declared, giving me the spiel that had opened wallets for six decades. "If people in the rest of the United States knew what we had here, they'd settle this valley up so fast that you wouldn't believe it."

Most of the parcels were too small for productive dry-land farming and far from the utilities that could transform them into second homes for the winter-weary. Yet midwesterners and North Texans snatched them up.

One day during the thirties Lloyd Bentsen, Sr., brought

one of his young sons along to hear him deliver his gospel to a group of potential buyers. "I must have made a rather convincing argument on what the future of this land would be and why," he told me. "My little boy finally just butted into the conversation and said, 'Dad, if this land is that good, why are we selling it?' "

The Longoria family wielded tremendous economic power on both sides of the border. The fortune began with Octaviano Longoria. In 1887, when he arrived in Nuevo Laredo, on the Mexican side of the Rio Grande 220 miles northwest of the Gulf, it was little more than a warehouse and customs checkpoint. Don Octaviano built the town's first factories and established the rich and powerful Banco Longoria. But despite his business successes, he was given to deep depressions. In 1931 he locked himself in a little room above his bank and blew his brains out with a pearl-handled revolver.

The eldest of his five sons, enterprising Octavio "Chito" Longoria, assumed control of the family empire. Balanced by his more cautious brother Federico, he made the Longorias the czars of Mexican cotton. Their fifty-two gins processed one sixth of the nation's crop. The Longorias also acquired four hundred thousand acres of Mexican ranchland and set up twenty-seven branches of their bank all over northern Mexico. At his death in 1986 at the age of eighty-one, the press hailed Chito Longoria as the last of the border lords.

Chito's passion was wild game. On his first African safari in the 1950's he'd noticed the similarity between the landscape and climate of Kenya and that of his ten-thousand-acre ranch near Laredo, Texas; he decided to stock the ranch with exotic antelopes, zebras, and wildebeests, something no other rancher was doing at the time. There was one obstacle: Because hoof-and-mouth disease was epidemic in Africa, U.S. law forbade importing live game from that continent. Any animal brought in had to undergo sixty days of quarantine, then spend the rest of its life in a zoo.

So Chito made a deal with the San Antonio Zoo. He agreed to donate 120 African animals, the largest single importation of wild game; the zoo, in turn, promised to give him an equal number of the animals' offspring and split the subsequent offspring fifty-fifty. By the early 1980's Chito Longoria had thirty-five hundred exotic beasts representing thirty-five species from Africa, India, Japan, Europe, and South America, including giraffes, wildebeests, ostriches, llamas, zebras, greater kudus, and fifteen hundred nilgais (five-hundred-pound Indian antelopes). He'd also started a fad. Ranchers all over South Texas were trying to outdo one another in the foreign beast department.

As was the custom among wealthy Mexicans, in thanks for his good fortune, Chito Longoria constructed the Church of the Holy Spirit and gave it to Nuevo Laredo. He asked the tall, willowy, very blond wife of his friend San Antonio businessman Morris Jaffe to help him decorate it. Blending folk art, priceless religious antiques, and contemporary surrealistic sculpture, she captured the flamboyant spirituality at the heart of upper-class Mexican taste. Shortly after the church was dedicated, Jeannette Jaffe got a quickie Juárez divorce. Seven months later, in March 1968, she married Chito, who'd been widowed five years earlier. He was at least six inches shorter and thirty years her senior.

To house his very *norteamericana* bride, Chito Longoria built Casa Kismet, a thirty-five-thousand-square-foot two-million-dollar arabesque fantasy on a hill in Mexico City. But he also spent much of the year at 300 Almeda Circle, the only street in San Antonio with conspicuous mansions.

The white stone house in San Antonio was *la Jeannette*'s, part of the spoils of her divorce. The decor was fearless—a living room done in Moroccan and Egyptian furniture, ebony inlaid with semiprecious stones. (Sra. Longoria was the Moroccan consul to Mexico.) Two deep-cushioned white satin couches faced each other in front of the fireplace. Trompe l'oeil murals of heavy drapes decorated the walls. But the most revealing part of the house was the trophy room in the basement. Floor to ceiling along the zebra-striped wallpaper were dozens of mounted heads: lesser and greater kudus, an oryx, a puma, a hyena, a leopard, a warthog, a lion, various antelopes and gazelles, and snarling baboons. Pairs of elephant tusks, some over six feet long, arched like pagan shrines.

The longest framed an oil portrait of Jeannette Jaffe Longoria, which hung among all those proofs of predatory prowess as if Chito had bagged her, too, on safari.

The HK Ranch lay 230 miles northeast of the Lower Rio Grande Valley; but it was still in South Texas, and life on the HK was fairly typical of life on the big spreads in that region.

"Every day on the ranch is different," Henry Clay Koontz, heir to the HK, told me as I toured the ranch in 1985. "One day we may have people coming in from other countries to buy bulls. Another day someone will be in to make an oil lease. Another day we'll be mending fences."

The nearest town, Victoria, was twenty-eight miles away. Before most of the ranchers thereabouts found oil on their property, Victoria was a modest little ranching community of fifty thousand. During the oil boom it vied with Midland for the most millionaires per thousand population. But Victoria's rich knew how to hang on to their millions, and they clung to old habits—like liquidity. In the early 1980's one oil heiress drove an ancient car and kept ten million dollars in her checking account at the Victoria National Bank.

"South Texans may have pretensions, but they can drop them," said Koontz's wife, Mary Sue, a Victoria doctor's daughter. "We can go to all these wonderful places with all this glamour and glitz and then come home and eat beans off the stove."

Until a car wreck on an East Texas cattle-buying trip in 1986 killed him at age fifty-one, Henry Clay Koontz was Victoria's favorite eccentric. His dark hair, rakish grin, and voice as smooth as Falfurrias butter were appealing, but his practical jokes were legendary. Even his wife bore the brunt of his pointed wit. At the time they began dating, she was a self-described "very Junior League" divorcée living in town in a comfortable house with a swimming pool. She wasn't sure she even wanted to go out with Koontz. "He was known around the state as quite a playboy," she said, adding, "I'd heard about him wrecking one Lincoln Continental after another."

A few months after the marriage Koontz announced that

he couldn't run his ranch from twenty-eight miles away. The HK's main ranch house was a grand Tara-style mansion, complete with two-story columns and an Olympic-size swimming pool. But it was the residence of Koontz's aunt Emma, the first female Brahma breeder in Texas. She'd kept the ranch together through good times and bad, even when that had meant giving up her San Antonio debut and subsisting on pinto beans for a few years. Nothing, not even Armageddon, was going to dislodge her. During the Cuban missile crisis she'd constructed a bomb shelter behind the house and stocked it with several years' supply of permanent wave lotion and food for her pet pekinese. Resembling a grass-covered hillock with a stovepipe sticking out the top, the shelter has two bathrooms: one for Emma and her family; the other for the servants.

If Henry Clay Koontz wanted to reside on the ranch and not live with his aunt Emma or in her relatively commodious bomb shelter, he had to provide his own house.

About that time a Pentecostal church in Victoria came on the market. It was a white building with a cross-shaped sign proclaiming JESUS SAVES in blue neon. Henry Clay bought it and had it moved out to the ranch. Mary Sue was so furious that she refused even to discuss the renovations he had in mind for the building. Then, one day, he called and ordered her out to the ranch immediately. He'd finished converting the church. He told her to pay particular attention to the transom above the front door. He'd replaced it. Facing outward was the ornately carved headboard of his bed; facing inward was the footboard. "That's just to remind you," he explained, "that there were plenty of girls in that bed before I met you, and if you don't want to move out here, there can be plenty more after you hit the road."

The one thing Henry Clay Koontz took seriously was his cattle breeding. Ranchers came from as far away as Brazil and South Africa to buy the registered red Brahmas his family had been raising for more than a century. (The Afrikaners were dour and pious, he observed; the Brazilians knew how to party.) Brahmas tolerated heat well; but some lines had nervous temperaments, and none of them produced very good beef. So in the late 1970's, Henry Clay Koontz engi-

neered a new breed, three eighths Brahma and five eighths
Saler—fertile, meaty French beef cattle. He called his new
breed Bralers.

Because Bralers' coats were rich russet, they attracted
less heat than the black coats of Brangus, the older Brahma-
Angus cross. But the main advantage was aesthetic. "A
rancher coming to pick a bull is as finicky as a woman picking
a hat," Koontz opined. "There's nothing more beautiful than
red cattle on the green pasture."

Using artificial insemination, embryo flushes, and the
whole high tech repertoire available to registered cattle breeders, Henry Clay Koontz got richer and richer. He wouldn't
say *how* rich, just as he wouldn't tell me how many acres or
how many head of cattle he owned. But he did admit that
his cattle operation turned a healthy profit; he wasn't dependent on oil and gas leases to hold on to the ranch.

"Henry feels that some of this dirt is in his blood," Mary
Sue Koontz said as we talked alone that spring day in 1985.
"Definitely he should be buried here. I can't imagine ever
putting him in any kind of stereotyped situation, including
a cemetery."

Even though it lay along the region's northern border,
San Antonio was the urban focus of South Texas. Until well
after World War II there were few paved roads in the brush
country, and the dirt roads were impassable after rains, so
rich ranchers had houses in San Antonio, where the wives
and children lived during the school year.

There was one other sizable South Texas city, Corpus
Christi. But even with a population of 360,000, Corpus
seemed like a small town. It curved along a shallow bay,
protected from the Gulf of Mexico by the north tip of Padre
Island, a 138-mile-long sandbar. Corpus had its share of
Texas Big Rich; most of them belonged to the Corpus Christi
Yacht Club (whether or not they had boats) and lived along
Ocean Drive, a shoreline boulevard studded with palms and
eclectic architecture. Offshore oilman Jimmy Storm bought
and refurbished Al Capone's yacht. Socialite Topsy Dough-
erty King built her Bahamian pink mansion to resemble the
four houses she'd owned in Nassau. The late Ada Wilson

drank champagne with her nachos and lived in a scaled-down fieldstone copy of a Norman castle; her prize possession was a five-pound ruby with her profile etched into the surface. Yet, somehow, Corpus Christi lacked the critical mass to raise it above the provincial.

San Antonio, on the other hand, was a magnet, and not just because 1.24 million people lived in the city and its suburbs. Founded in 1719, when Texas was the remote northern frontier of New Spain, it was the oldest city in the state; it had a population of two thousand in 1770. San Antonio was to Texas what Boston and Philadelphia, combined, were to the original Thirteen Colonies. The Texas War of Independence may have been won at the Battle of San Jacinto, just outside modern-day Houston, but everyone remembered the Alamo, which sat on the edge of the central business district in the shadow of Deco-embellished brick hotels and office buildings dating from the 1930's and 1940's. At what became the shrine of Texas liberty, for thirteen days 188 Texicans, as they called themselves, held off twenty-five hundred Mexican troops led by Generalissimo Antonio López de Santa Anna. Just before dawn on March 6, 1836, Santa Anna's army stormed the now-familiar chapel and slaughtered the defenders. But the siege bought former Tennessee Governor Sam Houston enough time to put together an army able to defeat Santa Anna six weeks later.

In the twentieth century the Alamo was defended by the Daughters of the Republic of Texas, a statewide cadre of four thousand strong-willed ladies who could prove their ancestors had lived in Texas between 1836 and 1845. In 1907, when developers wanted to tear down part of the Alamo to build a hotel, Daughter Clara Driscoll Sevier, a wealthy rancher, purchased the property and then persuaded her husband, a state representative, to pressure the Texas legislature into buying it and putting the DRT in charge.

Scattered throughout San Antonio were other relics of the eighteenth century: four more missions, an aqueduct, San Fernando Cathedral, and the Spanish governor's palace, an unpretentious but comfortable stucco house with golden carp in its courtyard fountain. The local economy rested somewhat precariously on the tourism generated by the city's historical shrines and on its five massive military bases.

San Antonio's first European settlers—apart from monks and soldiers—arrived in 1731, the year before George Washington was born. Reasoning that the only way to protect the northern region of New Spain from French and English encroachment was to colonize it, the Spanish king, Philip V, offered thirteen families of middle-class Canary Island farmers substantial land grants and the title of Don. All they had to do was sail across the Atlantic and the Gulf to Veracruz, trundle their livestock and household goods across seven hundred miles of rocks and cactus, and make the wilderness productive.

Spurred as much by social ambition as by patriotism, the Canary Islanders took up the challenge. Leaving the hard physical labor to the Indians, whom they cruelly exploited, the colonists established themselves as an insular provincial elite. "They were not people of great gentry," said one of their descendants, San Antonio investment banker Walter Nold Mathis. "However, they were very grand-acting."

For more than a century the Canary Islanders intermarried. Then, in 1830, a young beauty named María de Jesús Curbelo broke rank, taking her substantial dowry with her. She joined the Episcopal Church and married Virginia-born merchant John William Smith, who later became the last runner sent from the Alamo and then San Antonio's first Anglo-American mayor. María Curbelo's daughter Josephine produced ten children. Disenchanted with the Hispanic custom of sharing one's husband with a mistress, the girls married into some of the most prosperous Anglo ranching families in South Texas and the adjacent Hill Country—Schreiners, Armstrongs, Steveses, Tobins, and Wests. A century and a half later María Curbelo's descendants still held reunions—big, festive, well-organized affairs at which family members sported ribbons to show their lines of descent.

"Some of those ranchers weren't as rough-and-tumble as you'd think," said Walter Mathis, a bachelor who, with his sister, Agnes Edmonston, inherited the 1867-vintage Mathis House at the Gulf Coast town of Rockport. Even in the mid-nineteenth century the house was stocked with silver and fine European furnishings from New Orleans.

Mathis himself was something of a pioneer. During the mid-1970's, when he learned that San Antonio's new Mc-

Allister Freeway would cut through his cottage in Terrell Hills, a fashionable suburb on the city's near north side, he bought a massive yet graceful stone Gothic house in the King William district; once home to wealthy German burghers, this area next to downtown had fallen into neglect. To protect his investment, Mathis bought fourteen more houses in the neighborhood and fixed them up to sell and rent.

"People thought I was crazy to move down here," he told me. But the effort paid off. The King William district earned a spot on the National Register of Historic Places, and for his contribution to preserving the state's heritage, Mathis was made a knight of the Order of San Jacinto, founded by Sam Houston while he was the Republic of Texas's ambassador to France. "We have history here," Mathis said, "but we try to remember you have to *do* something with it. You can't just sit around and drink martinis."

Compared with the Canary Islanders, San Antonio's German settlers were relative newcomers. Arriving in the 1840's, most of them were young, well-educated political idealists. They joined with the Canary Islanders and the English and Irish ranchers in establishing a social order in which family connections were more important than money or achievement.

Housed in an antebellum mansion built by homesick Scottish cattle barons, San Antonio's very exclusive Argyle Club listed among its members the top ranching clans in South Texas, as well as much of María Curbelo's line. Yet the decidedly old-shoe decor included exposed pipes in the ground-floor dining room. Luxury was not the point; inclusion was. In a state where money not only talked but bellowed, this was one membership wealth alone couldn't buy.

San Antonio was the only major city in Texas where dynasties were the rule rather than the exception and where fortunes had to have been established in the past century to be considered Old Money. The oil millionaires who fled south from Oklahoma around 1940, when that state instituted an income tax, were still New Money fifty years later.

Paradoxically "San Antonio society doesn't think of itself as society, and they're not eager to be considered society," said late local *grande dame* Margaret "Mag" Tobin, who served on the boards of New York's Metropolitan Opera and the Santa Fe Opera. Mrs. Tobin's late husband, Edgar, a Curbelo descendant, made his fortune in the twenties and thirties drawing aerial maps for such fledgling petroleum prospectors as the Texas Company, which became Texaco. When they were short of cash, they paid him in stock. "People don't care about how much money you have *or* your accomplishments," Mrs. Tobin added. What they did care about was family.

When a young CPA named Jim Nelson asked to marry Carroll Devine, whose mother, Joanne Steves Devine, traced her ancestry to María Curbelo, Carroll's aunt asked where he was from. Nelson replied that he considered himself from San Antonio since he had moved there at the age of two. "No, no," the aunt corrected. "When a Steves asks where you're from, she means, 'Where did your great-grandfather die?' "

That was a far cry from the attitude of the upper crust elsewhere in Texas. "You can move to Houston with twenty million dollars and be accepted overnight," said Mary Sue Koontz. "You can move to San Antonio with fifty million, and they'd never know who you were."

What might have seemed snobbishly insular to outsiders could feel relaxed and pleasantly noncompetitive to those within its cloistered walls. "I've heard it said that San Antonio is a closed society, but I don't think about that much," said Wanda Ford, widow of O'Neil Ford, the late dean of San Antonio architecture. "I guess when you're born in the middle of it, it doesn't make any difference."

Those who were part of San Antonio's inner circle enjoyed certain freedoms from conformity. At black-tie parties, longneck bottles of Lone Star beer bristled from ice sculptures, and debutantes kicked off their shoes to dance to a peculiar South Texas blend of rock and *conjunto*—Mexican music with a polka beat. A number of middle-aged men with impeccable social credentials remained conspicuously unmarried.

Henry Clay Koontz recounted a meeting between Margaret Tobin and Houston *grande dame* Oveta Culp Hobby, owner of Houston's NBC affiliate and then-publisher of the

Houston Post. The occasion was a luncheon, and Mrs. Tobin glittered resplendently. "Mag, you know one doesn't wear diamonds before two o'clock in the afternoon," Mrs. Hobby tsk-tsked. Mrs. Tobin replied, "I always thought that, too, until I had them."

Every April Old San Antonio toasted itself during Fiesta. The custom, inspired by Spanish parades during which the gentry pelted onlookers with flowers from lavishly decorated floats, began in 1891. From the single Battle of Flowers Parade, the festival expanded to scores of events. Many of them were public, but as with New Orleans's Mardi Gras, the socially exclusive parties were the ones that mattered.

The seven-thousand-member Battle of Flowers Association, a women's group, staged the parade. But the Order of the Alamo, an old-line men's club, chose the Queen, the Princess, and the twenty-four Duchesses—twelve from San Antonio, twelve from South and West Texas families with strong San Antonio connections. Carroll Devine was Queen. Like their great-aunt Emma, Henry Clay Koontz's two daughters were Duchesses; so were his nieces.

The order required excellent and usually ancient social credentials of the girls it honored, most of them daughters and nieces of members. Yet one knowledgeable daughter of the old guard told me anonymously that many of the girls selected had to take out loans to pay for their private parties and elaborate gowns. Unlike couture ball gowns, which might be worn on subsequent occasions, Fiesta court dresses were highly stylized one-time-only creations. Each reflected a different aspect of the theme chosen for that year. Laden with layers of silk, velvet, beading, and appliqué, the trains could be so heavy that ball bearings had to be fastened underneath to allow the girls to move across the Convention Center stage for their presentation. Five ateliers of Mexican seamstresses did nothing all year but design and sew dresses for the Fiesta court.

By the 1980's serving as Queen cost between fifty and seventy-five thousand dollars, about the price of four years at Harvard; being just a Duchess ran about twenty-five thousand dollars. "When you put 'em up there, you can tell who has spent fifteen thousand on her dress and who has spent thirty thousand," my source said. Year after year families decided that belonging to San Antonio's tightly knit inner circle was worth the investment.

Occasionally, but not often, a member of Old San Antonio society resigned his membership in the Order of the Alamo on egalitarian principles. One of these few was gadfly attorney Maury Maverick, Jr., who defended more conscientious objectors during the Vietnam War than any other lawyer in the country. Maverick's great-grandfather Samuel Augustus Maverick, the only Yale man in the Texas Revolution, took unbranded cattle in payment of debts, a practice that gave the English language a new synonym for unconventionality. Nonconformity became a family tradition. One evening during the Depression, Maury Maverick, Sr., then San Antonio's mayor, was returning home from a formal event when he felt a call of nature and asked his chauffeur to stop by the banks of the San Antonio River. As he relieved himself, Mayor Maverick slipped and fell into the dank water, which was afloat with old tires and less savory debris. Fuming that something had to be done about the mess, he persuaded the federal government to clean up and landscape the part of the river that wound through downtown, transforming it from an eyesore into a tourist attraction.

Another exclusive men's club, the Texas Cavaliers, sponsored the first big Fiesta event, a nighttime parade down the San Antonio River. With a flotilla of 130 decorated barges, it cost about $130,000. The Cavaliers also picked one of their members to reign over Fiesta as King Antonio and accompany the Queen on official visits to schools and hospitals. On the first day of Fiesta the civic potentate arrived at the Alamo for his inauguration in a gold-plated carriage pulled by two palamino horses, their manes and tails plaited and laced with flowers.

While the Cavaliers' 1926 charter dictated their raison d'être as honoring the fallen heroes of the Alamo, they did this by sponsoring extravagant public revelry. Originally they'd staged jousts. Their sky blue tunics and crimson pants with sky blue stripes resembled the uniforms of a particularly gaudy high school marching band. "We can get away with them at home," said banker Jack Meyer, who reigned as King

Antonio LXIV during 1986. "But if we try wearing them in any other city, people mistake us for bellmen."

Yet some of South Texas's highest-born sons—among them Hearst Magazines president Frank A. Bennack, Jr., Southwest Airlines chairman Herb Kelleher, and Richard "Tio" Kleberg III of the King Ranch—were Texas Cavaliers, proving that this part of the state valued belonging over dignity.

★

CHAPTER TWENTY-THREE

Galveston

Gilded Gothic

Like San Antonio, Galveston Island was a Texas social anomaly. It floated languidly two miles off the Gulf Coast, a sliver of the Old South set adrift. Moist sea breezes ruffled the palm trees, black-faced sea gulls wheeled lazily overhead, and oleanders painted blazes of coral and fuchsia in front of ornately columned Victorian verandas. Thirty miles to the north, at the Johnson Space Center, astronauts trained to man space stations; twenty miles beyond that, Houston's towering pastel skyscrapers shimmered like a post modern Oz. But here on Galveston the twentieth century had never quite taken hold.

Names of families that settled Galveston when Texas was an independent republic—Sealy, Hutchings, Harris, and Mills—continued to dominate civic boards and club rosters a century and a half later. The Artillery Club, founded in 1840 as a civilian militia, made San Antonio's Argyle Club seem arriviste. In its subdued dining room descendants of antebellum cotton factors rubbed shoulders with scions of Texas's first insurance dynasties. The clubhouse architecture was bland fifties *moderne*, but banners and uniforms stood at attention in glass cases like ghosts of the heroic days when club members helped break the Union blockade during the Battle of Galveston, the only significant Civil War engagement fought in Texas.

In the mid-1800's, when the rest of Texas was raw frontier, Galveston was the largest and most sophisticated metropolis in the state. It had Texas's first gas, electricity, telephones, trolley lines, and medical school. In 1842 Gail Borden, the man who invented condensed milk, founded the *Galveston News*, the oldest continuously published newspaper in Texas.

Before the development of modern hydraulic dredging in the late 1800's, Galveston was the Gulf of Mexico's only deepwater port west of New Orleans. The eastern press hailed it as the Queen of the Gulf and called its main commercial thoroughfare—the Strand—the Wall Street of the Southwest. In 1880 the goods packing Galveston's warehouses were second only to those filling New York's. Ocean-going square-riggers brought fine wines from France, crystal from Austria, grand pianos from Germany, and ambitious immigrants from every country in Europe. The merchant princes who made their fortunes in this trade entertained so lavishly that in 1857 the British consul complained to the Foreign Office that he couldn't reciprocate on his official allowance.

Among this mercantile elite the main arena of competitive display was architecture. Stately stonework, ornate cast concrete and polychrome brick designs, and imposing iron fronts embossed with neoclassical columns celebrated the stability of the businesses that sprang up along the Strand. Residences were even more extravagant. Sons of Virginia gentry erected Greek Revival mansions; Swiss and German immigrants commissioned castles that could have overlooked the Rhine. The merely prosperous countered by building large wood houses encrusted with layers of elaborate machine-tooled gingerbread.

On September 1, 1900, Galveston's boom ended abruptly. A hurricane packing 120-mile-per-hour winds and an accompanying storm surge killed six thousand of the island's thirty-eight thousand residents and destroyed two thirds of the city's buildings, wiping out the previous period of pomp and prosperity. Ninety years later the 1900 storm still ranked as the greatest natural disaster in U.S. history in terms of lives lost. While Galveston was busy rebuilding, Houston entrepreneurs dredged a ship channel that allowed oceangoing vessels to dock fifty miles inland. Spindletop, the first Texas gusher, came in on January 10, 1901, but Galveston's once-proud banks were in no condition to finance the development of the rich field; that business went to Houston.

For the next seven decades, while mainland Texas gained population and economic importance, Galveston became a genteel backwater. In a Herculean effort the Army Corps of Engineers erected a seventeen-foot seawall and raised the grade by jacking up every structure and pumping in dredging spoils. By 1910 the city was relatively safe from hurricanes. But the melancholy knowledge that anything built by human beings, no matter how fine or beautiful, could be wiped out in a single night seemed to have destroyed the city's spirit.

There were other problems as well. The bankers and cotton factors who ran the Galveston Wharf Company from 1854 until the city took over in 1940 set prices so high that they drove business to Houston. And this same close-knit group appeared uninterested in bringing in new blood or outside capital.

While the rest of Texas quadrupled in population, Galveston didn't even double. By 1970 it had sixty-five thousand residents, one out of ten of them unemployed. The erstwhile Wall Street of the Southwest had become an agglomeration of down-at-the-heels warehouses and seedy bars catering to merchant seamen.

There was one bright side to this civic somnolence: Of the buildings that survived the 1900 storm, more than a thousand were still standing, saved from the wrecking ball by benign neglect. Spurred by the restoration fervor of the Bi-

centennial, Junior Leaguers, doctors at the University of
Texas Medical Branch, and refugees from the urban bustle
of Houston bought and rehabilitated the derelict commercial
structures on the Strand and the crumbling Carpenter Gothic
houses in the adjacent East End. The Galveston Historical
Foundation became the city's chic cause. Within ten years
trendy restaurants, artsy shops, and the refurbished nineteenth-century square-rigger *Elissa* were drawing tourists
year-round.

One of the restoration movement's pioneers was Robert
Lynch, a fourth-generation scion of old Galveston wealth.
He chaired the $4.5 million *Elissa* project, which involved
locating the rusting hulk of a ship that had called on Galveston in 1883, towing it back from Piraeus, Greece, and
spending a decade fixing it up, largely with volunteer labor.
And he bought and rehabilitated nine buildings in the city's
old commercial district.

Born in 1950, Lynch was the great-grandson of I. H.
Kempner, a Polish Jew who had emigrated to the island in
1870. Kempner made his fortune as a wholesale grocer and
cotton factor; one of Lynch's first undertakings was buying
his great-grandfather's warehouse and converting it into
postmodern flats.

I. H. Kempner established a financial dynasty much
more akin to low-key New England and midwestern Old
Money than to a Cowboy Capitalist clan. The family business
interests ranged from Imperial Sugar to the New York cotton
brokerage of Schwabach & Perutz. But most Kempners
seemed to view their wealth as a family rather than an individual asset. They eschewed ostentation and contributed
both time and money to cultural and civic causes. Framed
with oval mats, photos of sober, mustachioed I. H. Kempner
and his wife hung on their walls.

As quietly old-shoe as the Kempners were, the Moodys,
another, even richer Old Galveston family, were flamboy-
antly eccentric, although their behavior was less typically
Texan than it was Southern Gothic.

In the years immediately following the Civil War, Galveston was especially attractive to high-ranking Confederate

veterans. Other cities in the South languished during Reconstruction, but on July 1, 1865—fewer than three months after Robert E. Lee's surrender at Appomattox—President Andrew Johnson reopened the port to international trade. The promise of social and cultural advantages and economic opportunity drew Virginia-born Colonel William Lewis Moody to Galveston in 1866. The young attorney prospered in the cotton trade and in banking. He presided over the Cotton Exchange and helped found the Gulf, Colorado, and Santa Fe Railroad. He also commissioned the man who had created the New Orleans harbor to design a system for eliminating the sandbar that prevented deep-draft vessels from passing through Bolivar Roads into Galveston Bay.

The colonel had a reputation for coming out ahead on every business deal. When he bought cotton from farmers, he discounted the bales for water weight, then let them sit on the dock for a week sopping up humidity before selling them. In the wake of the 1900 storm he snatched up the grandest mansion on Broadway—a graceful Romanesque red and gold brick fantasy of arches and turrets—for ten cents on the dollar.

Building on the fortune his father had founded, W. L. Moody, Jr., expanded the family interests into ranching and established the Galveston-based American National Insurance Company in 1905. By 1986 its assets totaled $3.5 billion, making it the largest insurance company west of the Mississippi. Its headquarters—an architecturally undistinguished white tower, the city's only skyscraper—loomed over downtown, casting its shadow on the more graceful structures along the Strand.

During the 1920's Moody also went into the hotel business. When a Young Turk Texan named Conrad Hilton got into financial trouble with his early ventures, it was Moody who helped him out.

Rich as he was, the colonel's son warned his heirs against "necessitous buying" and advised them to look on each dollar as a soldier in their Grand Army; like the good general, the canny capitalist should seize his objectives while losing as few troops as possible.

W. L. Moody, Jr.'s grandson Shearn took the advice to

heart and traveled with a briefcase packed with ten thousand dollars in twenties. One February in the early 1970's he invited Henry Clay Koontz and his wife, Mary Sue, to join him on the Moody jet for a jaunt to Jamaica. Noting that Carnival was about to begin, they flew on to Rio de Janeiro, on impulse and without hotel reservations. The Grand Army easily secured them a suite overlooking the plaza. During the course of the festivities Shearn declared that he knew what Galveston needed to perk up its economy—penguins. The tuxedoed birds would bring a little class to Sea-Arama, the island's modest marine theme park. The entourage headed off for Tierra del Fuego, the frigid tip of South America.

Leaving Mary Sue and the pilot on the mainland, Shearn and Henry Clay hired a fishing boat to ferry them across the Strait of Magellan. Using blankets, the Texans managed to shanghai nine or ten large penguins and load them on to the boat, but on the voyage back, the outraged victims rushed around, pecking and biting their tormentors. Here the Grand Army proved useful in an unexpected way. While Henry Clay distracted the crewmen, who might have deep-sixed their passengers had they known how much cash they carried, Shearn slipped the rubber bands off his stacks of money and wrapped the birds' beaks.

Ultimately the excursion was for naught. The Argentinian authorities refused to let Shearn take the penguins out of the country without papers saying they'd be allowed through U.S. Customs.

In subsequent years Shearn Moody's adventures evolved from entertaining eccentricity—such as remodeling the house on his six-hundred-acre Galveston ranch to include a slide leading directly from his bedroom into the swimming pool—to the realm of the sinister. Driving this metamorphosis was his grandfather's fortune, placed tantalizingly out of his reach.

Either W. L. Moody, Jr., didn't trust his heirs' judgment or he believed that great inherited wealth sapped character. When he died in 1954, he left virtually all his $440 million estate to the foundation he and his wife, Libbie Shearn Moody, had founded twelve years earlier, restricting its grants to Texas charities. Mrs. Moody's separate trust provided an income of about four hundred thousand dollars a year for each of her grandchildren, and eventually, through lawsuits, the heirs gained control of another two or three million.

W. L. Moody, Jr., left the family mansion and his foundation in the hands of his favorite daughter, Mary Moody Northen, a well-meaning but sheltered sixty-two-year-old widow who had never even written a check before she took over the reins. Mrs. Northen had her own share of the family's eccentricities. She wore mended stockings and bought her Christmas trees on Christmas Eve, when they were reduced to half price, then left them up until Easter because she loved the twinkling lights. She was generous enough distributing the Moody Foundation's eighteen-million-dollar annual income, but she apparently never appreciated its potential. With that kind of money, she could have underwritten a university of Stanford's stature and turned Galveston into an academic Athens by the sea. Instead, she scattered her educational bequests and spent them on bricks and mortar. Virtually every college and university in the state had a Moody Building or a Moody Dormitory.

In 1969 the foundation acquired more vision when sociologist Edward Protz came aboard as grants coordinator and steered it toward arts groups, medical research, and historical preservation, an area in which Mrs. Northen had a keen interest. The foundation converted the Art Moderne Santa Fe Building into a railroad museum and underwrote much of the Galveston Arts Council's rehabilitation of the 1894 Grand Opera House. It also bankrolled the Galveston Historical Foundation's restoration of the home of Republic of Texas financier Samuel May Williams, contributed more than $1.5 million to the *Elissa*, and set up a revolving fund, allowing the GHF to buy threatened historical structures and hold them for sale to people who would refurbish them. After their aunt Mary's health began to fail in the early 1980's, Shearn and his brother Bobby ousted Protz.

Like many private foundations, the Moodys' reflected the individual interests of the family members who constituted its board. After Bobby Moody's nineteen-year-old son Russell received a serious head injury in a 1980 Jeep accident,

the foundation established Galveston's five-million-dollar
Hope Arena and surrounding Moody Botanical Gardens. In
seeking treatment for his son, Bobby Moody had discovered
that horseback riding and work with plants provided promising alternatives to tedious physical therapy for the seriously
brain-damaged. Yet no place in Texas offered them. As one
of three board members of a four-hundred-million-dollar
foundation, he could design and staff such a facility and
locate it in his own backyard.

Shearn Moody, also a board member, favored potentially
self-sustaining, if somewhat lowbrow, tourist attractions like
the *Colonel*, an ersatz paddle wheeler that toured Galveston
Harbor. Under Shearn's influence, the foundation launched
an annual summer season of two musicals at the Moody
Amphitheater in beachfront Galveston Island State Park. He
made his close friend, former Las Vegas dancer James Stoker,
director. To help give the production more show biz pizzazz,
Shearn got the foundation to buy a "dancing waters" machine to act as a curtain. Jets of water drenched in gaudy
ever-changing hues shoot into the air, synchronized with the
music.

"I've always been fascinated by lights and colors," he
explained. The dancing waters cost about the same as launching a new production, he added. "I didn't think our theater
was complete until we had something like that."

Some of Shearn's interests touched on the extreme. He
assembled a personal collection of Hitler memorabilia, including a print of the Nazi propaganda film *Triumph of the
Will*. He was fascinated by terrorism and FBI sting operations. And he talked incessantly about the need to reform
the judicial system and legal profession that were, he said,
destroying capitalism.

He was especially intent on changing the laws governing
foundations to assure that the families that accumulated the
wealth could keep control—"instead of just getting the greediest Mexican-American, the greediest woman, the greediest
Negro they can find to run them," he said in a telephone
interview in December 1985.

At the time Shearn was hiding out at the Moody family's
Hotel Washington in the nation's capital. W. L. Moody and

Company, Bankers, Unincorporated—the small private bank that his grandfather had founded and that Shearn had bought in 1968—had been declared bankrupt, and the courts wanted him to testify about its affairs. He was still steamed about the 1976 bankruptcy of Empire Life, his Alabama-chartered insurance company, and the charges of negligent mismanagement and breach of fiduciary duty.

If Shearn Moody had a growing sense that people were after him, it was more than simple paranoia. In the fall of 1986 he was accused of funneling Moody Foundation funds to his associates through obscure grants to obscure causes. A U.S. marshal delivered the grand jury summons to him at his aunt Mary's funeral. One grant for six hundred thousand dollars went to a dentist, allegedly to study the dental characteristics of convicts to determine whether individuals who looked peculiar had a greater tendency to end up in prison. The dentist made out checks to people on a list provided by one of Shearn Moody's cronies. Little, if any, of this money wound up in Shearn's pockets; however, it did go to lawyers who'd represented him in his insurance bankruptcy and to other creditors.

A year after he was charged, Shearn was convicted in federal court of swindling $1.3 million from his family's charitable trust. In December 1988 he began serving a five-year sentence in the Fort Worth Federal Correctional Institution.

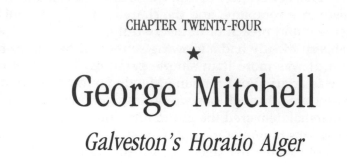

CHAPTER TWENTY-FOUR

★

George Mitchell

Galveston's Horatio Alger

Not until the 1970's was some-
one from outside Galveston's old guard able to penetrate the
power structure of this insular city. And even he was a
BOI—born on the island. Like a mythic hero, George Phydias
Mitchell, son of an illiterate Greek immigrant, left home to
make his fortune. Then, armed with hundreds of millions of
dollars he'd made in the Oil Patch, he returned to reshape
Galveston according to his own vision, which included its
gilded past.

George Mitchell was one of the nation's largest independent oil and gas producers; he was also a real estate
megadeveloper with an uncanny ability to exploit every possible government funding source, and he was a futurist who
hosted international conferences on problems that wouldn't
become acute until after his lifetime. He was one of the rarest
of corporate chief executives in that he owned 62 percent of

his publicly traded company, Houston-based Mitchell Energy and Development. Mitchell was also one of the few Texas oilmen who could take a $120 million loss in 1988 and emerge with his corporation and his personal bank account in good health. That was because he never fell into the boom-days trap of heavy borrowing. Even with most of his wealth tied up in energy and Houston-area real estate, Mitchell emerged at the end of 1989 with a net worth of $590 million.

With a sheen of self-confidence and vitality that knocked fifteen years off his age, George Mitchell looked prosperous but unassuming—not like one of Texas's legendary self-made men. No crowds parted as he moved around Galveston, dropping in on his myriad businesses there or running down to the marina for a bucket of bait fish to go bay fishing. He drove his own Cadillac Seville. The knit shirts he wore on weekends didn't always match his plaid slacks. His forehead was high; his dome, bald. The only thing remarkable about his face was his intense dark brown eyes.

Mitchell was born in 1921, the third son of a Greek goatherd named Sava Paraskivoupolis, who left a dirt-floored rock hovel in the Peloponnesus in 1901 at the age of twenty. Emigrating to the United States, the young Greek worked his way across the country on a railroad gang, almost getting fired in Arkansas because the Irish paymaster couldn't pronounce or spell his name. To keep his job, he took the paymaster's name—Mike Mitchell.

When he settled in Galveston, Mike Mitchell opened a dry cleaning shop called the Neat Dressing Club. His four children—Christie, Johnny, George, and Maria—grew up in a neighborhood of immigrants known locally as the League of Nations. Mike's wife never learned to speak English, but she insisted that all her children go to college. The eldest son, Christie, bounced around from one English or journalism department to another, eventually returning to Galveston to cover the social and entertainment scene for the *Galveston News*. Maria, the youngest, graduated from Mary Hardin Baylor College and married Houston surgeon A. J. Ballantyne. Johnny went to Texas A&M to study chemical engineering. Six years later George also enrolled in A&M, where he pursued a dual degree in petroleum engineering

and geology and rose to captain of the tennis team and major
in the tradition-laden Corps of Cadets.

His entrepreneurial drive already in top gear, "Greek"
Mitchell, as his classmates called him, operated a laundry
concession, bused tables, and sold expensive personalized
stationery to lovesick Aggies eager to impress their girl
friends. (In those days the school was all-male.) By his senior
year, 1940, Mitchell was making three hundred dollars a
month from the stationery alone, enough to send money
home to Galveston and to Johnny, who was drilling a succes-
sion of dry holes using a dilapidated old wooden rig like the
one that had brought in the Spindletop gusher in 1901.

Less than two weeks before Pearl Harbor, aboard a chartered train returning to Houston from the Texas A&M-Uni-
versity of Texas Thanksgiving Day football game in Bryan,
a stylish hazel-eyed young woman from New York was des-
perately trying to dump her blind date, a drunken buddy of
her twin sister's boyfriend. An hour north of Houston Cynthia Woods leaned over to her sister's companion and whispered, "Can't you find a poker game to lose this guy in?"
As the two men stumbled toward the card car, a twenty-
two-year-old lieutenant in a crisp Army Corps of Engineers
uniform appeared as if from nowhere, introduced himself
politely, and took a seat. Two years later he became Cynthia
Wood's husband.

Since that incident on the train George Mitchell had demonstrated again and again his eye for opportunity and his
instinct for making the right move at the right time. After
World War II Mitchell, who had worked briefly for Amoco
before enlisting, opened a one-man consulting practice,
doing geology on retainer. He also teamed up with his
brother, who was better at finding investors than he was at
finding oil. "I did the engineering and geology, and Johnny
would go down and sell the deals at the Esperson Drug
Store" in downtown Houston, George Mitchell explained
four decades later.

Johnny brought in financier H. Merlyn Christie, who in
turn brought in multimillionaire oilman R. E. "Bob" Smith
and Woolworth heiress Barbara Hutton. Johnny also snagged
Houston's Oshman and Weingarten Jewish merchant clans

and Sam Maceo, godfather of Galveston's gambling clubs, which, though illegal, were winked at until the early fifties. Maceo became so enthusiastic about his new, legitimate business venture that he trucked his pasta machine out to oil rigs and prepared Sicilian spaghetti dinners for the roughnecks.

From the start George Mitchell had a natural gift for discovering oil. Of the thousand wildcats he drilled out of four thousand total wells, one in five was productive; the industry ratio of successful wells in unproven locations was one in eight. Knowing the geology and being able to calculate the risk factors were important, but the secret, Mitchell explained in an interview, was art and instinct. "You can't computerize it," he said.

In 1953, with George doing the engineering and geology but also, according to *Forbes*, responding to a tip from a bookie, the young production company of Christie, Mitchell, and Mitchell discovered and brought in the huge Wise County play west of Fort Worth. Ranked as one of the biggest gas strikes in the industry's history, the field produced 10 percent of Chicago's natural gas supply for twenty-eight years and was still pumping in the late eighties. The profits were enough to prompt both Merlyn Christie and Johnny Mitchell to retire from the company in 1963. Christie sold out to the two brothers. Then George and Johnny split their shares seventy-thirty, with George getting the bigger slice because according to Johnny, George wanted to work harder.

No sooner had George taken control of Mitchell Energy than he formed a subsidiary, Mitchell Development of the Southwest, which bought Pelican Island, a three-thousand-acre industrial area across the harbor from Galveston's wharves. Five years later he donated a hundred acres to Texas A&M to establish the Mike Mitchell Campus, devoted to marine sciences. During the seventies Mitchell lured Pennzoil, Shell, and other offshore operators and service companies to Pelican, persuading them that it provided the ideal centralized access to the Gulf of Mexico.

In the late sixties Mitchell began picking up beach property on Galveston's West End, figuring that expanding Houston would appreciate a second-home getaway on the Gulf. It took his first subdivision—Pirate's Beach—ten years to turn a profit. In the meantime, lucky George found oil and gas on his property. "I bought it for the real estate, but then I started studying the geology," he explained twenty years later.

Suspecting that the oil and gas under Pirate's Point was the edge of a larger pool, Mitchell went looking for the rest of the field. He discovered that the rock under the island and several miles out to sea was saturated with oil and gas. The problem was getting it out. Two of the most promising places to drill were directly under the beach and straight out in the Gulf, a mile off Gaido's motel and seafood restaurant at Fortieth and Seawall Boulevard. Assuming that offshore drilling went hand in hand with oil-blackened beaches, which would damage wildlife and kill the tourist trade, the Sierra Club and other alarmed Galvestonians formed a coalition called Save Our Shores—SOS for short. To quiet fears about oil spills, Mitchell bought a twenty-two-acre slice of Fort Crockett, part of the World War II system of coastline fortifications. It included an old Army gun emplacement with elevated bunkers of seven-foot-thick concrete. He planned to sink wells on the property, then surround them with a hotel and condominiums to screen them from view.

But presented with the prospect of oil wells virtually on the beach, the Galveston City Council sent Mitchell back offshore. He worked the seawall himself, calling on the owners of tourist-dependent businesses personally. For the final hearing—for which, he said, SOS rallied a thousand protesters—he not only brought in such industry experts as blowout specialist Red Adair but bused hundreds of his own employees down from Houston to "make it look as if there were a great deal of general feeling in favor of the project," according to the chairman of the local Sierra Club executive committee, Dr. Mason Guest.

Two decades later Galveston's only major oil spills had emanated from ships at sea, not from Mitchell Energy rigs. Even Guest conceded that George Mitchell operated his offshore rigs as carefully as he had promised he would. Environmental precautions doubled the cost of drilling the wells, Mitchell said, "but it was still profitable."

Between 1972, when the first well came in, and 1989,

Mitchell Energy's Galveston oil and gas paid eleven million dollars in royalties, with the city of Galveston receiving 16 percent. It also generated more than five million in state and local taxes. Combined, Mitchell's Galveston energy and real estate interests employed approximately a thousand people and paid about a million dollars a year in taxes.

To an island city with much of its limited land occupied by nontaxable entities like the Galveston Wharves and the University of Texas Medical Branch, that economic impact was crucial. It meant that when George Mitchell asked for something, he usually got it. But not always.

In 1983 Mitchell lost a bid to buy and demolish Magnolia Homes, a public housing project located between the Strand historic district and the University of Texas Medical Branch and occupied mostly by blacks. The city council simply wasn't convinced that the alternative low-income housing Mitchell proposed to build elsewhere would be adequate for the displaced residents. He also tried unsuccessfully to get permission to construct a subdivision with canals on Eckerts Bayou, the highest, most wooded point on the island. Environmentalists insisted the area, a popular rest stop for migrating waterfowl, was far too sensitive to support dense development.

And Mitchell suffered defeat in his 1986 attempt to ban parking across from Mitchell Development's 244-room, thirty-eight-million-dollar San Luis Hotel and Condominiums. Perched at Fifty-third and Seawall Boulevard, atop the Fort Crockett bunkers, the fifteen-story San Luis put to shame every other hotel on the Texas coast. The subdued sea-foam and sand beige decor echoed Boca Raton. Palms and hibiscuses surrounded the large free-form pool, complete with swim-up bar. "You think you're in Ixtapa or Acapulco, except you don't get sick," Mitchell said proudly.

Even the public beach across Seawall Boulevard was classy. Mitchell trucked in fifteen thousand cubic feet of soft, clean sand—forty thousand dollars' worth—enough to fill in the seventeen-foot drop between the top of the seawall and the rocks below. It kept washing away, but he kept replacing it. Dotted with rental umbrellas and folding chaises in polo turf green, it looked downright elegant.

The San Luis shook Galveston out of its inferiority complex and overturned the local axiom that all tourists came to the island with a ten-dollar bill and a dirty shirt and didn't change either one. But it also upstaged and intimidated the local establishment. The hotel opened on June 2, 1984, in a shower of designer fireworks by the world-famous Gruccis. To George Mitchell's declared consternation, the city of Galveston canceled its traditional Fourth of July fireworks on Stewart Beach that year, claiming that the show couldn't hold a Roman candle to Mitchell's earlier blowout.

The question that had been brewing for more than a decade was becoming explicit: Was the island going to sit back passively, mired in its traditional malaise, and let George Mitchell make all its decisions?

By charging prices competitive with less luxurious beachfront hotels—about $120 a night for a double—Mitchell had no trouble keeping the San Luis full on weekends from April through October. But there was one problem: Those cars and pickups parked along the south side of the boulevard just didn't go with the tropical paradise image. George Mitchell asked the Galveston City Council to ban parking for three blocks in front of the hotel. On Thursday, May 1, 1986, it obliged. The following week, after much local outcry about limiting public access to public beaches, the chagrined council reversed itself.

"I didn't get mad at George for asking," said Les Daughtry, publisher of the *Galveston News*, whose editorials opposed preferential treatment for Mitchell. Outlawing parking along the whole length of the seawall would improve the view, Daughtry explained, but it shouldn't be instituted without an off-street alternative. Mitchell was stung that people hadn't told him before the stink how they felt.

"I met with Daughtry the next morning" after the editorial appeared, Mitchell related, "and I said, 'You know, if you build a thirty-eight-million-dollar project, you oughta get some help with the parking problem. The Galvez [the Marriott-operated hotel that then belonged to heart surgeon Denton Cooley] spent twelve million; you oughta give them one block. We spent thirty-eight million; you oughta give us three blocks.' " Mitchell smiled, but his tone was wounded. Three years later the conga line of pickups and surfer buggies still stood between the San Luis and the beach.

Whatever some may have thought of Mitchell Energy and Development's projects, Galvestonians were virtually unanimous about the nineteenth-century Strand district commercial structures George and Cynthia Mitchell had spent forty million dollars restoring. Mitchell got into restoration in 1974 for two reasons. First, from the time she moved to Galveston as his bride in 1943, Cynthia Mitchell had been appalled by the beautiful old buildings she saw being torn down. Secondly, he was persuaded that Galveston could have an economically viable tourist industry only if it extended its season from five months to ten or twelve. And George Mitchell seemed determined to demonstrate that Galveston had far more potential as a tourist destination than its old guard had recognized.

The Mitchells' most ambitious restoration project—the refurbishing cost twenty million dollars—was the Tremont House Hotel one block off the Strand. The hotel took its name from a Galveston hostelry that had been built in 1839 and housed six Presidents, but the structure the Mitchells restored was the delicately detailed merchandise mart from which, in the 1880's, Leon J. Blum, then hailed as the "Merchant Prince of the Southwest," had sold $7.5 million a year in goods.

Working with the building's vast spaces, Ford, Powell, and Carson—the San Antonio architectural firm responsible for many of the restorations along that city's River Walk—designed a four-story atrium that washed the interior with light. With a period decor in crisp black and white and hand-glazed Italian tiles and warming racks for towels in the bathrooms, the 108-room Tremont was a Victorian restoration for people who found the period claustrophobic. "I hate Victorian," said Cynthia Mitchell, explaining, "It's one of the worst periods in the history of design, from the standpoint of furniture and coloring and almost everything."

Although "Mitch," as Cynthia Mitchell called her husband, originally was disappointed that the black-and-white theme ruled out Oriental rugs, he later pronounced the interior "stunning." "It's something like you'd see in Paris in the 1880's," Mitchell declared. It was also the only hotel in the Strand district, which he envisioned as a year-round tourist attraction.

"If we get history going, we'll have a much stronger economy," Mitchell added animatedly. "We can get people to come in November. They don't care about the beach. They want to see history."

To buttress his point, in 1986 George Mitchell revived the island's decades-defunct Mardi Gras, bringing in jazz clarinetist Pete Fountain and floats and giant papier-mâché heads barged over from New Orleans. The weekend of nonstop partying attracted two hundred thousand visitors and cost the Mitchells $250,000.

Island residents complained about the streets being torn up for seventeen months for the resurrection of the trolley, another Mitchell-promoted project. Using $9.5 million in federal transportation grants, the city laid tracks across the island, then bought diesel-powered replicas of turn-of-the-century electric trolley cars. The grants were intended to beef up public transportation systems, on which the poor depended to get to work, but the Galveston trolley's main function was to circulate tourists from beach hotels to the Strand's shops and restaurants and from the Tremont House to the beach. True, Mitchell Energy and Development and the Moody Foundation did chip in seven hundred thousand of the $10.7 million total cost. But the trolley still amounted to a clever way of getting the nation's taxpayers to subsidize Galveston's tourist industry.

Using public money and maximizing tax breaks were Mitchell specialties. To finance the Woodlands—Mitchell Development's twenty-thousand-acre mixed-use community in a pine forest twenty-seven miles north of Houston—he snared fifty million dollars in federal loan guarantees and nine million in federal grants covering sewers, roads, and public buildings. By using an experimental surfacing material, he even got the government to pay for jogging trails. When his nineteenth-century Washington Hotel in Galveston burned down before he had a chance to refurbish it, leaving less than the 50 percent of the original structure required for a historic preservation tax break, George Mitchell persuaded the government to consider it two buildings and give him credit on one.

"Any tax benefits that can possibly be found in anything, he finds them," Cynthia Mitchell observed.

For a man only recently invited to join the Artillery Club, George P. Mitchell spoke mildly about the Old Money dynasties accused for generations of keeping New Money out of Galveston. Their fault, he said, wasn't intentional; it was a matter of failing to see that hydraulic dredging would deprive Galveston of its natural advantage as a port.

"Technology changed, and they should have seen the change and done something about it," he asserted. It's not an uncommon mistake, he continued; the oil crash had placed Houston in a similar position.

True to form, George Mitchell wasn't waiting for others to take the initiative, even in Houston. Priming the pump with a donation of land and five million dollars in seed money, he persuaded Houston's Texas Medical Center to establish its new research operation at the Woodlands, where the lab windows looked out at loblolly pines. With the lure of 250 acres and $8.2 million, he also talked the Houston Area Research Center—a consortium of the University of Texas at Austin, Texas A&M, the University of Houston, and Rice—into locating there.

Overcoming the problem of academic turf required a private-sector effort, Mitchell declared. To encourage that entrepreneurial input, he anted up five million dollars to establish Woodlands Venture Capital. During its first three years it raised ninety million dollars to back entrepreneurial spin-offs of biomedical research. Most of them never got very far, but that didn't seem to faze him. "It's like wildcatting," he said.

Mitchell dreamed of seeing the Woodlands transformed into the Research Forest. By 1989 this New Town, designed to allow people to live, work, and shop in the same pleasant, master-planned environment, had twenty thousand residents and 290 companies employing 6,500 workers, although most people who lived there still commuted to downtown Houston. By 2010, when the last subdivision was scheduled for completion, Mitchell anticipated between 160,000 and 180,000 residents. Sometime before that, he hoped the city of Houston would annex the community.

Every two or three years the Woodlands sponsored a conference on a complex international problem related to growth, a reflection of George Mitchell's interest in futurism, which began when he heard Buckminster Fuller speak on limits to growth in 1959. For each meeting Mitchell and his wife awarded a hundred thousand dollars in prizes for the best papers on growth-related issues.

"My interest is in global problems," he declared. "We can't even cope with five billion people. How can we make the world work with ten billion?"

In 1987 the Woodlands Conference subject was how technology could be shared between nations to "diffuse the time bomb in Mexico," as Mitchell put it. Most Texas oilmen considered former President Jimmy Carter anathema; Mitchell had him as his keynote speaker. Mitchell, who classified himself politically as an independent moderate, praised Carter for his vision and criticized Reagan for calling futurists, like members of the Club of Rome, to which Mitchell belonged, doomsayers.

George Mitchell wanted to get major corporations to use their resources and connections to address such long-range international issues as overpopulation, disappearance of the forests, and degradation of the environment. "If the business community doesn't use their talent and organizational ability and their resources to understand these things, they will devastate their own enterprises," he said.

As for Texas, it was time for it to make a break with its rural past. "All the emphasis has been on land and minerals," he asserted. "We have to figure out how to make our universities the powerhouses they are on the East and West coasts. We have to figure out how to develop our high technology. And we have to have tourism."

George Mitchell's own wealth and his corporate financial clout gave him the luxury of being able to think in terms of decades rather than years, to invest in ventures like the Woodlands that might not pay off until the year 2000. And they allowed him to operate on a grand scale to demonstrate that properly managed, projects that improved the human condition could also make money.

Even more than he liked finding oil and gas, George Mitchell liked showing the world that it could be made better at a profit.

★

CHAPTER TWENTY-FIVE

Hi-Yo, High Tech

As oil and gas began losing ground, Texas jumped into the high tech sweepstakes. Economic development councils trumpeted that in no time at all Texas would catch up with California and Massachusetts. With the state's low tax base and fawning attitude toward free enterprise, high technology would soon restore Texas to its rightful position as the richest, the biggest, the best.

The initial overreaction was Texas size. When the Microelectronics and Computer Corporation, a consortium of eleven technogiants working in harness to develop artificial intelligence, announced in 1983 that it would base its efforts in Austin, it set off a manic building boom that swallowed the capitol in a hodgepodge skyline. MCC had stated clearly that its initial efforts would bring only 250 well-paid jobs to the city, but giddy and greedy developers envisioned the streets of this unpretentious town teeming with Ph.D.'s toting six-figure salaries. When the nitrous oxide cleared a few years later, dozens of postmodern office towers and scores of pricey spec houses stood vacant.

By 1986 Texas had begun to wake up. Laissez-faire regulations and football-fan boosterism may have pumped up the oil industry, but luring and nurturing high tech companies demanded investment in some of the very areas where the state had been stingiest, especially public schools. Techies were a different breed of entrepreneur from wildcatters. They had to be sensitive to the market. They had to be visionary. They had to be exacting. Once it came out of the ground, there was no difference in price or quality between a barrel of West Texas intermediate crude extracted by Bass Brothers Enterprises and one brought up by Mobil. But the difference in features, speed, and price between one company's personal computer and another's could be dizzying.

Techies were also less dependent on luck and location. Computer manufacturers, software designers, and systems analysts weren't tied to what was underground. They could be anywhere. Except for the slight edge afforded by its mild climate and its position midway between both coasts, Texas had no natural advantages over, say, Montana.

Still, the independence from geography cut two ways. Parts of Texas remote from oil and gas had a near-equal chance at high tech.

Because the closest oil field was 150 miles away, El Paso had always been outside the Big Rich loop. In fact, stuck way out in the desert at the western tip of the state, closer to San Diego, California, than it was to Houston, El Paso was hardly part of Texas at all. It was even in a different time zone.

Flanked by the arid Franklin Mountains, El Paso sat on the Rio Grande at the point where it tumbled out of New Mexico and veered southeast to form the Texas-Mexico border. From the air El Paso blended with Juárez, twice its size, immediately across the river. More than 60 percent of El Paso's 480,000 residents were Hispanic—a higher percentage than in any other city in the United States. The local economy revolved around Fort Bliss and international trade, including the *maquiladoras*—American-owned factories employing Mexican labor in a duty-free zone just across the border. El Paso's one bona fide member of the Big Rich—former Mayor Fred Hervey, founder of Circle K convenience stores—decamped for Phoenix.

Yet even rocky, sunbaked El Paso was fertile ground for high tech. In 1971 a young civil engineer named Hector Holguin, whose grandparents had moved north to escape the Mexican Revolution of 1910, had an idea that would eventually make the drafting table as obsolete as the slide rule. He used a computer to lay out a new subdivision. Instead of drawing the same rectangle, the same curve hundreds of times, he drew it once, then got a computer to duplicate it.

As computers became smaller and more reasonable, Holguin polished his computer-aided design (CAD) system. By 1982 the Holguin Corporation was the second-largest supplier of CAD workstations in the country and fourth in the world, and architecture, engineering, and product design firms from London to Tokyo were buying his specialized computers for fifty thousand dollars apiece. About once a year Hector Holguin and his crew of thirty engineers dreamed up a new improvement in their system, and those firms anted up for the latest model. By 1989 his three thousand customers included Nikon Camera in Japan, defense contractor TRW, and futuristic Canadian architectural guru Douglas Cardinal.

The company grew exponentially. It did five million dollars in business in 1982. In December 1986, with its annual sales volume at thirty million dollars, Holguin merged with Accugraph, a Toronto-based CAD company a quarter its size but part of Canada's giant Kimburn conglomerate.

With his relatively fair complexion, hazel eyes, and salt-and-pepper hair with neatly trimmed white sideburns, Hector Holguin looked as if he'd always been prosperous. But starting out, he'd had to overcome both resistance to a revolutionary idea and ethnic prejudice. Although Texas had its successful Mexican-American entrepreneurs, they continued to face formidable obstacles.

''I had a very difficult time securing the bank financing

I needed," said Holguin. "It was much harder for a Hispanic to get the kind of backing he needed to start a new business, even in El Paso." But, he added, "When I see a wall of discrimination, I walk around the wall and find the opportunities on the other side."

While oil was heading south, pulling Texas real estate and banking behind it, on the northwest outskirts of Houston, Compaq, tied with Apple as the world's second-largest manufacturer of personal computers, was springing up faster than a mushroom in an East Texas cow pasture after a good rain.

Twenty-five miles from downtown Houston's iridescent postmodern skyscrapers and another fifteen miles from the belching petrochemical plants along the ship channel, redbrick walks linked eleven four- and eight-story buildings sheathed in smooth medium gray metal as clean as graph paper. A jogging trail wound through the ninety-four-acre corporate campus dotted with picnic tables. The air was full of mockingbirds improvising in counterpoint to the breeze through the treetops. It was almost too serene. But inside those techie-chic buildings, the pace was anything but sleepy.

Compaq had made *Fortune*'s list of America's five hundred top-grossing corporations quicker than any other company in history—just three years after it was founded in February 1982. The previous record holder, Apple, had taken five.

Coming out of nowhere, the infant company had gone head-to-head with IBM. Its initial product—the first IBM-compatible portable (or more precisely, at twenty-eight pounds, luggable) personal computer with the qualities and features of top deskbound PCs—became an instant yuppie cult object. It was speedy, agile, well designed, and at least as pricey as Big Blue's comparable stationary models. And because it could be hauled back and forth from office to home or even Aspen condo, it imparted to its possessor an air of both indispensability and freedom.

Before long a Compaq materialized on the desk of J. R. Ewing in the prime-time soap *Dallas*. London's Royal Botanic

Gardens at Kew was keeping track of its exotic fauna on Compaqs. Superstar Stevie Wonder was using two Compaqs onstage during his live performances.

Compaq was no one-trick pony. In October 1983 the twenty-month-old company introduced its first desktop PC. With the nimblest product development in the business, Compaq leapfrogged IBM, shipping the world's first PCs based on Intel's 386 microprocessor in September 1986. By 1988 one in every sixteen personal computers in America was a Compaq, and the Houston-made machines were sold in forty-two countries. Both the techie magazines and the business press were using Compaq—not IBM, not Apple—as the benchmark against which they compared the quality of new entrants into the computer arena.

Compaq was the result of a collective mid-life crisis. In 1981 three friends—Rod Canion, Jim Harris, and Bill Murto—all family men in their middle thirties, decided to leave secure jobs at Texas Instruments and set out on their own.

"I've often wondered why I ever did that," Canion admitted as we sat around the round table in the conference room off his office, looking out on the trees. It was April 1988, two months after Compaq had announced setting another American business record by surpassing one billion dollars in annual sales faster than any previous company. "I thought that I'd probably be with TI my whole career," he added candidly. "I didn't think a start-up company could compete with electronics giants like TI and IBM."

Born in 1945, Joseph Rodney Canion, Compaq's chief executive officer, was a new breed of Texas tycoon. He was low-key and well spoken (partly thanks to speech lessons he took to help him face Compaq's shareholders), free of Cowboy Capitalist brashness and egocentricity. With his thick light brown hair, oval face, and direct hazel eyes, Rod Canion looked like what he said he was: a nice guy—bright and self-confident but not pushy about his authority. He stood over six feet tall, with the fit look of a runner who did a little weight work on the side. He favored elegantly tailored but conservative suits, white pinpoint cotton button-down shirts, and black Italian loafers. Instead of the notorious "Texas Timex"—a gold Rolex President—he wore a twenty-five-dollar black plastic digital watch.

Texas not only loved to claim Rod Canion; it would have liked to clone him. But the fact was that unlike Clayton Williams and Bum Bright and Stanley Marsh 3, he might have come from anywhere. He grew up in a modest middle-class neighborhood on Houston's near north side. His passion was cars. While he was still in junior high, he saved enough money from his job at a neighborhood grocery to buy a '53 Ford. He couldn't get a driver's license yet, but he was happy taking the car apart, changing out the rear end, and rebuilding the engine and transmission. As a senior at Jefferson Davis High School he traded the '53 Ford in on a faster '55, better for drag racing.

"I liked understanding how things worked and making things work," he said. "Cars provided that."

Canion was a good student, especially in math and science. In 1962 he enrolled in the University of Houston. At the time UH didn't have superconductivity pioneer Paul Chu, an Architecture School building designed by Philip Johnson, or much of a reputation. Locals derided UH as Cougar High, after its football mascot, but for a commuter school it had strong mathematics and engineering departments.

Although he started out as a math major, Canion soon found that he preferred electrical engineering. "It was applying theory to practical use, like working on a car," he explained.

Meanwhile, he became fascinated with computers. "The first time I was in a programming course, I fell in love with it," he said. "It's consistent with the idea of an engineer making something work, except that programming is much more straightforward. It always does what you tell it to do if you tell it right, whereas in engineering the real world doesn't always quite work like the textbooks say."

Rod Canion's original intention was to earn his Ph.D. and then teach, but when he'd finished his master's degree, he couldn't come up with a dissertation topic that excited him. Deciding he needed a break from academia, he took a job with the Houston division of Dallas-based Texas Instruments, designing computer peripherals.

It was 1968, and a computer was still a big, expensive mainframe fed by keypunch cards. If you wanted the company computer to figure something out for you, you had a

PBX operator punch out the data, then took the stack of cards down to the computer room. The next day you came back and picked up your printout. It made for great bottlenecks.

Canion's first big assignment was to design a remote printer, a predecessor of the computer terminal. From there he went on to other design projects. He never did go back for his Ph.D.

"I was pretty satisfied with what I was doing," he said. "I was given a lot of freedom to pursue product ideas. Even though you had to fight for that freedom, you were allowed it."

By the late 1970's Canion could see that the small, relatively inexpensive computers that Apple and Tandy had pioneered had applications for business that went beyond accounting and inventory control. Texas Instruments saw the potential of a small business-oriented computer designed to increase personal productivity, but the huge, unwieldly corporation didn't quite know how to get into the game. It assigned three separate divisions to design products. Then the company started, stopped, and changed directions several times.

"Top management was trying to do the right thing, but there was a lot of wasted effort," Canion said. To make things worse, early in 1980 Canion's supportive boss was transferred to Europe and replaced by a division manager "who was not very people-oriented."

The single bright spot was that TI had assigned Canion and two simpatico colleagues, Jim Harris and Bill Murto, to develop a new product—a high-capacity Winchester hard-disk drive. That involved their traveling around the country talking to existing manufacturers who might have technology TI could buy. Rod Canion had never seriously considered going into business for himself. "I'd really never had confidence in my own ability to start a company or manage it," he admitted. "I figured that I needed the support of a big company." But there he was, meeting with little high tech shops that were producing good products and making profits. "This whole mental block that it couldn't be done, that you had to be a lot smarter than me to really do it, gradually broke down," he said.

Meanwhile, it was becoming clear to Canion that the personal computer revolution might be the biggest thing to happen to the business world in his lifetime. "A lot of people have drawn a parallel to the automobile," he said. "While I think there are a lot of differences, there are a lot of similarities in the magnitude of the change personal computers are going to make to society. Every person in business, from secretaries to top management, will use them to become more productive, so how things work will change. We're still just scratching the surface on that."

In June 1981, while he was sitting out by a hotel pool in Las Vegas, Rod Canion, age thirty-six, decided it was time to leave Texas Instruments. All through the rest of the sultry Houston summer he, Bill Murto, and Jim Harris kidded each other about starting a company. In August they began meeting at Murto's on weekends and brainstorming. They followed essentially the same methodical process they had on the hard-disk project. First they wrote down their goals. Then they wrote down their business ideas. Not wanting to overlook any ideas, they included a Mexican restaurant chain and even a car-oriented amusement park modeled on Malibu Grand Prix. "We laughed a lot about some of them, but we put them down," Canion recalled.

Once the entrepreneurial bug bit, the trio moved at hyperspeed. While they saved and borrowed enough to support their families for six months, plus a thousand dollars each to chip in for travel and incidental expenses, they held on to their jobs at TI. Meanwhile, they went about finding funding. None of the three knew anything about launching a business.

Canion spent a lot of time in the downtown Houston public library looking for books on venture capital. Since nothing much had been written at the time, he had to rely on magazine articles explaining how to write a business plan that would impress venture capitalists.

In October Canion, Harris, and Murto drafted a business plan around what Canion later admitted was "a pretty weak idea"—a Winchester disk drive for the new personal computer IBM had introduced in August—and took it to Ben Rosen and L. J. Sevin, who'd just opened shop as a venture capital firm in Dallas. Sevin and Rosen didn't think the product had much future, but they thought the three would-be entrepreneurs did; S-R wanted to study the proposal further.

Meanwhile, Canion, Harris, and Murto waited for Murto's wife to have her baby. It was due in November, and for insurance reasons Murto was reluctant to give notice at Texas Instruments until he knew whether the child was healthy. The little girl was born on December 2, and she had a problem, a large cyst. Bill Murto decided to stick with TI. Rod Canion and Jim Harris submitted their thirty days' notice on December 4.

"It was very exciting," Canion told me. "The real excitement was when we severed our ties with our old company. You can't imagine how exciting it became."

A week after he and Harris handed in their resignations, Sevin and Rosen announced that they wouldn't be funding the Winchester disk drive.

"This was the holiday season, but we didn't party a lot," Canion said. "We were mostly trying to figure out how we were going to earn a living next year."

On January 8, 1982, Rod Canion hit on an idea. "There were one hundred fifty companies building personal computers," Canion recalled. "Every two or three people who could get funding were starting a computer company." The trick was to find something the market needed that wasn't being supplied. Osborne had tried portable computers but couldn't match the desktops in quality and reliability. Canion figured that he could build a PC that could do everything an IBM PC could do and put it in a box the size of Osborne's.

Everyone else was talking about making portables smaller; Canion figured his niche was to make them better —and capable of running IBM software. IBM was keeping the nation's software houses so busy that they didn't have time to design for other companies' machines.

By January 21 Canion, Harris, and Murto (working in his spare time) had developed a second business plan ready for Sevin-Rosen. This one worked. Sevin-Rosen anted up five hundred thousand dollars. And there was more good news: Almost miraculously in late January Bill Murto's daughter's cyst disappeared. He quit TI and joined the team. On Feb-

ruary 12, seven months from the time the trio had begun
talking about setting out on their own, they incorporated,
with Rod Canion as president and CEO, Benjamin Rosen as
chairman, Jim Harris as vice-president for engineering, and
Bill Murto as vice-president for sales. Four days later they
hired four design engineers. Everybody worked long hours.
To show their appreciation, one of the company's principals
would stop off on the way to the office to buy free coffee
and Cokes for the employees.

The first step in developing a top-drawer portable was
to buy an IBM PC and take it apart to see how it worked,
then figure how to squeeze a sixty-pound machine into a
twenty-eight-pound package. By June they had a workable
design, sketched out on a paper place mat at the House of
Pies. They began production in September and unveiled their
portable PC in November, at the same time changing the
company handle from stodgy-sounding Gateway Technology to hyperevocative Compaq.

"If nobody's heard of you before and you want name
recognition, you pick a company name that can also be the
name of the product," Canion said. "And if it has a little bit
of meaning to it, that's good, too."

When the first Compaqs rolled off the line in January
1983, the business world snatched them up. Three private
offerings brought in thirty million dollars in capital, but it
wasn't enough. That December Compaq went public, raising
sixty-seven million. The company's first-year sales were
$111.2 million, another record.

Although Compaq spawned the IBM clone industry, initially Canion, Harris, and Murto didn't see themselves as
competing with IBM. But by June 1984, when their Deskpro
line of desktop personal computers debuted, there was little
doubt in Houston or on Wall Street that the upstart company
was nipping at Big Blue's heels. In September 1986 Compaq
introduced a sizzling fast series of desktops and portables,
the world's first PCs based on Intel's 386 microprocessor.

The road wasn't entirely smooth. Along with other PC
manufacturers, the company suffered from shortages of the
Intel microprocessors on which they all depended. And the
Telecompaq, a cross between a telephone and a PC, was a

conspicuous flop. But Compaq was smart and young and agile enough to drop it in a hurry.

The company also lost one of its key men to a spiritual epiphany. With enough stock to give him a comfortable income for life, Bill Murto left in April 1987 to pursue a master's degree in religious education at the University of St. Thomas, a Catholic liberal arts school in Houston. The decision was a compromise. His wife had balked at his original plan to become a missionary in Africa.

Five years after Compaq's birth the December 1987 issue of *Business Month* (formerly *Dun's Review*) named it one of the five best-managed companies in America, placing it alongside the venerable Ford Motor Company, Pepsico, Walt Disney, and Merck. One of Canion's management secrets: The soft drinks were still free.

On October 17, 1988, the company finally brought out a fourteen-pound battery-powered laptop capable of fitting on a tray table in Continental's coach class. Three days later Rod Canion announced an infusion of $150 million in long-term financing from Prudential.

Earnings for 1988 were double those for 1987. By the end of the year Compaq had forty-six hundred people on its Houston payroll and was talking about adding at least four thousand more jobs locally by 1992. Mere rumors that the company might conduct that expansion elsewhere—say, in Austin—sent the Houston Economic Development Council into paroxysms. HEDC quickly bundled up $7.75 million in incentives and presented them to Compaq: millions of dollars in tax and utility breaks, customized training programs at area junior colleges and universities, and an eight-lane freeway in place of the little farm-to-market road that ran in front of Compaq's headquarters.

All of a sudden Rod Canion was one of the most powerful men in Houston. He was also well on his way to Big Rich. Despite a recent divorce settlement that halved his assets, in June 1989 he held 150,000 shares of his company's stock, worth more than fifteen million dollars.

Rod Canion didn't look or sound like a Texas Cowboy Capitalist, but there was one trait he shared with his wildcatter cousins in commerce: a belief in luck.

"To get where we are today, there certainly was a factor

of luck involved," Canion said. The timing was lucky. Five years earlier potential customers wouldn't have understood what personal computers could do for them; five years later someone else would have produced a good portable PC. Luck was on Compaq's side in that neither Digital nor Hewlett-Packard predicted the flight of business computer users to PCs. And, Canion admitted graciously, it was lucky that IBM had set a high standard for the first personal computers.

"But as far as picking the right products and the right dealers to sell them, we earned those through a lot of hard work," he added.

The company Michael Dell founded was smaller than Rod Canion's, but he owned more of it. At the end of 1988 his Austin-based Dell Computer was the country's seventh-largest manufacturer of PCs, and his 73 percent of the stock was worth $125.5 million.

He was twenty-three years old.

Dell was the latest in a generation of technobrats—the high tech entrepreneurs who founded multimillion-dollar computer-related businesses before they were old enough to buy beer. Bill Gates was nineteen in 1974 when he dropped out of Harvard to start Microsoft, the Seattle company that owned the copyrights on BASIC, MS-DOS, and much of the other software that made personal computers do their magic. Steve Jobs was twenty in 1975, when he founded Apple Computer in a garage in Los Gatos, California. Michael Dell was nineteen in 1984 when he quit the University of Texas to incorporate the computer business he'd been running on the side his freshman year.

Except for his beautifully tailored suits and health-club-fit six-foot-one-inch physique, Michael Dell looked like a stereotypical computer nerd. He wore black-rimmed glasses as thick as Coke bottles and kept his dark, curly hair close-cropped. Like the smartest kid in your high school math class, he seemed to be trying hard to suppress a smug smirk.

When Dell talked about his company in his eager, buoyant, enthusiastic voice, his youth was at once disarming and intimidating. People at corporate headquarters called him Michael, but they spoke his name with an awed tone.

"Some people say, 'You're so young,' " he said during

an interview in March 1988, three months before he took his company public, hitting the market at eight and rising three points in five months before it dropped back down to the mid-sevens. "And I say, 'Well, I've always been young. What do you want me to do?' " Smiling an asymmetrical little smile, he added, "Time will change it."

Growing up in West Houston, where the lots were large and the houses sixties vintage, Dell was no narrow hacker. "I had this computer interest and this business interest, and they met in the middle," he told me. His father was an orthodontist; his mother, a stockbroker. They discussed finance around the dinner table. During junior high and high school his parents encouraged his lucrative hobbies—buying and selling stamps, gold, and stocks. For his sixteenth birthday they gave him his first computer, an Apple II. He'd wanted one ever since he got to use a terminal connected to a mainframe in seventh-grade math.

While other upper-middle-class kids used their PCs to play games and tap into electronic bulletin boards, Dell used his to make money. At the time he had a job selling subscriptions to the *Houston Post*. Instead of making cold calls the way the paper's other telephone solicitors did, he hit on a more effective approach. Compiling a list of the marriage licenses issued by the county clerk's office every week, he used the Apple II to send a personalized note to each couple. "Congratulations on your wedding," it read. "Now, here's a special offer."

He made twenty thousand dollars.

Meanwhile, Dell began buying computers, souping them up with additional parts, and selling them to his friends. "Sometimes I'd make it better; sometimes I'd make it faster," he explained.

He followed his older brother into premed at the University of Texas, but he soon grew impatient with the prospect of so many years of schooling for what he saw as such little satisfaction. Dell was a lot more taken with the growing cottage industry he operated out of his apartment north of campus. Computer-savvy UT students provided a market for his customized PCs, and he increased his profits by purchasing the machines wholesale.

Soon he was doing eighty thousand dollars a month in business. When his parents called from the Austin airport to announce a surprise visit, he stashed the nine IBM PCs he'd been tinkering with in his roommate's bathtub and spread open biology books on the dining-room table. But by spring break Dell had told his father that he wanted to drop out of school and devote full time to the business. Alexander Dell negotiated a compromise: Michael would complete the semester, then devote the summer to his computer venture. If he could make a go of it, he could quit UT.

Dell's first step was to lease a thousand square feet of office space. "I decided I'd be a whole lot more credible if I had a location instead of operating out of my car," he said. "Maybe I ought to get a tie; maybe not. Maybe I should go out and get an office and *hire* some people with ties and basically get the thing going."

If anyone asked what a nineteen-year-old wanted with a thousand square feet of office space, Dell didn't hear it. "I kind of ignore things that don't make sense to me," he explained.

That May, using a thousand dollars of his April profits, he incorporated. He also sold $180,000 in supercharged computers. By August there was no question, even in his parents' minds: Michael Dell wasn't going back to school.

The next year Dell Computer made the jump from selling customized versions of other companies' PCs to designing its own. Michael Dell brainstormed with his design team but left the actual architecture to them. His mind was on marketing.

One thing had struck Dell as he took apart Apples and IBMs: They were built from relatively inexpensive parts. "Being the young, persnickety fellow that I am, I said, 'Hmm, there's something funny going on here,' " he said. He figured that the difference between the cost of the parts and the retail price of the PCs must be due to inefficiencies in the way the computers were distributed.

"It was pretty evident to me that selling computers through dealers was not the best way to do it, because they paid the dealer about a forty percent markup, and the dealer added very little to the value of the computer," Dell explained. "You went to Computerland and paid them three thousand dollars for a computer; two thousand went to IBM or Compaq, and one thousand went to the dealer. It just didn't make any sense."

He decided to cut out the distribution network and market his IBM-compatible PCs direct, advertising in computer magazines and business journals and landing large corporate clients by mail and phone.

Dell didn't sell components; it sold individually tailored systems. Each model came with dozens of options for monitors, modems, printers, software, and expanded memory and storage. To keep track of the customer's configuration, an order list followed each machine through production, like an order slip in a restaurant. Despite the hefty ten million dollars it spent on advertising, Dell offered its computers for about 40 percent less than PC setups with comparable features from IBM or Compaq.

"We actually sell a computer for about the same price Compaq does, except that we sell it to the customer, and Compaq sells it to the dealer," Dell asserted. The company also offered service and support for whatever it sold, helping businesses integrate its PCs into their existing systems.

"Over time people will become much more familiar with this technology and much less dependent on getting in their car and going to a dealer to see a machine or have a machine serviced," Dell added.

The direct-marketing strategy worked predictably well with computer-literate Young Turks, but it was also phenomenally effective with novice business types. In 1988, 25 percent of Dell's customers were first-time computer users. Dell more than doubled its revenue annually during its first four years, soaring from $6.1 million in FY 1985 (its fiscal year ended in February) to $159 million in FY 1988.

Like any young, fast-growing company, Dell Computer faced the challenges of luring bright, experienced people from more established corporations like Apple and IBM and finding suppliers willing to provide parts on a predictable schedule. So many promising high tech ventures had skyrocketed into prominence and crashed just as quickly. Even though the company was private, Dell decided to publish an annual financial statement to reassure suppliers and potential customers that his outfit was around to stay.

If it hadn't done so much so well, Dell Computer might not have been. The company certainly made some critical mistakes. The most serious was a design flaw in its first models. In its eagerness to make its PCs as fast as possible, the company designed some circuits that didn't meet existing electronic emission standards set by the Federal Communications Commission. By the time the FCC raised emission limits in 1986, Dell had changed the offending board to comply with the previous norm.

Michael Dell dismissed the FCC action as "not such a big thing," but in the highly competitive world of personal computers, word of the slip spread in nanoseconds, and the company was still having to respond to questions about it years later.

Another problem was the matter of identity. Rather than give his computers the name of his company, Michael Dell christened them with the unfelicitous handle of PC's Limited. Not only did that connote unspecified but troubling limitations, but it was also confusing. In 1988 he changed the label on his machines to Dell.

Early in 1986 Dell brought E. Lee Walker, an Austin venture capitalist twenty-four years his senior, on board as a business consultant. By the end of the year Dell had made Walker chief operating officer and president, reserving the titles of chairman and chief executive officer for himself. "There was a clear fit between what he knew how to do and what I knew how to do, and our personalities meshed well together," Dell explained with a shrug. "Lee has a tremendous way with people and brings a lot of operating experience to the company."

He also brought some credibility-enhancing gray hairs.

Nonetheless, Michael Dell's youthful impatience gave him a competitive edge in the computer business. When a new operations manager suggested a computerized system for maintaining a complete parts history for every machine, Dell gave his okay within the hour, even though the system would cost several hundred thousand dollars. More than a year earlier the operations man had proposed the same system to his previous employer, IBM; Big Blue was still mulling it over when he left. Dell used another computerized manufacturing approach—Just in Time inventory. Rather than stock parts for ten thousand PCs when he only shipped four hundred a day, he got suppliers to agree to provide him with a steady flow of necessary materials, freeing millions in capital.

By 1987 Dell Computer was the darling of the techie press. *PC World* said in its November 1987 issue: "In the fast-moving compatibles market, PC's Limited is one of the most ambitious and nimble-footed players." Dell's 386 also got kudos from *PC Magazine* and *Info World*. And they all marveled at how problem-free the machines were on delivery.

That was no fluke. Michael Dell took the zero defect approach in operating his eighty-two-thousand-square-foot factory; no machine left the plant until it had had a thorough run-through.

Michael Dell was the crown prince of Austin, the manifestation of the city's fantasy of becoming the Silicon Gulch. At the end of 1988 he employed eight hundred people at his plant and five miles away at the intersection of Capitol of Texas Highway and Research Boulevard in his stylish corporate headquarters. Dell Computer planned to stay put as it added several hundred jobs a year.

"This is a great place," Michael Dell declared. "Austin is the center of the universe as far as I'm concerned."

Dell lived six miles from his office in Northwest Hills, a neighborhood with sweeping vistas of Austin's limestone hills and narrow lakes. Except for admitting that he jogged, swam, rode his bike, and played racquetball, he rivaled Sid Bass in reticence about his personal life. He wouldn't even confirm that the red Porsche convertible in his labeled parking space was his.

But he didn't mind confiding his ambitions.

Michael Dell had no intention of retiring early to enjoy his wealth. "Ten years from now I'll be running a much, much bigger, billion-dollar Dell Computer," he declared confidently.

★

CHAPTER TWENTY-SIX

H. Ross Perot

Beyond Cowboy Capitalism

$\mathbf{F}$rom the time I first began work on this book, my list of the Big Rich Texans was headed by Dallas computer services magnate H. Ross Perot. After all, he was the richest man in the state; *Forbes* pegged his fortune at $1.4 billion in 1984, $2.5 billion in 1989. But what was more important, he seemed to embody the best of Cowboy Capitalism—the energy; the confident individualism; the willingness to take risks, not just with his money but with his person. In December 1969, at the height of the Vietnam conflict, Perot had flown to Hanoi with a planeload of Christmas dinners for the American prisoners of war. The mission had failed (he'd been refused landing rights), but he had succeeded in publicizing the POWs' plight. Ten years later, after two of his employees were imprisoned during the Iranian Revolution, he'd gone to Teheran, over the strenuous objections of his company's attorney, to oversee personally the daring jailbreak and get his men smuggled out of the country.

Yet much of the stuff Perot was made of was antithetical to true Cowboy Capitalism. He'd racked up his first millions not by finding oil and gas but by pioneering a new industry. He had a reverence for higher education, even in the liberal arts. He had no patience for blind optimism. He and his wife, Margot, avoided ostentation. And his patriotism (which he preferred to call love of country) wasn't a jingoistic cloak for self-interest but a reflection of his recognition of public problems and his eagerness to apply his time and money to solving them. And what he said and did, I was convinced, emanated from genuine goodwill. If we were lucky, post-Cowboy Capitalist Texas would produce more Ross Perots and fewer Bunker Hunts.

It took me almost four years to get an interview with him. Perot was no recluse, nor was he publicity-shy like the Bass brothers. He had, after all, cooperated with Ken Follett for the real-life thriller about the Iran rescue, *On Wings of Eagles*, and had even allowed himself to be portrayed in the film version for NBC. When reporters for daily newspapers and business magazines wanted his opinions, he returned their calls promptly. But Perot was very careful where he appeared, and how. When I asked to interview him for a *Town & Country* profile, he kept postponing appointments and finally phoned personally to explain that he didn't want to be in that particular magazine.

"I'm not social," he declared. "Margot's not social. We don't go to Palm Beach. We don't play polo."

Finally, in 1988, Ross Perot agreed to an interview for my book. The subject of our talk would be the Texas economy, but it would range well beyond that.

Physically H. Ross Perot was unimposing. At fifty-eight he stood only five feet six inches and weighed about 150 pounds. His nose was knobby (he'd broken it breaking a bronco as a boy), and his ears stuck out. His hair was thinning at the crown, like a monk's pate. He spoke with a Northeast Texas twang, and when he wasn't talking, he kept his lips pressed tight and straight, like George Washington's in Gilbert Stuart's famous portrait, which hung in his office.

On the wall behind Perot's campaign-style partner's desk was another Stuart, "The Spirit of '76," the painting depicting a wounded but proud fife and drum trio. A few good western bronzes stood on end tables beside red high-backed armchairs. The tops of bookcases and credenzas were crowded with photos, mostly candid snapshots, of his wife, his four daughters, and his son, Ross, Jr. There was no computer. Neither grand nor skimpy, Perot's office on the seventeenth floor of a North Dallas high rise seemed an intensely personal space.

Placed prominently in the elevator foyer outside his suite was a bronze American eagle inscribed with his employment policy: "Eagles don't flock. You have to find them one at a time." The halls and reception areas displayed original Norman Rockwell illustrations.

Henry Ross Perot grew up in a Norman Rockwell setting, Texarkana in the thirties and forties. The community's only claims to fame were that it straddled two states and had produced ragtime composer Scott Joplin. Perot's father was a cotton broker; his mother, a tiny, iron-willed woman of strong principles.

"I lived in a very simple, small-town world," Perot said. "You went to Sunday school. A little bit of that rubbed off —not as much as should have, but a little bit. I was in the Boy Scouts, and a little bit of that rubbed off, too."

Although he'd never seen the ocean, he set his heart on going to the U.S. Naval Academy and began showering Texas's senators with requests for sponsorship. By sheer luck, lame-duck Senator W. Lee O'Daniel had a 1949 slot open and rewarded Perot's persistence. Perot served two terms as president of his Annapolis class.

In 1957, after four years in the Navy, Perot went to work as a salesman for IBM. He was phenomenal. By the third week in January 1961, he had earned the maximum commission Big Blue allowed during an entire calendar year. Perot was disgruntled that he couldn't bring home any more and unhappy as well that management had nixed his idea of setting up a service division to help customers use the company's expensive new high tech hardware effectively. On his thirty-second birthday, June 27, 1962, Ross Perot quit IBM and, using a thousand dollars of his wife's savings, founded Electronic Data Systems, based on the idea IBM had rejected.

In building his staff, Perot was partial to military veterans and reluctant to hire anyone who'd been divorced. He demanded long hours and stressed company loyalty. Like IBM, EDS had a dress code: Women wore suits or low-key dresses; men wore blue or gray suits, white shirts, quiet ties—and no facial hair. In principle, Perot didn't have anything against individualistic attire, but most of his employees worked in clients' offices, figuring out a company's computer needs and designing a combination of hardware, software, and procedure to meet them. He wanted his people to blend in and be treated as professionals by even the most conservative clients, and he figured much of his business would come from banks.

Some of it did. But most of it came from Lyndon Johnson's Great Society. EDS designed the computer systems for Medicaid and Medicare. Perot, the ultimate entrepreneur, built his company by aiding government programs many of his peers decried as dangerously close to socialism.

When Perot took EDS public in 1968, Wall Street jumped on it like a duck on a june bug. Within days his 78 percent of the company's stock was worth $1.5 billion, and Perot was one of the richest men in America. From that point on he kept his salary at $68,000 a year and took no bonuses, although he handed them out generously and immediately for good performance. The message was clear: Ross Perot was tying his personal fortune to the fortunes of his company.

That position earned him a rare distinction: When EDS stock took a nose dive in 1969, he lost six hundred million dollars overnight—more money in one day than anyone else in history. Eighteen years later he was luckier. He sold all his stocks during the summer of 1987, several months before October 19, Black Monday.

"Everybody said, 'Gee, you must have been so smart,' " he recalled during our interview five months after the crash. "No, I wish I had been. I'm not an economist. I don't have *any* business training. But I could figure out that it was *Looney Tunes* time up there, and if I couldn't understand it, I shouldn't be a part of it."

In June 1984 Ross Perot sold EDS to General Motors for $2.5 billion in cash and GM stock and a seat on the GM board. Even though it would be a subsidiary of General Motors, EDS would remain in Dallas and retain its name, and Perot would stay on as EDS chairman. He had no intention of being a rubber stamp for management. In fact, he saw the merger as a chance to revamp the world's largest corporation, using computer systems to make GM competitive with Japanese auto manufacturers.

But Ross Perot wasn't chairman of General Motors; Roger Smith was. In January 1985 Smith announced to the business press, "EDS is a way for us to get into the twenty-first century." But fewer than six months later Perot was criticizing GM—not only in the boardroom but in public. He seemed constitutionally unable to function in a bloated bureaucracy and equally incapable of keeping quiet about it.

Rather than make the rounds on the greens at the Grosse Pointe Country Club, Perot visited GM plants and showrooms, talking to the people who made and sold the automobiles. Anything that separated the people who ran the company from the people who worked for it should go, he said. He urged the corporate brass to forsake the executive dining room for the employees' cafeteria. He pronounced the practice of giving directors a new car every ninety days ridiculous; if they believed in the company's product, they should buy their own Cadillacs. And they should fire their chauffeurs. How else would they know what it was like to drive a GM car?

But what really got to Perot was the pace at which General Motors moved.

"The first EDSer to see a snake kills it," he griped to the *Dallas Times Herald*. "At GM, first thing you do is organize a committee on snakes. Then you bring in a consultant who knows a lot about snakes. Third thing you do is talk about it for a year."

Ross Perot was not a patient man.

"Revitalizing General Motors is like teaching an elephant to tap dance," he told the *Times Herald* in October 1986. "You find the sensitive spots and start poking."

But by that time the elephant had had enough poking.

Two months later the board agreed to buy back the 11.3 million shares of GM stock that made Perot the largest individual shareholder. It was willing to pay more than seven hundred million dollars—twice the stock's market value— to have him resign from EDS, give up his General Motors directorship, and go quietly away.

As part of the buyout, Perot agreed to refrain from criticizing GM in public or face a seven-million-dollar fine. Still, he got in a parting shot.

"There's something wrong," he told an audience of seventy-five hundred at the Detroit Economic Club on December 8, 1986. "We just closed eleven plants and laid off thirty thousand people, and we just threw seven hundred million bucks at a guy who didn't want it."

To a corporate raider, that seven-hundred-million-dollar buyout would have meant victory. To Perot, it was a consolation prize. He would have much preferred the satisfaction of revamping General Motors, creating, as EDS announced in a brochure published during that brief honeymoon, "the most advanced and effective CAD/CAM/CAE [computer-aided drafting, manufacturing, and engineering], robotics, 'factory-of-the-future,' and artificial intelligence systems products."

Perot may even have been after Roger Smith's job.

"Money can only operate in a very narrow spectrum of a person's life," the third-richest man in America (after discount king Sam Walton and Metromedia tycoon John Kluge) said during our March 1988 interview. "It can do certain things, but when you try to get it to do things it can't do, it doesn't work."

He talked about speaking to business school classes, warning against status seeking and materialism. "I tell them, 'Go to Palm Beach, where the yachts are. Go to the Riviera, where the yachts are. Go to those private clubs. And look at the faces of the people. Nobody's smiling,' " he whispered. " 'They've got every *thing* money can buy, and nobody's smiling. So they're not having any fun, even though they have sure bought a ticket. Now, go to Yellowstone Park. See ordinary people camping out with their families. They're laughing and they're talking and they're having fun with their buddies. What a paradise!' "

Considering his means, Ross Perot's life-style was relatively frugal. His main residence was a twenty-two-acre estate in North Dallas, complete with tennis court, swimming pool, and stables, and he had vacation homes in Aspen and Bermuda and a cottage forty miles north of Dallas on Lake Texoma, where he liked to spend weekends charging around in one of his three speedboats, one with jet engines. His wife drove a Jaguar; but he drove a 1984 Oldsmobile, and his suits were standard executive issue bought off the rack.

Perot's greatest extravagance was acquiring historical documents and works of art related to the concepts he held most dear: individual liberty; universal education; love of country. In addition to his two Gilbert Stuarts, he owned Jean Antoine Houdon's bust of Revolutionary War naval hero John Paul ("I have not yet begun to fight") Jones, the John Neely Bryan deed for the land that became Dallas, and the most stirring relic of the Texas Revolution, William B. Travis's February 24, 1836, letter from the Alamo penned ten days before its fall—a letter requesting reinforcements, pledging, "I shall never surrender or retreat," and ending, "Victory or Death."

In 1984 Perot paid $1.5 million for King Edward I's 1297 revision of the Magna Carta, which he pronounced "the basic document of all our personal freedoms," then donated to the National Archives. And he lost a Sotheby's bidding war for an original copy of Lincoln's Emancipation Proclamation to Malcolm Forbes, who got it for $297,000.

A year later Perot offered seventy million dollars to woo the neglected Museum of the American Indian from New York to Dallas. Despite the museum board's enthusiastic support for the move, by the end of 1989 New York state and city officials were still battling to keep the MAI in Manhattan and merge it with the American Museum of Natural History. As a result of Perot's attempt, the AMNH pledged to house the collection in a new fifty-six-million-dollar venue, financed half by public funds, half by private donations.

The New York press had sniffed that Dallas was trying, once again, to buy culture. But Perot's attitude was that the world's largest collection of North and South American Indian artifacts shouldn't be stuck away in a crime-ridden neighborhood north of Times Square; it should be located where people would see it and appreciate the virtues that it represented, especially the Indians' ability to adapt to a changing environment.

Perot set great store by concrete symbols of abstract ideas. Freedom, courage, and enlightenment, he believed, became more real if you could see and touch, or at least come within inches of, some *thing* intimately connected with them.

"Seeing documents has a special meaning for people," Perot said at the January 21, 1986, press conference announcing the University of Texas's acquisition of the Pforzheimer Library of English Literature. "We couldn't have that spirit if Travis hadn't been able to write."

The late New York investment banker Carl Pforzheimer had assembled the collection, the last of its kind in private hands, during the early twentieth century. It contained the first book printed in English, Raoul Le Fevre's *Recuyell of the Historyes of Troye*. It also included eleven hundred fifteenth- through seventeenth-century volumes of Chaucer, Shakespeare, Donne, Milton, and other masters.

"I would likely *crawl* to New York just to get a chance to look at that collection," said Decherd Turner, director of UT's Ransom Humanities Research Center, where the books were to be housed and displayed. "Mr. Perot has changed bibliographic geography."

Perot did that by shelling out fifteen million dollars shortly after the literary treasures went on the market, before museums and other institutions had a chance to figure out where they'd get the funds to buy them. Then he gave the collection to UT with the understanding that it'd try to raise the money to reimburse him, but he didn't seem too concerned about getting his millions back.

"What does a guy who was trained as a sailor and worked all his life in high tech know about great books?" Perot asked the crowd gathered at the HRC. "The answer is, not much."

To Perot, the literary importance of that 1475 edition of Le Fevre was secondary to its sociological significance: The fact that the book was in English marked a major step toward universal access to knowledge. But he also knew that the collection would attract top humanities scholars and that they, in turn, would raise the level of liberal arts education at the state's major university.

"The worst mistake we could make is turning out large numbers of technological robots," he announced. "The memory of the race, the rights of the next generation cannot be taught in high technology."

Over the years Ross and Margot Perot had given more than $120 million to charity, mostly in large gifts with an important string attached: that the projects supported be "world-class." "We love mediocrity in this state," he complained. "We'd rather have two hundred bad universities than one good one."

Perot donated ten million dollars toward Dallas's I. M. Pei-designed symphony hall in 1984, then announced that he wanted it named not for himself but for his loyal friend and then EDS president Mort Meyerson. Three years later Perot chipped in another two million so that the building could have African cherry-wood paneling and marble floors.

In 1987 he gave San Antonio fifteen million dollars toward creating a fifteen-hundred-acre biomedical research park. And when the FDIC put the failed First RepublicBank Corporation, the largest bank in Texas, on the block in 1988, Perot acted as a catalyst for the sale to the NCNB Corporation by pledging to make up the difference if the North Carolina holding company couldn't raise the necessary $210 million.

But Perot's biggest philanthropy was his twenty-million-dollar gift to the University of Texas Southwestern Medical Center at Dallas. Two of the medical school's faculty, Drs. Michael S. Brown and Joseph L. Goldstein, had won the 1985 Nobel Prize; that meant Southwestern had a good shot at becoming world-class.

Perot's help hadn't always worked. In the early 1970's his friend and then Secretary of the Treasury John Connally asked him to invest in two large brokerage houses, Du Pont Glore Forgan and Walston & Company, whose financial troubles threatened to push the New York Stock Exchange to the brink of bankruptcy. Perot obliged, but despite his efforts, the Wall Street behemoths failed. The stock exchange survived, but Perot lost sixty million dollars in the abortive rescue. Fifteen years later he pledged $4.2 million in an unsuccessful attempt to obtain videotapes of American soldiers still imprisoned in Laos.

Although the press often presented him as a jingoistic right-winger, Perot was, instead, a political pragmatist. In 1984, when Colonel Oliver North asked him to put up money to secure the release of the Beirut CIA chief of station William Buckley and other U.S. hostages in Lebanon, he deposited two million dollars in a ransom account at Crédit Suisse Bank of Zurich. Then Perot called on future Democratic presidential candidate Jesse Jackson to do the negotiating, paid Jackson's expenses, and sent along an associate to help. A year earlier Jackson had persuaded Syria to release Navy pilot Robert Goodman; to Perot, he was obviously the man for the job.

"I've been doing this since 1969, when there were Americans in distress around the world," Perot told *Nightline* on December 1, 1986.

His support for America's military efforts wasn't blindly gung ho. During our interview in March 1988 he slammed the Strategic Defense Initiative. "We're three trillion dollars in debt, and Reagan wants to spend three trillion dollars on Star Wars," he scoffed. "Suppose you get this Buck Rogers thing up there. I, with no new technology, can pop a space mine within half a mile of it, and it just sits there like a gorilla. We're back to square one again. We've just sapped the vitality of the country with this stuff, and it doesn't give us any protection."

Perot had praise for only one world leader, Mikhail Gorbachev. "Gorbachev is probably *the* most effective international figure on the scene today," he opined. "He's doing things inside his own country that are massive risks for him to take. We don't have any leaders who are wading in and saying, 'Hey, this is wrong. We gotta fix this.' "

Leaning forward across his desk, he added: "We live in a society now where if you whine about something enough, you think you've fixed it. When you've got potholes, what you need is someone with a shovel and some asphalt. You don't need a press conference on potholes."

Of Reagan's phenomenal popularity rating, Perot snorted, "That's levitation." He likened Reagan's political approach of denying deep-rooted problems, like declining American productivity and the worsening deficit, to a man with chest pains denying that he may be having a heart attack. "The only guys who can make the race are the feel-good-now boys," he complained. "You listen to President Reagan's radio address Saturdays and you wonder where he lives."

The national economy was like a submarine, Perot explained, using his hands to shape the vessel out of air and point it toward his desktop. Nobody knew just how much pressure it could take before imploding. But even though all the dials and gauges were far into the red zone and all the alarms were going off, we kept going deeper. And we refused "to even let a candidate *surface* who wants to talk about it in an intelligent way."

America needed to do a lot of things—fast. The government had to clean up the corrupt savings and loans and help the faltering banks back on their feet. It needed to get Japan and Europe to reimburse our military for their defense. It should save a hundred billion dollars a year by eliminating "welfare for the rich," entitlements for affluent individuals over sixty-five. "For me to get Social Security or Medicare or anything is a joke," he said. Individuals had to quit running up consumer debt. And we had to wean ourselves and our children from television.

"The people who most need to become competitive, who most need to endure the rigors of learning and developing their minds, are subjected day and night to a materialistic, feel-good-now message," he said. "About the most complex thing they'd try to think through is the true meaning of the Spuds Mackenzie, party animal ads."

Above all, we had to face the problem.

Ross Perot read, and he read widely. He'd pored over Thoreau's *Walden* three times and had just finished Tom Wolfe's *Bonfire of the Vanities*. But the most recent catalysts for his thinking had been Alfred Malabre's treatise on America's economic dilemma, *Beyond Our Means*, and an Ann Landers column on what a trillion dollars would buy—a hundred-thousand-dollar house and a ten-thousand-dollar car for every family in Kansas, Missouri, Oklahoma, and Iowa, with enough left over for schools and hospitals and plenty of teachers and nurses to staff them. Instead, Perot said, we were planning to spend three times that on Star Wars. It was a sign of how much trouble we were in.

"I'm going to tell you in plain Texas talk," he declared. "We've got to clean out the stalls. The stalls have been neglected a long time. The quicker we pick up the shovel and do it, the quicker we'll be finished."

But he refused to reveal whom he'd support in the upcoming presidential race. "I'm an independent voter," he said. "You'll see the words 'rock-ribbed Republican' applied to me. I find that amusing. The few cases where I've been asked if I'm a conservative or a liberal, I've said I don't know. I don't think in those terms. I've spent years of my life and millions of dollars of my money working to resolve problems that I see a lot of limousine liberals wringing their hands about."

Perot's ideas on law and order gave liberals plenty of cause for hand wringing. Ever since he took on the Governor's War on Drugs during Republican Bill Clements's first term, 1979–83, he'd recommended revising the Constitution to favor the defendant less and law enforcement more. Why should police need a court order to wiretap a suspected drug dealer? Why shouldn't otherwise sound evidence obtained through an illegal search be admissible in court?

"Our Constitution is two hundred years old; its founders thought we'd be changing it at least after ten years," he argued. "But we're all afraid to touch it. I, for one, am not. It wouldn't hurt to have a roaring debate about it. I really deplore the fact that it's such a traumatic thought that people don't even want to discuss it."

As Governor Clements was about to leave office in 1983, he asked Perot to head the Select Committee on Public Education, set up to examine why Texas ranked forty-fourth among the fifty states in the percentage of its students graduating from high school. Under someone else's leadership, SCOPE might have been a mired-in-molasses study lasting years, costing millions, and resulting in a few vague conclusions. Ross Perot tackled the task on his own terms, without public funds or state employees. Assigning EDS staff to work full time on the effort, Perot set up a series of hearings in communities around Texas. Each hearing ran eight to twelve hours, with experts addressing an audience of concerned citizens and Perot asking incisive questions and listening.

"Where do the dropouts of Texas *finally* go to school?" Jim Estelle, the director of the Texas Department of Corrections, asked at one SCOPE hearing in Dallas. They went, he said to TDC, where 85 percent of the inmates hadn't finished high school.

"How many people that you get have been told that they're dumb or stupid?" Perot queried the prison director. Some, Estelle answered, had even been told they were uneducable. He pointed out that it cost less per year to send a young man to Harvard than to keep him in the Texas Department of Corrections.

When Ross Perot took on SCOPE, the only thing he knew about public education was that he'd had a good one. ("If I could wish just one thing, it would be for the average kid in Texas to have teachers like I had," he told me in 1988. "We had these world-class teachers because only women from the finest Texas homes went to college, and the only job they could get was teaching.") But he was a quick study. The first SCOPE hearing began on July 13, 1983; the last ended on March 15, 1984.

A month and four days later the committee issued its recommendations, a forty-four-page document packed with specific suggestions worded in clear, tough language.

Texas erupted in a furor.

Among other things, the SCOPE recommendations called for every teacher to pass a test of basic academic skills, for degree-mill teachers' colleges to raise their standards or close, and for the state to step in to equalize the funds available to tax-poor and tax-rich school districts. But the reforms that created the most controversy were those that attacked Texas's most sacred institution next to the Alamo: high school football. SCOPE declared that no student could participate in intramural sports (or any other extracurricular activity) who didn't maintain a grade of seventy or higher in all subjects. No pass, no play. It also demanded that practice be held after school, not during the academic day, as it was in many districts.

"Sports drive the school system, not education," Perot said four years later. "You don't get in any trouble teaching bad English. You'll get fired if you're not a winning coach."

Yet the most strident resistance came not from the coaches but from the parents, the very people who should have been most outraged that their children were receiving second- and third-rate educations. "Life's too short to face a cheerleader's mother," Perot declared. Those women were addicted to reliving their youths by watching their daughters jump up and down during midday practice. After school wasn't convenient; the moms had to be home preparing dinner. "Drill team mothers are just as interesting," Perot added. "We were spending four hours a day, six days a week training kids to prance and dance, fifteen minutes a night per subject, typically, on homework."

Governor Clements had started Perot on his education crusade, but it was his successor, Democrat Mark White, who pushed for the reforms to be implemented. And an angry coalition of parents and teachers—once firmly in White's pocket—shoved him out of office after one term and brought Clements back in.

But virtually all the SCOPE reforms went through. Although those revamping the education system didn't expect results in terms of test scores and graduation statistics for a decade or more, Texas schools began to improve. In 1989 the state ranked forty-third in high school graduates and fifteenth out of the twenty-two states requiring the SATs.

Like the hero in an old-fashioned western who rides into town, dispatches the bad guys, and then rides on down the road, Ross Perot preferred to tackle specific public problems, solve them, and get on back to Dallas. "I've taken on projects," he explained. "Whatever success I've had, I believe has been primarily because I was *not* a part of the system and couldn't be intimidated by the system. And I never ask the system to supply any of the funding, so they can't control me by the budget, and they can't control the resources. I can come, I can do the job, and I can leave. Normally, by the time it's done, they're glad to see me go."

He added: "Sometimes you realize in midstream, 'Gee, they didn't really mean to fix it.' But the people who work with *me* mean to fix it, and if we can, we fix it."

A President from either party would have been fortunate to have Perot as his secretary of education, but when I asked him if he might be interested, Perot threw back his head, gave a loud laugh, and retorted: "Absolutely not. Cabinet officers report to guys who blew up balloons during the campaign. If you spend any time around Washington, you find all these little power-hungry characters around the White House. I wouldn't go within a thousand miles of that fire drill. My advice to the next President is: Thank all the guys who helped you win, and then go find people who can help you run the country, because it's two different sets of skills."

Neither did Perot have gubernatorial ambitions. "Everybody's been asking me that since 1968," the year he became an overnight billionaire by taking EDS public, he complained, a peevish note tinging his Texarkana twang. "Surely at some point people are going to stop. Public life is not for me. I'm a businessman. If I have a role in life, it's to create jobs and create taxpayers. And that's not a bad role."

But Perot wasn't all that pleased with the raw material he had to work with. "I've been to the best business schools, and they don't teach leadership [which he called "getting ordinary people to do extraordinary things"], and they don't teach product design and engineering," he complained. "Other countries' best and brightest are creating new things, while our best and brightest are doing more extreme and damaging things on Wall Street. What we produce in our business schools is a bunch of greedy, selfish, upwardly mobile corporate gypsies, who go from rung to rung up the corporate ladder, taking as they go, giving back very little, and playing the corporate game at the expense of thousands and thousands of decent working people."

The eighties' wave of corporate takeovers, he said, amounted to "piracy—pillage and plunder and loot." The result was that once-solid companies, like third world countries, were burdened with debts they had little hope of repaying.

"Wall Street's function is to provide the capital to create jobs," he announced. "But what they had going there was Las Vegas East. It was a giant slot machine. Anytime you see twenty-eight-year-old boys making half a million dollars a year, you know·something's wrong. There's only two places you can do that: One's Wall Street, and the other's dealing dope."

Computer *wunderkind* Michael Dell, then twenty-three, was different, Perot conceded: "He's building a company. He's creating jobs."

Perot was appalled by all the young M.B.A.'s he was meeting whose definition of success was making a lot of money. "I don't want anybody around me that has that as their goal," he said. "I want people around me who want to be the best at what they do—build a better product, provide a better service. If you do that, you'll *make* money. But you've got to be driven to be the best at the thing the customer needs."

American managers, Perot advised solemnly, should put a picture of the first car Mr. Toyota sent to the United States in front of their desk. "Worst-looking thing you ever saw," he said. "But what did he do? Instead of going away in embarrassment, he sent people over here to see why people didn't like it. Now Toyota City is the automobile capital of the world, not Detroit."

During my interview Perot jumped up every fifteen or twenty minutes to field calls from Just Say No or one of the scores of other causes that solicited his help every week. Yet he had the tightly wound look of an active man enduring forced inactivity.

Perot had plenty to do. His energy company, Petrus Oil & Gas, was operating at a profit, partly because he hadn't used a penny of borrowed money to fund it. He owned twenty-two thousand acres of real estate in growing cities; his son, Ross, Jr., was helping him develop a chunk of it into an industrial park and airport north of Fort Worth. He personally reviewed the forty proposals submitted each week to his venture capital company; he'd decided to bankroll, among other projects, the development of a contraceptive vaccine for dogs and cats. And he'd put twenty million dollars into ousted Apple Computer cofounder Steven Jobs's new company NeXT, which aimed to produce a personal computer system delivering mainframe processing speed and graphics capability in a sixty-five hundred-dollar package.

With his long hair and jeans, thirty-three-year-old Jobs would never have passed EDS's dress code. But Perot seemed excited about working with him. "Steve never sleeps," Perot observed. "You hear from Steve in the middle of the night. I heard from him yesterday, and of course, I enjoyed it. Steve is such an interesting person."

But being involved vicariously in another entrepreneur's passion wasn't enough for Ross Perot. Neither was managing one of the world's largest private fortunes. He was eager to start building another company.

In June 1988 Perot formed a new company, Perot Systems. The money he used came from a family investment partnership called HWGA, for "Here We Go Again." The first project, he announced, would be designing a computer system to make the Postal Service more efficient.

General Motors cried foul. When Perot had broken with GM, he'd signed a noncompetition agreement. Here Perot was, sixteen months later, fielding a team to design computer services and even raiding the EDS ranks; five of his first seven hires were EDSers. Perot countered that he wasn't really competing because he wasn't going to make a profit on the postal job.

That July the General Services Administration nixed the Postal Services contract because it hadn't been let out for bid. But the following April Perot won a partial victory when a circuit court ruled that his fledgling company could offer computer services, provided it didn't make a profit until December 1989, when the noncompetition agreement expired.

The court also said that Perot was free to raid the ranks of his former company, provided his recruits had been employed by EDS before December 1986. So the corporate commando could regroup his eagles.

As he waited impatiently to launch his new venture, Ross Perot talked about Texas. The state emerging from the oil bust of the eighties was as different, he said, from the Texas of the first three quarters of the twentieth century as that Texas had been from the land of the cattle barons.

"Texas has been a rich state because it had a large land-mass rich in natural resources and a relatively small popu-lation," he explained. "We've been pretty ingenious at discovering the natural resources and taking them to market, whether they were wild cattle or oil and gas or sulfur or you name it. Our population has grown dramatically. Our land-mass has stayed the same. And we're depleting our natural resources. So for Texas to be a rich state in the future, we must build a diversified industrial base. This represents a huge change in thinking. We can no longer go find something and sell it. We have to create things."

We didn't operate in economic isolation anymore, he pointed out. Then he uttered the ultimate Texas heresy: Low oil prices were good because they benefited millions, while expensive energy benefited a few. The worst scenario for the state would be a disruption of the world's oil supply—say, all-out war in the Middle East—pushing up prices. "If it does happen," he said, "my greatest fear is that everybody would say, 'Well, it's back to normal times again.' "

What the state needed to do, he insisted—even if money was tight, even if it meant raising taxes—was to invest what-ever it took to create a world-class public school system.

"Businesses are going to come where they can get the best work force," he declared. "Let's assume that our taxes are low but our work force is brain-dead. The kind of world we're going to be living in in the future, you don't need people who can string barbed-wire fencing for you. Those same people can be made highly productive *if* they are ed-ucated through a good, rigorous public school system."

We also had to solve some of our other social problems, like lingering ethnic prejudice. "We've got to grow up," he said. "We don't have time to slowly evolve out of adolescence in terms of how we deal with people of different races and different backgrounds."

In a faint reprise of Cowboy Capitalist optimism, Perot added: "There's no question in my mind that Texas's best days can be in the future."

Then the wealthiest individual in the state said, "It's not that things are so bad right now in Texas; it's that things have been so good. If God hadn't put so much oil and gas under Texas, we wouldn't think we were so rich or so smart."

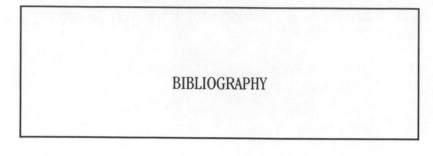

BIBLIOGRAPHY

Ashman, Charles. *Connally: The Adventures of Big Bad John.* New York: William Morrow and Company, 1974.

Bainbridge, John. *The Super-Americans.* New York: Holt, Rinehart and Winston, 1961.

Barrett, Neal, Jr. *Long Days and Short Nights: A Century of Ranching on the YO 1880–1980.* Mountain Home, Texas. Y-O Press, 1980.

Best, Hugh. *Debrett's Texas Peerage.* New York: Coward-McCann, Inc., 1983.

Brooks, John. *Showing Off in America;* Boston/Toronto; Little, Brown and Company, 1979.

Broyles, William, Jr. "The Last Empire." *Texas Monthly* (October 1980). About the King Ranch.

Burka, Paul. "The Man in the Black Hat." *Texas Monthly* (June and July 1984). About Clinton Manges.

Cartwright, Gary. *Blood Will Tell: The Murder Trials of T. Cullen Davis.* New York and London: Harcourt Brace Jovanovich, 1979.

_____. "The Last Roundup." *Texas Monthly* (February 1985). About the 06 Ranch.

_____. "The Sleaziest Man in Texas." *Texas Monthly* (August 1987). About Shearn Moody.

Chadwick, Catherine. "The Big Country." *Texas Monthly* (February 1985). About Texas ranches.

Davidson, John. "The Very Rich Life of Enrico di Portanova." *Texas Monthly* (March 1982).

_____. "The Empress of Fort Worth." *Texas Monthly* (February 1987). About Big Anne Bass.

Elkind, Peter. "Going for Broke." *Texas Monthly* (October 1986). About John Connally.

_____. "Can Ross Perot Save America?" *Texas Monthly* (December 1988).

Follett, Ken. *On Wings of Eagles.* New York: William Morrow and Company, 1983. About H. Ross Perot's Iranian escapade.

Frantz, Joe B. *Texas: A History.* New York: W. W. Norton Company, 1976.

Garreau, Joel. *The Nine Nations of North America.* Boston: Houghton Mifflin Company, 1981.

Grimm, Jack, and William Hoffman. *Beyond Reach: The Search for the Titanic* New York/Toronto: Beaufort Books, Inc., 1982.

Hoffman, William. *Texas: A Year with the Boys.* Dallas: Taylor Publishing Company, 1983.

Hurt, Harry, III. "The Most Powerful Texans." *Texas Monthly* (April 1976).

_____. *Texas Rich: The Hunt Dynasty from the Early Oil Days*

Through the Silver Crash. New York. W. W. Norton & Company, 1981.

Kowet, Don. *The Rich Who Own Sports.* New York: Random House, 1977.

Love, A. J. "Expensive People." *Texas Monthly* (May 1978).

Mackintosh, Prudence. "The Greatest Experience of Your Life." *Texas Monthly* (May 1975). About Texas's elite summer camps.

Nocera, Joseph. *Bidness.* Austin: Texas Monthly Press, 1986.

Patoski, Joe Nick. "The Long, Strange Trip of Ed Bass." *Texas Monthly* (July 1989).

Payne, Richard, and Geoffrey Leavenworth. *Historic Galveston.* Houston: Herring Press, 1985.

Pickens, T. Boone, Jr. *Boone.* Boston: Houghton Mifflin Company, 1987.

Seal, Mark. "Doin' the Social Climb." *Texas Monthly* (March 1986). About Twinkle and Bradley Bayoud.

Sedgwick, John. *Rich Kids.* New York: William Morrow and Company, 1985.

Thompson, Jacqueline. *Future Rich.* New York: William Morrow and Company, 1985.

Thompson, Thomas. *Blood and Money.* Garden City, N.Y.: Doubleday, 1976.

Veblen, Thorstein. *The Theory of the Leisure Class.* New York: The Macmillan Company, 1912 (1953 Mentor edition by American Library, with an introduction by C. Wright Mills).

Yoffe, Emily. "Boone Pickens and the Roach Motel." *Texas Monthly* (June 1988).

Index

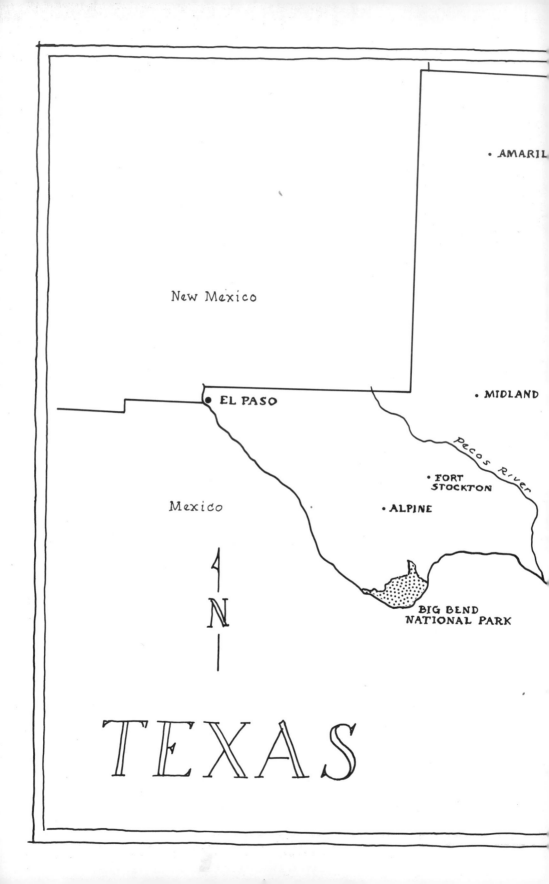

New Mexico

• AMARIL

• MIDLAND

● EL PASO

Pecos River

Mexico

• FORT STOCKTON

● ALPINE

N

BIG BEND NATIONAL PARK

TEXAS